AF584415

A Maker of Books

Alec Bolton and His Brindabella Press

A Maker of Books

Alec Bolton and His Brindabella Press

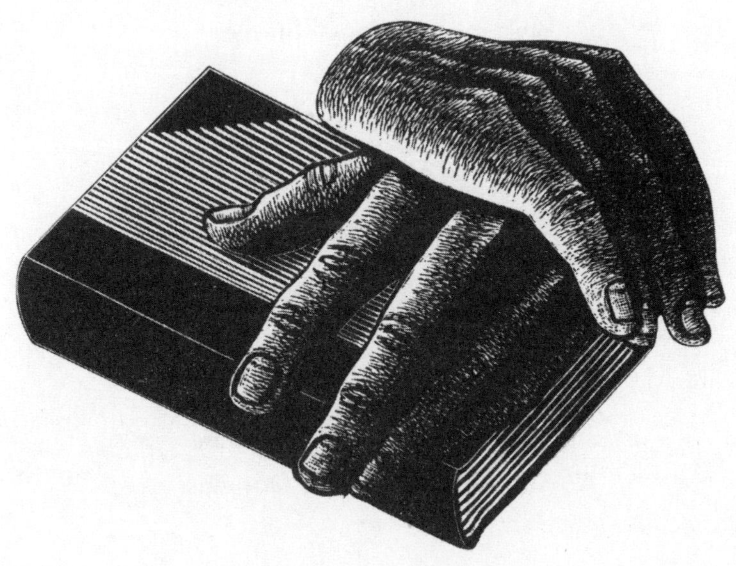

Michael Richards

Dedicated to
Bill Thorn (1932–2014)
Librarian, bookman, mentor and friend,
who took a chance on me

and

Anne Richards (1926–2021)
Traveller, reader, family historian and mother,
who taught me to read

Once you learn to read, you will be forever free.
Attributed to Frederick Douglass

Contents

Foreword

Alec Bolton was the founder and sole operator of the Brindabella Press. He was also an editor, publisher, photographer of literary figures, oral history interviewer and husband to poet Rosemary Dobson. He linked the traditions and sensibilities of his training as a commercial publisher with the literary and aesthetic ambitions of the private press movement, publishing fine editions of some of Australia's leading poets, as well as bringing younger and overlooked writers to attention. Although writing about her task as a poet, Rosemary's exhortations in her poem 'On Museums' echo Alec's approach to producing books: 'Learn still; take, reject,/ Choose, use, create,/ Put past to present purpose. Make.'

He played a similar role at the National Library of Australia, where he was the founding head of Publications. The Library had been producing books since its establishment, largely research guides and bibliographic publications but, in 1971, Alec arrived with a brief to 'share fully and effectively' the Library's collections and to infuse new life into our books. He set about searching for stories in those collections, producing the first publication under this new imprint in 1972 and building a reputation for high-quality books, one that National Library of Australia Publishing enjoys to this day, as the program enters its fiftieth anniversary year.

We are therefore particularly pleased to publish *A Maker of Books*. It celebrates the art of bookmaking (as do we), the contribution to literary culture of our first publisher and it was written by a Library alumnus in Michael Richards, a former Director of Exhibitions and now keen amateur letterpress printer. The Library holds the most substantial collection of Brindabella Press books and ephemera in existence. We also hold oral histories and manuscripts that document Australian literary life in the twentieth century, including the papers of Alec Bolton, which Michael has used extensively in *A Maker of Books*, and the papers of other poets and artists published by the Brindabella Press, including Les Murray, David Campbell, Rosemary Dobson, Barbara Hanrahan, A.D. Hope and Manning Clark. Alec Bolton's portrait photographs in the Library's collection are a valuable resource for literary biographers and historians. He also worked as an oral history interviewer for the Library, writing the first manual for National Library of Australia interviewers.

My personal connection to this story goes beyond the Library's walls. Rosemary Dobson was one of the subjects of my Ph.D. and became a very dear friend in her later life. Rosemary was a crucial part of the Brindabella story, however self-effacing she was about her contribution. She learned how to print letterpress while still at school, producing her first book of poetry herself, and Rosemary's early encouragement of Alec's interest in hand printing was highly significant. One of my most treasured possessions is a one-off edition of Rosemary's 1992 *Untold Lives*, a beautiful creation of the Brindabella Press. Not long before Alec's 1996 death (by which stage I knew both Alec and Rosemary well), I asked Alec whether he had any copies of this volume for sale.

The answer was no—but a few weeks later, Alec and Rosemary asked me to their home for lunch. Alec then presented me with the beautiful gift of a copy made just for me.

Alec's work celebrates the primacy of the book as the means of scholarly, cultural and poetic communication. His poetry volumes are still to this day 'Blowing, bright coloured, all about the world,' as Rosemary Dobson imagined poetry would.

Dr Marie-Louise Ayres
Director General, National Library of Australia

Prologue

In which the author takes the reader on an imaginary journey into the mind of the printer

How much type do you need to set the text—maybe four pages at a time, or even two? What typeface? Do you have it? Can you still get it in Monotype?

Make a dummy of the book in miniature to plan the imposition. Which pages will be printed side by side, what goes on the back of each leaf? This depends on the order of pages in each signature. How will each opening look? Where should the illustrations go? What sort are they? Have the artist and the writer met and do they agree? What will the artist give you to work with and how will it be reproduced? You are working with old technology: an early twentieth-century press, based on principles of relief printing developed in Europe in the Middle Ages (much earlier in East Asia). Printing in more than one colour is possible but tricky.

Paper. What works with the type, with the wood engravings or line blocks? Which way round to print on it for best folding and binding? Can you get it in this country or do you need to order from overseas?

What leading works best? Cut strips of leading to exact lengths. Set the type. Take each individual letter, each punctuation mark, from the type case. One at a time set them upside down and back to front in a composing stick, with leading between each line. Any mistakes when you read the line as a first proof? Keep lines of type exactly the same length, adding quads and spacers so that the block of lead is snug in its holder. Every few lines carry it to a galley tray and put it with previously set lines. One fumble and you will have to sort the pied type and start again.

When you have a full forme, move it to your stone. Build the furniture around it and lock everything into a chase with quoins. Is it tight? Can you pick up the chase and its contents without anything falling out? One loose piece of furniture, one loose line of type, and everything collapses. Is any of the type sprung? Before you tighten the quoins for the last time gently plane the type.

Next, make-ready. New tympan paper, perhaps. Where should the quad guides go? Ink up the disk. When the rollers are moving freely there is a smooth, sucking sound that says the ink is ready. (No good on a really cold day, unless you can warm things up a bit.) Take a proof. Hold it up to the light and check the impression. Think about how it looks. Clean everything up, go back to the forme, correct typos, adjust the quads and spacers, move type, maybe alter the leading, balance the blocks of black ink on the white paper. Is the type too worn? Are there rivers? Have you got the size right? Have you got the same face in a different size? Work with thin paper to get the make-ready right so that each part of the page is printed with equal pressure. Would it print better if you dampened the paper? That means less ink, and it's what the great printers of the past did, but it changes paper handling and presents challenges when you print the reverse of the sheet.

Ink up again. Is it right? Start feeding sheets of paper into the press, one by one, turning it by foot with its treadle. Have you picked up any ink on your fingers? Does the ink density look much the same from sheet to sheet? Put the sheets somewhere to dry.

Who is signing the colophon? Number the copies. Who is binding it? Method, materials, colours, cost. Mail prospectuses. Do they do any good? Who knows. Write invoices. Wrap and mail copies.

Start again. You've been working for a while on the next book.

Introduction

Today we take books for granted, at a time that sees more books printed than ever before—while self-appointed prophets forecast the death of the book and some neuroscientists warn that we may be losing the ability to read and comprehend book-length texts. Prophets (always self-appointed, aren't they?) are usually wrong, and the transition to literacy itself changed our brains in ways that the wise men of the day (also self-appointed) decried, as Maryanne Wolf shows.[1] The future may not be bookless: the digital revolution in communications may simply free it up to be a more powerful mode of speaking than ever before. But while the ease with which a book can be produced and distributed today is astonishing in comparison with all previous periods of history, a great many contemporary books will be short-lived, both in content and because they are poorly edited, printed and bound. This book is about a man who set himself against much of this as a private avocation during a lifetime in mainstream publishing. He consciously chose old, painstaking and incredibly labour-intensive ways of making books of significance and beauty while printing standards fell elsewhere, and his achievement is important.

At the same time, Alec Bolton was no Luddite. He was simply, in every aspect of his working life, a maker of books who believed that if they were worth publishing they deserved high standards of printing and design. As sources of type dried up and his texts became longer, he moved from hand-setting to machine-setting, and finally accepted computer-setting. He started with a second-hand Chandler & Price upright platen (which demanded procedures as imagined in the Prologue) but later acquired more sophisticated presses and from the start eschewed the teaching of the handpress purists against mechanical inking. He worked with the equipment available to him in Australia, which largely meant the legacy of late nineteenth- and early twentieth-century printing, rather than the flat-bed Albion, Columbian and other handpresses of the first private press movement. What he shared with it was a commitment to relief printing—to the bite of type and wood, making the indelible impression of good ink on good paper. But like those who resist waves of modernisation, change and mediocre standardisation without being fossilised—I think of writers such as Wendell Berry and John Berger, communities such as the Amish—he consciously negotiated the transition of his practice into the modern era, accepting the new when it was sensible or necessary but only if it did not compromise the essentials of what he was doing. In many ways he was a forerunner of the letterpress revival of the early twenty-first century. His small, crowded printing office, with its Chandler & Price upright platen press, Western proof press and Wharfedale stop-cylinder press, would today be a highly desirable set-up for an aspiring letterpress printer.

The goals of the Brindabella Press were made quite explicit when, in 1976, he threw down a challenge to what was happening in Australian publishing at the time. Taking a collection of poems by James McAuley recently printed in a cheap, ephemeral format by the firm that had trained him, and whose treatment had greatly disappointed their author, he printed a limited edition, which today is scarce and sought after by collectors. *Time Given* won prizes in its day and still commands respect as an elegant book by a significant Australian poet. Although he would go on to produce many much finer books, learning along the way from his self-acknowledged shortcomings as a printer, in many ways *Time Given* is the exemplar of what he stood for as a private press printer.

The books of the Brindabella Press did not emerge from nowhere. Many factors were at play. Among them were Alec's early working life as an editor at Angus & Robertson, at the time Australia's leading publishing house, then with another publisher, Ure Smith. After that came a further stint with Angus & Robertson in their London office, and finally many years of pioneering work as the National Library of Australia's publisher. His long and happy marriage to the poet Rosemary Dobson and their shared passions for Australian literature and good printing were crucial (the poet Alan Gould has remarked that Alec was more deeply knowledgeable about Australian writing than any other non-writer he knew). And finally there was his discovery of the world of the private presses during that brief sojourn in London, where he was able to enrol in night classes in printing at a time when letterpress was still taught as foundational to good printing despite the fact that offset lithography and phototypesetting was sweeping it away from the world of mainstream publishing.

And so a journey into letterpress that began as a weekend pursuit became his personal statement of defiance against declining standards of printing. The later works of the Brindabella Press are among the finest of twentieth-century Australian private press books. But there is more to say than this. While his private press work drew on a lifelong career in publishing, the publications of the press can also be seen to represent something of much larger significance to many today. Alec came from the editorial/managerial side of publishing, not from a career as a printer. The discovery of a personal avocation as a letterpress printer was one he made in midlife. Moving in small and manageable stages, from cards and pamphlets through quite straightforward, commercially bound books to fine printing of a very high standard, he constantly sought to grow as a maker and to achieve a better result next time. Whatever one's vocation, his example is inspirational. At the same time, his deep engagement in his spare time with the hands-on practicalities of letterpress printing gave deep grounding to his professional career as a publisher. This fed back into his achievement at the National Library of Australia, where he was responsible for so many fine books.

While it is tempting to classify the Press as being simply part of the twentieth-century private press movement—a late Australian outlier of the Arts and Craft printers inspired by William Morris and his followers—it is not as simple as that. What began as an attempt to hold the line against technological change and the concomitant loss of standards in the printing revolution of the 1970s and 1980s then became a bridge between the design achievements of the best commercial printing of Alec's younger years and the letterpress revolution/artist book movement of today. This is another significance of the Brindabella Press now, more than two decades after Alec's untimely death and the closing of his Press. Alec was an inspiration to many and was generous in mentoring young and new letterpress printers at a time when they were few in number. He began with the advantage of familiarity with the Australian literary milieu of the day and found a few key allies in his passion for letterpress—people he treasured and learned from. He learned also from his own mistakes, with persistence and determination to continually improve his technical and design skills. His ability to negotiate contested territory also grew through failure as well as success. As he slowly built up a community of like-minded people with whom he could reflect on his experience, he brought openness, precision and honest self-appraisal to the discussion. At every step of the way his beloved wife Rosemary travelled with him. She was his key advisor, a partner in the development of the press, and always an enthusiast for its work.

This book is in the form of a biblio-biography, tracing Alec Bolton's life through the lens of the books he made. I have devoted most attention to his later books, partly reflecting the richness of their documentary record, but also because they are the superb productions of a fine printer, books that make a significant contribution to the history of book design in Australia and for which he was inducted into the Australian Publishers Association Hall of Fame in 1996. At times, as also with the years before the Brindabella Press, I look at other aspects of his life in order to tell a more complete story. My major ambition, however, is to tell the story of the Brindabella Press, and I give only passing attention to the books he published at the National Library and elsewhere. In tracing its history, and in following his quest for the more perfect book, I hope to pay tribute to an inspiring man and to stimulate others to follow in his course.

I was fortunate enough to meet Alec in 1986, his last year at the National Library of Australia, when I joined that great institution as a young librarian. He was kind and friendly, both then and when, a little later, I had the opportunity to curate the Library's Bicentennial exhibition, *People, Print & Paper: A Travelling Exhibition Celebrating the Books of Australia, 1788–1988*. Indeed, he was extraordinarily generous with his time and knowledge, giving me my first lesson in letterpress printing after we set up a small treadle platen press in the exhibition to print souvenir bookmarks. Later, I wrote a brief tribute to his work, *A Licence to Print* (published by the Friends of the National Library of Australia), by which time I had become a keen collector of his books. His sudden death in 1996 was one of those jolting reminders of mortality with which one charts one's own life. I refer to him throughout this text as Alec, the name most of his friends used, even though it was only towards the end of his life that he first used this in a colophon (in *Granite Country*) rather than the more formal 'A.T. Bolton'. This may seem informal, but is a measure of the love and respect I have long had for a remarkable man and his equally remarkable wife, Rosemary.

1

Beginnings

In the early 1980s Alec spent time tracing his family history and discovered, to his delight, that he was descended (through his paternal grandmother Martha Elizabeth Devlin) from John Small and Mary Parker, two convicts transported to Australia on the First Fleet. He was, he calculated, their great-great-great grandson. Martha's father Arthur Devlin, moreover, had been one of the leaders of the United Irish rebellion of 1798–1803.[1] Devlin was charged with treason and exiled for life to New South Wales in 1805.[2] 'All this hot-blooded stuff is an interesting contrast to the proprieties that I associate with the Rev. Robert Thorley Bolton, founder of the Bolton family in Australia,' he told one of his oldest friends.[3] Perhaps what matters most about all this is Alec's pleasure at finding a First Fleet ancestry, which in Australia in the early 1980s had become something to be proud of rather than the convict stain of earlier generations. His Aunt Beulah also knew of the Devlin connections 'and was not especially thrilled by them', he told Fischer. But Alec himself had a rather more conventional upbringing. Convict and Irish rebel ancestry notwithstanding, his own childhood was solidly middle-class and stable, despite the loss of his father far too young and his mother's straitened circumstances.

He was born at Drummoyne in Sydney on 22 January 1926 and christened Alexander Thorley Bolton, a name he shared with his father. Although he was usually known as Alec, some called him Alex. (In his Brindabella Press colophons he generally abbreviated his name to A.T. Bolton, but towards the end of his life changed this to Alec Bolton—and then, in his last book, reclaimed the name Alexander.) His mother was Amy Bolton née Crouch. He was the second of two children: his brother John, 18 months older, was the constant companion of his childhood. His father worked as superintendent providore for the Sydney firm McDonald Hamilton, agents for several shipping lines including P&O[4], and was keen on music and horse-racing. In his spare time he was also an accomplished cabinetmaker. Alec's paternal grandfather, another Alexander Thorley Bolton (1847–1918), had been a successful stock and station agent in Wagga Wagga and served briefly as a Member of the Legislative Assembly for Murrumbidgee (1885–1887) before moving to Sydney. He settled his family in Randwick, although after his death they moved to Hunters Hill. The name Thorley, common to all three generations and continuing into the present, came in turn from his father Robert Thorley Bolton, a clergyman, also of Wagga Wagga.

Amy Crouch belonged to a large, well-to-do family and attended Sydney Church of England Girls' Grammar School at Darlinghurst. She was interested in music and books; in later years Alec recalled that she 'had aspirations, I think, to a more intellectual life' than was possible in a large family (she was the second youngest of ten children) dominated by seven brothers with a passionate interest in motoring. 'So, I think the conversation in the household was mostly about vehicles and not about the life of the mind, which my mother would have appreciated more,' he told Heather Rusden in an extensive oral history completed for the National Library of Australia shortly before his death.[5]

The Crouch money had been made in the Casino district by Amy's father, Frederick George Crouch (1843–1922), an English-born storekeeper and cedar trader, who lived there from the 1870s until he retired to Sydney in 1894.[6] He too had been an MP for a short time, representing Richmond in the New South Wales Legislative Assembly (1887–1889), and was several times Mayor of Casino.[7] Amy Crouch had a close school friend who was also a reader, Beulah Bolton, and it was Beulah's older brother Alexander whom Amy married. The Crouches also lived in Randwick, where the family were stalwarts of St Jude's Anglican Church, and it was in Randwick that Alexander and Amy Bolton made their first home after their marriage at St Jude's in 1923.[8] This was in a flat in a large two-storied house in Arthur Street, overlooking Randwick Racecourse and known as The Laythes. It had been the Crouch family home since the 1890s.

Alec's uncle Harry left a vivid description of family life at The Laythes in the early years of the twentieth century. Meals were formal, with Frederick Crouch leading the family in lengthy prayers and Bible readings every morning after breakfast and a 'House Parlour maid' in attendance at every meal. There were three domestic staff and a gardener living with the family. Randwick was on the urban fringe in those days: as well as a garden big enough for two tennis courts, vegetable and formal gardens, and a large fowl run, a neighbouring paddock was rented for the family cow, which was milked twice a day in the stables by the gardener. The family got about mostly by horse and carriage, with the gardener sometimes in livery when driving Ada Crouch in her phaeton, until Frederick bought one of the first cars in Sydney. It was a French De Dion-Bouton: later he owned a Humber and a Buick, among others. Despite the patriarchal formality of the era, the family atmosphere was clearly relaxed, at least for Frederick Crouch's sons: 'Fred and Bert at times would steal Dad's car to go for a run. They would push it out into the street and start up the engine some distance from home so that Father would not hear the engine being started up'.[9]

Despite growing up in the Eastern Suburbs, it was Sydney Harbour that dominated Alec Bolton's recollections of his childhood. It was the place of his father's livelihood and the two boys often accompanied him on board the liners that his firm provisioned. After moving to Hunters Hill when he was eight, the harbour was his playground, first while playing at being sailor with ropes bought from a ship chandler in George Street ('friendly deckhands would splice eyes into these ropes and we would lasso various things') and then as a young teenager aboard a ten-foot wooden canoe in which he ventured up the Parramatta River and down the harbour as far as Balls Head. Sometimes he went alone, and sometimes with a friend. 'Well it was often quite rough,' he told Heather Rusden:

Because from Gladesville Bridge down to where we lived at Hunters Hill there was quite a long fetch of water and westerly gales could blow up quite a choppy sea … certainly a choppy sea for a canoe. One of the strange things, when I look back, is that it was an era in which precautions were not taken in the way they are today. I never had a lifebelt of any description. I could certainly swim, and swim quite well, but it would have been quite a long swim to the shore if I'd capsized. But I got through without any disasters. I remember one occasion where my mother was extremely worried because I was sort of missing and there was a big westerly gale blowing, but I was safe close to the shore and all was well. No, I never had any misadventures.

'Today it's an exciting place of recreation and tourism,' he said of the harbour:

But in the 1930s it was very much more a working harbour. There was a great deal of shipping activity and there were a great many workboats, steamboats of all descriptions using the harbour, working the harbour. Timber would be unloaded from Scandinavian timber vessels in Snails Bay and long rafts of logs would be towed by these small steam tugs up to timber yards beyond Gladesville. That was all of intense interest to me. I think of the light raking over the harbour and the air being often, of course, full of smoke, as it was in those days, from steam trains, but that was something of which one was not conscious. I found all that intensely interesting and exciting and from quite early days I used to read the shipping notices and be aware of what ships were coming in or what ships were in harbour and when they were sailing, what the tides were, things like that became of absorbing interest to me …

> *There's a famous photograph by Harold Cazneaux called When Liners Tear Themselves Away, which has often been reproduced and which shows a ship about to pull out from Pyrmont or the Quay with a huge crowd on the wharf and a huge crowd of passengers lining the deck and streamers flying. A great romantic photograph. That photograph was true to life and it happened perhaps every other Friday at the Quay. We were sort of witnesses and partakers in a way of that experience, simply by passing by in the ferries all the time when this was happening and watching the tugs as they eased these liners from their berths.*[10]

The Sydney he grew up in was still a colonial city of the Victorian era, with inner-city terrace houses and town-planning regulations borrowed directly from British models. While little remained of the Georgian town of the first decades of British invasion, with its windmill-filled hillscapes and reminders of the brutalities of the convict era, Sydney was yet to be hacked apart by the demolitions and massive building of roads, skyscrapers, carparks and freeways associated with its postwar sprawl. Car ownership was increasingly common, but public transport was still dominant in what was then a relatively compact city centred on its port—even though buses and trains had taken over from what had once been one of the largest tramway systems in the world. The magnificent new symbol of the city was the Sydney Harbour Bridge, opened by Premier Jack Lang in 1932 and quickly adopted as the iconic image of the state and indeed of Australia as a whole. The city's other bridges were still low level so road traffic had to stop when boats passed through at places like Gladesville and the swing span of the bridge opened.

Construction of the Sydney Harbour Bridge had begun in 1923, in the prosperous years that followed the First World War, but by the time it was declared open by Lang (after a fascist attempt to pre-empt him) the country was in the middle of the most savage recession in Australian and world history, with a third of the workforce unemployed and Australian political life in turmoil. Outward signs of all this were in some ways perhaps muted in Hunters Hill, a quiet, still semi-rural suburb, 'pastoral, warm and golden'[11], where well-built sandstone houses with big gardens shared narrow, steep lanes with modest cottages, but the Depression could not be ignored there either.

Many writers, business and professional people lived in Hunters Hill, including prominent legal families such as the Windeyers, distant relatives of the Boltons. The opening of the first Gladesville and Iron Cove bridges in the 1880s had brought the city to little more than eight kilometres away, by which time it was already considerably suburbanised. A few suburbs to the east, at Mosman and Balmoral, bohemian artists' colonies had once flourished. They finally surrendered to suburbia in the 1920s, although the area was favoured by artists and writers for a few more years, before 'Bohemia [was] … annexed by El Dorado'[12], as Gavin Souter, one of Alec's future authors, put it.

Hunters Hill was an altogether more respectable place: 'a desirable residential resort', as writer, publisher and maverick political activist 'Inky' Stephensen described it, 'peaceful and genteel', but it too has a distinctive history, which would have been highly visible to a boy growing up there. It was for a time nicknamed 'the French village' because of the many houses (some 200 of them) that the Joubert brothers had built there in the mid-nineteenth century, and whose Lombardy stonemasons were imitated by later generations. Alec's ferry trip each school day also took him near Australia's largest graving dock at the end of the Hunters Hill Peninsula at Woolwich, although according to Stephensen this industrial zone 'scarcely disturbed the Arcadian peace of the suburb. The noise, grime, and ugliness were all at the tip of a peninsula three miles long, and out of sight'.[13] Even as late as the 1970s, wrote author Ruth Park, 'a purring contentment' was

> *the resident spirit of Hunter's Hill. The adorable old houses … radiate the same serenity as do the dozens of mousy, one-storey cottages with veranda, two front windows, centre door, like a child's drawing. (But they are in old worked stone of soft grey and fawn.) Nearly every street has a blue glimmer at the bottom; some have romantically misty vistas of headlands and bays across the way.*[14]

One can't help but suspect that for young Alec, the bustle and grime of Woolwich would have been part of the attraction of the place: signs of the vital, working harbour he loved, and just as interesting as romantic vistas of headlands and bays. Some years later he wrote a series of poems set on the Hawkesbury River, north of Sydney. One is about a fruit boat, one of the steam lighters that used to carry crates of fruit from the orchards along the Hawkesbury to the morning markets in Sydney, which he might have seen crossing the harbour during his ferry trips as a child. The second stanza is, perhaps, tinged by childhood daydreams:

Here's a man with a job that I could envy—
This river-pirate in his wheelhouse, dreaming
Just as his fancy takes him, all the morning,
With nothing to do but watch the water creaming
Rinsed and fresh from the bow, the curving sweep
Of reaches slipping quietly past until
The houses over Wiseman's swing to sight
(Thrown up or down?) scattered about the hill.
How pleasant, then, to raid the packing-sheds
Beyond the town, and hear the graders stop,
To meet the growers on their tumbling wharves
And talk the season's prices and the crop;
Drink tea with them, and yarn, and take aboard
The bursting orange-cases, row on row,
That rise to shoulder-height above the deck,
And feel the ship with treasure overflow.
A cheerful life! And best of all the homeward
Run for the distant coast, the throbbing flight,
Urgent and fast down all the sleeping river,
Magnificently fruitful through the night.[15]

But the reason for the move to Hunters Hill was anything but happy. Alec's small world had been turned upside down with shocking suddenness when he was barely eight. In April 1933 his father died of meningitis at Kobe, during a work visit to Japan. That the impact of his sudden death was devastating can be clearly measured in financial terms, and it must have been the same emotionally. He had not been a wealthy man and the loss of his income left Amy and her sons quite poorly off. Indeed, family lore was that he had been so badly paid that his marriage to Amy had only been made possible by the flat provided by her mother at The Laythes and a small weekly allowance. A £500 payout from his life insurance was her only capital, although as a resident of New South Wales she would have been eligible for the new widows' pension and child endowment established by the Lang Labor government in 1926 and 1927.

The next blow came barely two months later when Amy and the children lost their home as well, after Ada Crouch too died suddenly.[16] This meant that The Laythes had now to be sold, in accordance with the terms of Frederick Crouch's will.[17] There would be an inheritance of some £2,000 for Amy after her father's estate had been wound up (her father had divided his estate unevenly, with the sons each receiving twice as much as the daughters), but the income from this would at the very least have halved her entitlement to the widows' pension (if she claimed it), leaving her with perhaps a pound a week from this source while she still had children under the age of 14, and it also probably now rendered her ineligible for the state's child endowment payment.[18]

Money must indeed have been tight, as Alec recalled more than 50 years later. It helped that she was evidently good at living carefully: 'Amy's household expenses were infinitesimal. No one could possibly be more economical than she, in every respect, but she lived a very happy life: happy with Allen and later happy with her two boys,' wrote her brother Harry.[19] Of course, many Australian families of the day lived in poverty. Minimum wage for a married man lucky enough to have a job in 1933 was £3 and 3 shillings a week (approximately $250 today): not a great deal more than Amy might have earned from her small capital, assuming a healthy return of around 6 per cent. A good deal of her income went in rent: 21 shillings a week, in Harry Crouch's recollection. Amy's close attention to the detail of her daily household expenses, and her determination to stay within budget, was typical of her generation and of the children who grew up in the shadow of the Great Depression, but it is also surely where Alec first learned to be careful about money. His meticulous costing of the books he was to print, and his principle of working within his budget no matter how committed he was to a project, was likely a legacy of these difficult years.

Throughout this troubled time, the Crouch and the Bolton families remained close. Harry in particular 'helped her to manage her limited finances and managed her accounts and used to ring her up almost every day and was really a wonderfully supportive person', Alec recalled in his oral history interview. And they moved to live near the Bolton family, renting a weatherboard cottage in Ferry Street, near the waterfront at Hunters Hill, and close to where Amy's four sisters-in-law lived in an old book-filled house named Kareela at 6 Mount Street.[20]

The aunts at Kareela became a large presence in Alec's life. Beulah Bolton read widely, judging by books from her library that Alec inherited, and also had literary connections through her work. One, for example, was with Robert D. FitzGerald, whose first small collection of poems, *The Greater Apollo*, privately printed and circulated by the author in 1927, was inscribed by the author to her in February 1927. (FitzGerald later mentioned that copies were distributed 'in memory of my mother', so perhaps she and Beulah were friends.[21])

But it was Constance Bolton, eldest of the four aunts and Alec's godmother, whom he later recalled as the major force in this household of four sisters and one servant ('Miss Moir, my aunts' servant and friend'). 'Hardly anyone influenced or overshadowed my life so much,' he wrote after her death in 1960. She was quick-witted, restless and intelligent, he recalled. 'She had a masculine mind in many ways, and other masculine characteristics too, you might say. She always concealed her emotions and had no feminine softness about her.' (As the poet Mairi MacInness says of her tutor at Somerville in the 1930s, 'one could still say such things then. To have a man's mind meant simply that you had an eye to what was important, and you had a range of interesting ideas that you weren't afraid to try out'.[22]) At the same time, she was 'first and foremost, a person of great kindness. From my earliest childhood … she was marvellously good to me, and to John too. She took us on numberless outings (often to the pictures, of which she was fond), and was always knitting us things and giving us things … Her kindness was almost oppressive at times; it was a love that would not let go, somehow'. She 'set great store by hospitality', he recalled, and liked 'to think of other people having a good time, or being successful at what they were doing. For herself, she did not mind what happened. She never went for a holiday'. (This, it might be said, could be seen as a characteristically feminine trait of the time.) 'She was a wonderful and amazing woman; difficult in many ways, but courageous and strong-minded, and inexhaustibly generous.'[23]

Despite the move to Hunters Hill, Alec and John stayed on at their primary school in Coogee and travelled to school on their own. The coastal suburb of Coogee borders Randwick;

when they first started, it would have been a short walk to school. Now they caught a ferry from Hunters Hill to Circular Quay and then a tram to Coogee. 'In those days the last leg took only 20 minutes,' he recalled, for there was much less traffic back then. The ferry journey allowed time for reading as well as for making friends with the crew, imagining themselves as deckhands (even, he remembered, being allowed into the wheelhouse at times to steer the ferry), and although he lamented that his reading was unguided, and that he often re-read favourite books to the point where he knew them by heart, the importance of books in his childhood is apparent in his recollections. Hugh Lofting's *Doctor Doolittle* series was a particular favourite; years later he was to be delighted when his eldest son Robert read them as well, and Robert remembers his father saying later still that he thought of Hugh Lofting as a great humanist.

As for so many children of the era, another big influence in his life was radio, and particularly the ABC children's programs. And while his mother did not really approve of the movies, he and John were avid filmgoers, splurging their savings on newsreel cinemas in particular. She read aloud to them, often Kipling. The family could not afford to buy many books, and he thought later that they were not well served by libraries either, but there was enough in the kitty for trips to the Sydney Symphony Orchestra, to which Amy subscribed. She sang in church choirs, and although Alec came to regret not having learned an instrument, he too sang, particularly rejoicing in Bach in his Sydney University days. He would remain a keen chorister for much of his adult life.

He was lucky in his schooling and remembered his first headmaster as a great influence: indeed, almost as a substitute father figure. This was William Nimmo, the remarkably long-serving headmaster (1914–1965) and founder of the Coogee Boys' Preparatory School, which was a private preparatory school for Sydney Grammar and The Scots College. Alec was at Coogee Boys' for seven years. (Amy seems to have managed the fees, despite her tiny income.) He then won scholarships to both Grammar and Scots and chose Grammar, where his father as well as John and his uncles had been students, starting there in 1940. He had a half scholarship, earned from athletic prowess as a sprinter, rather than talent as a scholar. This began early: in his first year at Coogee Boys' he won the 50-yard under-seven sprint in the annual school sports meeting in 1933, and he is remembered by colleagues at the National Library as a jogger.[24] In his last year at school he was stroke of the school eight, implying a high degree of proficiency as a rower. If asked what he wanted to do after school he would answer 'join the merchant navy', even though his teachers warned him he would need to improve in maths and physics if he was to cope with navigation. But it is evident from his oral history interview, and from talking to him myself in 1993, that going to sea was his only clearly defined ambition for life after Sydney Grammar. The family's resources evidently were not exhausted; there was enough coming in for his mother not to have to work outside her home. Nor did he have to leave school to work as soon as he was old enough to do so, and he perhaps lived somewhat in the moment, enjoying his time there.

So, to the extent that Alec's childhood can be described in class terms, he grew up in a middle-class, business-oriented family. This was true also of the four Bolton aunts, all of whom worked outside the home. One went into a bank, another to a major finance company, and one taught cooking. Beulah, his mother's friend, was the secretary of the Victoria League in New South Wales (1917–1961) and secretary of the Bush Book Club of New South Wales for most of those years, and was awarded the MBE when she retired. (The Bush Book Club ran libraries in country districts, while the Victoria League, founded in the UK during the Boer War and established in New South Wales during the First World War, did such things as providing hospitality for Army nurses in Sydney and, after the war, meeting war brides from the UK when their ships arrived.[25] It was one of numerous imperial propaganda organisations that spread from Britain between the 1880s and the First World War, and was primarily a women's organisation. It survives as the Victoria League for Commonwealth Friendship.[26])

Sydney Grammar, too, was at the heart of Sydney's business and professional establishment. While it took sport seriously, the school had a strong scholarly ethos and a connection to Sydney University going back to its foundation under the Sydney Grammar School Act of 1854, as well as a headmaster with scholarly credentials in Frederick George (Sandy) Phillips (head 1940–1950). Alec recalled later that a benefit of taking up rowing at Grammar was the long tram journey to the school's rowing shed at Gladesville, which gave him plenty of time to read, and in general he did better in history and literature than in maths or science. Another of his contemporaries in his last year at school recalls talking about books with him and finding a shared admiration for *The Great Gatsby*.[27]

Phillips was important to him also in setting standards of conduct and promoting concepts of service and duty that Alec happily accepted, although he did not particularly warm to him as a person. 'Young people are always rather awed by senior teachers or senior people who swim into their lives, cross their paths in one way or another,' he told Heather Rusden, revealing more perhaps about himself than young people generally. Other old boys remember Phillips, who had previously been Head of English at the school, as an inspiring teacher. He was Max Dupain's English master in his last year at school in 1930: in 1976 Dupain recalled that it was thanks to him 'I learned to love Shakespeare and can still quote numbers of salient extracts which we were required to learn by heart'.[28] Bruce Storey, a boy from a working class background who also attended Sydney Grammar in the 1940s and who went on to a career as a distinguished paediatrician, spoke in similar terms: 'it was my connection with that great Headmaster, Sandy Phillips, that left such an indelible impression. To me the ethos of Grammar started in Big School and Sandy's assemblies, a place which reminded one of the scholastic deeds of some and the sacrifices of many'.[29]

The Second World War was the other huge presence in Alec's adolescence. Students from his year at school died on active service: Sydney Grammar as a whole lost 208 old boys, more than 15 per cent of those who served in the forces.[30] While the war may have been a somewhat remote event for many Australians in 1939, with the Second AIF far away in North Africa and Greece, after 1941 Sydney was caught up at the edge of the Japanese assault on Australia. Although Alec makes no mention of the submarine attack of 31 May 1942, the events of that confused night, in which an attack on Sydney Harbour killed 21 Australian and British sailors, as well as the crews of all five Japanese midget submarines, took place not too far from the further reaches of his canoeing. Sydney people were alarmed by the attack: some moved inland, while others prepared for possible evacuation. As far away as Canberra, slit trenches were dug in the gardens of the Provisional Parliament House and broadcast facilities were set up for the new government-controlled radio news service to avoid the possibility of capture in Sydney by a Japanese invasion. Volunteer defence units kept watch along much of the coast while aerial attacks continued in the north until the end of 1943.

Even though Alec was an enthusiastic member of the Sydney Grammar cadet corps, at the end of his life his strongest memories of school in wartime were of watching his friends perform in school debates. Alec Bolton, as his friends often remark, was a gentle, judicious and sometimes shy man with a usually quiet manner, and this was probably true of his adolescence as well. Nonetheless, as soon as he turned 18 he enlisted in the Royal Australian Navy—where, rather to his surprise, despite those youthful adventures in his canoe, he found himself seasick most of the time. It was the seasickness that really got the sea out of his system, he said, and while still in the navy he began studies as an external student of Sydney University. His induction at Flinders Naval Depot (at Western Port Bay, south of Melbourne) was also a shock. It was:

> *a rather hostile environment where unpredictable things happened and discipline was severe—not that I minded that, I took quite easily enough to discipline, but I took less kindly to the unpredictable nature of people's conduct and also to the fact that I was exposed to a much wider range of people from different backgrounds whose style was different from perhaps the sheltered style that I had grown up in.*

After initial training he attended the Royal Australian Naval College, in those years also based at Flinders Naval Depot, before taking up duty on HMAS *Echuca*, a minesweeper working out of Darwin on surveying work in the Arafura and Timor Seas, in April 1945. He was promoted to acting sub-lieutenant in July 1945 and confirmed in that rank in January 1946. When the war ended in 1945 *Echuca* was refitted in Brisbane and sailed south to Bass Strait on minesweeping duties. Alec served there until February 1946, when he was transferred to shore-based duties at Rushcutters Bay. The Navy moved him there on compassionate grounds so he could live at home and care for his mother, who had suffered the first of a series of strokes. He was demobilised in February 1947 and received a war gratuity of £66.[31]

In early 1947, John (who had been demobilised early in 1946) was sent to Fiji by his employer, the Colonial Sugar Refining Company, where he was to remain until 1960. With him abroad, Alec became his mother's primary carer, although family memory is that John would have willingly shared the burden if he had still been in Sydney. The two brothers were close, as they would be for the whole of their lives, and they shared a highly developed sense of personal and family responsibility. Amy was able to stay at home until 1949, when her condition worsened and she moved to a private hospital at Drummoyne. She died in 1950. And so the prevailing note of seriousness in Alec's life continued after he left the Navy and became a full-time student at Sydney University in 1947. Although his voice sounds perfectly equable as he talks about those years in the National Library interview, he did allow in retrospect that he had become 'highly anxious and nervous' at the time. He did only moderately well in his Arts degree and sidestepped the allure of student politics at Sydney University, although he recalled an attempt to recruit him to help oust a group of leftists from control of the student newspaper. 'I didn't offer to take part in that. Why [Geoff Pretyman] chose me, I don't know.' He was more interested in singing Bach with the Sydney University Musical Society, and in his own writing:

> *I became interested in scriptwriting and was helped and influenced a lot by Gwen Meredith, the writer of the ABC's serials* The Lawsons *and* Blue Hills. *She was a niece of a great friend of my mother and at one stage—actually after my mother had gone to hospital—Gwen Meredith and her husband, Ainsworth Harrison, lived briefly in our house at Hunters Hill. She was then madly writing* The Lawsons, *or it may by then have been* Blue Hills *… and I was impressed by the fact that she would sit there at this large dictating machine, which came on a trolley like a traymobile, and she would dictate these episodes at the rate of knots. She knew I was interested in radio and encouraged me. I think it was largely through her influence that I came to write two or three short radio serials, which were broadcast in a Sunday program that fell under the responsibility of a very nice man named Kenneth Henderson, who was the head of the religious affairs … department of the ABC in those years. So, I wrote these serials, which were kind of adventure serials but with a kind of moral or religious twist in them. They didn't rise out of any particular conviction on my part of a religious nature at that time, but they were a means of trying to break into radio.*

His first episode, for a serial called *The Young Company*, was broadcast in 1947. He earned five pounds an episode, and kept it up for two or three years, selling at least enough episodes to buy himself a typewriter, but eventually came to feel he was writing in the wrong area. Again with Gwen Meredith's encouragement, he then wrote a few trial episodes for a serial on commercial radio, but this came to naught. 'I really didn't have enough experience of life to attempt to be writing it,' he later concluded.

2

Angus & Robertson

Perhaps Alec was drifting somewhat at this time. A sea anchor of self-confidence and firmly implanted loyalties was firmly attached, and he was in no danger of sinking, but it was luck that took him into publishing. Up until then he had been thinking semi-seriously of teaching: indeed he had been interviewed for a position as a trainee teacher, and had sought advice on teaching from his former headmaster at Coogee Boys'. Then one day in 1950, quite by chance, he met a schoolfriend who was about to head off for the UK, creating a vacancy in the editorial department at Angus & Robertson. At his friend's suggestion Alec went to see Beatrice Davis, head of editorial, and then George Ferguson, head of publishing, who hired him almost immediately. It was to be the watershed of his life, and yet it also depended on a great deal that had gone before. Above all, I suspect, it mattered that he was comfortable around women, for it was one of the most formidable women in Australian publishing who was to be his next major formative influence, and the office he joined was otherwise female at the time. Alec liked women and respected their intelligence, dedication and hard work: he had been much loved and cared for by them from his earliest years, and he had grown up with an ease and an ability to communicate with women that many men of his time (and still today) simply could not comprehend. It is striking that so many of the writers, artists and binders with whom he would later work in creating the Brindabella Press were also women of talent and achievement, as were many of his future colleagues at the National Library of Australia. Although to some Alec appeared quiet, even shy at times—he had a trick of turning away from you when talking to you—his capacity for friendship, and the warmth with which his friends (both male and female) still speak of him, is memorable.

The small Angus & Robertson editorial department worked in a crowded office in the attic of 89 Castlereagh Street, the lower floors of which formed the firm's flagship bookshop (and which had famously begun life as a livery stable). It was then the best-known bookshop in Australia, with a legendary history as the base of the leading publisher of its day, located in the most celebrated bookselling precinct in the country. Here his book-soused life really began, where, as A.G. Stephens had put it two decades earlier:

The Gilded Tomes stand proudly up
The Sets are ranged in piles
The Small Octavos, cheek by jowl, would stretch for Several Miles
The Boxes spill their Dusty Wealth
The Windows make Display

It is the Street of Lots of Books
Along the Castlereagh.[1]

The heart of the business was Angus & Robertson's role as a bookseller, he later reflected, with sales so substantial that at one time print runs for some books were held up in the UK until its order, which could be for thousands of copies, had been received. But even as publishers, the firm still dominated the Australian market, producing about 100 new titles and editions a year in the 1950s. It had a strong backlist, had bought the Australian rights to many popular overseas books, and its wholly owned printing business, Halstead Press, was relied on by many other publishers. Oddly though, and despite its bookselling credentials, with its own publications Alec later considered that 'the firm tended to put more effort into producing books than selling them'. Halstead Press too had this strange tendency, sometimes even giving priority to printing rival publishers' works over Angus & Robertson books to meet crucial deadlines such as Christmas. These weaknesses would in the end help bring the firm down.[2]

Alec's new boss was Beatrice Davis, whom he admired and whose influence he would feel for the rest of his life.

> *She was a very sympathetic person, very encouraging of her staff, very supportive of her staff at all times, very generous to me, a good person at training people and a person who imparted her standards.*

Davis had joined Angus & Robertson in 1937, when she became the firm's (and probably Australia's) first full-time editor. Alec also worked closely with Davis' deputy Nan McDonald, who taught him copyediting, and who was also to remain a friend for life. Rosemary Dobson, Elisabeth Hughes and Janet Bennett were the other permanent staff in the small section. 'They were an enthusiastic and dedicated team of editors,' commented Anthony Barker, who worked in the editorial department at Angus & Robertson in the last years of Davis' time there (1966–1973). He cited both Alec and Rosemary Dobson extensively in his short tribute to Davis, published by the Society of Editors as a celebration of one of its most distinguished members:

> *Trained to Beatrice's high standards, they were expected to be 'patient and self-effacing, tactful and courteous—and self-controlled', meaning that if any rewriting was needed they should not use their own voice but the author's voice at its best. It was a histrionic gift, Beatrice considered. It was also a bit like invisible mending: the better the handiwork, the less likely it was to be noticed.*

'Beatrice imparted a lot of training through her conversation, which was largely work-oriented,' Alec Bolton recalled.

> *She was not a dominating person, but she had great strength of personality and persuasiveness. People who worked for her tended to absorb her values. Her department was of one mind about most things. It was a harmonious setting.*[3]

Davis followed Oxford style—possibly, he later remarked,

> *even more strictly than they followed it at Oxford. Manuscripts would be cleared of their roughnesses, ambiguities and inconsistencies; and*

> *if they were non-fiction they would be rigorously checked too. It must have been like working at the New Yorker … Proofreading was equally careful … I don't think you will find a printer's error in an A&R book of that era.*[4]

'In my early days the thought that something might slip through contrary to house style would practically keep me awake at night,' he recalled on a different occasion, although on reflection he questioned the remoteness of Angus & Robertson's editing from many authors.

> *It was quite the usual thing for a heavily edited MS to go to the printer without the author being aware of what had been done to it until he saw the galley proofs. What is amazing to me now is that more of them didn't kick up a fuss.*[5]

As an editorial trainee Alec's major task was to sift through the flood of manuscripts coming in, as well as learning how to be a copyeditor and how to index. Davis had brought rigour and a commitment to literary publishing to Angus & Robertson, which prior to her arrival preferred writers in the tradition of its past successes with bush poets such as Henry Lawson and 'Banjo' Paterson and novelists such as the hugely successful Arthur Upfield, creator of the 'Bony' detective series, and E.V. Timms, who wrote historical romances with print runs of around 15,000.[6] Davis established two important annual anthologies, one of Australian poetry and the other of short stories, and by the time Alec arrived in 1950 had transformed the firm's poetry and fiction lists. In addition, Angus & Robertson also published a great deal of non-fiction, from school textbooks and practical manuals on topics ranging from tailoring to the diseases of sheep, to history and biography titles. It had sold hundreds of thousands of copies of the *Commonsense Cookery Book*.[7] 'The training at A&R was rigorous,' one editor of the time recalled. 'Everything that I worked on was looked over … I worked very hard to avoid the embarrassment of having my errors of omission and commission pointed out to me with little mercy.' Nonetheless, she went on to comment:

> *Those who know only the harassed existence of an editor of the 1990s cannot imagine the joys of being an editor in those early days. We were vastly underpaid (women automatically much less than men), housed in an attic that was a firetrap, but enjoying the most amusing and informative tea-breaks I have ever known. Nan McDonald the poet poured the tea, and we talked not only 'shop', but about the theatrical events of the day, the books we were reading, and the gossip of a small publishing world.*[8]

This was a world largely without literary agents; publishers such as Angus & Robertson mostly dealt directly with authors and their manuscripts, and there were a great many of the latter. Alec recalled:

> *The firm was receiving huge numbers of unsolicited manuscripts, all of which were conscientiously dealt with. Lots of novels were coming in that had been entrants in literary competitions conducted by the Sydney Morning Herald. The Sydney Morning Herald ran a number of novel contests from 1945, '46 onwards. The first of them was won by Ruth*

Park's novel, The Harp in the South. These competitions attracted thousands of entries and in the course of time these came flooding in to Angus & Robertson to be dealt with. There were lots of non-fiction manuscripts coming in, lots of people who had been prisoners of war of the Japanese were writing their experiences and submitting them. Endless numbers of children's books were submitted. So, there was a vast amount of material coming through all the time.[9]

Although Angus & Robertson was the dominant Australian publisher of the day, with a growing and diverse list that 'rode the post-war boom in Australian books'[10], its hegemony was no longer absolute. It is telling that there is no publisher among the cast of literary types in Arthur Upfield's *An Author Bites the Dust* (1948), a thinly disguised attack on those who dismissed his own work as mere 'commercial fiction' rather than serious writing. Instead, the maker and breaker of careers in his cast of villains is a producer for ABC Radio. 'Publicity is an author's very breath of life,' announces the writer Mervyn Blake, just before he is murdered, and the general opinion of the fictional Australian Society of Creative Writers is crucial to the careers of its members.[11] For Alec, though, there was no doubt that he had arrived at the right place and the perfect job. 'It seemed to me,' he told Heather Rusden, 'to have an element of rightness about it, as if a cloud had lifted and some kind of future could be discerned.'

Surely this was also because, as well as finding Angus & Robertson generally a congenial place to work, he quickly fell in love with one of his fellow editors. Rosemary Dobson was a young poet who won the 1946 *Sydney Morning Herald* Literary Competition prize for poetry with 'Ship of Ice'.[12] Her second collection of poems, *In a Convex Mirror*, had been published by Dymock's Book Arcade in 1944, by which time she had been published in *The Bulletin*, as well as *Southerly*, *Poetry* and *Meanjin Papers*. A sociable, self-assured and beautiful young woman who was already a presence on Sydney's literary scene, Rosemary introduced Alec to a coterie of Sydney writers including Douglas Stewart and his wife, the artist Margaret Coen, and through them Norman Lindsay, who had a studio in the same building where the Stewarts lived and painted two portraits of her.[13] While she and Nan McDonald were on at least calling terms with Dame Mary Gilmore[14], Rosemary also became friendly with many of the younger people who frequented the Angus & Robertson editorial department, among them the poet Francis Webb (later to be godfather to Ian Bolton) and the other writers, young and old, who looked to Beatrice Davis for advice and support. This included James McAuley, Elizabeth Riddell, Peter Hopegood, John Blight, Ethel Anderson, Hugh McCrae, Xavier Herbert and Ruth Park. And, apart from her proofreading and editorial credentials, as a promising poet herself she was highly regarded by her employers. Poetry was central to George Ferguson's understanding of how the firm could contribute to Australian culture. Neil James, director of the Plain English Foundation, has calculated that of 136 poetry titles published in Australia with Commonwealth Literary Fund sponsorship between 1939 and 1973, Angus & Robertson published almost half—and they were often early works by new writers, with little prospect of being profitable.[15]

Alec and Rosemary married in June 1951 and set up home in the flat at Neutral Bay where Rosemary had lived for some time, part of a house owned by the deputy Mitchell librarian, Heather Sherrie, a close friend of Beatrice Davis (and through whom Rosemary herself had met Davis). The wedding was a small affair, mostly close family, followed by a honeymoon on a rented Halvorson cruiser on the Hawkesbury River. They travelled together to work every day, mostly by ferry, and Alec remembered those early years as quite idyllic. At first they had some concern about the six-year difference in their ages, Rosemary mentioned in her oral history interview, but she felt strongly that he was the wiser of the two despite being younger, and the age gap never mattered. Their happiness was marred by one great loss, the death of their first child, Alexandra, who was born six weeks prematurely in October 1953 and who lived for only a few hours. Years later Alec was to recall his sadness then, writing with characteristic empathy to a friend whose wife had just had a miscarriage:

> *at the time we thought we would never get over it, but of course we did. But I do quite often think of the unrealised potential of that life, and wonder what course it might have taken.*[16]

Rosemary's poem 'The Birth (ii)', published in her next book (which she dedicated to Alec), mourns that same loss.[17]

Lissant was born a year later in 1954, followed by Robert in 1958 and Ian in 1961. Rosemary left work outside the home when they started a family, as was common at the time, which halved their income. At around this time Alec began writing a regular Sydney Letter for the *Toowoomba Chronicle*, a job he inherited from his friend, the poet and journalist David Rowbotham. 'I used to spend every weekend grinding out these Sydney Letters, and it used to take most of the weekend,' he later recalled. He was a great admirer of *The New Yorker*, and said he modelled his writing on its Talk of the Town section. Each letter earned him two guineas, a useful supplement to his weekly income from Angus & Robertson, which by then was 13 pounds a week (he had started on eight), and almost enough to pay the weekly rent, but the loss of Rosemary's income meant they had to be quite careful about money.

Alec and Rosemary had a great deal in common. Apart from their work and their shared passion for books and writing (indeed, Alec too was a published poet, with six poems accepted by *The Bulletin* between 1950 and 1952, although he seems to have stopped writing poetry soon afterwards), they had both lost fathers while young and both had grown up in straitened circumstances.[18]

Rosemary de Brissac Dobson was born in Sydney in 1920, the daughter of Arthur Dobson, an English-born civil engineer (he was a son of the poet and essayist Austin Dobson, and, like Amy Crouch, one of ten children), and Marjorie Dobson (née Caldwell).[19] Arthur and Marjorie had met at a meeting of Sydney's Dickens Society.[20] Rosemary was the second of their two daughters and was five when her father died, leaving the family hard up. After three unsettled years sharing a house with her grandmother's large family, matters improved when one of her English aunts, Lissant Dobson, visited Australia and discovered just how poor they were. (Rosemary recalled later that the Dobson family in England, although it did its best to stay in touch after Arthur's death, for several years had no real idea of her mother's circumstances. 'They used to send books "for the nursery" and we were living three in a room,' she told Heather Rusden.) Her introduction of Marjorie to Susannah Williams, head of Women's College at the University of Sydney, led to a further introduction to Winifred West, headmistress of Frensham, a progressive girls' boarding school at Mittagong. This transformed all their lives. Marjorie became a housemistress at Frensham and both Rosemary and her older sister, Ruth, were offered free places in the school. Ruth went on to a distinguished career in the Australian Public Service, serving as Australia's first female ambassador (in Denmark and Ireland), while Rosemary, as Joy Hooton has recorded, found the school

> *possibly the perfect environment … She revelled in the school's well-stocked library, in its beautiful setting and family atmosphere and in the unusual ethos established by Winifred West … and her encouragement of the students' creative endeavours in a spirit of community.*[21]

Rosemary later recalled that one of the big impacts her mother had on her life was 'the way she made things possible'. It is an observation that her own son Ian makes about the way Rosemary and Alec lived also.

When she turned 21 Rosemary came into a small legacy. It was enough to live in Sydney without having to earn an income for two years, she calculated, so she gave up her job at Frensham, where she was now a pupil-teacher, and moved back to Sydney. 'My education had equipped me with an eagerness to continue being educated,' she later reflected, 'and to write—if not to write *and* paint.'[22] The English Department at Sydney University allowed her to attend lectures and submit essays, and at the same time she studied design one day a week with Thea Proctor. (As an unmatriculated student, she could not sit exams or take a degree. Many years later she would be awarded an honorary doctorate by Sydney University, to her great satisfaction.) Towards the end of the war she also worked briefly as a naval cipher clerk at Elizabeth Bay before joining Angus & Robertson in 1946, firstly as a proofreader and then as an editor.[23]

Printing came up early in the relationship between Rosemary and Alec, when she told him he ought to have a press of his own. She also gave him a copy of Herbert Simon and Harry Carter's *Printing Explained: An Elementary Practical Handbook for Schools and Amateurs.*[24] She had herself been an amateur printer in her youth, printing her own first volume of poetry in an edition of about 200 as a student at Frensham in 1937 (including the cover paper, which is a linocut signed with her initials), and later working on the Frensham Press when she joined the staff of the school. The press was a modest affair, established by Joan Phipson, the librarian/printer at the school (she was later a distinguished writer of books for children, and remained one of Rosemary's lifelong friends). Living in London at the time, Phipson went to see Leonard Woolf at the Hogarth Press in 1936, in search of advice. The school bought an Adana 8 x 5 inch benchtop press and one fount of Garamond type as a result. Rosemary's interest in printing continued at university, when her major essay during her two years as an unmatriculated student was on 'Typographical Design in the Twentieth Century'. Years later, in 1973, soon after the Boltons returned to Australia from London, she spoke about that essay:

> *It was a curious work into which I pasted all sorts of ephemera like bus-tickets. Architecture may be said to be the custodian of the arts, but typography is the custodian of all arts and of all knowledge. Picasso is probably the greatest innovator of our time, but the man whose innovations have been most pervasive is surely Stanley Morison who, as begetter of that great typeface, Times Roman, and as reviver of such notable types as Baskerville and Garamond, has revolutionized the appearance of the printed word in our time. Consciously or unconsciously we are all indebted to him. Typography, which in a peculiar way brings together literature and art; which demands restraint but which can also allow for extravagance and eccentricity, is a subject of compelling interest to me now, as it was then.*[25]

The gift of *Printing Explained* was to have a 20-year gestation, Alec later said, but Rosemary's long-term enthusiasm for letterpress printing was to be central to the foundation and the conduct of the Brindabella Press. It's there in their early years together, evident in her poem 'The Alphabet', first published in *Child with a Cockatoo* in 1955, in which 'my twenty six, my leaden men' rest for the night upon a 'bare and silvered hill', which could be a press platen or a galley.[26] And it would be there for the many years of their long and happy marriage.

In 1953 Alec was seconded to *The Australian Encyclopaedia* to work on its second edition. First published in two volumes in 1925–1926, the new edition was a considerable expansion at ten substantial volumes and was edited by the journalist and ornithologist Alec Chisholm. It was intended to be one of the firm's flagship publications, meant to 'give a comprehensive picture of Australian life, both past and present'.[27] Alec was one of three assistant editors, and at the same time served as assistant editor of the journal *Southerly*.[28] Early in 1958 Chisholm's successor as general editor of the encyclopaedia, Bruce Pratt, revealed something of the difficulties in building a reliable editorial team for such a large project. There were many failures because of 'a sheer inability to conform to the mental discipline that is essential in the preparation of an authoritative work of reference', he said.

> *The assembling of all this material and the presenting of it as an alphabetical work of reference made a formidable undertaking. More than 380 contributors, each an authority in his own field, had to be commissioned to write articles or groups of articles. Often their authority was more in evidence than their reliability. Some promised to supply contributions and then forgot all about them; some departed for distant shores, without saying good-bye, leaving their work half-done; others looked on the Encyclopaedia as a medium of propaganda and shaped their writing accordingly.*[29]

'There was a sense of national purpose about it really,' Alec told Heather Rusden. 'It was a pretty high-minded enterprise and I learnt an awful lot about Australia.' He reflected just before publication in 1958 that the impending end of the encyclopaedia brought mixed feelings.

> *On the one hand it will be good to throw off the load that we have carried for so long; on the other, it seems certain that nothing else one could ever do at Angus & Robertson's would be so satisfying or worthwhile. The Encyclopaedia represents a really creative enterprise.*[30]

The *Australian Encyclopaedia* project was so large and all-encompassing that it perhaps made a return to the normal routine of work in the editorial department difficult for Alec, and it also led him to think about the nature of the career he had chosen—a timely reflection, for the coming year would prove to be an especially difficult time for Angus & Robertson, where such enterprises as the encyclopaedia were for a time viewed with suspicion. There is a long reflection on what he saw as paradoxical in editorial work in his most substantial attempt at keeping a regular journal, in 1958:

> *It is obviously true that editorial work for the Encyclopaedia, more than almost any other work you could think of, requires the utmost care and attention to the accuracy of detail. Everybody concerned with the enterprise acknowledges this to be so. Yet the person who, like Janet [his colleague Janet Bennett], really stands by this idea, and holds out for perfection, is despised and persecuted … There seem to me to be two reasons for this extraordinary state of affairs. One is the genuine economic reason. After all, books must come out, and the longer they are delayed in editing the greater is the overhead and the smaller is the productivity. Where the basis of the whole enterprise is in the last resort commercial, it is obvious that pressure will be brought to bear by the management or the editorial chiefs to see that processes are speeded up as much as possible. That is one reason. The other is less obvious, but perhaps more devastating. My experience is that the class of editorial person who takes 'average' 'reasonable' care <u>may</u> be unable to bear to see his own shortcomings so painfully revealed by the example of the absolute perfectionist. He grows restive under the example, and perhaps feels and may even begin to murmur that the perfectionist is going too*

> *far, is too fussy, is wasting time over things that don't matter or that could be sidestepped. There may be justice in the last of these claims. Anyway, what happens (I believe) is that the people who are average, reasonable editors, the mediocre majority, that is to say, unconsciously league together against the perfectionist, and unconsciously conspire for the perfectionist's downfall. I put these views forward to Rosemary Dunlop today. She thought I was going too far, as perhaps I was and am. Still, I know the psychology of the mediocre editor well, being of the class myself.*[31]

Perfect or not, the *Encyclopaedia* was not promoted strongly and did not sell as well as expected. It was one sign among many that the firm was vulnerable and that its status as the leading publisher in Australia was declining even though it was still making a profit. At the same time it owned considerable assets, above all in real estate, and therefore was inevitably bound to be the target of a takeover attempt. The next few years were to be torrid for Alec, and indeed for most of his colleagues.

The slow and perhaps inevitable take-down of Angus & Robertson began when Walter Burns, a real-estate developer who had been buying shares in the firm for some years, came onto the board in 1958. Within two years he had taken control of the board and had become managing director, with the publishing director, George Ferguson, reporting to him. As well as splitting Angus & Robertson's publishing, bookselling and printing operations into separate companies, Burns restructured the publishing division, ostensibly run by Ferguson, and created a new position as director of publishing. To his horror, Alec was given this new job. Instead of it being Beatrice Davis, the most experienced editor in the country, with unrivalled contacts in literary Australia, it would now be his task to find new bestselling authors, to commission new books, and to bring new commercial rigour to the firm's publishing operations. While he was in no position to refuse the promotion, and Davis understood that the situation was not of his making, he was now her supervisor.

Alec was 'distressed and embarrassed', as Davis' biographer put it.[32] He lasted only a short time in the new post, resigning angrily towards the end of 1960. Although such decisions as the sale of the *Australian Encyclopaedia* to the Grolier Society 'for a ridiculously low £100,000'[33] may have been part of his motivation, he later remembered its prime cause being the treatment of a senior colleague who lost his job because of a dispute with Burns.

> *It sounds very high-minded to say so, but I resigned on a point of principle because I thought that it was a disgraceful thing to have happened and so I left. That was a pretty upsetting thing to happen because Rosemary and I by then had two children, one of whom was one or one-and-a-half or something, very small, and I was sort of on the beach for several months and trying to scratch together a living as a freelance.*[34]

Given his generally equable temperament, let alone these responsibilities as a family man with a wife and young children to support, plus a mortgage (they had bought a house in Gordon, an Upper North Shore suburb of Sydney), the pressures causing him to 'storm angrily' into George Ferguson's office and to resign must have been extreme.

As it happened, Burns' days in charge were also numbered. An extraordinary coalition of Angus & Robertson's leading authors and publishing staff (prominent among them George Ferguson, the founder's grandson; Beatrice Davis; and Colin Roderick, the head of technical and educational publishing, who turned out to have finely honed tactical abilities), along with the publisher Sam Ure Smith, gathered enough support from shareholders at the end of 1960 to elect a new board and to overthrow Burns. It was a fascinating moment in Australian cultural history: the last act of a hegemony built in the early years of the twentieth century, with its hard-bitten views of what Australian writing could and should be. This is not the place to dwell on the subsequent history of the firm, except for the brief period when Alec returned to it, but the story was not over and in the end Colossus fell.[35]

After some freelance work for the Adelaide-based publisher Rigby, Sam Ure Smith gave him a large manuscript to edit: a translation of an important Japanese account of the conquest of Malaya in 1941–1942.[36] This led to five years working at Ure Smith, a tiny publishing outfit with a small crowded office in the Sydney CBD, who had had one recent runaway bestseller, Nino Culotta's *They're a Weird Mob* (appropriately, turned down by Angus & Robertson). Tellingly, his was not simply an editorial position; again he was tasked with finding new authors:

> *Ure Smith … felt that there was a kind of royal road of best sellers which was going to be produced, and that was a slightly anxious responsibility because although it's nice to have bestsellers, you can't always find them.*

Perhaps his biggest success was in tracking down the author of a series of newspaper articles about spoken English in Australia, which became the phenomenally successful *Let Stalk Strine* (Ure Smith, 1965). (This was Alastair Morrison, who used the pseudonym Professor Afferbeck Lauder.) Alec edited a couple of Norman Lindsay's books at this time[37], and also rescued John Meredith's significant first collection of *Folksongs of Australia* from a publishing doldrum in which it had languished for several years.[38] Alec was happy at Ure Smith, and considered Sam Ure Smith to be both 'friend and mentor'.[39] He took several months to decide whether to accept an invitation to return to Angus & Robertson, but in 1966 the offer of a posting to London to establish an editorial outpost there persuaded him. 'Boltons To Be Transported' he told family and friends in July 1966. They would leave in November and expected to be away for three years.[40] Given the choice of going by air or sea, they opted for the six-week sea passage, which gave them their first sight of Asia, the Middle East and the Mediterranean as a bonus. It was a treasured experience for generations of Australians, and Alec's letters home to his family show that the Boltons relished it too.

Angus & Robertson had had an office in London for many years, initially to manage its substantial purchases of British books for export to Australia. Although the old Great Russell Street premises were gone—sold during the Burns years—George Ferguson wanted to develop sales of the firm's books overseas. He has been described as 'a pioneer Australian book exporter, particularly to Britain', and he had ambitions in the American market as well as Asia. By the late 1950s Angus & Robertson were publishing up to 17 titles a year in Britain. Added to British sales of books published in Australia, 'combined sales in Britain were averaging 82,000 copies a year'.[41] The firm's office was now in Bartholomew Close, near the Smithfield meat markets and Barts Hospital: 'out of the publishing swim', as Alec said, but still in the heart of the city:

> *it was a place where you could go into a pub for lunch and there would be white coated people there, some with blood on them who were from the Smithfield markets, and others, probably without blood on them, who were interns or whatever from Bart's Hospital. But you couldn't always tell who was who by looking at them. It was an interesting location to be.*

There were publishing successes for Alec in these years, although no bestsellers. He noticed that a local woman in Richmond, where they lived, had developed an exercise program for women to do at home with the catchy title of 'Slimnastics', and commissioned her to write a successful book by the same title, which was later sold to Penguin. Reading magazines for ideas he came across a piece on sailing for women and commissioned the author to write *The Sea-Wife's Handbook*, which was also highly successful when translated by a German maritime publisher. He travelled to the US and bought the rights to publish titles in the British publishing zone, which included Australia.

> *So, we had quite an active program and I think we came to be quite well accepted on the London scene. London was full of very big and influential publishers and very big and influential agents and we rated nowhere in that. But, nevertheless, England is a place where small niches can be carved out and we carved out one.*[42]

Meanwhile, they got on with family life in London. They had chosen Richmond for its closeness to the Thames and Richmond Park, and quickly made friends there. The children liked their schools and were doing well. They bought a Renault 4— 'it was the nicest car I've ever had'—which gave them the opportunity to travel widely in the UK on holidays. There was a trip to Venice, and one to the Outer Hebrides. Alec joined a choir and went to many concerts, sometimes with Rosemary and sometimes with Catharine Carver, a distinguished editor with a New York background who would remain a friend of both Rosemary and Alec for life. And it was now that Alec enrolled in evening classes at the London College of Printing.

Printing, which thus began as an evening avocation, would over the years become his passion and his overwhelming interest. What, then, did he bring to this new pursuit? For a start, it seems self-evident that his years of working at Angus & Robertson and Ure Smith are central. In an interview with Heather Rusden for the Library he spoke of his early interest in the

> *processes of publication, the ways in which manuscripts were transformed into print and the excitement of the physical object … and the fact that one had played some kind of a part in that transformation from turning a manuscript into a book.*[43]

When he began as a member of the editorial department at Angus & Robertson, he was generally quite removed from the printing aspect of publishing. But this was, as he put it in a talk to a History of the Book in Australia meeting in 1994, 'the last great decade of letterpress printing', and for him it clearly became the standard against which all printing would be measured. There were people who brought him closer to production as well. He was friendly with Henry Mund, the production editor of the *Australian Encyclopaedia*, who was 'a gifted typographer' as well as having 'immense learning about books', someone whose influence he often mentioned.[44] Mund 'imparted to me a feeling for production that I had not had before', said Alec. 'That was a kind of seminal influence to me, which became very important.'[45] Another was Leslie Apthorp, chief printer at Angus & Robertson's Halstead Press, who gave a series of talks to the firm's editorial staff.[46] Apthorp, who had come to the firm from the great printers Jarrolds of Norwich, was a Monotype enthusiast. 'You would see him around the factory in his immaculate white coat, an avenging angel among the rather happy-go-lucky compositors and printers of that period', Alec recalled, adding that although Halstead Press was a Linotype shop, its small Monotype department was usually responsible for the better-looking books of the day.[47]

Furthermore, all his life Alec mirrored Angus & Robertson's single-minded focus on publishing and selling books over anything else—books that mattered, and not necessarily profitable ones. As George Ferguson put it in 1954, 'we have always concentrated all our thoughts and all our efforts on books'. He later explained:

> *I think on the whole we were interested in what we saw as the basic essential worth of the book rather than what it would make. If it would make a profit, well and good. If it didn't make a profit, we'd probably know that before we started, but we'd still do it if we thought the book itself was worth it … We knew we had to think about money to some extent too, but basically we thought about books.*[48]

The books of the Brindabella Press would be driven by a similar idealism, which most publishers today would dismiss as quite unworldly.

Later, at Ure Smith, Alec learned a great deal about typography and art from Sam Ure Smith, whose books had primarily been art books up to then and who 'did all his own production'.[49] After his return to Angus & Robertson, in London, Alec was again involved in production as well as commissioning and buying titles. There he oversaw production of titles such as James Lipton's *An Exaltation of Larks*, reprinted photolitho from the attractive American original, and at times drew on his hobby of photography in designing new jackets. He remembered one in particular that featured Lissant's hands breaking an egg into a bowl, for the Angus & Robertson reissue of *The Other Half of the Egg*, when it took several dozen eggs to get the right shot: 'it was actually a jolly good cover ... I was a kind of photographer manqué, I suppose'. It is a striking and effective jacket. (He also photographed bookshops, including for the back cover of early impressions of Helene Hanff's unexpected bestseller of 1971, *84, Charing Cross Road*, published by Andre Deutsch.) Indeed, he was beginning to look for a possible new career path in production as his uneasiness with Angus & Robertson grew:

> *I felt that I was to some extent running out of steam as an editor. I didn't think that I had particularly good ideas and I was probably not enough of a reader to be a really good editor.*[50]

Under different circumstances, his enrolment at the London College of Printing might not have taken him into the usually letterpress-oriented world of the private press. Fortunately, he enrolled at a time when hand composition of metal type and letterpress machining were still very much part of the trade curriculum. While machine composition of type was by then dominant, the production of books had until very recently been done on relief presses that, despite their sophistication, were directly descended from those of the fifteenth century. Even though offset printing was taking over, knowledge of the earlier processes was still seen as relevant and useful to good printing.[51]

Alec was much older than the other students, but they accepted him, and 'there were very, very good instructors there, senior people who knew a tremendous amount and from whom I learnt a lot'.[52] At this time he also became friendly with the illustrator Richard Kennedy, whose youthful memories of working at the Hogarth Press were about to be published as the first book of John and Rosalind Randle's Whittington Press[53] (and whom Alec commissioned to illustrate a children's book for Angus & Robertson[54]), but he later recalled that it was primarily his lunchtime visits to the St Bride Library and displays put on by the National Book League that introduced him to the private press books that inspired him.

> *I got bitten by this idea and the idea began to form in my mind that if I returned to Australia I would like to start a press of my own and do some printing.*[55]

It is telling that his children still recall the seriousness with which he approached his evening classes.[56] It is also worth noting that the Frensham connection to printing emerged again around this time, when during a brief return to Australia on business in 1971 he was introduced by Winifred West (founder of Frensham School and the Sturt Workshops at Mittagong) to the printer/engraver Mary Quick of the Juniper Press. It was to be their only meeting, and nothing came of West's proposal that he might teach letterpress printing at Sturt, but he remained an admirer of Mary Quick's work as an 'under-recognised pioneer of our trade in Australia' for the rest of his life.[57]

The following October—just before they left London for Canberra—Alec printed the first production of what was to become the Brindabella Press. It was a small broadside poem by Rosemary called 'Knossos', in an edition of 24 copies on an Adana 8 x 5 inch tabletop platen press he bought in London. The typeface was 10 point Univers, an interesting choice he never made again. The recipients were family and friends: a list that included the book collector Walter Stone; the poets David Campbell, R.D. FitzGerald and Douglas Stewart; and Lady Casey, artist and aviator. This small, unpretentious piece embodied much of what was to come. It was printed letterpress, about which Alec was to become so passionate. He kept his first little press, a common starter press for people becoming interested in letterpress printing, for the rest of his life, and it is now in the National Library of Australia, where his papers are kept.[58] *Knossos* was produced with his wife, a key partner in the press as it grew. It was distributed within a circle of people as concerned with poetry and writing as Alec Bolton and Rosemary Dobson were. And Alec documented its distribution, just as he was to keep meticulous records of the production and distribution of later works.

There are some differences from what was to come. *Knossos* was not illustrated. It used a modern sans serif type instead of the Baskerville that Alec came to prefer, and he used larger presses for his later titles. His subsequent print runs were to be more substantial, although never more than 450. And it is impossibly rare today. There are two copies at the National Library, including one in the Bolton Papers, and he gave a copy to the Fryer Library, which was very early in seeking Brindabella ephemera. It comes on the market occasionally. (The poem itself can be read in Rosemary Dobson's *Over the Frontier*, 1979, and in her *Collected*, 2012.[59])

In later years he was to be somewhat disparaging of the printing of *Knossos*, and this too was typical. He could see the shortcomings of his own work even when others praised it; he looked to do better next time. 'Printing is like religion,' he said. 'We live in sin, but with the hope of perfection before us.'[60] But this did not stop him from having a go. 'If it's worth doing, it's worth doing badly' was the other side of this pragmatic attitude—in this case shared with a younger colleague who went on to become a much admired director-general of the National Library, and who says today it was the most important of his many words of wisdom to her and others at the Library.[61] So, despite his later reservations about this incunabular work, when the time came to deposit the first tranche of his papers at the National Library he annotated its folder with the words 'the first publication of the press, before it had a name'.

3

The National Library of Australia

In 1971 Alec accepted the newly created post of director of publications at the National Library of Australia, and the family returned to Australia and to a new home in Canberra—a place he came to love. Indeed, for a while he was to think of his own publications as particularly Canberran. The modest house they bought in the inner south suburb of Deakin, just over the road from Ruth Dobson, had been previously owned by a sculptor and had a separate studio with a concrete floor—perfect for a printshop.[1] In September 1972 he bought a reconditioned Chandler & Price New Series treadle platen press from Dolphin & Hannan Pty Ltd, the Sydney specialists in reconditioned printing machinery. It had a 10 x 15 inch chase, in the old terminology a crown folio (in metric terms 381 x 508 millimetres), which mostly limited him to printing two pages at a time. With two chases, it cost him $415.[2] Although it was already some 50 years old, and he later added two other presses to his printshop, it was to be his workhorse as he taught himself the craft of printing and he spoke of it fondly for the rest of his life. He also kept the Adana, which was used for book labels and small items such as the first Christmas card he printed in 1972.

There are differing explanations as to how Alec was recruited by the National Library. As he remembered it, Rosemary's mother saw an advertisement for a new position as director of publishing, which she cut out of the paper and gave to him when he was in Sydney to meet Gordon Barton, the new owner of Angus & Robertson. He rang Allan Fleming, the National Librarian, to discuss it. (The cutting is in his desk diary for 1971.) He went to Canberra and met Fleming before applying for the post, but heard nothing for months until invited to a further interview at the Australian High Commission, after which he was offered the job.[3] On the other hand, Fleming's biographer says he headhunted Alec at the suggestion of George Ferguson, in his last days before Richard Walsh succeeded him as publisher at Angus & Robertson.[4] Ted Vellacott, a senior member of the Library's staff for many years, who met Alec on the day he came to the Library and took him upstairs to meet Fleming, had no doubt that this was the man who would be appointed to the job, he recalled in a conversation in 2017. George Clark, then head of corporate affairs at the Library, who interviewed him with Fleming, also recalled that Fleming made it clear Alec was the right choice for the position from the start.[5] He was appointed at the top of the possible salary range, Clark told me, a further measure of how keen Fleming was on the appointment.

Allan Fleming was something of a controversial figure in the small world of Australian libraries. He had had a diverse career as a journalist, soldier, trade commissioner, public servant, intelligence chief and, for two years, the Commonwealth Parliamentary Librarian. Other than this he had never worked in libraries and had no library qualifications, which caused a pursing of lips by some in the profession. It has to be said that this was mostly outside Canberra, and that, as one of his successors put it, 'his performance soon silenced his critics'.[6] Fleming was a formidable operator, with extraordinary networks, a forward-looking imagination and demonstrated competence as a public service leader of the highest rank. He had been keenly interested in the possibilities offered by information technology since his time in the Defence Department in the 1950s, when he had bought one of the first computers owned by the Australian government, and he was convinced that the Library needed to be outgoing in its orientation and to meet the information needs of the entire community. Within the libraries he ran he enjoyed wide support, but eventually the attitude of some in the professional library community perhaps helped him decide to take early retirement at the age of 61 in 1973.[7] Recruiting a strong, widely experienced publisher from outside Canberra and the public service was typical of him.

And so Alec came home. He returned to Australia at a time of accelerated change in the publishing sphere. Angus & Robertson had now been taken over by Gordon Barton, briefly but famously successful as an entrepreneur, founder of the interstate freight company IPEC while still an undergraduate, and also momentarily a charismatic leader of liberal thought in Australia. (His full-page ad in *The Australian* opposing Australian participation in the

Vietnam War, published during the visit of President Lyndon Johnson in 1966, led to the foundation of the Australia Party. Make Sydney Gay for LBJ was the awkward official slogan for the visit.) Barton's enterprises tended to become interwoven: for a while the Australia Party, of which the author was a youthful member, appeared to be run out of Angus & Robertson, despite its claims to participatory democracy. It is unlikely that Alec would have been happy under the new regime there, but there were also strong family reasons for a return to Australia.

London was thrilling and vivid for all of them, he reflected many years later, but 'I think the sufferer in all of that—although that's really an exaggerated word—was Rosemary because she was cut off from her roots in a way that made it difficult for her to do a lot of writing'.[8] Rosemary was herself conscious of this, even though she had long since rejected a narrow nationalism in the subject matter of her work. 'I am an Australian poet, and I write best and most prolifically in Australia,' she said soon after their return, 'even though I may be writing poems about Greece in the second century A.D., as I'm doing at present.'[9]

This aside, Angus & Robertson's dominance of Australian publishing was increasingly a thing of the past. Apart from competition from British firms, notably Collins and Penguin, its position was challenged by 'the emergence of a swag of pace-setting independent publishers, such as Outback Press, Lonely Planet and McPhee Gribble'.[10] Printing was increasingly done in Asia, while technological change made it easier and cheaper for new businesses to get into publishing. The industry was forced to become more competitive with the abolition of retail price maintenance in 1972, while co-publishing with American imprints accelerated. Paperbacks gained new currency, and were particularly popular with students.[11] In the words of Richard Walsh, installed as the head of Angus & Robertson by Gordon Barton in 1972, 'the famous Old Firm was more of a beached whale. Still recognisable as a former leviathan, it was in fact close to death'. (By 1986, when Walsh left to head up Australian Consolidated Press, he argues, the firm was again highly profitable 'and the most prolific publisher of Australian books'.[12] By then Rupert Murdoch's News Ltd owned it.)

What, then, were the National Library of Australia's expectations for its new publisher in this competitive and volatile market? The Library had been a publisher for many years, well before its incorporation under the *National Library Act 1960*. Its bibliographic and historical publications had a long history going back almost to its beginnings. Between 1914 and 1925, in its earliest guise under the direction of the Library Committee of the Commonwealth Parliament, it had undertaken the 'ambitious and difficult production of the first series of the *Historical Records of Australia*'[13], a 26-volume compilation of documentary records beginning in 1788. In 1936 it had taken the lead in establishing a national bibliography with the first *Annual Catalogue of Australian Publications*, and after the war had established the Australian Public Affairs Information Service, an index to Australian periodicals.[14] Such projects as the massive Australian Joint Copying Project (1945–1997), which microfilmed material of Australian interest in British archives and in which the Library took the lead as 'first among equals', could also be considered as publishing of a sort, given the distribution of microfilm to partner libraries. Librarians across the country knew and relied on such resources, albeit with at times a grudging acceptance of the National Library's leadership aspirations, as did many scholars, but outside these worlds little of its role and collections was known to the majority of Australians. Fleming and his colleagues set out to change this.[15]

A new emphasis on publications was only one aspect of what was going on at the National Library. In 1968 it had moved into a striking new building prominently located on the shores of Lake Burley Griffin and close to what was then anticipated would be the site of a future new Parliament House. This was nothing to do with Fleming; the building was the result of years of lobbying by Harold White (later Sir Harold), the head since 1947 of the Parliamentary Library. Although the new role defined by statutory independence in 1960 meant the National Library lost some of its previous wide-ranging functionality, in that it was no longer directly responsible for parliamentary library services, the Library's visibility on the ground in Canberra was enhanced under White. He had opted to move with the new agency to the new building, where he served as the first National Librarian, and, although he is often remembered primarily as a champion of collection building, he had also taken an interest in Library outreach. As a result, the new National Library building had space for exhibition and display when it opened, both in the imposing Tasmanian Blackwood showcases in its large foyer, and on a mezzanine floor above the foyer. (In 1972 the fit-out of a major new exhibition gallery—an extra 3,000 square feet of display space next to the theatre on Lower Ground Floor 1—was approved. Twenty years later it was relocated to the ground floor, displacing the old cataloguers' workspace. A bookshop and a restaurant today flank the foyer, with its superb Leonard French windows.)

The Library's new home was markedly different from its former premises, spread between a relatively modest building on Kings Avenue (opened in 1931 and known as the National Library long before it existed in statutory form); desperately overcrowded rooms at the ageing Provisional Parliament House; and various somewhat ramshackle annexes. The result had been that, before 1968, priceless works from magnificent acquisitions such as the Rex Nan Kivell collection had been barely visible—sometimes hung in parliamentary corridors closed to the general public, but often kept in crammed storerooms and difficult to retrieve. Some were even more off limits, in parliamentarians' or staff offices: famously, White himself had Tom Roberts' 1918 painting *Allegro con brio: Bourke Street West* in his office at Parliament House and took it with him to the new building, although it at least was accessible if need be. Other artworks owned by the Commonwealth were lent to state galleries, or displayed in Australian missions overseas. A few works were lent to the Prime Minister's Lodge. It would be several years after the establishment of the National Gallery of Australia before this latter practice ceased. (The Gallery too gained its own act in 1975, although the Menzies Government had planned its establishment in 1965. The Queen opened its building in 1982—mirroring the Library by the lake, with room between them for the Parliament House that would in the end be built elsewhere. The substantial collection of artworks acquired by the Parliamentary Library and Historic Memorials committees, and by the Commonwealth generally, in the years since Federation was divided between the two institutions.

The Library had few readers in its earlier buildings: a handful each day, apart from at the relatively busy Parliamentary Library. Now they had a large new building and vastly larger public and specialist reading rooms. Alec Bolton's remit was simply one aspect of a more general focus on outreach and greater visibility for the Library's collections and services. It also included improving the technical standard of its publishing. The general standard of government publishing was low at the time. Frank Thompson, one-time director of publishing at the Australian Government Publishing Service (and much more, in a wide-ranging and significant career in publishing), said, of the 1960s:

> *the federal government was receiving considerable public criticism over the poor design of its published material, the sometimes turgid and impenetrable bureaucratic prose, and the sheer inability of citizens to discover which department actually published what and, more importantly, where it could be obtained.*[16]

The Australian Government Publishing Service, incorporating the existing Government Printing Office that had come to Canberra with Parliament in 1927, was created in 1970 to remedy this situation, but, as Thompson remarks, it was dominated by its printing personnel and struggled to behave like an entrepreneurial publisher. The National Library, along with some other government bodies, decided instead to develop its own expertise in-house, building on its long history as a publisher as well as the nationally significant material in its collections. Meanwhile, and in common with the rest of government, there were also new expectations about outreach as well as public access to information about the work of government. Agencies such as the Library were operating in a new environment, especially after the election of the Whitlam government at the end of 1972, which would include Freedom of Information legislation enacted in 1974. They would no longer essentially report simply to their minister and parliament, but to the people of Australia.

Coincidentally, in 1970 UNESCO had proclaimed 1972 would be International Book Year, choosing the theme of 'Books for All'. One of Alec's first tasks would be to contribute to the development of a national travelling exhibition, *Book Design in Australia*, which was to be sent out to the state libraries. Alec's previous employer Sam Ure Smith contributed a brief foreword to the exhibition brochure, arguing that the development of a cadre of professional book designers meant that 'standards of presentation have risen to a level that merges with standards prevailing in British, American and European book production'.[17] There were some fine books displayed, beginning with a historical section including John William Lewin's *Birds of New South Wales* (1813) but also showcasing contemporary publishers such as F.W. Cheshire, Georgian House, the Melbourne branch of Oxford University Press, Sydney's Edwards & Shaw, Ure Smith, Angus & Robertson and even one of Alec's favourite small presses, Mary Quick's Juniper Press of Burradoo. Clearly, there was an expectation that the Library's new publications program would soon be of a similar standard.

Alec later said that there were unrealistic expectations of miracles when he started in the new job.

> *The Library felt that it was sitting on vast treasures which ought to be shared with the public at large, and that was an invincible concept and I was expected to give form and substance to it.*

Moreover, although the Library was indeed already producing a range of bibliographical publications, 'they were being produced to what I think everybody would agree was a very, very poor standard'. This included the printing work sent out to local printers 'whose work was pretty rough, and that's really praising it'.[18] At the same time, developments in the computer-based automation of publications such as the Australian National Bibliography offered opportunities for significant improvements in production. Alec would be intensely occupied for several years with the upgrading of these bibliographic publications, while also searching the Pictures collection for material suitable for reproduction as cards—there was a Library shop, but almost nothing to sell from it when he arrived. But it was books he was really interested in publishing, and he recalled that the chairman of the National Library Council at the time, Senator Sir Alister McMullin, was also urging him in this direction. (McMullin, President of the Senate 1951–1973, had long been an ally of Harold White, supporting him earlier as well in establishing the Parliamentary Library's trail-blazing Legislative Research Service.[19])

Alec found himself in a new and somewhat unusual position at the Library. It was very different from his previous working life, he later recalled:

> *when I was at the Library it always seemed to me that the world of commercial publishing, from which I had come, was like warfare being*

> *conducted by guerillas in a spirit of great competitiveness and anxiety and tension and conflict and drama, and the Public Service, by contrast, was like the ceremonial aspect of the Brigade of Guards. That's how it seemed to me. It was a very different world. A strange world to get used to, and my position at the Library was an unusual one because I was really the one person, the one senior person at any rate, with responsibility in this field. All other people in the Library were very helpful to me and very nice to me, and I had a lot of friends, and because I was on a separate plateau or at a separate standpoint, I seemed to be immune from some of the tensions that probably existed between competing sections of the Library, sections of the Library, that is, competing for funds or attention or the development of projects in which they were keenly interested.*[20]

Notwithstanding this, there were four things Alec's work as a government publisher and his personal avocation as a private press printer had in common. These were elegant and well-considered book design, quality printing, punctilious editing, and a solid scholarly apparatus to accompany the collection material being published. All these are evident in such National Library of Australia titles as *The Private Journal of James Burney* (1975), *Letters of Vance and Nettie Palmer* (1977), *Cazneaux* (1978), *The Autobiography of John Shaw Neilson* (1978), *Augustus Earle Travel Artist* (1980), *Flower Paintings of Ellis Rowan* (1982), *The Challicum Sketch Book* (1987), and *The Hunter Sketchbook* (1989). Most notable, perhaps, was *The Bligh Notebook* (1987), when the Library ventured for the first time into the world of the limited edition, but these principles are evident also in the bibliographic and statutory publications on Alec's watch. This began almost immediately. The contrast between the Library's *Annual Report* for 1970–1971 and that of the following year is striking: the first is a drab brown pamphlet illustrated by only one photo (of the council chairman) and with densely set pages, while the next is both well-printed and well-designed, with frequent illustrations of material from the Library's collections and of Library activities. The cover features the floodlit Library building at night instead of the logo of the early years, which had been an intriguing but obscure representation by Douglas Annand of a gryphon holding a book—a reference to the Library's location by Lake Burley Griffin, but of no immediately apparent meaning to most. (The next logo was an equally obscure vortex. It was not until 1991 that the Library reverted to the building itself as its avatar, as prefigured in 1972.) And while it took some time to build up a publishing momentum—as appropriate material in the Library's collections was assessed, authors and editors were commissioned, and designers and printers found—when Alec left 15 years later there was both a distinguished list in place and many works underway that had their origins in the Bolton era.

One graphic designer he worked with a great deal was Adrian Young, who settled in Canberra in 1973 after growing up in Boorowa (a nearby country town) and working in London for HMSO for some years. Although he was employed by the Australian National University Press he was permitted to undertake private work, and in fact a meeting with Alec had been his first job-seeking appointment on getting back to Australia. Although his first commission was small—wrapping paper and paper bags, featuring his own brushwork drawing of the National Library—he quickly became the Library's most frequently used designer.

He recalled the design process for the Library's award-winning book of photographs by Harold Cazneaux in a conversation in 2017. There was no written brief, but rather a long chat between the two about type, layout and grouping, with copies of the photographs under consideration before them, after which Adrian produced a mock-up. Alec would generally agree with his suggestions regarding typeface, and in this case the Library imported the paper Adrian specified from the US (S.D. Warren's Lustro Offset Enamel Dull). The page spreads are design-led, grouped by tones as much as theme, and using five different duotone colours throughout the book—two colours in some individual images. Although the printer generally did a good job, there was an issue because the paper was guillotined without a vacuum, which only became apparent with the first print run, meaning that specks of loose paper interfered with printing on some pages. More paper had to be imported but the first impression of the book still had some pages with this tiny but just visible flaw. It was perhaps this that led Alec to criticise the printing of the book in his pseudonymous persona as Martin Em in the *Australian Book Review* (see Chapter 10).

Another project they worked on together was *The Bligh Notebook*, an edition of one of the Library's newest treasures, which was the ship's log kept by Bligh after the *Bounty* mutiny. It had been bought at auction in 1976. With funding provided by Morris West, then chairman of the National Library Council, the publication included a two-volume limited edition of 500 copies published in 1986, with a facsimile of the log bound in full calf by the Library's preservation bookbinder, Brian Hawke. Adrian's daughters did one page with hand-coloured detail at their home, he recalls, although when a press photographer visited it was thought best for him to be the one to pose with a brush for the camera. Both this and the trade edition published in association with Allen & Unwin in 1987 sold well, amply repaying the Morris West Trust Fund investment in the publication and underwriting future National Library publications. (At $280 a copy, gross returns from the limited edition would have been in the vicinity of $140,000. The Library later also entered into a co-publication agreement for a trade edition with the American Book-of-the-Month Club.)

Although Adrian was by no means the only designer with whom Alec worked, the two had similar views on book design. Both men were deeply influenced by Beatrice Warde's notion of the crystal goblet, of the best typography being one in which 'type well-used is invisible *as* type, just as the perfect talking voice is the unnoticed vehicle for the transmission of words, ideas', but they also relished the opportunity to do something different each time.[21] Warde's metaphor asked whether one would prefer to drink fine wine from the clearest crystal or an opaque vessel, however beautiful. (While many typographers of the time disagreed with this 'evangelist of a reborn classicism' and looked for alternatives to the conservative book typography that dominated the UK in particular, and that was closely associated with Warde and her second partner, Stanley Morison, Alec was self-evidently not one of them.[22])

Some years later (see Chapter 30), Adrian designed a patterned paper for the Brindabella Press, a characteristically harmonious and elegant design. His design practice was also influenced by Hugh Williamson's book, *Methods of Book Design* (Oxford University Press, 1956), but he particularly treasures the gift from Alec of his own copy of Jan Tschichold's influential book *Asymmetric Typography*[23], which intriguingly is a key text in an avant-garde design tradition that Alec was not much inclined to explore in his own books. The journal *Visible Language*, to which Adrian subscribed, was yet another resource that Alec could call on through his circle of Canberra book people, and he regularly borrowed copies.[24] And they met often at the monthly meetings of the Colophon Society. Founded in 1977 at a meeting chaired by Pat Croft, editor of the Australian National University Press, the Colophon Society survived until 1986. Although editors were its major instigators, it had an interest in all aspects of book publishing and for some years awarded an annual prize for its Canberra Book of the Year, for books written, designed, printed or published in the ACT. The National Library won this in 1980 with *Augustus Earle: Travel Artist*, also designed by Adrian Young, and Alec shared the prize with Adrian in 1982 (for *The Continuance of Poetry* and *A Day in the Life of Australia* respectively).[25] While there were other designers in Alec's stable—Arthur Stokes and Alison Forbes in particular—the working relationship between Alec and Adrian was to be close and harmonious forthe rest of Alec's life.

Canberra, at the time the Boltons settled there, was still both a small country town and a company town, the company being the Commonwealth government. The cultural life of the national capital was restricted in comparison to Sydney and London, but a strong tradition of community engagement continued alongside the paternalist and heavily bureaucratic administration of the city by the Department of Territories. Alec himself helped establish one of Canberra's quintessential community-based institutions, the Canberra Lifeline Book Fair, albeit initially at the behest of Allan Fleming. The other National Library staffer given the task, in partnership with Alec, was Anthony Ketley, another recent arrival who at the time managed Canberra's public libraries, then part of the National Library. In a conversation in 2014 Anthony Ketley recalled that the idea came originally from Russell Oldmeadow, director of Canberra Life Line (now Lifeline), a telephone-based personal crisis and suicide prevention counselling service, who asked Fleming for help in establishing a book fair as a fundraiser.[26]

Neither Anthony nor Alec had any previous involvement with Lifeline, nor had they run a book fair before, but a previous boss told him that the first principle of such affairs was simply that there should be no books left over at the end of the sale. Lifeline administered the fair and found a place for the two of them to sort and price the books, which they divided into just three categories: fiction, non-fiction, and children's. Ketley's public library branches also served as depots for donations. The first book fair was held at the Albert Hall in Canberra over three days in June 1973, and raised more than $2,000 for the charity from donations of more than 12,000 books.[27] Alec also had the idea of asking local poets to give manuscripts of their poems for sale, and provided the auctioneer with notes on them, although the idea did not catch fire—a highpoint of the auction, according to *The Canberra Times* report, was instead a signed original of the cartoon by Larry Pickering that had won the 1972 Walkley Award for best newspaper cartoon, which made $33. Alec's list and his notes on the poets are nonetheless interesting. Many were from Canberra, or had connections there. He was able to get donations from Dorothy Auchterlonie (Dorothy Green), David Campbell, J.M. Couper, Bruce Dawe, Rosemary Dobson, Michael Dugan, A.D. Hope, Evan Jones, James McAuley, Les Murray, Roland Robinson, J.R. Rowland, Tom Shapcott and Douglas Stewart.

It is an impressive list, eight of whom were, in one way or another, to be published by the Brindabella Press. Many of the special books auctioned were Australian titles signed by their authors, presumably also at Alec's request.[28] His involvement lasted for only another three or four years, Ketley remembers, but the book fair (and a strong tradition of National Library staff involvement, especially in retirement) has become a venerable Canberra institution, at times raising more than $500,000 from each of its major biennial fairs.

'Life gets better / As I grow older / Not giving a damn / And looking slantwise / At everyone's morning', Rosemary wrote, concluding her poem 'Canberra Morning', one of two manuscripts she donated for Alec's poetry auction.[29] Canberra itself, clearly, had quickly become a congenial home for the newly arrived Bolton family.

4

'Christmas Greetings from the Boltons'

Venite, Angeli sancti (1972)

Alec Bolton's first use of his new Brindabella Press imprint was ephemeral and, while attractive, not his own design. It was, if you like, an apprentice piece: a Christmas card he printed in 1972, soon after settling in Canberra. *Venite, Angeli sancti* is a single sheet of pale grey paper, folded once, which inside reads 'Christmas Greetings from the Boltons', in red italics, and with 'Brindabella Press Canberra' as the colophon on the last page. Intriguingly, the main text, printed in alternate lines of 12 point Monotype Baskerville (black) and 12 point Monotype Baskerville Italic (red), was a nine-line carol chanted by followers of the Dominican friar Savaranola on the streets of Florence at Christmas time, at the end of the fifteenth century.[1] I have not been able to find other examples of its use as a religious text.

Rather than being evidence of religious enthusiasm, however, Alec simply borrowed both words and layout from a book by John Mason, *Paper Making as an Artistic Craft*, as he later told the librarian Nancy Bonnin.[2] He printed the card on his little Adana press. He overlooked it when he and I compiled the list of the press' publications in *A Licence to Print*, but had given copies to Jürgen Wegner's Brandywine Archive and the Fryer Library, the first university library to show a serious interest in the press. As the first use of 'Brindabella Press' as an imprint, the card has significance despite its ephemeral nature.

Years later he joked that he briefly thought of calling his press The Month of Sundays Press, because everything took so long, but later was glad he had resisted the temptation to be whimsical. 'We lived within sight of the Brindabellas and I thought it was a lovely name with literary associations with Miles Franklin and Douglas Stewart,' he told Heather Rusden.[3] In 1985 he changed to Officina Brindabella when he discovered the name Brindabella Press had been registered by someone else, but he happily reverted to it in 1992 when that registration lapsed. The Brindabella Range is at the northern end of the Australian Alps and forms the western border of the Australian Capital Territory. Although never rising above 2,000 metres (Bimberi Peak, the highest point, is 1,913 metres), the hills are visible from most of Canberra, especially when dusted with snow in winter. The writer Miles Franklin lived there as a child.

Many years later Alec spoke about what had led him to found the Brindabella Press. Given that this is the beginning of that journey, however modest, these later reflections are relevant to this ephemeral card as well as the books that followed.

The idea that 'small is beautiful' is attractive to many people, and I am one of them ... it is not a reaction against the fact that I work for a government authority, where procedures tend to be unwieldy, and the budgetary future is unpredictable in a way that makes forward planning difficult. If you will excuse a personal digression, I will tell you how I got to this stage of cherishing small-scale activity. In my early days, you tended to acquire a narrow range of skills and to stick to that line of work. In the Editorial Department at A&R, you prepared a manuscript for the press, and wrote the blurb that would appear on the front flap; and you might not see the work again until it was printed and bound. Those questions of design and presentation and publicity, which I find so absorbing today, and which I now see as part of the follow-through of editorial involvement, then belonged to different departments, in a kind of assembly line. Of course there was consultation, but I think it is fair to say that books were handled with an amazing demarcation of responsibility. It is no surprise that they often looked such a mess. For my part, I became more and more interested in design and production, and picked up clues wherever I could. A Polish friend named Henry Mund, now dead, taught me a bit about typography, and I learnt a lot from Sam Ure Smith, who has great flair and versatility. I wouldn't say that the appearance of words became more important to me than the words themselves, but I did become obsessed about print; and when I was living in England in the late sixties, working in publishing by day, I went to the London College of Printing at night to learn hand composition and letterpress machining. In that way I became an amateur printer, and my Brindabella Press, which I established when I returned to Australia has become the absorbing leisure interest of my life, and the thing for which I feel I need another life altogether. I mention this because it was an interesting experience of living to me to discover at

> *what a late age one sometimes gets on to a thing that really matters, and how unimportant and inessential a lot of former interests then become. I used to fool about with carpentry and home repairs and things like that. I can hardly bear to think of the wasted weekends when I could have been printing—except of course that I didn't know it was in store for me. My advice is that you should always keep yourself tuned in for intimations about changes in direction.*[4]

Wasted weekends or not, the next few years were to show that Alec was certainly keeping himself tuned in.

5

'And pretty awful too'

Rosemary Dobson, *Three Poems on Water-Springs* (1973)

In March 1973 Alec printed *Three Poems on Water-Springs*, again on a single sheet, folded into three, with three poems and a drawing by Rosemary. It was, he noted, 'the first item printed in Deakin on the Chandler & Price. And pretty awful too'.[1] The drawing was printed in red and he again used Monotype Baskerville, supplied by Brown Prior Anderson Pty Ltd of Burwood in Victoria.[2] Baskerville, the revival of which was at the heart of the private press movement of the early twentieth century, was to become his most used typeface.[3] The block for the drawing was made locally, by *The Canberra Times*. The edition was 150. The distribution list, kept in both their hands, again features family and friends, but with a few libraries added—the Mitchell, the State Library of Victoria, and the National Library of Australia.

The first name on that list was Beatrice Davis, the redoubtable editor who had taught both of them their trade at Angus & Robertson, and with whom they maintained a lifelong friendship. With her are many literary and artistic figures, including writers and academics James McAuley, Stuart Sayers, Roger McDonald, Frank Webb, Maie Casey, Leonie Kramer, Alec Hope, Dorothy Green, David Campbell, Geoffrey Blainey, Tom Shapcott, Bob Brissenden and Fay Zwicky; artist Rosalie Gascoigne; librarian and bibliographer Geoffrey Farmer; and book collector and publisher Walter Stone. This was a formidably well-connected couple. And although Alec later disparaged this work, it was well received. Walter Stone, who was to be a strong supporter for the rest of his life, loved the press name—'how neatly "Brindabella Press" fits into speech. It sings its own song. Miles Franklin would have been ecstatic about it'—and praised the printing.

> *It belongs so well to the poems and the illustration by Rosemary and the paper and the inking, without that excessive blackness that marks so much of the private press work that is done, that it is hard to see anything but the completed piece. Unity is the word.*[4]

High praise for a work that is indeed modest, but that unity of production was to be something that Alec strove for in all his work, and it is not a bad piece of presswork for an almost complete beginner.

Later in 1973 Alec printed his second Christmas card, with the poem 'Five Days Old' by Francis Webb, an old friend and godfather to his son Ian. Webb was able to sign a few of about 150 copies printed before he died. Webb thought the poem was the best he had ever written[5] and Alec later described it as 'the most precious of all these small productions'.[6] He again kept a list of the people they sent it to: new names, presumably all met since they settled in Canberra, include library colleagues Bill Thorn and Catherine Santamaria, designer Adrian Young, furniture designer Fred Ward and historian Manning Clark.[7]

The third and final Christmas card of the press was also to be a poem, 'Brindabella' by Douglas Stewart, with a drawing by Stewart's wife Margaret Coen. This time Alec offered Stewart and Coen half the print run by way of remuneration, a formula he was to use for many years although proportions varied.[8] So, further patterns that the press would develop are showing: a pairing of verse and illustration, deep engagement with authors and illustrators, as small a financial outlay as possible for what was still very much a pastime, but high production standards despite the modesty of the work.

6

'I am more or less pleased with it'

David Campbell, *Starting from Central Station* (1973)

These characteristics are apparent in *Starting from Central Station* by David Campbell, the first book of the Brindabella Press. Campbell was a close friend, with whom Rosemary co-wrote two collections of 'imitations' of Russian poets, 're-created in English'.[1] He farmed near Canberra and belonged to a circle of writers who would later feature in the press' books, including Alec Hope, Bob Brissenden and Manning Clark. An Angus & Robertson author of the 1950s (although his first book was published in England in 1949), he had also been published by Edwards & Shaw, the fine commercial press that had grown out of the Barn on the Hill private press, and which maintained distinctive and high production and design values throughout its history. Alec was an enthusiast for their work, which struck a sympathetic chord with his own.

Although modest compared with his later books, it was still a step up, and Alec later said

> *It was an alarming prospect, but I enjoyed the work and still look at the result with affection. You really get to know a poem when you set it, proof it, correct it and print it: it's a real test of any poem.*[2]

He used Beckett Text, a hard American paper sized for offset printing, and found it difficult to print satisfactorily, especially since he disliked printing with heavy impression. (His training in London had emphasised the search for the perfect 'kiss' impression, evident in the trial pieces he brought home from evening classes.) 'Despite dampening I achieved only a mediocre result,' he later told the New Zealand printer Bob Gormack, of Nag's Head Press[3], and the impression is indeed uncertain. His subsequent search for good letterpress paper quickly became 'almost an obsession with me'.[4] The poet suggested a Canberra artist, William (Bill) Huff-Johnston, who had taught him ceramic wheel throwing at the School of Art.[5] Huff-Johnston's pen and ink drawings were made into line blocks at *The Canberra Times*, and Alec hand-sewed the pamphlet. He did not mix enough ink for the full print run of the drawings, so there are variations of shade. 'Yet I am fond of this work,' he later commented, 'and many lines from the poems are indelibly in my mind.'[6]

Three important Brindabella Press correspondences with friends who had similar interests began with this work. Alec sent one copy to Gerald Fischer, a Sydney archivist whose Pump Press (founded 1956) frequently used a similar format. 'I am more or less pleased with it,' he told Fischer, 'but the presswork is not very hot … I don't like printing that is done with too much ink and too much impression; it has that awful Braille effect when viewed from the other side.'[7] Fischer was to be an enthusiastic supporter of Brindabella, and he praised the book's 'character and typographic sureness'. Alec sent another copy to the Sydney book collector, printer and publisher Walter Stone[8], seeking his advice on how best to distribute the 100 copies left for sale after giving 40 to the poet, 20 to the artist and keeping 60 to give away. He wondered if something between $1.50 and $2 would be about right, and demurred when Stone advised $3, settling on a retail price of $2.50. Stone suggested he approach James Bennett, a library supply firm, and Bennett's were to be agents for the press later on, but Alec preferred to distribute via a Hobart bookseller, James Dally.[9] Quickly, though, he became unhappy when Dally marked the book up to $4.

Finally, Alec sent a copy to Geoffrey Farmer, Tasmanian librarian, bibliographer and enthusiastic promoter of the private press in Australia. He told Farmer that the Campbell book had taken much longer than anticipated, and he had taken a short break from printing. 'I'm interested, at least for the moment, in pursuing work of local association or by writers of local association,' he told Farmer.[10] Farmer praised the design and noted the impression difficulties: apart from that, it 'is as good as any contemporary work I have seen from any little press'.[11] These three confidants—Fischer, Stone and Farmer—were to be constant supporters in the years to come. Alec would add others to the list of those he wrote to regularly, seeking advice and sharing his output. Indeed, the press became, in a way, a means of maintaining deep connection with longstanding friends.

That fine-grained engagement in turn created opportunities to extend the network as people who cared deeply about the press brought newcomers into the circle. (Alec also sent details of the pamphlet to David Chambers, editor of the influential British annual checklist *Private Press Books*, in which it was duly listed in the 1973 issue. This was a listing only, as there were no reviews in the checklist.)

Starting from Central Station had one other incidental impact: it was much admired by a group of young Canberra poets, including Alan Gould, David and Alison Brooks, and Paul Balnaves, who after a congenial dinner at the Bolton house and a visit to its printery decided to buy a printing press of their own. In a telephone conversation with the author in 2016 Alan Gould recalled that Alec helped in recommending a suitable press, a Chandler & Price platen like his own, which was bought for $300 from a Queanbeyan printer going out of business, and then suggested Dolphin & Hannan as supplier of a treadle to power it, type and other necessities. ('I think I fired them to start printing, which is a pleasant by-product of my own interest,' Alec told Bob Gormack.[12]) The Brindabella Press set the standard they aspired to, although Alec's search for perfection and the growing complexity of his 'immaculate' books and their binding was more than they sought for the Open Door Press (so named because the press was at first housed in a garage, needing the door open for there to be enough light to print). From 1975 to 1980, when the press was sold, Open Door printed 'twenty six broadsheet poems, four foldout sonnet sequences, and five booklets of poetry', mostly in editions of between 100 and 180. They were illustrated and signed by the authors, who included many of Australia's best-known poets as well as younger writers. The broadsheets were sold for 50 cents each. They are well printed and attractively designed, working within the possibilities of a limited range of typefaces, and are now scarce.[13] Open Door Broadsheet number 1, 'The Stake, 1633', a poem by Bob Brissenden, was published on 1 January 1975. Brissenden was by then also a Brindabella Press author, as were to be many others over the next five years of Open Door's life, including Philip Mead, David Campbell, Rosemary Dobson, Judith Wright and Les Murray. Broadsheet number 3, David Campbell's poem 'The Poetry Reading', dedicated to A.D. Hope and illustrated on this occasion with a drawing by Anne Kent from a photograph of Hope by David Brooks, aptly captures the camaraderie of the Canberra poetry scene of the day, which often crossed generational boundaries and schools of thought.

7

'Perhaps we could experiment?'

Bob Brissenden, *Elegies* (1974)

For his next book Alec turned again to a friend, the Australian National University (ANU) academic and writer Bob Brissenden. A long-term Canberra resident, Brissenden (1928–1991) specialised in English literature of the eighteenth century, but had wide-ranging interests in other fields and was both a poet and a novelist. When I interviewed him in 1993, Alec described *Elegies* as having been printed too lightly, with not enough impression or ink, with a binding that was too tight.[1] This is particularly evident in the individual poem titles, but at least the creamy Monadnock Mills Caress Text 118 gsm paper was more suited to letterpress than the Beckett Text of *Starting from Central Station*.[2] The book was illustrated by Robin Wallace-Crabbe, who lived not far from Canberra at Braidwood, with one drawing extending across two pages in the central spread of the book. It was again a simple sewn pamphlet. It's a melancholy collection: poems in memory of Janis Joplin, Percy Bysshe Shelley, Kenneth Slessor, Michael Dransfield and the poet's grandfather, bound in a sombre black card which is, indeed, too stiff for easy opening.

Considering the possibility of illustrations, Alec said to Bob Brissenden:

> *I guess I am hoping for pen or brush drawings that can be printed from line blocks, but if it seems that halftone effects are needed, I am willing to try my best. Perhaps we could experiment?*[3]

Brissenden was the initial point of connection with Wallace-Crabbe, but artist and printer quickly entered into a dialogue about how the book would be illustrated and Alec was in the end 'really delighted with the drawings … They expand one's appreciation of the poems, which is what good illustrations should do'. This was almost a throwaway line, but it reveals an approach to illustration that was to cause him problems later on, and that he would eventually modify. On this occasion he was mostly concerned that some brushstrokes in the original drawings had not been replicated in the line blocks, but thought the result still acceptable. 'The job will take four or five months,' Alec suggested, 'as alas it is only a Sunday and occasional evening pursuit with me'[4], and despite both the title-page and colophon bearing the date 1974 the actual date of publication was, judging by Alec's correspondence, early in February 1975. The edition was 303 (not 310 as stated in the colophon); 40 went to the author, 40 to the artist, 135 were made available for sale and the remainder were given away by the printer, or retained.[5] (As mentioned, his other printing task in 1974 was his third, and last, Christmas card, the appropriate poem 'Brindabella' by Douglas Stewart, with a drawing by his wife Margaret Coen. The couple were old Sydney friends. Thereafter there was to be little such ephemeral printing unless it directly related to his books, such as prospectuses and newsletters, and it would be some time before Alec even got round to printing his own letterhead.)

Elegies sold for $3. James Bennett took 40 to sell to libraries, and for the first time copies were sold to the public through bookshops in Sydney, Melbourne and Canberra: Margaret Woodhouse, The Bookshop of Margareta Webber and the ANU Co-Operative Bookshop respectively. 'Of all the bookshops I know in Australia,' he wrote to Webber's, 'yours is, to me, the most sympathetic.'[6] These, with Michael Treloar in Adelaide later on, were to be his mainstays for retail sales for some time. It is an interesting list, featuring some of the most distinctive Australian booksellers of their day. In particular Margareta Webber's store, which she opened in 1931, was famous for its comfort and gracious style. Webber employed only women and kept up good relationships with many significant English publishers, both mainstream and small. Laurel Clark, a librarian with a particular interest in the history of the book trade, points out, for example, that as well as stocking Virginia and Leonard Woolf's Hogarth Press, she was an early Melbourne stockist of Penguins. She sold the store in 1973, so Bolton's dealings were with her successors. Despite a difficult transition to new ownership, the distinctive style of the firm was evidently maintained as far as Alec was concerned.[7]

One recipient of *Elegies* was the poet Dorothy Green, who praised it:

> *the delicate confidence of the setting, of the poems on the page—the colour of the paper—This is how poetry should be presented, it is obvious. And in small doses, instead of in those unending Wagnerian compilations in blaring white light that we are stunned with nowadays.*[8]

Alec sent copies to John Ryder, whose book *Printing for Pleasure* 'was one of the things that started me off',[9] and to David Chambers for his annual review *Private Press Books*, this time with a short letter outlining his ambitions as a printer and disclaiming any expertise as a collector of books. (*Elegies* was shown as obtainable from The Bookshop of Margaret Webber in its entry.) And copies of *Elegies* accompanied other letters, as Alec set about looking for like-minded printers, suppliers and future authors.[10] 'I am sure it must be a common thing among private printers to feel the need of being in touch with others,' he wistfully remarked to David Chambers. 'There is a lot of backyard, semi-amateur printing in Australia today, mostly of poetry, and nearly all by small offset. Amateur letterpress printing is, I think, rather rare at present.'[11]

8

'On the whole I think I am getting more ambitious'

John Rowland, *Times and Places (*1976*)*

Dwelling on these very early productions of the Brindabella Press may seem disproportionate, given their modesty. Nevertheless, they deserve close attention because their printing in many ways foretold what was to come, and also because as rarities they can be hard to come by for collectors. I now turn to consideration of the first casebound books of the press, which were to be Alec's breakthrough.

In 1974 he discussed a more ambitious volume of verse with John Rowland, Australia's ambassador in Vienna. He suggested that there might be a series of poems 'dealing in one way or another with the life you have had in other countries'[1], adding soon afterwards that his interest in works associated with Canberra meant that he was 'interested in writers of local association, but not necessarily in local subject-matter'. Rowland had published two previous collections, both with Angus & Robertson, and Alec urged him to consider commercial publication as well as a Brindabella edition. 'Angus & Robertson is in disarray at present,' he wrote, but 'if the firm should fail, there will be others.'[2] Rosemary had told him that Rowland was an accomplished artist, so Alec asked him to consider illustrating the book himself. The two went back and forward for some months, with Alec reassuring Rowland that publication by him would not preclude later, more commercial publication. The virtue of a limited edition was its uniqueness, he said:

> *I suppose it's obvious that a limited and private edition of something must necessarily be singular and distinguishable in some way. I am not really an exclusivist by nature. I am just interested in poetry and printing, and in the idea of trying to produce something that is a satisfying bit of craftsmanship.*[3]

Times and Places took most of 1975 to print, and although the colophon dates it to 1975 it was not finished until 1976. The hand-set type was Monotype Baskerville with Perpetua Light titling, and the paper again Monadnock Caress Text, printed dry with a light impression.[4] There were six line drawings by the author. The book was casebound by a commercial binder, E.C. Chapman & Co. of Surry Hills in Sydney. Alec had asked for it to be sewn in five sections but accepted the binder's advice that it should be done in three to avoid the paper tearing.[5] Alec folded and collated it. He also did the labelling and put the acetate dust wrapper on.[6] Although the inking is overly light, especially on the titling, Alec was pleased with the book. It was 'the most harmonious production of the press' up until the Shaw Neilson, he said later: 'right in proportion, colour, and set for the first time in 12 point Baskerville, not the 10 point I had used until then'.[7] (He would return to Rowland with *Granite Country* (1994), also an attractive book.) The edition size was 230, of which 130 were for sale at $5. Sales realised $390, allowing for a 40 per cent discount to booksellers, and outgoings were $373.50, not including paper. The profit was thus $16.50, which went to the author.[8] This was not a profit-making enterprise, nor was it meant to be. Many praised the book's beauty, but the letter that probably meant most was from his one-time mentor at Angus & Robertson, Beatrice Davis, now employed by Nelson's after her peremptory dismissal from the firm she had helped make great. She called it 'the most beautiful small book I've seen for years'.[9] But Alec was conscious of its shortcomings, although partly attributing them to his press:

> *Although I feel that with more practice and skill I can improve on the results I am getting with my Chandler & Price platen, I do sometimes regret my inability to print solids and halftones, and have more or less decided that when my ship comes in I will look for a hand-operated cylinder proofing press capable of accurate registration, such as a Vandercook or Verax. To me, this would be the ultimate.*[10]

Writing in a similar vein to Gerald Fischer, he said:

> *I must say I miss it when I am not printing. It becomes steadily more important to me, and on the whole I think I am getting more ambitious … I feel I need another life in which to print all the things I would like to.*[11]

'I find myself constantly turning to pieces of print that are especially pleasing in their style and proportions,' Alec had written to Fischer a little earlier. He was trying to devise a pressmark, and was thinking of printing a Brindabella Press manifesto as well.[12] (A pressmark, in this usage, is a unique printer's device indicating who printed a book, and not an indication of a book's shelf location, as in early libraries. Such devices were common in the early years of printing and were revived in the late nineteenth century.)

Although these were years of turmoil in Australian political life, much of it taking place only a short stroll away from the National Library at the Provisional Parliament House (now Old Parliament House), there is little sign that Alec felt any strong connection with the troubled public life of the time, with neither the dismissal by the Governor-General of the Whitlam government nor its replacement by the Fraser government in November 1975 drawing any evident response. (While Rosemary was prepared to sign a public statement praising the Whitlam government's arts policy during the election campaign that followed its dismissal, Alec would have been constrained from public comment by his role as a public servant.[13]) Rather, his correspondence of the time reflects a deepening immersion in printing as his principal personal avocation, accompanied by occasional efforts to break out of the isolation imposed by living so far from the centres of the letterpress revival and the continued tradition of fine printing in the US and the UK.

Unlike his friend, fellow printer (Duyfken Press) and National Library colleague Bill Thorn, he did not seek to compensate for his isolation by becoming a collector of the books he admired. Apart from people already mentioned, he began writing occasionally to Bob Gormack of the Nag's Head Press in Christchurch, New Zealand. (Gormack also printed an occasional limited edition for James Dally of Hobart under the imprint Sullivan's Cove.[14]) He also wrote to the American wood-engraver and printer Michael McCurdy, sending him a copy of *Times and Places* in 1976 after admiring two of his Penmaen Press books at the National Library. 'I suspect that more interesting work is being done in your country than in England,' he wrote. 'There is not a great deal of activity in Australia.'[15] That letter took three months to arrive, and McCurdy's reply a month. Nonetheless, despite the slowness of the mail, the exchange continued. McCurdy was to contribute a frontispiece to Dorothy Green's *Something to Someone* (1983), the tenth book of the press, although the two never actually met.[16]

Some years later, when he made what was for him a rare political comment to the poet Philip Hodgins, his disengagement from politics remained evident. 'It is getting towards the end of election day. I feel pretty discouraged about it myself. Whoever wins will be a government elected by the unconvinced.'[17] The most public political statement Alec ever made had been several years earlier, during the controversy over Jørn Utzon's resignation as architect of the Sydney Opera House, and it says as much about his attitude to artistic endeavour as to the political process. On that occasion he lamented the lack of an 'intelligent, sympathetic mediator' able to interpret the views of a great artist and the 'prudent banker's attitude' of the NSW state government to each other. 'The fact is that where a work of art is concerned, money may cease to have ordinary meaning,' he argued. 'All that counts is the work itself and the necessity of acquiring it.'

While he agreed that the state government was correct in seeking to rein in the rising cost of the Opera House construction, the cost of Utzon's departure was also high.

> *Australia will face the awful fact of having spent many millions of dollars only to end up with a less than original, less than perfect building. This would be the most bitter cost of all—again something quite beyond reckoning in terms of money alone.*[18]

9

‘It is harder today … to define a role for a private press’

James McAuley, *Time Given* (1976)

It was the low standard of contemporary book design that Alec emphasised when he approached James McAuley in 1975 to see if he had any suitable poems for publication by Brindabella, contrasting his aesthetic judgement with that of McAuley’s latest title from Angus & Robertson. ‘I have seen a copy of *Music Late at Night*, and wish I had been its printer. The poems are most beautiful, but the presentation is wretched,’ he said.[1] *Music Late at Night* was a 48-page stapled pamphlet in Angus & Robertson’s *Poets of the Month* series, an interesting attempt by the previously dominant publisher of Australian poetry to match the flood of cheap, offset-printed, small press formats characteristic of the New Australian Poetry movement of the 1960s and 1970s[2], but its printing was indeed undistinguished.

Alec and Rosemary had been friendly with McAuley for many years—he was someone she had known at Sydney University when she was studying there in the 1940s, and they had moved in overlapping friendship circles in the years since—and although they differed politically it was Alec who had suggested the name *Quadrant* for the anti-Communist literary and cultural journal founded by Richard Krygier of the Australian Association for Cultural Freedom, of which McAuley was the founding editor.[3] He had also tried to persuade Rosemary to join the editorial advisory board, along with A.D. Hope, Manning Clark and Leonie Kramer, among others, but she refused 'because she did not wish to be seen as "part of the right"'.[4] It is typical of the way Alec and Rosemary rose above the cultural feuds of the time that they had maintained their old friendships, often with people who had themselves fallen out quite bitterly. Seeing *Quadrant* for sale still gave Alec satisfaction 40 years later:

> *The idea came to me when I'd got in the tram that ran from Neutral Bay wharf up to the junction—a very ancient four wheeled tram, I think the ends of which seemed to overhang the wheels in an amazing way. I sat in this tram and I suddenly had this inspiration … a title that was apt for a magazine that was to be a quarterly, and it had other sort of implications as well, the quadrant being a navigational instrument and Quadrant having, shall we say, navigational aspirations about ideas and so on. So, it seemed apt and I put it forward and they accepted it very happily. I think they paid me five pounds, which I thought was pretty handsome. So, I've always had a sort of gratification about Quadrant and I still get a flicker from it when I see copies in the newsagent or wherever.*[5]

Ian Bolton also remembers that Rosemary long treasured a clipping of McAuley's praise of one of her early books in the *Catholic Weekly*, annotating it as 'very precious'.[6] And in the present case Alec and McAuley agreed fervently on book design. McAuley replied to Alec's letter with the comment that 'I would hope that never again would I have to deal with A & R on this score: almost three years to bring out one of the nastiest designs and productions that ever disgraced Australian publication', and he agreed to the suggestion of a Brindabella title. It would include all the poems from *Music Late at Night*, with some new material, and at McAuley's suggestion would be called *Time Given*. Alec admired the poems:

> *They are lovely. It is their crystalline quality that appeals to me, the sense that you have got down to the pure substance of what you are saying. I think they are very beautiful and moving, and I would be proud to print them.*

The comment is a reminder that Alec was a reader, and indeed an editor, of discrimination. He printed and published writing he admired. That was the point of all the effort.

Printing *Time Given* was a race against terminal illness, and McAuley died before it was completed. Alec showed him pages as they were printed and recalled later holding his breath while McAuley looked at them for a long time. '"Now that is *very* nice," he finally said. I was greatly relieved that he approved.'[7] Deferring to his author's cautious approach to illustration, and at Gerald Fischer's suggestion, Alec approached Rod Shaw to create handwritten titles for a book 'that is otherwise rather severe'. 'These poems … are very restrained and classical,' he said to Shaw, 'they are not morbid, but some of them are written against a background of mortal illness.' The notion of calligraphy was suggested by the love he shared with McAuley of the chancery italic of Ludovico Vicentino degli Arrighi, an Italian Renaissance type designer and scribe whose letter-forms were drawn on in the twentieth century by several type designers, notably by Frederic Warde and Stanley Morison for the Arrighi italic designed to accompany Bruce Rogers' Centaur typeface.[8] Both Alec and McAuley had themselves adopted italic handwriting as adults, in Alec's case under the influence of Henry Mund at Angus & Robertson.

As for Rod Shaw, Alec had long admired his work as a commercial printer, although he was not a close acquaintance. The books printed by Edwards & Shaw are striking, with generous margins, conservative but elegant typography, and good paper. Despite a distinguished record of printing art-related works, the firm did not generally share Alec's interest in illustrating poetry. 'The best contribution a publisher can make to a writer is to present his work in the most readable way,' they argued.[9] The rule was sometimes broken—for example, with the dancer Meredith Kinmont's poetry collection *I Am the Green Grass* (1964), which was illustrated with photographs, and Ethel Anderson's *The Song of Hagar to the Patriarch Abraham* (1957), which had striking calligraphic decorations by Rod Shaw. Alec asked Shaw to consider 'italic capitals suggesting Plantin with flourishes'. (He chose Plantin to print with, although he later thought it was perhaps too dark.[10]) Shaw, who had known McAuley since the 1930s, drew a great many alternatives for the title-page and half-titles and refused payment.[11] 'Jim would have loved these titles,' Alec replied. 'It's sad that he is not still around to see them.' Rod Shaw's generous contribution to the book belies post-Cold-War views of the primacy of left and right binaries; despite McAuley's social and political conservatism, and Rod Shaw's own close identity with progressive causes, they shared a history in Sydney cultural circles of the 1930s and 1940s, as did Alec and Rosemary.

Alec appears to have had some issues with the binding of some copies of the book. 'I have used a very good paper and have put many months of loving care into the printing, so that I will appreciate your most careful attention to this job,' he wrote to the binder.[12] He later estimated that around 40 had what he called binding faults.[13] In a conversation with the author in 2022, Bill Chapman had no recollection of his firm having received any complaint from Alec, and suggested the slight cockling of one copy described to him over the phone ('cockling' means some pages have ripples) showed that the paper might have been printed with the grain running the wrong way, from spine to fore-edge—a problem Alec would have again in 1983, with *Something to Someone*. (Machine-made paper has a grain in which the majority of fibres run in one direction, which is most easily discovered by tearing. A book bound with the grain running from top to bottom edge will turn more easily.) Whatever the rights and wrongs of this matter, and bearing in mind that Alec returned to Chapman to bind his next book a year later, the problem cannot have been a deal-breaker.

Given the strong demand from McAuley's many friends and admirers, including an allocation of 100 copies to be given away by Norma McAuley and by Alec himself, the 90 or so copies now available for retail sale were sold out within days of publication.[14] *Time Given* has always been the most difficult Brindabella book for collectors to find, perhaps partly for this reason. There are usually only one or two copies on the market at any given time. It was sold for $6.50. Paper, binding and freight cost $502, and the planned sale of 130 copies to the trade at $3.90 would have netted $507, so overall there must have been a small loss for the press.[15]

Walter Stone praised it as the work of the best Australian private press of the day[16], and it is indeed a lovely book, which won the design and production award in the fiction, poetry and belles lettres section of the Australian Book Publishing Association competition for 1978. Alec himself acknowledged that its design was conservative, but thought it was the best bit of printing he had yet done.[17] He generally avoided such awards, he said many years later. They required up to six copies per entry, and, as he explained to the journalist Ian Healy, 'I like the books to be well thought of, but I am not interested in awards'. The only other book he would enter in this competition would be *Greek Coins*, which he thought was a better book.[18]

The Sydney paper supplier B.J. Ball & Co. imported a small batch of Basingwerk Parchment from the UK for him to use in *Time Given*, which he thought was the first time this paper had been used for an Australian book.[19] The impression is assured and the red handwritten titles are highly effective. 'The Basingwerk Parchment that you imported for me is a lovely paper to work with, and wonderfully sympathetic to letterpress printing on a platen,' he told his paper merchant. 'I have always known and admired it, but printing on it is a new pleasure.'[20]

Beatrice Davis wrote from her exile at Nelson's to thank him for her copy: 'what a lovely book TIME GIVEN is! … I'll treasure it. Henry Mund would have highly approved'. She also suggested he approach Dorothy Green for a manuscript.[21] Green herself wrote:

> *James … needs no other memorial—the one you have given him is as near perfection as anything this imperfect world could give. To find printed pages as near in spirit to the words which must be mediated is a happiness not many poets ever experience; it is good that J. had a foretaste of it. All who love poetry owe you a great debt … I wish you could do nothing else but work like this—I am sure it's the only way to publish poetry: to cover expenses, perform a labour of love & take the whole thing out of the market-place.*[22]

And indeed, Alec was beginning to wish that he could devote himself to printing full-time, telling one friend 'I would like another life in which to give myself to it entirely'.[23] This would become a regular comment in letters to friends until he did take early retirement, but for now he contented himself with the purchase of a new press. And, importantly, he began to articulate a new mission for the Brindabella Press.

10

Interlude: Alec Bolton as Reviewer

'Long live letterpress' proclaimed Alec, concluding his purchase of his new press, which came from the Dominion Press in Melbourne.[1] It was a Western proof press, an English version of a Vandercook.[2] It was a fortunate purchase, as it was only nine years old and in very good condition. Its early disposal by both previous owners—Melbourne University Press and then Dominion Press—was typical of the times, as letterpress gave way to offset in most printshops. The time would come when surviving proof presses such as this, comparatively simple to operate but capable of extremely accurate registration, would be much sought after by a new wave of letterpress printers. For now, the Western cost him only $400 and he was able to commission a Melbourne firm to overhaul it[3], something that letterpress printers in Australia today have to learn how to do for themselves.

Alec stood on the cusp of two printing eras, with the advantage that the old was still relatively easy to obtain and maintain. To him, the dying world of letterpress came to symbolise quality in printing, as general standards fell during an age of rapid technological transition. Compared with the slough of phototypesetting that book design fell into in the 1960s and 1970s, before the digital transformation of later years, letterpress was thus not only the technology he was most comfortable with but also an infinitely better mode of printing.[4] A disadvantage of his stance was that in Australia he was mostly a lone voice in trying to maintain the traditions of excellence letterpress was capable of. The absence of a community of like-minded hand-printers is also perhaps one reason why he did not follow the example of those British and American private presses that gave priority to the iron hand press traditions of an earlier age, using flat-bed presses such as the Albion or Columbian; or perhaps it was simply that such presses were always hard to find in Australia. He worked with readily available presses that he knew were capable of good work. Tellingly, the platen and proof presses with which he equipped his workshop would later become the overwhelmingly dominant combination used by the women and men of the letterpress revival of the early twenty-first century: as in so much, Alec was a forerunner.

Some of these considerations were perhaps in his mind when he accepted an invitation to succeed 'Peter Pica' (publisher and bookseller Andrew Fabinyi, who died in 1978) as a pseudonymous reviewer of Australian book design for *Australian Book Review*.[5] Writing under the name of Martin Em, he contributed ten BookShapes columns over the next four years.[6]

His comments are frequently critical, once even of one of his own prize-winning publications at the National Library.[7]

The first column sets the tone, chiding publishers gathered for the Australian Book Publishers Association design awards for 1977–1978 for their inattentiveness during the presentation:

> *It seemed that many publishers who were present did not feel obliged to pay attention, their complacency abetting rudeness. One could almost hear them saying, 'Well, yes, this was a disaster area up 'til the sixties, but we've fixed it now. Everyone knows that Australian books today are the equal of the world's best'.*

He attributed many of the improvements that had occurred in the 1970s to his predecessor's frequently critical remarks and promised to follow suit, beginning with a trenchant critique of a recent Angus & Robertson biography of Sir Robert Menzies as a 'shoddy production':

> *The author appears to be emphasising numerous lines and even paragraphs by the use of bold type; but then we realise that these are photoset correction lines that have emerged from the processor with a heavier density but which have been stripped in regardless. The two lines of the centred title are not quite centred, and for that matter not parallel either. Page numbers … wander nervously in and out of the margins … A portrait drawing on the front of the jacket is repeated in reverse on the back, as if left and right were all the same to this subject. What we infer from this book is that nobody in the publisher's office could have cared for it. There is no worse fate.*

And of a recent Macmillan title, Elyne Mitchell's *Light Horse*:

> *The work has an inviting appearance. So far as I am concerned, however, it is damned to hell by Letraset chapter titles that are not straight: letters not upright; letters not quite sitting on the baseline. This should be declared a notifiable disease! I am at a loss to know how any publisher can spend a fortune on a worthwhile book and neglect such details.*[8]

He praised such elements as 'generous pages and a confident use of white space; illustrations and text working together without strain', good judgement in leading and typeface selection.

His columns are well worth reading in their entirety, and give important clues to his own ambitions at Brindabella. 'I like books that are coherent and all-of-a-piece,' he said.[9] He had the advantage of being able to scan the daily intake at the National Library, a venerable tradition (still maintained) in which newly catalogued and labelled books were placed on open shelves for staff to inspect before being taken off to the stacks. I remember Alec as a frequent browser at those shelves. The entire output of Australian publishing—or at least of those publishers who lived up to their legal deposit obligations—was thus in view as Martin Em sat down to write his column. (Incidentally, this practice was not simply for the sake of maintaining general current awareness among Library staff but was also used by others as the principal source for compilation of *Australian Books: Select List of Recent Publications and Standard Books in Print* and also to identify edited collections of articles for indexing in APAIS, the Australian Public Affairs Information Service index of scholarly articles in the humanities and social sciences.[10])

Poor design, he argued, was not so much a matter of technological change per se, but of not investing in the education of young publishing staff in the standards they should be aspiring to. 'In typesetting, as in everything else, you get what you pay for and—more important—what you have been educated to insist on.'[11]

Speaking to a group of professional colleagues a few years later, in about 1980, he remained critical of prevailing editorial standards, but less so of design:

> *In the National Library where I work I scan the daily intake of copyright copies deposited, and in the Australian National Bibliography I see the catalogue entries for what has appeared, and the cataloguing-in-publication data for books in the pipeline. I am frankly stunned by the quantity of what appears, and I am mystified as to where it ends up … I find it so hard to believe that a lot of what is published can be more than marginally viable. In the non-fiction field, particularly with practical titles, so many books look like the same book. So many titles seem to be publisher-generated, dreamt up in the office … I get the impression sometimes that books are being created by a cloning process, without individual authors as their begetters. Publishable authors seem to be rare in Australia …*
>
> *I am depressed by the low editorial standard of a lot of material that gets published, even under respected imprints. The level of literacy in books has declined. It must have something to do with education, but it is also related to the reluctance of publishers to finance the very high costs of detailed editorial preparation and proofreading … Can you really wash your hands of responsibility for mistakes, when students and school children and others who are learning the language may*

> *happen to read it? Can you afford to print a book but not afford to care if it is correct, even though you can afford an appealing four-colour dustjacket to help it sell? What is the point of being a publisher in these circumstances? These are disturbing questions to me.*[12]

Years later he was still critical of declining editorial standards in particular, something that was just as important to him as book design, and the maintenance of which was a key aspect of his legacy as the founding publisher at the National Library. This was evident in his private thoughts on the Peter Ryan/Manning Clark controversy in 1993, when Ryan (Clark's former publisher at Melbourne University Press) attacked Clark, who had died two years before, over errors in Clark's *A History of Australia*.

> *Manning was certainly prone to error, but his publisher is the last person in the land who should attack him for that. MUP should have mounted a bigger editorial effort to clean up the factual details, that is all you can say about that. They could have afforded it too. To expostulate over Manning's carelessness on the occasion when someone wandered up from the warehouse to point out the mistake in the new book about the number of times Phar Lap won the Melbourne Cup is just ridiculous. It was the editorial department of MUP who should have hung their heads in shame. Manning was the goose who laid the golden egg for MUP. He just had to be protected from slips of that kind. I was very unhappy about this episode, but thought how nobly Dymphna handled it.*[13]

He was less critical of Australian book design and production in later years, attributing its improvement to a small group of pioneers: Sydney Ure Smith; Frank Eyre of

OUP, Melbourne; Edwards & Shaw; Andrew Fabinyi (again) of Cheshire, 'a publisher who brought a European mind and educated taste to the Australian scene'; Margaret Horder, 'who did much to raise the standard of children's books from the early 1950's'; and the typographer Leslie Apthorp, 'who refashioned the image of books from A&R … and who tried to establish the superiority of Monotype over Linotype in the company's publishing' (a cause always dear to Alec's heart). The ABPA book design competition was also a factor, as was participation by Australian publishers in the Frankfurt and Bologna book fairs. And, despite the loss of skills involved, the move to printing in Asia made full-colour printing of a high standard possible even for books with small print runs.[14]

11

'The printing of these small books takes me literally months and months'

Rosemary Dobson, *Greek Coins* (1977)

'My thoughts take fire from the printed page' wrote Rosemary Dobson at the end of the first of her books to be printed by her husband. Its contents had appeared before in various journals and newspapers, and it was her fifth volume of original poetry to be published. The *Greek Coins* poems were also to be included in her next volume from a mainstream publisher, *Over the Frontier*.[1]

Such words remind us of her unqualified enthusiasm for Alec's avocation, as well as her key role in its success. And perhaps this is an appropriate point to say something of her importance to Australian writing generally, which amounts to a great deal more than the three Brindabella books she would write. In the course of her long life (she would live until 2012) she published 16 books of poetry, as well as other work. As librarian and literary scholar Marie-Louise Ayres commented in her obituary:

> *throughout her life [she] was regarded as one of Australia's most important poets, with a completely distinctive voice. Her career was one of steady commitment to contemplation, traditional forms, and the discipline of discovering and rendering anew oft-repeated themes and concerns.*[2]

Rosemary's interest in art continued long after her brief time as a student with Thea Proctor and is reflected in the illustrations she did for *Three Poems on Water-Springs*, *Greek Coins* and *The Continuance of Poetry*. She also wrote a pioneering monograph on the Australian artist Ray Crooke, and many of her poems concern paintings. As Peter Kirkpatrick, a scholar of Australian literature and cultural history, puts it, her interest in using one art to reflect on another embodied an ancient idea:

> *the concept of ekphrasis, the poetic description of a work of visual art: painting, sculpture, architecture … Across her long career, Dobson was celebrated as a poet who could take the reader beyond the immediate image to another insight. From early on her skill with traditional forms was balanced by a willingness to loosen them in more conversational ways, so she responded better than some of her postwar peers to the cultural shifts of the 1960s and beyond.*[3]

Writing about Ray Crooke in London, at a time when she found writing poetry difficult, Rosemary began by describing him as 'a single-minded painter who believes that in restating the same themes the artist can penetrate ever deeper into a mystery'.[4] This notion of mystery is there in her own work as well: as she put it in 1989, hers was 'a search for something only fugitively glimpsed'.[5] Similarly, her presence may not always be easily discerned in the books of the Brindabella Press, but it is there nonetheless.

Greek Coins is a 'miniature sort of book'[6] in an oblong format reflecting both the shape of the four-line poems (one to each page) and her line drawings of coins accompanying them, which were printed from line blocks made by a local commercial printer, Pirie Printers. One features on the dust jacket, the only printed dust jacket on a Brindabella book, and this perhaps reflects the fact that Rosemary had strong views on the importance of spine labels, according to one of her later printers, and the book was so slim that a spine label would have been difficult.[7] The poems reflect her debt to Pausanias' *Guide to Greece*, written in the second century AD, and in its last line there is perhaps a reference also to her admiration of Peter Levi's Penguin edition of the work. (She sent Levi a copy.) *Greek Coins* is a lovely example of book design allowing poetry room to breathe, and it was admired by its recipients. The contrast with the treatment of the same poems on their mainstream publication in book form is stark, for they were shoehorned into three pages.[8] Dorothy Green said it was 'one of the most beautiful books ever made in this country', and that she 'held my breath when I came to the Sappho poem, but there was the essential word—looking as if it had grown there as naturally as the grass'.[9] Which word that might be is not entirely clear to me; I assume it is 'love', but it could as well be 'suffering', or indeed 'offering':

Sappho on Lesbos. An island is a ring,
A burning-glass for love and suffering.
To her a crown of violets, the moon,
And a round-dance of girls as offering.[10]

Harold Stewart expressed admiration for both the poems and the craftsmanship of their printing and Ray Crooke, who had himself previously illustrated some of her poems, responded to the gift of a copy with a suggestion he might be interested in illustrating a future Brindabella title with screen-prints, although nothing came of this proposal.[11] Indeed, Alec's distribution list shows that many copies were gifts, given to a diverse collection of people including Margaret and Gough Whitlam, Manning Clark, Fay Zwicky, Peter Levi, Leonie Kramer, Judith Wright and Tom Shapcott, as well as many previous recipients of Brindabella books. One hundred and forty-five copies out of an edition of 240 were allocated to three bookshops and Bennett, the library supplier.[12] It is one of the scarcer Brindabella titles on the market, perhaps partly because of its unusual size.

Alec also printed a prospectus for *Greek Coins*, which he asked Walter Stone to help distribute.[13] This appears to have been his first, and he produced them for most of his subsequent books, even though he was later to doubt their value. The prospectus is a common marketing tool for many private presses, and the printing of one for *Greek Coins* suggests that he was beginning to think of his press in more commercial terms—a considerable change from his attitude in the early years, when most of the books he printed were intended as gifts to friends, or to be shared with the poet and illustrator. The prospectuses also say why he thought something merited publication. 'Each coin-sized poem shines with wit and creates a world of meaning and suggestion,' Alec wrote this time. 'It is a characteristic achievement of the poet that so brief a text should evoke so much.'

Greek Coins featured strongly in *The Sydney Morning Herald*'s regular round-up of books received for review, appearing in a substantial review with two of Rosemary's illustrations and details of where it could be purchased.[14] This appears to be the first time the press had received such attention at the time of publication of a book. Alec also entered it into the annual design competition of the Australian Book Publishers Association, this time without success—although it was the year in which his National Library of Australia publication, *Cazneaux*, designed by Adrian Young, won the ABPA prize as Best Designed Book of the Year.[15]

The body of the work was set in 12 point Baskerville Italic, with headings in smaller (8 point) Baskerville Roman capitals, which foregrounds the distinctive shape of the quatrain poems. The display type is Imprint Shadow. Alec again printed on Basingwerk Parchment, although the inking is a little less even than in his previous book, and once more had the case binding done by E.C. Chapman in Sydney. 'As the printing of these small books takes me literally months and months of my leisure and as the editions are very small, I just cannot bear to lose copies at the binding stage,' he told Bill Chapman. 'I really feel I must ask you to give GREEK COINS your personal supervision and attention at all stages.'[16]

In some copies (for example number 77, acquired by the author in 2021; the deposit copy at NLA; and number 45, advertised for sale by The Grisly Wife Bookshop in 2021) Alec fully signed the colophon page beneath Rosemary's signature. Another copy in my possession (number 128) is signed by Rosemary Dobson only.

At around this time a collection of poems by the Sydney surgeon Miles Little was also under consideration by the press, with the proposed title 'Chart of Events'. The initial suggestion came from James McAuley, who had been one of Little's patients, and was championed by Leonie Kramer (later Dame Leonie). 'Australia seems as never before a nest of singing birds,' Alec confided to Tom Shapcott in seeking his opinion of Little's work, 'but I read the work of poet after poet without a sense of recognising an individual voice with something to say. However, I do get this from Miles Little, and so I am interested in him.'[17] In the end, Little decided to withdraw his manuscript from consideration for a year[18], and a larger version of the book was published by Melbourne University Press later in 1977 under a different title.[19] Alec had floated the idea of an approach to Little's friend Sir Russell Drysdale to illustrate the Brindabella edition, although he could also 'think of one or two younger and relatively unknown people who I think could illustrate the five sections of the sequence in an attractive, non-literal way'.[20] As it happened, the MUP edition of 1977, issued both in cloth-bound trade and leather-bound signed editions, the latter of 150 copies, was indeed illustrated by Drysdale.[21] Alec had hoped there might be room for a Brindabella edition alongside the trade one, but this time he had been edged out by what he himself acknowledged as a beautiful book.[22]

12

'With printing, it seems to be a case of "off with the old love, on with the new"'

A.D. Hope, *The Drifting Continent* (1979)

Brindabella's new Western press was hand-operated but with power inking. It had a larger platen size than the Chandler & Price, which meant Alec could print four pages at a time rather than two. 'It ought to be possible to do really elegant work,' he told one of his friends in the paper trade.[1] As a cylinder proof press, it had the power of impression and the precision to allow him to experiment with more versatile illustration, which he tried with his next book in 1979. This was *The Drifting Continent*, with poems by A.D. Hope and drawings by Arthur Boyd. 'This was an exciting book in every sense' he said later. 'The poems were thrilling and the drawings wonderful.'[2] He used a coarse screen to print some of the drawings line and half-tone. (Line and half-tone printing plates combine lines, photographed on an unscreened negative, and half-tone areas photographed through a screen. These are then combined by the platemaker to produce a single metal plate. Examining the tone areas of the final print under magnification shows they are made up of tiny dots, printed at various levels of density.[3])

Alec had approached Hope for a manuscript in 1978, saying that he preferred unpublished work.

> *It would be a great distinction for the press to have something by yourself. I have no preconceived ideas about illustrations; that would depend on the material, and of course it might be appropriate to omit illustrations altogether. However, some element of decoration seems called for in this kind of printing.*[4]

The two were already friendly. Indeed, Hope had recently been one of Alec's confidants in canvassing possible publications, one of which should be considered in some detail before moving on to Hope's own Brindabella book.

In 1977, Alec consulted Hope about the merits of a group of translations by Kaye Mortley of songs by Pierre Louÿs (from *Les Chansons de Bilitis*), in particular some that had been set to music by Claude Debussy at the beginning of the century. Hope had doubts about the worth of the translation, and more. 'Rosemary also mentioned your hesitations about extending the range of the Brindabella Press if you took on this publication, neither local nor in any real sense original,' Hope wrote. 'I make no comment on this, but I would say that if you decide to extend the range, it ought to be with something absolutely original and first-rate.'[5] One wonders if, in retrospect, Alec Bolton regretted turning down this early work by Mortley, at the time working with ABC Radio Drama and Features in Sydney but soon to depart for Paris and a career of great distinction as a radio documentary producer. Hope made no secret of his dislike for the original poems, and for free verse in general, and Debussy as well, but Alec's letter to Mortley seems almost chastened: 'I do like them, but on reflection I feel that they are perhaps a bit outside my range, which I see as being based on material of Australian content or authorship … I am most grateful for the opportunity, and sad to decline it'.[6] Privately, and again to Hope, he confessed that he was puzzled that Mortley's translations were 'less complete and explicit than the originals', and that what had really interested him was the possibility of accompanying the text with appropriate illustrations.[7]

In retrospect, it is perhaps not surprising that translations done for an ABC Radio program of the 1970s were somewhat toned-down; Louÿs' poems, originally presented as a claimed discovery of work by a contemporary of Sappho and complete with a fake biography of Bilitis, became, after their publication in French in 1894, an influential lesbian text (albeit actually written by a man). They were often printed as a limited edition *livre de luxe*, illustrated with erotic drawings.

However, consideration of the Bilitis poems, which he also discussed with David Campbell, helped Alec consolidate his ideas about just what it was that he should seek to be publishing—a question that occupied his thoughts 'more or less continuously' at that time, he told Hope:

The role of my kind of private press seems to have changed. In other days it could serve the gifted young writer who might not otherwise get published; but now I think it is easy (perhaps too easy) for the young writer of any talent to find a commercial publisher for at any rate his first book. The poet who is more likely to be in difficulties is the older writer who may be doing really good work but who is not quite famous or fashionable. That is where I think I should be looking, while at the same time wishing to print nothing but the best and the unusual. Of what I have printed so far, the Rowland comes closest to expressing that view. The Campbell and Brissenden books had special and local associations, and the McAuley was special in another way. As you know, I am just starting Rosemary's 'Greek Coins', and beyond that there is the possibility of something from Roger McDonald, whose work I greatly admire and who is now a Canberra poet too. I have wondered about Dorothy Green. And then I wonder about someone like R.D. FitzGerald and ponder whether, if he had a manuscript of his difficult, inaccessible poems ready, there would be a rush of commercial publishers to do it; I doubt it. It is pretentious to go on like this, because the capacity of the press is so limited. The limitations and the slowness of the whole process make it all the more important to choose well.[8]

Although he noted in a postscript to this letter that he had just heard that Angus & Robertson were about to publish a new book by FitzGerald[9], his later productions were to follow this pattern. Dorothy Green was to be a Brindabella author, and most of the books that followed were by older writers who were 'not quite famous or fashionable' (if one can include John Shaw Neilson and the artist Helen Ogilvie in that description), while the rest were younger writers whom Alec particularly admired. Hope was not his only confidant in this vein: at around the same time, sending his old boss Beatrice Davis a presentation copy of *Time Given*, he expressed similar sentiments and welcomed her thoughts on the subject.[10]

Hope discussed possible poems for his Brindabella book with Rosemary, with whom he had recently done an ABC radio program on the poet Pausanias, who had been her inspiration for *Greek Coins*.[11] At first they considered a non-Australian selection that might be published under the title 'Homage to Akhmatova'[12], including translations from the Russian, and also considered a theme dealing with Pausanias and Greece. In the end the volume focused on Australian places, animals and people. An elegy for James McAuley follows erotic vernacular verse; marsupial mice and echidnas walk its pages. Much concerns the Monaro district. The title poem, set on Canberra's Black Mountain, deals with continental drift as well as the likely short future for humankind.

Alec had once met the artist Arthur Boyd at Hope's home, and in July he approached Boyd to illustrate the book. 'It was a joy to work with these illustrations,' he later wrote to Boyd, 'they all come right out of the heart of the poems. I feel as if I had known them all my life.' But he had difficulty printing the halftones, particularly in one drawing for 'Beyond Khancoban', where he could not print Boyd's original wash as a halftone portion of the block lightly without losing density in the line part of the drawing.[13] He printed dry on Curtis Rag, a roughly textured paper that meant he could only specify an 85-line screen—very low for fine printing, and comparable to that used in newspapers. 'The technical problems of printing halftones by letterpress are enormous,' comments Clifford Burke in his influential book on printing letterpress poetry.[14] They work best when printed on coated paper.

'The bite of impression that makes type look so brilliant on rough stock makes halftones look terrible.' The finest Alec could have specified for printing on even a smooth text paper, at the expense of engraving on copper, would have been 150 lines to the inch. This is half that which is used in high-quality book illustration on smooth, coated paper. Burke goes on to say:

> *I used to consider myself a pretty good pressman until I tackled halftones … Artists often like to use grey ink washes with line illustrations as a way of obtaining tonal effects. Unfortunately, in order to reproduce these grey washes accurately they must be screened as halftones … which requires a second negative and invariably makes the whole thing look like it was cut out with scissors. Better to collar the artist before the drawing begins and insist on some other method, such as cross-hatching, to create the effect of shading.*[15]

The other difficulty Alec had was with the paper he had chosen, which he had specially imported from Massachusetts by Mitchell Ross & Co.[16] He was sure before he started printing that it would be 'a lovely sheet'. Michael McCurdy, himself an experienced printer, advised him to avoid Curtis Rag as a hard paper unsympathetic to letterpress but this suggestion came too late. Alec might have ignored it anyway, as it was a paper used by many letterpress printers at the time.[17] Incidentally, he mentioned in his prospectus that Curtis Rag was acid-free—the first time he had spelled this out. The Library was actively campaigning for publishers to switch to acid-free paper at the time and was using it in its own publications. This was largely at the behest of its conservators, faced with the issue of having to preserve vast holdings of nineteenth- and twentieth-century materials printed on acidic paper. In fact, Alec had generally used acid-free paper up to now, for example the Monadnock Caress Text used for *Elegies* and *Times and Places*, but had not specifically drawn attention to this aspect of the papers he chose. (When mentioned by him, this will be noted in the text following.[18])

The Drifting Continent was bound in quarter leather by Peter Marsh at the Dove Bindery in Melbourne.[19] The endpapers were black Grandee Text supplied by Edwards Dunlop & B.J. Ball. It retailed for $26.50 and quickly sold out. Overall costs were $2,814.27, which meant the final cash loss on 175 sale copies was $31.77. The edition size was 285. Hope and Boyd each received 34 copies, and the Boltons had 42 copies to send to friends, plus legal deposit and review copies sent to *The Age* and *The Sydney Morning Herald*.[20] It was reviewed favourably as 'a collector's piece of very high quality' by Douglas Stewart in *The Sydney Morning Herald*. Stewart liked the poems as well, although he found them surprising in their vernacular quality and their light-heartedness.[21] The prospectus listed the four bookshops and one library supplier from whom the book could be obtained, and stated firmly 'copies will not be available from the press'. (It would appear, judging from Alec's list of recipients, that he produced only about 50 copies of the prospectus.) His prospectus blurb gave brief details of the content, especially of the title poem, 'a long meditation on the fate of those who have voyaged aboard the drifting continent, Australia—monotreme, marsupial and man'. Arthur Boyd's drawings 'are by turns reflective, tender and ribald', he said, 'and offer a characteristically brilliant and individual interpretation of the texts'.[22]

Bolton moved on from *The Drifting Continent* very quickly: 'it has been excessively praised and I am a bit fed up with it,' he told one friend. 'The printing is not all that hot, especially of the 85-screen halftones; and I now feel that the binding, for the planning of which I was responsible, seems pretentious … With printing, it seems to be a case of "off with the old love, on with the new". I am now immersed in a little book of poems by Harold Stewart.'[23] As it happened, he was soon to be much more jaded with the Harold Stewart book, but for a different reason. It would test his belief in the value of illustrating poetry to the point where he seriously considered abandoning the book.

13

'A chance that was lost'

Harold Stewart, *The Exiled Immortal* (1981)

Bolton's first approach to Stewart was in mid-1977.[1] The two had never met, but Rosemary Dobson and Stewart were correspondents. Alec sent him a copy of *Time Given*, which Stewart greatly admired—'I can see that, like myself, you are a perfectionist in your chosen craft, something which I consider as being of the highest importance'—and he later sent him a copy of *Greek Coins* also.[2] Writing in May 1977 Alec asked about progress with *By the Old Walls of Kyoto* (the city where Stewart had lived since 1965), and in January 1978 broached the possibility of printing it as a Brindabella book now that he had a cylinder press with which he could print four pages at a time. This was after Stewart had sent an early manuscript to Rosemary. Stewart told him that it was committed elsewhere, adding later that he could only survive financially in Japan if he sought commercial publication[3], but soon afterwards offered a small selection of poems that had previously been accepted for journal publication, to be collected under the title *The Exiled Immortal.* A possible book of poems by Dorothy Green had been postponed, so as he finished work on *A Drifting Continent* Alec began concrete discussions with Stewart about text and, in particular, the illustration of *The Exiled Immortal.* These were to go on for some considerable time.

This was partly because Stewart made constant changes to the text. A supposedly complete manuscript arrived in March 1979, but it was not really final until January 1980. Even then, Stewart discovered a word he wanted to change from his typescript after receiving the first batch of books for signing, and to Alec's horror started asking previous recipients to hand correct the earliest batch of copies that he had already despatched to his friends.[4] 'You will appreciate my deep reluctance for general copies to go out with an alteration that looks like the correction of a printer's error,' Bolton wrote with characteristic tact, offering to insert an erratum slip. He stood his ground, though, in saying firmly that it should be labelled for what it was: as a 'Textual Amendment'. In the end they agreed to a slip headed 'Manuscript Mistyping', which was pasted to the title-page verso.

But all this was minor compared with the protracted and ultimately unsuccessful negotiations over the illustration of the book. After discussing the poems with Dorothy Green, Alec initially thought they could stand publication on their own. Stewart meanwhile approached Ueshima Masaaki, his one-time lover and still a friend. Masaaki was one of the artists who had illustrated Stewart's successful first collection of translated haiku, *A Chime of Windbells.*[5] Although the lyrical style of these drawings was not suited to Stewart's own poems, and he had previously expressed reservations as to whether Masaaki could meet deadlines, Stewart thought Masaaki could engrave and print four or so woodblock illustrations in a more suitable style for tipping in. Alec admired the drawings in *A Chime of Windbells*, but suggested Kiyoshi Saito, another artist proposed by Ken Henderson, editor of *Hemisphere*, the Canberra-based journal of Asian studies where the poems were first published. Four of Saito's coloured woodblocks had been printed in its July 1976 issue, with striking results. But even though he liked Saito's work, the expense of printing in three or four colours would be prohibitive. Blocks for four-colour printing would cost in the vicinity of $3,500 to $4,000, he told Stewart, and would also require different and more expensive paper than he had planned. (One senses a growing frustration in his remarks at this point.) 'Within the limitation of my resources, and of my skill, I like to work in a single colour, but could probably run to two colours, with say a black line and/or tone basis, and a wash in another colour.' Alternatively, the prospect of tipping-in up to 1800 original woodblock prints was also 'very daunting'. Further, he would prefer to have blocks made in Australia from the originals rather than having them printed in Japan, as Stewart had suggested.

He understood Stewart's reservations about illustration, writing:

> *You will appreciate, I'm sure, that the kind of book I do, deriving from the private-press tradition, seems to call for some touch of illustration or decoration. Are there, I wonder, classical or out-of-print woodblock prints of Kyoto places that appear in the poems? In other words, could the poems be illustrated descriptively rather than interpretatively, in the style of the*

> *Notes? On the whole I would like to use the work of a living artist, if anyone could be found. Another possibility, failing illustrations, might be to employ brush-drawn calligraphic titles. Please reflect on these notions and tell me what you think.*[6]

By out-of-print, he added, he meant out of copyright. Stewart, still unsure as to whether the poems needed illustrations at all, suggested several woodblock engravers whose work might be in the public domain. He could not afford to buy originals of their work for the purposes of reproduction, but was able to photograph copies owned by an American collector who lived in Kyoto. Alec rejected photographs as not being good enough for reproduction. He then asked Stewart for the names of Japanese artists he could search for in Australian collections, and also suggested Jörg Schmeisser—who had lived in Japan before a long tenure as head of printmaking at the Canberra School of Art (1978–1996)—as an outside possibility. This set off another hare, with Stewart suggesting that there were collections of books with woodblock illustrations from the Meiji or Taishō periods at the State Library of Victoria that might be appropriate sources. Alec had no luck tracking these down, and in return came up with another suggestion: Sydney-based Marianne Yamaguchi, who had recently illustrated an attractive book by Eric Rolls for Angus & Robertson with 'beautiful and meticulous' drawings.

Stewart was uncertain because he said Ruth Park had warned him that Yamaguchi's work might be 'too pretty', but Alec was enthusiastic after meeting Yamaguchi and commissioned her to do two trial drawings:

> *Her response to the poems is strong and perceptive … Also she understands that nothing pretty or sentimental is wanted; her approach to this work is, if anything, rather austere; an effect of woodcut simplicity is what she would like to achieve. She knows Kyoto well.*

Alec and Yamaguchi quickly got down to detailed planning of the book's layout and illustrative themes, with the artist building her ideas around the seasonal rhythm of the poems. She created a substantial portfolio of brush and ink drawings, with many alternatives offered for consideration. Stewart reserved judgement, saying only that 'the illustrations should combine the topographical references with the visionary quality at which I aimed'. But when copies were sent to him he condemned them in quite brutal terms:

> *Her sketches might well be acceptable in Australia among people who are not acquainted with the scenes and settings of the poems, but to anyone who knows them by living here or visiting Kyoto, they completely failed to capture either the appearance or atmosphere of the place … by not using her work, I have really saved her from embarrassment, since it would have been laughed at here, where standards in artistry and craftsmanship are so high that only perfection is good enough.*

Alec wrote despairingly to Yamaguchi:

> *Dear Marianne: it grieves me to report that he is not happy. To him, the drawings are too modern. They are not literal enough, not topographical enough. He has written me a long letter that I can hardly bear to read, much less to send to you … He just fails to see what the drawings add to the poems, and how they extend them. What he is implying is that*

> *only one conception is possible—his own. I am more downcast than I can say, by reason of his attitude, [at] the waste of all this effort and thought. I really can hardly bear to have misled you into producing beautiful drawings to such an end. The tone of his letter is such that I realise the impossibility of persuading him to another point of view. I am half of a mind just to give the whole thing away … My wife returns from Europe tomorrow, and I will discuss with her what is best to do. I am so very sorry, Marianne. But of course you will realise that a private printer is not like a publisher who has a contractual right with his author to produce a book entirely at his own discretion … It is a couple of days since I had his letter … I have been brooding on it since then … To hand-set and print a book on which one has gone cold is practically impossible. I am just appalled by this waste of your time and your great gift, not to mention the time I have spent on it with you too. I was happy to feel I had made a friend of you, and I don't want to unmake that.*

He asked if he could keep all the drawings (at that stage he had only paid for two) because his papers would eventually go to the National Library where 'if anyone ever studies the history of the press, he or she will have an opportunity to consider the problems of relationships between authors and publishers, and to see evidence, in the drawings, of a chance that was lost'. They are now at the National Library.

Alec once wrote that his 'habits of reticence' meant that his 'life is full of missed opportunities to tell people what they mean to me'[7], but this is not apparent in his warm and caring correspondence with Marianne Yamaguchi. Perhaps this is a measure of how upset he was by Stewart's veto of her illustrations, which he so admired. He decided to go ahead without illustrations at all, and was circumspect in telling the writer that he was

> *Very disappointed that you did not like the illustrations. For myself, I liked them very much, and felt that they add something to the poems, and extend one's appreciation of them … The book will be modest … and I will sew it myself into limp covers … Although it will be, for me, a rather austere production, I believe I can make it look well. Although I am disappointed that my original conception of the book has been changed, that does not affect my wish to make a beautiful job of it.*[8]

The book is indeed austere. It was sewn as a single section into paper wrappers, the only book apart from the Clark eulogy for David Campbell that 'I have bound entirely by myself … although I have always folded and collated the sheets by hand'.[9] The only illustration is Stewart's signature seal (his *inkan*) on the colophon page, designed by Ueshima Masaaki, the artist he first suggested.[10] It 'fell into something of a well of silence', Alec told Geoffrey Farmer. 'Even friends to whom complimentary copies have been sent have answered silently'.[11] In 1982 he apologetically sent a copy to Yamaguchi, who replied with great generosity. It was handsome, she said, and she praised the typography. Stewart's objections to her work did not disconcert her at all, she told Alec. He had surrendered to an outmoded concept of Japanese culture, and she contrasted him with her own father-in-law, a poet and musician descended from samurai, who simply dismissed the interpretation of Buddhism promoted by Stewart as barbaric.[12]

The Exiled Immortal was hand-set in Monotype Baskerville and printed dry on Basingwerk Parchment, on the Western proof press. The edition was 240, of which 150 were for sale at $9.50. It was published on 27 February 1981, not Spring 1980 as the colophon optimistically states.[13] Like many of the Brindabella books, it was in a tall format and as described in its bibliographic listing there is a small variation in size, at least one copy being 4 millimetres shorter and 6 millimetres wider. Production costs were $857.27. Booksellers took 138 copies, and 15 were sold by Alec direct. His estimated profit on some four years of effort was $70. The book is now quite scarce.

In retrospect, it is apparent that Alec Bolton and Harold Stewart were working from different perspectives. Alec aimed always at perfection, but knew that he would fall short of it. The point, as he said on several occasions, was to keep moving. 'The nice thing … about our kind of work is that any disappointment felt with a past project can be completely submerged by one's hopes for the next project,' he later told a young artist. 'In this sense, and provided one can learn something from mistakes, it is a very forgiving business.'[14] Stewart took his work just as seriously, but implicit in his world view, as a follower of Jōdo Shinsū, the Shin version of Pure Land Buddhism, appears to have been the possibility of achieving something that might be termed perfection. Or rather, in the language of his faith, Enlightenment. Others have also commented on how complex and narrow his understanding of Japan was. 'Friends recount that he lived in a Willow-pattern world, or mentally among a set of shifting woodblock scenes, of which the central print was imperial Kyoto into which he read the iconography of a Buddhist paradise', as his biographer Michael Ackland puts it.[15] The wonder is that the book appeared at all.[16]

And what of his epic poem, *By the Old Walls of Kyoto*, which Alec had earlier expressed interest in? It was published in 1981 by John Weatherhill Inc., a Tokyo and New York–based firm specialising in books on Japan. Some 322 pages of commentary, glossary and index accompanied 135 pages of poetry, far more than Alec could ever have contemplated printing by hand. A handsome production, it was illustrated with four-colour offset plates reproducing nineteenth-century woodblock prints of scenes in Kyoto thanks to generous support from Geoffrey Fairbairn, a historian at the Australian National University with a particular interest in Southeast Asia. The Literature Board of the Australia Council and the Australia-Japan Foundation also contributed to the cost of printing. A.D. Hope, an old friend from Stewart's Melbourne days, described it as 'the greatest poem in English this century', but, as Ackland comments, it too was largely ignored and remains little read in Australia.[17]

14

'The courage to take the step'

Rosemary Dobson, *The Continuance of Poetry* (1981)

In 1979 Alec and Rosemary's close friend David Campbell died. Manning Clark's eulogy for Campbell is one of the great Australian funeral orations and it became the seventh publication of the press (counting both books and pamphlets). Although it was only eight pages long, Alec had the text set in Linotype Baskerville as he felt a sense of urgency in sending it to Campbell's friends. He printed a halftone photograph of Campbell (taken by poet and writer Graeme Kinross-Smith) on the cover, using the Western proof press.[1] This was one of the reasons he had wanted to upgrade his press, so he could print better halftones. The front cover was printed in two colours on a light Lusterkote cover paper, and the text on white Glastonbury Antique. The edition was of about 400 copies, all given to Campbell's friends and none sold.[2] It is now one of the scarcer publications for collectors to find.

The Boltons then produced their own memorial to Campbell in the form of Rosemary's *The Continuance of Poetry: Twelve Poems for David Campbell.* The book was illustrated with her drawings and photographs by Alec of Campbell's property, The Run, and also of Lilli Pilli on the Eurobodalla Coast, south of Bateman's Bay. It was the most lavish Brindabella book to that point, with five blank pages among the preliminary pages and generously proportioned text on an attractive laid paper from Abbey Mills in the UK. (Laid paper, which can be either machine-made or hand-made, shows rib lines produced during manufacture in both vertical and horizontal directions.) Campbell's friends loved the book. Douglas Stewart, for example, told Alec and Rosemary he thought it was the finest product of the press[3]; Patrick White, who like Campbell had lived on the Monaro plains, said the poems were 'absolutely marvellous. I thought it would be more paintings and Greeks, but they're *marvellous*'.[4]

This brings me to a point I want to make about the circles of friendships within which the Brindabella Press functioned. In 1993, when I first wrote about the press, I spoke of its books as being 'engaged in a long conversation with each other'. They are the work of 'friends and acquaintances', I suggested.[5] What I did not fully appreciate at that time was how often it was the creation of the book itself that was the genesis of the friendship, nor did I know that Alec often approached writers and artists he did not know, or had only a passing acquaintanceship with. My close study of his letters has underlined this. Nonetheless, at the heart of it all there are many long, deep friendships, some going back to the 1940s and 1950s and the Angus & Robertson years, and others more recent but just as carefully maintained. As his daughter Lissant says, Alec Bolton had 'a gift for friendship'.[6]

Rosemary Dobson was of course also central to this web of close acquaintance. H.M. and Dorothy Green grouped her with the postwar reflective poets they labelled 'the intellectuals'. Others in the group included A.D. Hope, James McAuley, R.D. FitzGerald and Kenneth Slessor. The categorisation somewhat ignores work after the 1950s, but the Greens were correct in describing Dobson as a deeply reflective poet[7], and this element is also there in the friendships they both cultivated, as well as the books Alec printed. This, I think, is part of what distinguishes the Brindabella Press from the anodyne poetry of some private presses. The Brindabella Press was a place for poetry that Alec and Rosemary grappled with and believed in. Alec tenaciously built friendships and working partnerships, ignoring possible boundaries of generation, style and outlook. It was the poems that mattered, and their rightness for the present time. In 1977, reluctantly turning down an offer of work from the 1930s and 1940s by the art historian Bernard Smith, he said:

> *I think people would feel—and not altogether wrongly—that I had done the book for a wrong reason. It just seems to me that the moment has passed when one could publish these poems successfully for their own sake. My output is so small (say one book a year, at present) that I feel I should do things for their intrinsic rather than their associative interest.*[8]

Just a few years earlier, concluding her Herbert Blaiklock Memorial Lecture, Rosemary touched on the related theme of why poetry and art were so important for her.

What I want to try to say is that, as Drysdale and Judith Wright each gave us a landscape to which we could belong, so Kenneth Slessor gave us a time to which we could belong.

She felt, she said, 'a joy in belonging to one's own time and implicit in this is a sense of gratitude to the poets who have been, and are, my friends and contemporaries'.[9] Much as the press was Alec's domain, and much as she alway deferred to him in talking of it, it was in so many ways a joint endeavour.

It is also evident that Alec was, with regard to printing and book design, a conservative in the true sense. He looked to letterpress and what it did best in an endeavour to print the best books he could, given his resources. This was not out of a reactionary rejection of all that was new but an attempt to keep alive traditions of proven excellence that were in danger of being lost in a world flooded with books produced cheaply by new technologies that had yet to prove their long-term value. Much as he admired the boldness of people such as Mike Hudson and Jadwiga Jarvis at their Wayzgoose Press, their pushing at the boundaries was not for him. Despite this, it is worth noting that Brindabella was the only Australian private press Hudson would work with. More than this, though, and just as it was for Wayzgoose, printing was for Alec above all a matter of his own freedom of expression. In the case of *The Continuance of Poetry* he broke one of his own rules: 'photographs do not sit well with poetry,' he wrote, 'but this was a very personal book and I wanted to include them. I felt that if they meant less to some readers than to others, it just could not be helped'.[10]

The Continuance of Poetry is in oblong format, a shape that had previously been used for Rosemary's smaller *Greek Coins*. Although Alec generally preferred tall, narrow books, he also disliked breaking long lines of poetry. The typeface was 14 point Monotype Baskerville, which he later thought was 'really too big'.[11] It was the first time he had worked with 14 point; he had quite a lot of it, cast by Brown Prior Anderson in 1980 and ordered to pre-empt the firm's anticipated departure from Monotype casting.[12] He printed dry on the Western proof press.

The four tipped-in photographs were printed in green with blocks he ordered as 133-line screen halftones. [13] The decision to stick with such relatively low-resolution halftones suggests that he was still working in a trade publishing frame of mind with regard to how he printed illustrations, although it might also simply reflect the need to contain costs (these four blocks cost $20.18, half the cost of the line blocks). One authority on commercial printing of the era suggests that rulings 'from … 110 to 133 lines are popular for commercial job printing by both letterpress and offset lithography', while 150- to 250-line was normal for 'high quality printing and rendition of very delicate detail'.[14] As a result, the photos have a somewhat overexposed appearance, lacking precise detail and fading into the distance; perhaps, though, this is what Alec intended by way of requiem. He was, after all, a highly competent photographer; one should assume this is what he desired. There are also four line drawings of grasses by the author, printed from line blocks. The edition was bound in dark blue buckram with gold lettering on the spine and front board. The endpapers are Sage Glastonbury Antique and there was an acetate dust wrapper.

The Continuance of Poetry cost $2,556.52 to produce. This time most copies—210 out of an edition of 275—were for sale.[15] The costs of producing books were mounting, with the biggest single cost ($1,255) being the binding, done in Sydney by Stanley Owen Ltd. And in another sign that his hobby was becoming more business-like, Bolton now wrote off some of his capital costs against books, primarily of type. The book retailed for $18.50. As the great bulk of sales were through bookshops, the estimated loss on the entire edition, after allowing for discounts of 40 or 33⅓ per cent, was $100.08.[16] This presumably kept the tax office happy, and may also have been necessary to assure his employer that he was not engaged in outside work for profit, an issue that the Australian Public Service takes seriously.

He again printed a small prospectus, in the same oblong format as the book, which was probably mostly distributed by bookshops—a copy in the author's possession has the stamp of Henry Lawson's Bookshop, in York Street, Sydney. The reason Alec sent prospectuses and later a few copies of this book to a handful of booksellers other than his usual outlets was because he was beginning to think that one day, after retiring from the Library, he might want to make something out of what he had described until then as a hobby, and thus should start widening his distribution avenues.[17] Indeed, he had started to talk of becoming a full-time printer and publisher of fine books quite soon with some of his correspondents: 'in a year or two when the youngest of our children has flown from the coop I hope to have the courage to take the step'.[18]

The Continuance of Poetry was a joint winner of the local Colophon Society's Canberra Book of the Year for 1981.[19]

It was well reviewed and had sold out by early in 1982, although Rosemary Dobson was annoyed at *The Age*'s description of the poems as 'delicate'. 'She hates these drawing-room adjectives and appellations, which are quite inept to describe these particular poems about David Campbell and their friendship and literary collaboration,' Alec told his fellow-printer Jim Walker.[20]

15

'A satisfying music'

Philip Mead, *The Spring-Mire* (1983)

In early 1981 Alec sent a copy of the Harold Stewart pamphlet to Philip Mead, asking if he would be interested in publishing a small book with Brindabella and again suggesting Jörg Schmeisser as a possible artist. Mead, who had recently left Canberra to take up a post teaching English at the Geelong College, was 'delighted and flattered', and thought he had enough poems in hand for a small volume.[1] Alec's reply says something about his personal response to poetry, and also indicates his continuing interest in the poetry of place:

> *I was deeply impressed by your poem in the May Quadrant. It gave me the feeling of descending through layers of language and meaning to a quite new perception of a landscape. A sense of complete stillness and attention came to me while I was reading it. I am not able to say in*

> *what way this felt like something newly or differently experienced, but that was how it was.*

Although he does not mention it, it is also likely that Alec would have seen Mead's first small collection of poems, hand-set and printed in the A.D. Hope Building at the ANU by David Brooks and Alan Gould in 1975.[2] He offered to discuss a royalty payment instead of a substantial number of free copies, and told Mead also that he was thinking of putting the press on a more commercial basis when he left the Library.

Mead's manuscript continued to inspire Alec once received:

> *there are such beautiful poems in it embodying what I think of as a new language of perceiving the landscape and oneself within it … So many layers of meaning and such acute and yet dreamlike impressions. Other poems reveal themselves more slowly, but will be no less rewarding.*

For some time he continued to hope that Schmeisser would provide images, and sent a copy of the manuscript to him in Hamburg, but began to look for alternatives after receiving no response, first considering Queensland artist Ray Crooke (who had previously expressed interest in illustrating a Brindabella book) and then approaching Canberra artist Ian Sharpe. (Schmeisser later wrote to say that he found it difficult to envisage the Canberra landscape at a time when he was so immersed in his return to Germany.)

Sharpe was keen, Alec told Mead. 'I did not suggest illustrations to him, but rather the idea of graphic meditations … He has done some unusual posters and his work is often witty …

He draws extremely well'. Mead replied quickly to say the artist looked interesting[3], and by October 1982 printing was underway. It concluded in January 1983[4] and the book was available in May, according to its prospectus. Alec used his last stock of the Curtis Rag that the Hope volume had been printed on, which he hoped would result in at least 235 copies after spoils, and while the colophon claims an edition of 240 there appear to have been four fewer. This textured paper having produced only fair results with Boyd's line-and-tone drawings, Alec asked Sharpe for line drawings, which he printed in a very deep violet blue. He returned to Peter Marsh at the Dove Bindery, settling on a quarter leather binding with crash canvas (that is, a loose weave binding cloth) sides and a clear acetate jacket. And he discovered one typo (an authorial error) after printing 21 copies: 'I don't think I can afford to abandon those copies. We'll make sure they go to libraries, say, instead of friends'.[5]

The Spring-Mire was the occasion for a revealing discussion between Alec and one of his older friends, the poet R.D. FitzGerald, about its merits as poetry. Although in later years he commented that he 'admired these poems in a somewhat uncomprehending way, finding them just a little opaque'[6], he was more positive at the time. FitzGerald, to whom Alec had sent a copy while inquiring whether he too might have poems ready for publication by Brindabella, questioned whether they were in fact poetry as opposed to poorly constructed essays, although he conceded richness in Mead's use of imagery. Alec agreed that 'some of the lines are prosaic and that the syntax is sometimes perverse', but defended Mead as a poet:

> *I do hear a satisfying music in these pieces. If I hadn't, I wouldn't have spent months setting them up and printing them! No, I don't know what the line means about the spring-mire 'you can feel is valved and ascending'. It made me think there might be something in common between water rising in the earth and blood returning to the heart. That is the sort of metaphor I find in these poems.*[7]

Alec had loved FitzGerald's poetry since he was young, and also greatly admired both the printing and the verse in John Kirtley's epic production of his poem 'The Heemskerck Shoals'. He too 'would love to print a heroic book one day—but perhaps not in such a huge format as Heemskerck Shoals. It is hard to know where to put such mighty tomes'.[8] The acquaintance with FitzGerald went back to the Boltons' earlier days as a young married couple in Sydney, when 'Fitz', as Alec called him, was a major force in the world of Australian poetry, but it was of no avail when a Brindabella edition of 'The Heemskerck Shoals' was later to be vetoed by its author. Of this more anon.

The Spring-Mire retailed for $27.50, with 160 for sale, 30 to Mead, six review and legal deposit copies and 40 for the press, so the final print run was 236 copies. Binding, at $1,888 for the edition, was the single largest cost. Total costs were estimated by Alec at $2,804 and projected income at $2,805 in early 1983.[9] Critically reviewed by R.A. Simpson in *The Age*[10], it was not a runaway bestseller. I bought my own copy, one of 15 taken by the ANU Co-op Bookshop, at the recommended retail price six years later. The largest consignment sent to a bookseller was the 60 copies allocated to Webber. Alec gave copies to many of his friends and acquaintances: Patrick White loved the production qualities of the book and was 'impressed by some of the poems', and the photographer Max Dupain found the verse 'refreshing', as well as praising the production as 'exquisite'.

Notwithstanding such praise, there were some problems with this book. The solids in the drawings were difficult to print, Alec commented to Geoffrey Farmer, even though he printed them on dampened paper, and there are inking issues at some points in the text. The textured paper did not help. Nor are the drawings 'meditative', as Alec had hoped. Instead, they are quite literal illustrations to the poems, despite the artist having been given licence to freely explore the themes of the poetry. Sharpe went on to a successful career as a cartoonist for *The Canberra Times* (1988–2012), and has a distinctive and instantly recognisable style, but one can't help but wonder what Schmeisser might have made of the commission. All but one of the poems ('Evening') were included in Mead's next book, *This River Is in the South* (University of Queensland Press, 1984), illustrated in this case only by a painting by Fred Williams on the cover.

During the time he was negotiating with the author and possible artists of *The Spring-Mire*, the Boltons took a short but important break from life in Canberra. They spent a month in the US in April 1982, the first long holiday Alec had taken since starting work at the National Library more than ten years earlier. They met several letterpress printers, beginning with Sam Hamill, one of the partners at the Copper Canyon Press in Port Townsend, Washington. This visit—suggested by the poet Denise Levertov, who had stayed with them during a recent visit to Australia and who had herself recently been published by Copper Canyon—took them to Seattle.[11] In California they met

Lewis and Dorothy Allen of the Allen Press, Andy Hoyem of the Arion Press, and Leigh McLellan of the Meadow Press, and also visited the Mackenzie & Harris Type Foundry in California, where he ordered Centaur and Arrighi type. The new American quarterly *Fine Print*, published in San Francisco, had alerted him to a thriving community of letterpress printers surviving in the US—'heartening' news he told Jim Walker.[12] He had studied Allen's influential book *Printing with the Handpress*[13], as he told them when writing to ask if he might visit them.

> *Private printers in Australia are a small community, and are separated by great distances. Letterpress has all but died here, and there is now but one commercial typesetter still with Monotype, and he is too costly for private customers. With a friend I am now the owner of a Supercaster, which is in process of being set up on his farm. Thus I hope we will not run out of metal, even if sympathetic letterpress papers are extremely hard to come by and have to be imported. I have a Western register proof press and a Chandler & Price treadle platen. I am afraid you would not approve of the Western as it has power inking.*[14]

The visit to Copper Canyon Press was encouraged by Michael McCurdy of Penmaen Press, with whom he was in regular contact by letter and whom he also planned to visit in Massachusetts. (For some reason, and despite firm arrangements, they did not meet, although their correspondence continued for several years.) He had been greatly impressed by the Allens' work, he later told McCurdy, and had spent time looking at copies of their books at the Book Club of California. He had also been interested to see how the Copper Canyon Press was straddling the divide between being hand-printers and publishers happy to use offset printing for their commercial editions. He bought a copy of the trade edition of the Arion Press' *Moby Dick*, but was not so sure about some of their more experimental work.

> *Hoyem is into some rather eccentric poetry productions. The latest is a circular printing of a poem by John Ashbery, the lines like the spokes of a wheel. It is to be on hand-made paper from a circular mould. I think this is as far as he can go, and hope he gets back to books.*

Unfortunately the call on the Meadow Press did not go as well asthat to Copper Canyon; despite a friendly response by its proprietor to his initial overture, the two seem to have had little in common.[15]

Even though he visited only a handful of people, meeting like-minded printers clearly invigorated him, and the journey was a highlight in his regular summary of the year for Geoffrey Farmer.[16] With the advantage of hindsight, though, it seems a somewhat constrained itinerary when one considers the extent of the revival of fine letterpress printing on the West Coast from the mid-1970s on. There were many fine printers in California in 1982, of whom a large proportion were to be found in the San Francisco Bay area. But we need to remember that to an Australian planning a short visit from the other side of the Pacific in a time before the internet they were not nearly so visible or accessible. Apart from personal connections, his awareness of the American scene was partly based on what he could read in the National Library's holdings of Sandra Kirshenbaum's California-based magazine *Fine Print*—which began publication in 1975, but to which the Library only subscribed in 1981.[17]

Still, it is clear that Alec was generally aware of the strength of letterpress printing in North America, referring to this in his first letter introducing himself to Michael McCurdy in 1976.[18] He had seen two of McCurdy's books at the National Library and he saw the Private Libraries Association's annual survey volumes, *Private Press Books*, most likely through Bill Thorn. Yet there is no evidence that he had read Clifford Burke's highly influential book *Printing Poetry*, published by Scarab Press in San Francisco in 1980, although he later spent time studying the Library's copy of Adrian Wilson's lovely limited edition *Work & Play*, published in San Francisco soon after their visit there.[19] He had long admired Lewis Allen's *Printing with the Handpress* also, despite Allen's disapproval of mechanical inking, which he did not share[20], and later acquired a copy of the superb facsimile of the bibliography of the Allen Press, published by the Book Club of California in 1985.[21]

While he and Rosemary were away, the poet John Tranter wrote asking if he would be interested in printing an eight-page booklet with four poems written collaboratively by himself and John A. Scott, in an edition of 200. They could raise a small sum to pay for the printing. On their return Rosemary wrote a brief reader's report querying the success of the collaboration, and noting also that the manuscript was 'not suitable in length for Brindabella. Tranter has not grasped what the BP is about', but adding 'still, he is a good poet and a future possibility'. Alec's reply to Tranter was rather more diplomatic, making a virtue of what Rosemary had seen as a weakness of the collaboration by stressing the single voice of the work, while gently declining it on the grounds of brevity and asking for the opportunity to look at something longer in the future.[22]

The episode is a useful reminder that Rosemary Dobson was always a key figure in the life of the press, although she does not appear to have written such reports as a matter of course. What the press was 'about' was itself still evolving, especially in terms of the relationship between text and illustration, as negotiations during the next project were to demonstrate.

But, as it happens, at about this time Alec made what seems to have been his first major public statement of the aims of the press, in an article for the Book Collectors' Society of Australia's journal. Everything started with his longstanding professional interest in book design and production, he said, but even so it had taken him 20 years to respond to his wife's early enthusiasm for hand-printing. As soon as he started learning to print, though, he discovered it to be an absorbing passion: 'I would go home to Richmond by late trains from Waterloo dreaming of returning to Australia to start a private press'. His interest was in making books of poetry, and although his output to that time had been only 'a few slender books', he hoped to one day make it a full-time occupation:

> *Printing is exciting to me. It is a rewarding and also a forgiving occupation. There is always the wonderful prospect of the next book, and the next book is never burdened by mistakes that one has made in the past. You cannot say that of many things.*
>
> *Many people have helped me … And as well as people there is always the uplifting prospect of the work of other presses: the superb, really well printed books that one sees from presses like the Whittington Press in England. Theirs is the company of the elect to which I aspire.*[23]

16

'A powerful artist might run away with the book'

Dorothy Green, *Something to Someone* (1983)

In August 1977 Beatrice Davis had urged Alec to approach Dorothy Green for a manuscript, saying that she had to be asked because she could not bear submitting and being rejected.[1] Green, who lectured in English at the Australian National University and the Royal Military College, Duntroon, published her poetry under the name Dorothy Auchterlonie, and was well known to both Alec and Rosemary. By late 1977 arrangements had been made, with Green expressing delight at Alec's proposed 'low key, inconspicuous' production on an 'unsophisticated press'.[2] However, there then ensued many delays. It was a transaction that adds to our understanding of Alec's intentions as a private press printer at that time, and bears close reading.

To begin with, in June 1980 Alec withdrew from the project,

explaining that the Harold Stewart book had taken much longer to print than anticipated, and that he felt a sense of urgency about printing Rosemary's poems for David Campbell. He stressed that he liked Green's manuscript. 'The poems are strong and beautifully finished. Many of them are very poignant to me,' he wrote, although perhaps as a group they were not as coherent as some he had published. He appreciated that she would be disappointed, but wanted her to be free to pursue other options. Green's response was quite simple: she would rather he printed them than anyone else, and if it was just a matter of waiting a year—well, she would wait. All she really cared about was that he liked the poems enough to print them. He assured her he did, although he added now that he was also somewhat reluctant to be seen 'as if I only cared for middle-aged established writers', and that he might want to look for someone younger to follow *The Continuance of Poetry*. A measure of his frustration with the Stewart book followed:

> *I think I can truthfully say that, with Harold's book not quite half printed, there is nobody to whom I would be happy to give a promise, now, that his or her book would be the one to follow Rosemary's.*

'Private printing with its immense delays and general unpredictability seems to be so much a matter of timing,' Alec said in one of these letters, and it was not until early 1982 that he again canvassed a possible publication of Green, to follow Philip Mead, and he began planning in earnest in early 1983.

In the letter of March 1982 he spoke of wanting to 'devise some illustrative or decorative content', which was also to get him into unexpected difficulties. To begin with, he tried a new approach to finding an artist: wanting to find a wood engraver, a medium that greatly attracted him and that was central to the private press book revival of the mid-twentieth century, he advertised for one in *Art & Australia*. To begin with, his ad drew almost no response, but after some months a letter arrived from the writer and printmaker Barbara Hanrahan, then living in London.[3] It was to be the beginning of one of the most significant artistic partnerships in the history of the press, but ironically this first attempt ended in failure. Green was somewhat dubious of Hanrahan as a writer[4], but was willing to go ahead with her in her other persona as an illustrator. It was Hanrahan who, in the end, became the obstacle.

Alec told Green that, as soon as he saw examples of Hanrahan's work, 'I felt that her gift might be adaptable and sympathetic to your manuscript'[5], and he wrote the same day to Hanrahan to say that 'I am walking on air after receiving your letter, as I think we might collaborate in producing something really good—not only in Dorothy's book but in others beyond that. You will have to trust me as a printer, but I think you will be satisfied'.[6] And Hanrahan's initial responses were similarly enthusiastic, adding that 'I've always loved books, and can't resist buying great quantities of paper—Arches, Rives, etc.—for my prints and drawings'.[7]

In London, Hanrahan had studied wood engraving with Gertrude Hermes and Blair Hughes-Stanton, two leading artists among the group of modernists who had established a new style of wood engraving in Britain from the 1920s on. Mostly breaking from the Bewick tradition of fine detail and masterly use of black lines, they and their contemporaries used white lines and massed blacks and whites to create powerful images that were sometimes attacked by their critics as being merely derivative of photography. They had also been among the first to work in linoleum, a medium Hanrahan excelled in.[8] Both Hermes and Hughes-Stanton had been associated with the Gregynog Press in the early 1930s, when Hughes-Stanton's engravings for *The Revelation of Saint John the Divine* (1933) in particular received great acclaim.[9]

The private press revival of the 1920s was severely damaged by the economic crisis of the 1930s, but a second wave of fine book printing in Britain in the decades after the Second World War had created new opportunities for many wood engravers. While the revival of wood engraving in the early twentieth century had largely been based on the notion of producing affordable artistic work for domestic display, in the 1920s the revival of wood engraving to illustrate books had also gained support, albeit controversially, and was particularly promoted in the UK by Eric Gill and Robert Gibbings. The development of the electrotype process also made it possible to print long runs of high-quality illustrations from metal duplicates of wood blocks.[10] Some illustrators of the era were not prepared to work with private press books—Edward Ardizzone, for example, for a time refused to work with any limited edition, developing 'a style of illustration that could be satisfactorily reproduced in magazines and books using the technique of rotary printing on cheap paper', for partly political reasons; and many commercial publishers rejected wood engraving as outmoded and impractical.[11] But any engraver whose results depend on careful inking and impression, fine paper and sympathetic typography, and especially those using the medium of wood, which will lose definition over long print runs, is likely to be drawn to private press book illustration if the opportunity arises. So it is not at all surprising that Hanrahan was keen to work with Alec. What is surprising is how quickly their first attempt failed.

In October Alec wrote again to Hanrahan setting out what he aimed at in the relationship between text and illustration in books of the press. He enclosed some poems and stressed that if she decided she did not like them, and did not want to do the book, there was potential for later projects.

> *But I hope and think that you will find scope in these poems for some strong decorations to complement the text. I suppose that if I were the author of poems like these, the unspoken thought in the back of my mind would be that a powerful artist might run away with the book ... My view is that the illustrations in a book like this should be subordinate to the text, and I have no doubt that you will agree with this. The only book that I have ever printed that came close to threatening this principle was A.D. Hope's The Drifting Continent, which Arthur Boyd illustrated with prolific generosity. As the poems were immensely strong, it turned out to be a successful collaboration.*[12]

But Hanrahan did not agree with this view at all. She wrote immediately to say that she did not feel that her work would do the poems justice, because her style and that of the poetry were too dissimilar. Furthermore, she said:

> *I'm not an illustrator (I should have thought of this before, but I didn't). I don't like holding myself back to make my work illustrative. I just cannot work to the principle that the engravings in a book should*

> *be subordinate to the text. For me, text and 'illustration' should be equally strong, and my perfect 'illustrated' book would be one of Blake's.*

She went on to analyse why this might be in words that presage the two superb books she would later illustrate for the press:

> *I am afraid that the fact of being a writer as well as a printmaker is a further complication. It is easy enough to be decorative, but the 'writer' part of me gets in the way and I worry that if I did engrave for something I didn't relate to, it would seem I was enthusiastic, as a writer, about the text when I wasn't. I feel that I would like to have my engravings (not illustrations) published with writing that I related to intensely and felt deeply about—and the result would be a book where my work and the text would complement each other. Of course, the ideal book I could make engravings for would be one of my own.*[13]

Alec and Hanrahan would go on to create just such a book, and two more publications, during her short career (she died at just 52) of great distinction as both writer and artist.[14]

So despite an unpromising beginning, the contact Bolton had developed with Hanrahan would in the long run be a breakthrough. She, Mike Hudson and Rosalind Atkins would be the three artists with whom three Brindabella works were created, out of the total of 17 artists with whom Alec worked. Hanrahan, Hudson and Atkins were all wood engravers in the majority of their Brindabella guises, although Hanrahan especially used other mediums, and fine wood engraving by these artists and others was to become a central characteristic of Brindabella publications.

Alec too experimented with other techniques, and there is a natural synergy between wood engraving and letterpress, but there is one other factor that perhaps helps explain his enthusiasm for wood engraving. As previously mentioned, his friend Bill Thorn was in those years well advanced in building a significant collection of British private press books. His collection was particularly strong in contemporary presses, with a strong focus on wood engraving, in particular the Whittington, Incline, Old School, and Old Stile presses. Alec regularly visited Thorn, who lived in a neighbouring Canberra suburb, and spent time with the books that flooded in with seemingly every post.[15] Regular exposure to the work of these fine British presses, together with inspection of the books of a small range of contemporary British and North American hand-printers collected at that time by the National Library, thus kept him in touch with the output of a good range of the important letterpress private presses of the 1970s, 1980s and 1990s. Jim Walker was another of his printing acquaintances who praised the work of the Whittington Press in particular, and who also spoke of the revival of wood engraving in the UK at that time.[16]

With Alec's growing knowledge of the leading English private presses of the day, however, went a certain degree of narrowness. He had only limited exposure to his significant European contemporaries, as well as those of North and South America.[17] The annual TYPOMANIA printfest at Uelzen, Germany, for example, which Mike Hudson and Jadwiga Jarvis of the Wayzgoose Press in Leura participated in regularly from the mid-1980s on[18], was not on this horizon. As Jarvis has written:

> *Alec and the Typomaniacs (us included) came/come from different planets. We have different—I'd venture to say, totally incompatible—mental maps of private press and letterpress printers … Alec was a conservative who treaded a well-worn typographic path … The Typomaniacs laugh at convention. The challenging of received wisdom (conservative thinking) and the status quo has been TYPOMANIA's raison d'être since its inception thirty years ago. The challenge is not merely typographic (the contributor's work is invariably creative, but that is by-the-by), it is first and foremost political. Each TYPOMANIA portfolio is concerned with a current political and/or social issue and the stance is decidedly left-leaning. It is no place for conservatives—typographic or political.*[19]

Something to Someone is an elegant (and indeed conservatively designed) book printed in typically formal Brindabella style. The title comes from words by Victor Hugo, chosen by Green as an epigraph: '*Tout dit, dans l'infini, quelque chose à quelq'un*'. It was handset in Bruce Rogers' Centaur typeface and its companion italic, Arrighi (not Perpetua as I incorrectly stated in *A Licence to Print*), imported from the typefounders Mackenzie & Harris in San Francisco and, Alec thought, used for the first time in an Australian book. It was printed damp. Some of the type was bought with the cash prize awarded by the Colophon Society for *Time Given*.[20]

To begin with, there were some negotiation about which poems to include. He had 'enough Arches paper for a book of 36 pages in an edition of 220 to 235 copies', he told Green. Allowing for preliminaries and colophon, that would leave 29 pages for text, so seven of the 36 poems submitted had to go because some poems needed more than one page.[21] Deletions were up to Green in the first instance: 'It's your book,' Alec wrote later, 'but I think we should both be happy about changes and additions'.[22] He proposed some deletions, which were all accepted except for 'Parturition'.

Following Barbara Hanrahan's decision to withdraw, Alec sent half of the proposed contents to Michael McCurdy, asking if he would be interested in providing a frontispiece. Although McCurdy had come to mind because of a Penmaen engraving featured in the American journal *Fine Print*, which 'catches something that I feel about this book: its sense of the darkness and solitude of life, but of there being light in the distance'[23], the two had been exchanging letters and occasional publications since Alec's first letter to McCurdy in 1976.

McCurdy offered two sketches for consideration, and Alec was delighted with one showing bare trees stretching towards the sun, sparked by the poem 'Autumn Drought'. He sought the artist's advice on how best to print the engraving on his cylinder press:

> *I guess one must be careful not to apply too much impression, for fear of cracking the block. With this relatively small size, I doubt if it should be necessary to dress the cylinder. I would expect to underlay the block carefully to bring it up to the right height. Is that right?*[24]

McCurdy reassured him: the block was uniformly type-high, but needed more make-ready on the upper half. 'Keep the ink down to a minimum and keep up the pressure. You don't want to lose the fine lines,' he advised.[25] And indeed the printing of the engraving is assured. McCurdy was delighted with it, and hoped to work with Alec again.[26]

The mould-made Arches paper led to a binding problem, however, which caused much consternation. Alec realised too late that he had misread the direction of the grain in the paper before printing, which was manageable for the bound sections of the book but forced a late change in the choice of endpapers and, eventually, the whole style of binding, to avoid warping of the boards. He had intended to use the same paper for endpapers as in the text, but had to find an alternative—first hoping to use a grey from Dunlop & Ball, and finally settling on a paper that came close to matching the light red of the title on the title-page. He envisaged quarter binding in cloth, with marbled sides in a Cockerell design, but also considered full marbled sides and a cloth spine. He wanted a board with the best possible archival quality.[27] Peter Marsh suggested that a cloth spine with full marbled sides might not work well, pointing out that the problem with the grain direction meant that the book had to have a square back rather than a round one, which he thought should not be done with the spine only in cloth. Alec had also seriously underestimated the number of sheets of marbled paper the edition would need.[28]

After considering a range of options, he settled on a two-part binding in Oxford Library buckram, the spine and one-and-a quarter-inch sides in black, and the front and back in terracotta. This would work with the square back, and gold blocking on the spine was complemented by a gold rule on front and back where the two buckrams met. He now suggested the endpapers could be a Glastonbury taupe[29], but in the end they were a Brigadoon shade called Ancient Red.[30] Alternatives would be too expensive, he told Marsh. He was owed $1,500 on the last book by 'slow-paying booksellers' and was trying to keep the cost of this one down because 'the book itself, in terms of its content, is not one that I want to have to sell at a high price … Am I slipping?' he wondered to Marsh. "I hope not. But preoccupation with other things has caused some unhappy mistakes.'[31]

Marsh was phlegmatic—'You're probably a bit like me at the moment—trying to do everything and forgetting a few rules'[32]—but in an undated letter acknowledging receipt of the copies for binding told Alec that he had decided to retire and this would be the last book he did for Brindabella. This was partly for health reasons (he was losing his hearing) and also for financial reasons. 'I think you are getting better with age,' he told Alec. 'Your craftsmanship re typography, printing and paper choice is unequalled. I am an old fashioned bookfeller who likes to see some "impression" on the sheet and on this book, you have brought out the cut of the type to perfection.'[33]

Marsh left the edges of the pages untrimmed, suggesting that the slightly feathered fore-edge would help disguise the long-term buckling he predicted because of the incorrect grain of the paper.[34] Three decades on, this problem is not apparent in copies I have examined, although the pages are a little stiff to turn. Alec thought the inking was not as even as it should be, but told Marsh he was happy with the title-page and frontispiece opening. Printing damp had added considerably to the work involved.[35] He returned later to the grain issue in a somewhat more negative vein, noting that:

> *by mistake (my mistake) the paper was cut the wrong way, so that the book folds against the grain. As it is a mould-made paper, this is not too serious; but in some way I have always felt that I disown this production because of the mistake.*[36]

Because Dorothy Green was ill and in hospital at the time of publication, Alec offered to drop the idea of her signing the entire edition.[37] At least one subscriber's copy examined is nonetheless signed—but on the title-page verso rather than the colophon page, as was the press' normal practice. Perhaps its owner asked her to sign it after publication. Other copies, however, are unsigned.

Something to Someone retailed for $22.50. There were 30 copies for Green, two for the artist, six or seven review and legal deposit copies and 30 press copies for family and friends. As there were 170 copies for sale, the number of copies sent for binding was probably 238 (as opposed to 230 described in the colophon).[38] Binding, at an estimated $1,920, was the single largest cost, and paper cost $353. Total costs were estimated by Alec at $2,647.50. These were anticipated costs: unusually, Alec did not file a record of his final costs, although there is a brief note in his papers suggesting that he would break even on the book once it sold out, which it eventually did.[39]

Sales of *Something to Someone* were slow, possibly not helped by a critical review of the poems by the poet Judith Rodriguez in *The Sydney Morning Herald*[40], although Bruce Beaver, another poet, reviewed it more favourably in *The Weekend Australian* as 'a beautifully made book, one of the handsomest I've seen in recent years, a worthy home for Dorothy Auchterlonie's whole-hearted verses'.[41] Alec told one bookseller that he felt constrained from advertising his own books because of his position at the Library. There was a 'need to be non-commercial and anonymous'[42], he said, despite having again produced a prospectus that went to bookshops and his mailing list.

What were the matters that were pre-occupying Alec in

1983? One was family-related: he spent many weekends in Sydney in the second half of the previous year visiting, and then sorting out the estate of, his Aunt Beulah Bolton, who died at the age of 93, leaving her house jointly to him and his brother John. (The house was Kareela, at 6 Mount Street, Hunters Hill, Beulah Bolton's home since 1919.[43]) The house needed work, and then took a long time to sell in a quiet market.[44] Although a buyer was found early in 1983, the terms of the sale included settlement over almost four years. At about this time the Boltons bought a small terrace house in Glebe, initially for use by Lissant but also as a pied-à-terre in a part of Sydney they loved, and from which they could look down 'to see fishing boats and colliers berthed in Blackwattle Bay'.[45]

A minor matter, aimed at securing long-term availability of type, was an investment in a Monotype Super Caster Jim Walker of Croft Press had bought in about 1979 and in which Alec asked to buy a half-share. In an email from 2016, Jim Walker confirmed that Alec never actually cast type on it: 'the Supercaster is a complex machine to set up and use and I think Alec decided against using it personally for this reason'. The Super Caster came with mats to cast Univers, Garamond, Plantin, Rockwell, Gill Sans, Spartan—all in 8, 10 and 12 point, with 6 point in Plantin and Spartan as well—and 12 point Typewriter.[46] These were not types Alec used much, but he could have searched for others on the second-hand market. Although Walker learned how to use it[47], and Alec spent three days on a Super Caster at King Linotypers in Melbourne in April 1981, feeling that he had got the hang of casting with it, he remained unsure about fundamental issues such as changing point sizes. Overall he recognised that:

> *If I were faced with a machine tonight, two weeks after my apprenticeship, I probably couldn't change it over and get it going. But anyway I did learn a few things, including the need to be highly cautious of splashes. Mal King himself is extremely respectful of the hot metal … The thing that struck me about it all is that while I might be able to operate a machine in a fundamental sort of way, I would be completely floored by any happening or stoppage outside my experience.*

But, he added:

> *I was overwhelmed as never before by the beauty and refinement of the Mono system, and the extremely delicate tolerances of it all, as well as the mechanical wizardry, close to madness, of the casting processes; and I felt sad that the genius and sophistication of the system has been so suddenly eclipsed by photosetting. It is, in a way, like the art of the old wood engravers being suddenly abolished by process engraving. I returned to Canberra feeling both elated and chastened.*[48]

The Monotype Super Caster was introduced in 1928, and for the first time enabled Monotype operators to cast display faces to match its text faces.[49] (Display type is larger and/or more distinctive than that in the continuous text of a work, and is used for titles, chapter headings and the like.) It was a highly successful innovation—and both demanding and dangerous to operate. It should be noted that in the 1960s a trainee compositor at the Oxford University Press would spend six months in the Monotype Casters Department as part of his five-and-a-half year apprenticeship. It is hardly surprising Alec's three days were not quite enough![50] Bill Thorn had told him, after a visit there, that the Whittington Press had a Composition Caster, Alec later reported somewhat enviously to Walker, but they had several retired Monotype tradesmen living in the village who could work for them part-time, and such skills were rare in Australia. He even began to think of installing a Linotype machine 'at the printing end of this house', because at least it would be quieter to operate than a Composition Caster, but that would have to wait until he retired.[51] (This did not eventuate, but in the end he would be forced to use Linotype, albeit reluctantly.) So, apart from a small quantity of leads and rules, Jim Walker's Super Caster at Cobargo was not used to cast type for Brindabella.[52]

Rather more than these issues, it is most likely that his preoccupations were primarily to do with the situation at the National Library at that time. Allan Fleming's term as director-general was followed by the appointment of Dr George Chandler in 1974. Chandler came from a different library world, that of municipal libraries in the UK. His restructure of the Library was not universally embraced, nor did he develop an easy understanding of the needs of state and university libraries in a federal system.[53] His contract ended in 1980, when Harrison Bryan took over and served until 1985.[54]

The Library also lost staff and collections to the newly established National Film & Sound Archive in 1984, which caused internal trauma. Alec wrote to his friend Gerald Fischer, who as an archivist understood the impact of such deliberations on a collecting institution:

> *There have been many stresses and strains at the Library during the past year; some of them to do with moves to hive the Film Archive from*

> *the Library; possibly the sound recordings archive too. These matters are said to be before Cabinet at present. No one knows what will happen. The crisis atmosphere has passed, but there was some unpleasantness through a lot of the second half of last year.*[55]

Alec normally expressed himself in an understated way: for him to use a word such as 'crisis' underlines how significant and unpleasant the debate was. A policy originally lobbied for by the film industry, which wanted to see archival film collections managed by an institution dedicated primarily to their needs, ended up including an arbitrary division of recorded sound collections and a transfer of resources and collections that had previously been closely integrated with other aspects of the Library's collection development priorities.[56]

Another crisis faced by the Library at the time was the removal of asbestos, which had been used widely in the construction of the building in the 1960s, and which led to conflict between management and unions, followed by a fire that briefly threatened the entire building. By 1985, when Warren Horton took over as director-general, there was a perception in some Canberra circles that the Library was due for another major overhaul. This Horton did in his first seven-year term, but soon after he took over Alec would take early retirement.

17

'I was happy with this book'

John Shaw Neilson, *Some Poems of Shaw Neilson* (1985)

The Brindabella file on the next book includes a series of prints Alec labelled '12 stages of make-ready for "The White Plum Tree"'.[1] Make-ready is the process of adjusting the height of the printing surface so that all areas of the forme, in this case consisting of a woodblock engraved by Barbara Hanrahan, print with a satisfactory impression and thus, in the case of a woodblock, properly give effect to the intention of the artist when printing. Make-ready can involve tiny changes to the height of the block, underlaying portions with thin paper, or equally small changes to the bed of the press by way of overlays of paper on the tympan or cylinder. The process demands a great deal of trial and error, for a small change to correct the impression in one area may alter a previously satisfactory result in a neighbouring portion of the block. It is partly a question of judgement by eye and partly one of exact measurement; a precision type high gauge of the letterpress era measures in increments of one thousandth of an inch, although I do not know whether Alec owned one at this time. That it took him only twelve proofs to get to a satisfactory result demonstrates his growing skill: 'the making ready of a form[e] is a very intricate process, and requires much judgement and care upon the part of the workman'.[2] Its success also vindicates the decision to use the medium of wood engraving again. This was quickly to become Alec's preferred method of illustrating his books.

The genesis of this project was the correspondence between Alec and Barbara Hanrahan after her decision not to offer woodcuts for Dorothy Green's book. His immediate response, as soon as he received that letter, was to say that:

> *The points you make in your letter are all very reasonable and I feel that I understand your point of view perfectly. Let us set all that aside and see if there is any other project on which we might both be happy to work. Can you identify any other available or potential Australian text on which you would like to work to produce the kind of illustrated book you have in mind?*[3]

One possibility he canvassed was Christopher Brennan's poem sequence 'The Wanderer', and he proposed that the blocks and copyright would remain the artist's property. 'I am most reluctant to abandon the idea of our collaborating on something,' he concluded. 'It has been much in my mind for months!'

Hanrahan's response was immediate and enthusiastic.

> *The poet I would like to make engravings for is John Shaw Neilson. I have always related to his work since I was fifteen or so, and copied down his poems into an exercise book that was like my friend. I think I could do something good, as I feel very close to him—to his poetry and his life. I feel towards him as I do to Clare or Blake or Lawrence … I'm afraid I don't think I would relate to Brennan—but I haven't read 'The Wanderer'. But I would love to do Shaw Neilson.*[4]

Hanrahan's biographer also records her admiration for John Shaw Neilson, mentioning visits to see his cottage at Nhill in the 1970s.[5] Alec happily agreed on the choice of Neilson. The National Library had published Neilson's autobiography in 1978, so he had already been in contact with the owner of Neilson's copyright. He could not take on a very large selection, so asked for an editorial rationale for a book of 40 to 48 pages in length.

Hanrahan was 'intuitively attracted to two types' of Neilson's poems, she replied: 'the openly joyous "spring" ones and the more bitter-sweet ones that often have a macabre or slightly sinister undercurrent'.[6] She later expressed similar views introducing her selection, and also briefly and diplomatically repeated her argument that 'the engravings should be on equal terms with the text'. She wrote of when she had first read Neilson:

> *I had just left school and was working as a typist in the Mail Order Department of one of the big Adelaide stores. My own identity seemed to have been diminished by out-of-town orders for the Roomifoot comfort shoe, the Comfy-nite pyjama suit. I began spending my lunchtimes in the Public Library and it was there I discovered Neilson's poetry and a*

> *private vision so delicate, yet so strong that its potency restored me to my own imaginative world.*

She suggested 15 poems to begin with, and Alec asked for another seven, which was agreed. He wanted some page spreads to be purely text and proposed nine engravings; Hanrahan in the end did 13, a considerable undertaking, especially as seven of them were full-page in size. The size of the book was dictated by the size of the blocks Hanrahan had brought back with her from England; they were mostly three by five inches, so the book was quite small, a demy quarto. (The supply of suitable blocks for wood engraving was always a problem for Bolton and his artists. He experimented later with Australian timbers, but relied primarily on supplies from England, a somewhat cumbersome business when ordering by mail.) The typefaces were Centaur and Arrighi again, and the paper was Basingwerk Parchment, 'a lovely, smooth English sheet that is particularly sympathetic to wood engravings,' Alec told Hanrahan. He would have liked to try Zerkall Halbmatt, a German mould-made paper, but did not know how to get hold of any.

As the correspondence continued between the two, their initially quite formal relationship began to thaw. Alec confided to Hanrahan that he had declined an invitation to participate in a session at the forthcoming Word Festival (a Canberra literary festival) on the theme of 'Life with a Writer', as:

> *I thought that this would possibly become a competition in light-heartedness, and that in any case the deeper privacies of anxiety and frustration and success are not really suitable material for general consumption.*

Perhaps he was being too serious, he added, asking 'what does Jo Steele [Hanrahan's partner, a sculptor] think?' And later that month they made plans to meet, apparently for the first time. This was the beginning of a deeply caring friendship, which would continue through two more publishing projects and, tragically, Hanrahan's illness until her early death from cancer in 1991 at the age of only 52. Like many of Alec's friendships, it grew around the regular exchange of long, thoughtful letters, rich in their frank discussion of matters both literary and personal.

Their early letters, however, mostly concerned the design and printing of the wood engravings, and also the order of the poems in the book. Whereas their first correspondence had played a part in his learning about the relationship between illustrator and artist, this new series of letters was about him learning how to print wood engravings. Alec was not entirely happy with Hanrahan's first version of the image to go with 'Child of Tears', asking 'is there some strain in the rendering of the legs of the figure?' Hanrahan sent another version, agreeing that 'perhaps … this very crudity of the print as a whole … would destroy the unity of the book'.[7] Hanrahan in turn asked for more inking in three images after seeing the proofs: 'I'm afraid my Virgo perfectionist streak has been niggling me'. Alec found that he needed to hand-ink the blocks, at a 90-degree angle to the direction of the rollers on the press, as well as using the rollers, and printed them in a separate run from the text, as they needed different amounts of ink. 'I must tell you that the printing of the engravings will be slow,' he wrote, which perhaps also reflected how busy he was at the time. While experimenting with these proofs he was still finishing off the Philip Mead book and printing the Dorothy

Green—and all this on weekends. When he eventually got to the main printing of the book, in early 1985[8], it was done on both his large presses: the text on the platen press, and the engravings on the cylinder press.[9] He was terrified of cracking the blocks, he told Hanrahan, because 'a fair amount of impression is needed', but was pleased with the result.[10] He was also pleased with a 'wonderfully rich carbon-based ink' he had imported from the US, even though it dried 'unbelievably slowly'.[11] (This was probably a Daniel Smith ink, which he used in his next book.) 'Neilson's short lines and simple diction—so many words of one syllable—make for rather quick setting,' he told Gerald Fischer, adding:

> *It is a pleasure to work on his poems. There is a narrow dividing line between unearthly beauty and silliness in his work. I can't feel reverent about it all, but it has moments of wonderful beauty.*[12]

Although Alec asked Peter Marsh at the Dove Bindery to quote for the binding, Marsh was winding up his business (and his Queensberry Hill Press) and suggested it would be difficult to do the job in the time available—especially as private presses were notoriously unreliable in matters of timing, although he conceded Alec was 'pretty accurate and better than some people I could mention'.[13] Instead he turned to a local craft binder, Brian Hawke, whose day job was as the conservation binder at the National Library. Although the outcome was similar to the Dove Bindery treatment of *Something to Someone*—quarter leather divided from buckram sides with a gold rule, and the spine title blocked in gold—this marked an important change. From now on nearly all Brindabella books would be bound by craft binders. Pale green endpapers mirrored the green title on the title-page, and like the previous book the Neilson was supplied in a glassine wrapper. At $13 a copy, the binding was the most expensive item in the book's production costs, totalling $3,146. Fourteen copies were returned to the binder for remedial treatment because some pages began to show cockling.[14]

The decision to employ Hawke reflected a great deal more than simply the closing of a trusted trade bindery in Melbourne, although this was its immediate cause. In 1984 the groundbreaking Crafts Council of Australia exhibition *Contemporary Designer Bookbindings: Europe & Australia* toured nationally. It was on display at the National Library in November and December 1984, in association with the First National Conference of Craft Bookbinders, held at the Canberra School of Art and organised by the newly established Canberra Craft Bookbinders' Guild, which drew binders from all across Australia to the nation's capital. Both the exhibition and the conference were to be seminal events in the history of book arts in Australia. For the Brindabella Press in particular, the exhibition directly coincided with Alec's shift from commercial trade binders to craft binding and must surely have been a major factor in inspiring that transition, although he does not appear to discuss it anywhere. It is noteworthy that of the ten Australian binders represented in the exhibition, Brian Hawke, Robin Tait, Helen Wadlington and Ron Eadie were to do editions for Brindabella, along with Mike Hudson, who illustrated for the press.[15] At the same time as the international exhibition's Canberra showing and the conference, Petr Herel put on an exhibition of artists' books made at the School of Art's Graphic Investigation Workshop. Caren Florance has argued persuasively that this was a watershed moment in Canberra's history as a city of the book.[16] It could also be argued that the subsequent introduction of hand binding to the Brindabella mode of book production was similarly a key moment in its history, consolidating its identity as a private press.

Neilson's work was still in copyright, so Alec offered his estate three copies of the book and a royalty of five per cent of the copies offered for sale.[17] Hanrahan was to receive a royalty of seven-and-a-half per cent[18], but an unexpected additional cost was a claim by the publisher Lothian to an interest in all but two of the poems, for which there was a charge of $50.[19] Angus & Robertson similarly claimed an interest but did not charge a fee. Royalties cost $1,050, paper $268 and type $459. All up, the book cost the press $5,513, including some capital costs—that is, type and legal fees (the latter to do with registering the business name). After considering a range of prices on the 200 copies for sale, Alec settled on a recommended retail price of $40, which he anticipated would bring him a return of $5,546.[20] 'This is getting to be like publishing,' he told Gerald Fischer, but he thought the book would stand the (for him) high price. If he costed in his own time, it would retail for $100 or more.[21] Mike Hudson of the Wayzgoose Press chided Alec for selling it too cheaply: 'Between Brian Hawke/Barbara Hanrahan/yourself/the paper and typesetting—this slim effort has all the earmarks of missionary zeal—what happened to the good old Aussie profit motive?'[22]

Orders were brisk. By just before the official publication date of 23 August 1985, Alec had orders for 160 copies.[23] He sent review copies to *The Age*, *The Sydney Morning Herald*, and *The Australian*; to *The Bulletin* and *Overland*; and to the American magazine *Fine Print*.[24]

A small four-page prospectus featuring two engravings from the book was distributed to the 54 people and libraries on his mailing list and to bookshops, encouraging direct orders from the press by including the cost of postage as well as a recommended retail price. 'Booksellers are delightful people and we can't do without them,' Alec commented to Hanrahan, but they took a long time to pay their bills, and when he left work to become a full-time printer he hoped to have a higher proportion of direct sales.[25] '*Some Poems of Shaw Neilson* is the most ambitious piece of hand printing to appear so far under the Brindabella imprint,' the prospectus announced, and it highlighted also the binding 'by the award-winning Canberra hand-binder Brian Hawke'.[26] Judith Rodriguez reviewed the book enthusiastically in *The Sydney Morning Herald*: Hanrahan was a 'magical print-maker … It is a beautiful book'.[27] It was also reviewed by Bruce Beaver, who called it 'a combination of masterly book-making and lovely poetry', in *The Weekend Australian*.[28] Hanrahan was indeed a superb artist to put alongside Shaw Neilson, and her engraving for 'The Orange Tree' was later to be reproduced by University of Queensland Press as the cover image of a book asserting his importance as a major Australian writer.[29]

18

'While I still have the strength to heave type metal around'

Christina Stead, *The Palace with Several Sides* (1986)

The Boltons had become friendly with Christina Stead during the last years of her life, when she lived in Canberra. Alec greatly admired her work, especially *The Man Who Loved Children*, which he said 'made more of an impression on me than practically any modern novel I can think of', and thought she should have won a Nobel Prize.[1] Shortly after Stead's death Alec wrote to her literary executor, Ron Geering, to ask if he knew of an unpublished or uncollected short story that he might publish. He had discussed the idea with Stead on several occasions, he told Geering, and she had been interested, but it had not gone any further. His preference was for a short story, but 'an interesting piece of non-fiction or autobiography would also be very appealing, as would any group of letters on a theme'.[2] Geering's response appears to have been positive, as Alec followed up with a letter explaining the financial basis of his publications, and suggesting that 'in the future I am likely to be more commercial, especially when I retire from the National Library and become a fulltime printer'. It would appear that the journal *Southerly* had an option regarding unpublished material, but 'if there were a strong story that was too long for *Southerly*'s requirements, how happy would I be'.

Nothing happened for quite some time, during which the Boltons took a holiday in Europe. Crete was a highlight: Rosemary had visited it in 1977, but it was Alec's first visit. In England they saw Jack Lindsay, Randolph Stow and Peter Porter. It was not until mid-1985 that Alec had the go-ahead to publish Stead's short story 'The Palace with Several Sides', which Geering had found in three versions in her papers. It had been sent to her American agent in 1976 but had not been published. Geering served as editor for the Brindabella edition, and relied largely on the third version of the story, but he drew on the second as well.[3]

The book is a modest volume, small in size and bound in paper wrappers in a deceptively simple style. But it is still nearly 6,000 words long, and so was machine-set in Monotype Bembo by C.D. FitzHardinge-Bailey of the St Mark's Press in Sydney, one of the few remaining hot-metal type casters in Australia at the time. (FitzHardinge-Bailey was the name used by Charles Darrell Bailey for many of his productions at St Mark's Press, and also consistently in correspondence with Alec.[4]) Having set *Something to Someone* by hand, Alec was reluctant to take on anything much larger, and the cost of importing more type from the Mackenzie & Harris foundry in San Francisco was prohibitive.[5] By now, especially when contemplating such a long piece of prose and the possible transition to becoming a full-time printer, he had come to the view that 'the key to being truly productive will lie in obtaining machine setting. Hand printing is okay; it's the setting that is so time-consuming'.[6]

There were several innovations with this book. Firstly, after Michael McCurdy was unable to provide two or three wood engravings in the time available[7], Alec turned to a new artist who was also a printer: Mike Hudson of the Wayzgoose Press, who was about to move from Sydney to Katoomba in the Blue Mountains.[8] His search for new potential illustrators had until now not been particularly successful. A year previously he had written to the Society of Wood Engravers, in London, asking for assistance in finding one or two wood engravers he might work with in addition to Barbara Hanrahan—whom he planned to continue with—but this drew little response.[9] The sole extant response in his papers came from an expatriate Australian woodcut artist, Larry Macdonald; Alec was friendly in his reply, remarking that while he thought of 'the bolder style of the woodcut as calling for big formats', he was prepared to be proved wrong. 'As you will surely infer from the enclosed announcement,' he added in enclosing the prospectus for *Something to Someone*, 'I am a rather traditional sort of worker.'[10]

Hudson was recommended by Judy Hungerford, presumably the designer of that name who had been one of the founders of the limited-edition art-book publisher Craftsman House in 1981. Alec wrote to him in February of 1985, outlining his plans and asking if he would be able to provide wood engravings.[11] Secondly, he turned to a new binder, Robin Tait, with whom he was to work regularly thereafter. And finally, reluctantly, it was now that he changed his Brindabella Press imprint to Officina Brindabella.

Mike Hudson would ultimately illustrate three Brindabella books, while his own Wayzgoose Press, established in partnership with Jadwiga Jarvis, has been described as 'the apogee of Australian private presses of the recent—and, I would argue—whole history of private presses in Australia'.[12] Hudson had a strong background in photography and graphic design in the UK before he emigrated to Australia in flight from Thatcherism. He took up bookbinding in Sydney, along with wood engraving and calligraphy, and with Jadwiga Jarvis set out to turn the world of Australian book arts upside down. They were admirers of the books made by the Kickshaws Press in Paris—books that Jarvis described as 'mini typhoons which blew away the traditional limp-wrappered, limp-wristed slim volumes of limp poetry into their overdue oblivion'—and in general their and Alec's taste was poles apart. Nonetheless, they were able to work together, despite moments of difficulty.[13] And despite their differences, Alec would have agreed with Jarvis and Hudson that:

> *To those who love the printed word the concept of a private press need not be explained. The total experience of a well laid-out page, enriched by original artwork, well printed on archival paper and soundly bound is a thing of joy. The printed word is the repository of the knowledge and spirit of mankind, and the proper representation of this essence will ensure that both live on.*[14]

Hudson's response to Stead's 'bleak little narrative' was imaginative and powerful. The work, he told Alec, suggested:

> *a narrative imagery rather than an abstraction, as my reading of the text makes it a clear statement of lost opportunities, which can't be easily depicted (in the size allowed) as an abstract expression without it appearing too decorative for the overall feeling of European angst.*

His haunting portraits of Marchant and Hortense, the central characters, wonderfully reflect and extend the text. His enigmatic tailpiece, a chair draped in a dustsheet in the foreground of a room stripped of its contents, in which the only movement is that of a bird flying out of the scene, is a particularly powerful interpretation of the story. As Hudson wrote to Alec:

> *The format and scale of these blocks mitigate against the kind of complex detail needed for a visual investigation of a Grand French interior … but in any case I feel that the desolation factor inherent in the denouement is better expressed by the 'vacant' abandoned room and shrouded chair. The flighted bird (hopefully) is suggestive of a liberated soul (Hortense) though still potentially 'trapped' in an internal limbo as defined by the edge of the picture plane. Alternatively the bird represents a new regime of freedom intruding irreverently into the sepulchral environment—albeit after the event!*

This Alec liked, but he disagreed with Hudson's first proposal for the portrait of Marchant, querying his inclusion of a candelabrum in an exchange that underlines how engaged he became with the texts he printed:

> *I think that what worries me is that the Damoclesian candelabrum makes the drawing judgmental in a way that the story is not.*

> *Christina Stead is a writer who does not work like that. She tells you what he did and said, and what happened. You draw your own conclusions. I quite like the idea of the old man in the shadows, but not the sense of impending retribution. Can you agree with this? Is it possible to tackle the idea of the first drawing in another way? … Or is it possible to retain the basis of the first drawing in an extended setting of a shadowed interior? That is how I thought of the image in the first place, before you started.*

He was more than happy with Hudson's reworking of the drawing, responding to the delivery of the finished blocks in January 1986 with the comment:

> *the engravings are superb. I am really delighted with them. It's an heroic effort on your part — I do appreciate it. The book is advancing quite well. I printed two formes this weekend. It is looking okay. I will print the engravings last, and allow them plenty of time to dry. The Daniel Smith carbon-based ink that I use takes for ever to dry. The binding will be probably by Robin Tait of Canberra, and will be very simple, and limp.*

'I feel that I am a complete beginner in the printing of engravings,' Alec confessed in a later letter to Hudson. He shared his hopes of printing a half-size facsimile of John Kirtley's edition of *Heemskerck Shoals*, along with an essay by Geoffrey Farmer on Kirtley, and for that purpose had laid in a stock of 1,000 sheets of Mohawk Letterpress Text. He had also acquired 250 sheets of Zerkall Halbmatt,

> *the paper with which John Randle prints so many engravings at the Whittington Press ... The only acknowledgment he has ever given me that engravings present difficulties is to concede (this was when I last visited him, in 1985) that he prints them separately from the text. I can only say that within my pitifully small experience, I do the same. The amount of ink required is so much greater with engravings, I don't know how you could do them otherwise.*

The joy of having another Australian letterpress printer with whom to discuss paper and presswork is almost palpable in Alec's letters to Hudson. Their work together would continue well into the future and they shared a deep respect for the craft of printing, even though the output of their respective presses was so dissimilar. One immediate commonality was their joint disdain for a recent article in *Craft Australia* by James Taylor, with whom Hudson had been involved in founding the journal *Wayzgoose: The Australian Journal of Book Arts* (one issue, 1985), and who was later editor of the *Journal of the Australian Printing Historical Society* (two issues, 1986 and 1990). 'All efforts on behalf of the Book Arts are welcome of course but ENLARGING a wood engraving to fit a paste-up is not what I'd call a sympathetic treatment; it is from such things that I quit commercial activities,' wrote Hudson.[15] 'I was not thrilled by his piece', Alec replied:

> *The enlargements of engravings from my books horrified me, but I suppose he may not have been the one responsible for that. For myself, I do not mind his describing my typography as staid, but I did rather resent the use of the adjective precieuse to describe my books. I would*

> *have hoped that is the last thing they are. Anyway, what the hell. We press on regardless.*

Taylor's article began with a brief historical survey of Australian printing, dismissing most previous practitioners, and hailed Jim Walker's Croft Press of Cobargo as 'the best of Australian contemporary presswork'. Taylor had some regard for the Brindabella books, which he conceded were handsome and neatly executed, with commendable use of wood engravings. But his praise was sparing, and it was a not yet published edition of Froissart's *Battle of Poitiers*, to be published by FitzHardinge-Bailey's St Mark's Press in Sydney, with wood engravings by Hudson, which he claimed would give 'something of the imprimatur to Australian private press work'.[16] As it happened, this was never published, and although Alec mentioned his irritation at Taylor's critique to other correspondents he soon shrugged off his remarks.[17] Hudson's magnificent engravings were later published by Wayzgoose Press in an edition of ten copies.[18]

The second new development with regard to the book, building on the previous book, was to do with its binding. Alec had met the Canberra craft bookbinder Robin Tait some years previously, through their mutual friend Bill Thorn. Tait had been among the first intake for training as a paper conservator at the University of Canberra in 1978, and after working at the Australian War Memorial as a paper conservator had started to look for opportunities in book conservation. A Rotary Foundation Scholarship had given her the opportunity to spend a year studying book conservation at the Camberwell School of Art & Craft in London. Another Canberra binder, Helen Wadlington, had also been studying in London (at the London College of Printing) at the time, and also returned to Canberra at around the same time, as did John Tonkin, who studied the craft at the *Centro del Bel Libro Ascona* in Switzerland after initial training by Neale Wootton at the Canberra College of Technical and Further Education (TAFE). So suddenly there were a number of binders doing fine hand binding in Canberra, a development that led to the formation of the Canberra Craft Bookbinders' Guild in May 1981 and, as previously discussed, to the First National Conference of Craft Bookbinders held in Canberra in November 1984.[19]

Tait's first binding of a Brindabella book had been one copy of the Neilson poems, which she recalls she may have disbound from a copy in its original binding by Brian Hawke. In 1984 she returned to the UK for further studies with a leading English craft binder, James Brockman, at Headington, Oxford. This exposed her to a wide range of institutional and private clients, with many superb contemporary private press books coming through the bindery. She worked on the Gregynog edition of Dylan Thomas' *Deaths and Entrances*: 'being involved in that, and seeing how you go about doing three hundred plus books, all hand-sewn, all hand head-banded, it was just an extraordinary undertaking'.

Initially she proposed a quarter-leather binding with silk striped sides for the Stead, and was greeted with silence when she showed it to both Alec and Rosemary. Her subsequent suggestion of a very different wrapper-style binding was greeted more enthusiastically. It was a major departure from the Brindabella bindings of the past. Tait said:

> *I had been very taken by … a small book on medieval vellum binding put out by Chris Clarkson of the Red Gull Press and it had basically been bound the same way—it was sheets sewn together and then this wrapper cover put around it—I ended up having to pull this binding of my own apart to actually see how it was put together but it struck me as being an ideal binding structure for this particular book because Alec didn't want something heavy and clunky and because they are, as Bill [Thorn] used to describe them, 'slim volumes of poetry'—it needed something that looked elegant and was kept simple.*[20]

She recalls being a little hesitant in suggesting this binding, but Alec was enthusiastic, and the same structure was to be used again in *Iris in Her Garden*. She quoted $6 per book for the binding, based on the expectation that each copy would take 15 minutes to bind, and thus offering to reduce her usual rate of $30 an hour because the project interested her so much.[21] Alec refused to accept the reduction and agreed to pay $7.50 per copy.[22]

The structure Tait proposed used an additional four leaves at each end of the book. Alec was loath to use the Basingwerk Parchment he was using for the text for this, as it would deplete his stock of a paper that worked well for engravings. He proposed using either a Strathmore paper, with Velvet Gray for the cover and Pottery Green for the endpapers, or a fairly light (104 gsm) Kilmory Text for the cover and contrasting endpapers. Considering the alternatives of two or four leaves, he preferred four, with the cover folded over two leaves: 'this would leave 2 leaves as the endpaper— a more generous thing for anyone picking the book up, especially if the endpaper and text stocks were different'.[23] His final choice was for grey endpapers contrasting with a cool violet cover, with a label on the front cover and a blank spine. Tait recalled:

> *I would never have chosen this coloured paper and I learned subsequently from this edition that I could suggest things to Alec but I had to respect the fact that this was ultimately his book, or his and Rosemary's book, and therefore they would make the judgements in terms of what colours and what materials would be used.*

Rosemary Dobson was the silent partner in everything the press did, Tait emphasises. She was 'very much his backstop. She had the same … restrained taste … in what they wanted in their books coming out of their press'. The book lies open beautifully, something that Alec valued highly and that had at times eluded him.

Finally, the third new element with the book was a change in imprint. Alec had registered the name 'Brindabella Press' in New South Wales in 1984, but discovered he could not follow suit in the Australian Capital Territory because he had been pre-empted in 1981 by a firm named Brindabella Press and Publications Pty Limited. This business name had been registered by a firm otherwise known as Canberra Reprographic Printers, but only recently used by its former proprietor after his main business was sold. Alec visited him and found he had not known of the existence of the Brindabella Press when he registered the name. He was quite happy for Alec to continue using the name, but as he intended continuing to use it himself Alec preferred not to: 'it would not be an attractive prospect to me to be identified or confused with his business in the long term,' he told his solicitor.[24]

The Corporate Affairs Commissioner for the ACT then refused an application to register the name Brindabella Books, because it might have been confused with the other firm. However they did allow Officina Brindabella—the Italian word *officina* being commonly used for small and private presses—which was duly registered as a business name on 3 October 1985. Alec was to use this imprint until 1992: 'I suddenly noticed one day that Brindabella Press … was no longer in the telephone book' and he was able to reclaim the name.[25]

The Palace with Several Sides sold out within six months or so, with many copies ordered by American libraries to whom Alec had sent prospectuses.[26] The largest cost of production was again binding: 235 copies at $7.50, totalling $1,762.50. Typesetting, including the prospectus, came to $541.40 and paper $355.78, of which two thirds was for the cover and endpapers. Alec paid royalties of ten per cent on 150 copies sold for $30—that is, $450. The projected final cost of the book in May 1986 was $3,380.[27] Income from sales is not recorded but is unlikely to have exceeded this. Hudson received 30 copies in lieu of cash payment.[28]

Alec's long-running thoughts about early retirement from the National Library came to fruition at this time. He took long service leave in 1986 and retired at the end of the year.[29] Although financial considerations must have been a large part of his and Rosemary's discussions, he had some time ago confided to Gerald Fischer that:

> *it is the relative isolation of the life that worries me. I suppose I should not be so gutless about taking the final vows of the printing vocation … I was involved in some discussion at the Library about the publication*

of the Retrospective National Bibliography, the NLA's main effort for the Bicentenary. It gave me a funny feeling to realise that I will not be there when the work sees the light of day.[30]

Later in the same year, he told Fischer, he had become more resolved. The turning point was a brief visit to London for a conference on library publishing, during which he visited the Whittington Press of John and Rosalind Randle.

I was immensely stimulated by this visit … In part of a huge barn (about 1647) there is a Monotype shop with goodness knows how many fonts already installed, and others constantly arriving from printers fleeing into cold-type setting. I was staggered by the amount of stuff that Randle turns out; but then, as he pointed out to me, if you are printing full time, you do get through the work. This is a truth that has penetrated my brain, I think. David Chambers made the same remark to me in a long conversation by phone—I had not a chance to get to Pinner. I liked Chambers greatly from his voice and conversation. I felt as if we were friends—I would certainly like to hope so. Nearly all Randle's work is done on an old Wharfedale, acquired years ago for a song, perhaps it was a hundred pounds. He does the most beautiful work on it … the quality of the printing is superb, and the choice of materials is always so interesting. I would say the Randles are not by any means making a fortune out of the Whittington Press, but they are flourishing.[31]

The influence of the Whittington Press in the survival of fine letterpress printing in our times is substantial, and Alec was simply one of a legion of printers inspired by a visit there. David Chambers, too, editor of a long-running annual survey of private press books, was—and remains—a significant figure in the British private press world. But as well as reflecting Alec's growing certainty about taking up printing full-time, this brief passage says a great deal about the type of printing he aspired to: 'The quality of the printing is superb, and the choice of materials is always so interesting'. Fine printing on good paper, with well-crafted bindings: these would be his aims in the years to come. He was not so concerned with pushing the boundaries of design and book construction: in that sense, despite the beauty and aesthetic sensibility of his books, he was always to be a printer ahead of being a maker of artist's books, even though, as art historian Sasha Grishin comments, he was the latter as well—in effect a pioneer of the artists' book in Canberra who 'made a valuable contribution to both the Canberra handmade book scene and to the book world nationally'.[32]

Clearly, by 1986 Alec had completed his apprenticeship as a letterpress printer. He had begun as he had learnt to do: planning his page and forme layouts meticulously before he started to set type; and largely working within the boundaries of the conservative traditions in typography and book design he had met as best practice in his early years as an editor and novice publisher. Although he was influenced by the private press movement of the twentieth century, his was not an imitative appropriation of what went on at the great British presses. He adapted sound typographic principles, proven to work in the best commercial book design, in order to maintain the distinctive style evident in books he designed or published. Whether it is the ten volumes of the Academy Editions of Australian Literature (1996–2007), for which he would advise on the page design and more for the Academy of the

Humanities at the very end of his life, National Library of Australia books such as James Burney's journal, designed by his friend Arthur Stokes, or the books of the Brindabella Press itself, there is a family resemblance. They share many characteristics: good paper, generous use of white space, strong but not domineering typefaces, clarity and coherence in the way complex information is presented, and distinctive shapes—often tall and narrow.

Many of these elements are evident in Alec's next book, Elizabeth Riddell's *Occasions of Birds*, which coincided with his retirement. It was, Alec told me, 'one of the books I'm happiest with'[33], and he spelled out why to Gerald Fischer, telling him 'I have enjoyed working on this book; the luxury of printing on weekdays one after another has been pure bliss'. He had quickly realised that he simply could not return to the Library after his long service leave: 'certainly I missed friends, but hardly at all did I miss the work. The sense in which I did miss some of the work was quite overwhelmed by the feeling of freedom from administration, and in particular freedom from meetings'.[34] He was more circumspect at his staff farewell, telling his colleagues:

> *I have had a long interest in letterpress printing—really backward-looking stuff—and I have decided to devote myself to it full time, while I still have the strength to heave type metal around. I appreciate the fact that so many people have been able to sympathise with me and encourage me in this apparent folly.*[35]

His farewell gift was a subscription to the journal *Fine Print* and a copy of the recent book *Photoportraits: Henri Cartier-Bresson*, the latter aptly recognising his contribution to the library's photographic collections. Retirement was 'a dread word to me', he told one friend. He was leaving the Library simply 'to devote more time to printing and photography'.[36]

Retirement or not, it was at last possible to become a full-time printer; a half share in the proceeds of selling his aunt's house in Sydney, which had recently been realised when the seller's mortgage on the house was discharged, also helped make this slightly early departure from the Library possible. He was aged 61 (at a time when retirement for public servants was compulsory at 65), and therefore had full access to his savings in the generous superannuation scheme then common to all Commonwealth public servants and thus, after 16 years at the Library, a sizeable superannuation lump sum (which he seems to have withdrawn in full rather than taking a pension). All the Bolton children were by now launched on their careers: Robert as a journalist, Lissant as a museum anthropologist, and Ian as a viola player in the Elizabethan Sydney Orchestra (now the Opera Australia Orchestra). In 1984 Rosemary had won the Patrick White Award, an amount of $15,000 that would have substantially boosted the family's reserves. 'Poets don't earn very much,' she told *The Canberra Times*. 'My husband has supported me financially, as in so many other ways, for many years. Now I would like to contribute something of my own.'[37]

In the same year of Alec's retirement, Rosemary was made an Officer of the Order of Australia, a further indication of how highly she was respected as a writer of national significance. Which is not to say that all was happiness and light for her; she had suffered first one and then another haemorrhage in her right eye, beginning in January 1984, and was now confirmed as being irrecoverably blind in that eye.[38] (Years later she was to lose most of her sight in the other eye, although she had some vision almost to the end of her life.) Nonetheless, the transition to full-time printing was clearly a happy one for Alec, and Rosemary would continue to be, as she always had been, an integral part of the press. At about this time she wrote her only novel, an engaging work for young adults called *Summer Press*, about an Australian family who take up hand-printing during a stay in England. The heroine of the story also solves a minor mystery involving an Elizabethan gravestone inscription, as Rosemary herself had done when the Boltons were living there. *Summer Press*, which was published in 1987, was dedicated to Alec, as were many of her books of poetry.[39] Although she came to dislike it (just as she actively discouraged interest in her first book of poems), the book is yet another reminder of how central printing was to the Bolton household.[40]

19

Interlude: Alec Bolton as Photographer

Alec began developing his own films in 1966[1], and was a keen amateur photographer for most of his life. Photographs of the editorial offices of Angus & Robertson in the early 1950s that appear to be by him, for example, are a unique record of working life behind the scenes in a great publishing house. A three-page inventory of his photographic equipment prepared by his family after he died includes a Rolleiflex Twin Lens Reflex camera with a 75-millimetre lens and a Pentax MX SLR with a 35-millimetre lens, along with a small collection of other lenses, a substantial amount of photographic paper, developing equipment and chemicals. [2] He used his own photographs in only one of the press' books, *The Continuance of Poetry*, but was delighted at the suggestion that a small selection of his photographs of Australian authors should be included in my 1993 tribute to his work, *A Licence to*

Print. For this was his chief ambition as a photographer: to build up a good collection of portrait photographs of Australian writers as a gift to the National Library. Although it was therefore a given that they would be in black and white (the Library collected colour photographs reluctantly at that time, because they lacked archival quality), this seems to have been his preferred format anyway.

The project began while he was still working at the Library, although in his own time, and continued for many years afterwards. He went to immense trouble to make portraits of people in the rooms where they wrote, usually at their homes, and travelled beyond his and Rosemary's friendship circles to secure portraits of the people he thought mattered. Rosemary usually accompanied him and helped to relax his sitters, he recalled:

> *she has always described herself as being like the mother who goes with the small child to the dentist and distracts and encourages and amuses the child while the dentist does his work … She's often expressed that very idea to the people we're photographing and that seems to amuse them and relax them.*[3]

He occasionally sought technical advice from his friends Axel and Ros Poignant in London, but was largely self-taught. Rosemary felt that a crucial attribute in the success of this project was his empathy with people, his ability to get on with almost everyone.[4]

There are nearly 200 writers represented by his photographic portraits in the National Library collection, sometimes at different stages of their lives. One or two, such as a photo of Norman Lindsay with Rosemary, were taken early on, but the project essentially began in the early 1970s and gathered pace, taking up much of Alec's spare time in the years immediately before and after his retirement, with around 30 writers documented at its height in 1984 and 1985. It continued through the 1980s and into the 1990s, and he remained active to the end of his life. Although some of his subjects were also Brindabella authors—Dorothy Green, Les Murray, Judith Wright and John Rowland, for example—the majority were not. A handful were artists, such as Rosalind Atkins and Ray Crooke. Many were women, including his one-time mentor and first boss in publishing, Beatrice Davis, and often he took photographs of married couples together, such as Manning and Dymphna Clark, and Tom and Judy Kenneally. While there is a slight bias towards Canberra writers, most lived elsewhere.

The collection is regularly drawn on by biographers and other writers as well as by the Library itself, which for example in 1994 published photographs of Dorothy Hewett, Frank Moorhouse and Antigone Kefala as cards. Sometimes, one suspects, the photographs Alec took are the only portraits that are readily available of many fine Australian writers, and they are often the best.

20

'I hope to be very active and to produce quite a few titles'

Elizabeth Riddell, *Occasions of Birds* (1987)

Elizabeth Riddell's poetry was her passion, although she earned her living as a journalist. She once said:

> *Journalism is a trick in the trade but poetry's not. Poetry is art. Poetry is person to person, like a painting. You see you don't do poetry in the dark. You don't paint in the dark either. You're talking to somebody. But my poetry is very much influenced by my journalism.*[1]

She lived in Sydney and the friendship between her and the Boltons was well established by the 1980s. And she matched the criteria he had proposed earlier for the press: an older writer, of great distinctiveness but not widely published in book form (this was her first book for 25 years, he pointed out in the prospectus), whose poetry he and Rosemary greatly admired. 'A wonderful collaboration between printer, poet, illustrator,' Rosemary wrote on the folder when handing papers concerning this book over to the National Library.[2] The poems 'are about birds, about urban Sydney, about growing older', Alec said. 'They are attractive, free and youthful in spirit, and accessible.'[3]

Alec first approached Cressida Campbell, a young Sydney artist and the daughter of friends, to illustrate *Occasions of Birds*, but this did not eventuate. She was initially keen but became unhappy with the results of her work in black and white. The discussion between the two is interesting, nonetheless. He was clear about his limitations from the start, telling her that because he worked by letterpress, and on papers suited to line rather than halftone printing (hard-won knowledge!), 'essentially it is one-colour printing'. Wood engraving was ideal, he told her, and the print run would be small because everything was done by hand. 'If it all sounds rather unsophisticated publishing, I think that is how it is, although I believe the books look good and are usually well regarded.' One day, he speculated, he might well publish a book with a frontispiece or other illustrations 'hand or machine printed separately by lithography, and tipped in'. However, when Campbell suggested dry point illustration for this book he quickly retreated: 'I think I am right in saying that drypoints would have to be printed on an etching press, unless the images were such that line blocks could be made from them to be printed letterpress (my sole resource). We will have to discuss this. Line drawings might be easier'.

This discussion also says something of the design considerations Alec had in mind. He had been attracted to Cressida Campbell's work because 'she seemed on the right urban wavelength for the poems', he told Riddell. 'Also I liked the idea of involving a young person in the book—a salute to the youthful spirit it expresses despite occasional mentions of change and decay!' He 'could get the illustrations printed by litho and tip them in, but it would lessen the immediacy of the book while adding a lot to the cost', he added. (By this he almost certainly meant commercial photolithography, in the form of offset lithography, rather than art lithography.)

He turned next to another member of his and Rosemary's friendship circle, the Australian artist and sculptor Anne Wienholt, who lived in California but still had strong ties to Sydney. Wienholt had boarded at Frensham when Rosemary was a student there and the two were lifelong friends.[4] This time he was more specific in describing the printing process he had in mind. He suggested line blocks based on crayon drawings:

> *A friend of mine in England has printed some lovely drawings by Richard Kennedy originally executed, I think, in Conte crayon … They were printed from line blocks in a rusty red colour.*[5]

The reference is to the Whittington Press edition of *The Mirror and the Eye* (1984), a new translation of the *Rubaiyat of Omar Khayyam* illustrated by Richard Kennedy, which Alec appears to have discussed with John and Rosalind Randle when he visited the Whittington Press in 1983.[6] Later he recalled that 'they had found that drawings done with a 6B pencil, when made into line blocks, looked like original crayon work'[7], although this was a somewhat conflated recollection of Kennedy's technique (he used soft crayon) and Wienholt's work, which she did in her preferred medium of a 6B pencil. Alec then suggested she experiment with a fairly hard litho crayon 'on a paper with a bit of tooth or texture', for fear of having to print from halftone blocks again, and she tried both; in the end Wienholt's soft 6B pencil produced the most satisfactory line blocks. The printed drawings do indeed look as if they could be autolithographs, 'i.e. drawn direct on to stone or plate with a litho crayon'.[8] To this end, Alec printed the drawings in a Conte crayon colour. There was 'a little bit of variation in the illustration colour', he said to Wienholt, 'but I do not think it is too bad. It is very hard in printing to ink the press in a way that will give absolute consistency of colour'.

Here is a good example of how Alec made the most use he could of his rare encounters with other letterpress printers during his infrequent travels overseas. These visits, and journals such as *Matrix* and *Fine Print*, were highly significant to him. He later told Randle that the most important aspect of *Matrix* for him was 'its amazing editorial interest, which never flags, and which has reached its highest points for me in some of the correspondence you have printed'.[9] Being able to read such primary documents, from the very heart of the English private press tradition, gave this isolated practitioner a real understanding of how the books he admired had come into being.

By now Alec had learned to be careful in suggesting what he was looking for in terms of the relationship between text and illustrations:

> *The first question is whether you find things in the poems to which you might make a graphic response. The connection between poems and drawings could be free-ranging and tenuous, rather than illustrative; in*

> *fact, better that way. Perhaps you should just read them through a few times and reflect on them before responding.*

Including an element of illustration had been one of the first things he had canvassed with Riddell:

> *even if confined to a frontispiece and a tailpiece at the very end. At the same time I would not like to produce a book that was too obviously 'charming'; it would be wrong for the poems.*

Similarly, he carefully sought her views on possible artists, including Wienholt, and showed her the first trial proofs. He also proposed a new title for the collection, *Occasions of Birds*, 'wondering if "From the Midnight Courtyard" is a little too sombre, or too unlike you'.[10] (She left the decision up to him, but the latter title, a phrase from the poem 'The Party', which Alec had earlier suggested, was used for her next book.[11] This included all the poems from *Occasions of Birds*, although their earlier publication therein was not acknowledged in the new volume.)

Occasions of Birds was hand-set in Centaur and Arrighi, with Bulmer for display. He had used Centaur twice before, in *Something to Someone* and *Some Poems of John Shaw Neilson*, but for this project he bought new type from Mackenzie & Harris in California.[12] Rosemary and Lissant were in North America in April for a poetry festival in Toronto, returning via San Francisco: he had them bring some of the type home.[13] Again he mentioned that he was using acid-free paper for this book, made at the historic Rising Paper Mill in Housatonic, Massachusetts. And he asked another of Canberra's pioneer craft bookbinders, Helen Wadlington, to bind the book, at a cost of $13.70 per unit, including paste paper sides made by the binder. 'I hope to be very active and to produce quite a few titles,' he told her, and 'a collaboration between us could be mutually beneficial. If we work at it, I think it could turn out well.'[14]

Paste paper is made by using coloured binder's paste to decorate paper, with patterns then done by hand. Wadlington's paste paper has warm red tones that complement the ochre red of the illustrations, running in a band through blues and browns. The technique has been used by Western bookbinders since the late sixteenth century. The effect in this book is striking, and was to be repeated in the other books Wadlington would bind for the press. Alec printed a paper label for the spine for the first time, and also printed the prospectus, using the same paper and reproducing two of Wienholt's drawings.

The edition was 275 copies, with 211 for sale at $45. Bolton gave 20 copies each to poet and artist in lieu of royalties. Binding was completed in May 1987, and by August it had sold out.[15] The author had provided a strong list of potential buyers, many of whom ordered it. One was Patrick White, who, she reported with relief, thought it was wonderful.[16] Alec recorded 102 sales at full price—that is, to people who bought directly from him—84 through booksellers at a one-third discount, and 21 to libraries and others to whom he offered a ten per cent discount. Total revenue thus amounted to $7,960. The major cost was again binding, at $3,850, along with paper ($270) and block-making ($405). He calculated the final cost of production at $5,000, with a unit cost of the copies for sale of $23.81. So, for the first time he had set out to pay himself a modest amount for his time as the printer, and succeeded.[17] Chris Wallace-Crabbe hailed the book as 'likely to be the best book of poetry for 1987'[18] and it was favourably reviewed by Peter Ward in *The Weekend Australian*.[19] *Occasions of Birds* also won the Grace Leven Prize for Poetry for 1987, a highly regarded annual award for 'the best volume of poetry published in the preceding twelve months by a writer either Australian-born and writing as an Australian, or naturalised in Australia and resident in Australia for not less than ten years'.[20] Despite such success, and the high regard her peers had for Riddell as a writer, the book is surprisingly undervalued on the market today.

21

'Kirtley's heroic but rather crazy enterprise'

R.D. FitzGerald, *Heemskerck Shoals* (not published)

While all went well with *Occasions of Birds*, after the initial difficulty in finding an illustrator, the same could not be said for another of Alec's projects at the time. He had long been an enthusiast for the work of the Australian printer John Kirtley, a self-taught printer who had been a co-founder with Jack Lindsay of the Fanfrolico Press in the 1920s. Like P.R. (Inky) Stephensen, who became associated with Fanfrolico in 1927, Kirtley's political views eventually got him into difficulty. He was interned after war broke out with Japan as a supporter of the banned isolationist Australia First Movement, even though he was not personally a member of the AFM but rather a long-term friend of Stephensen, its co-founder.[1] Stephensen and a small group of his political associates were also interned. Kirtley was interned from

March 1941 until February 1944, and after the war ended was not among those of the Australia Firsters exonerated by a judicial inquiry.[2]

Kirtley was nonetheless a superb printer whose determination to establish fine printing as a lasting strand in Australian cultural life produced one magnificent book, a folio edition of R.D. FitzGerald's poem 'Heemskerck Shoals', published at his Mountainside Press at Fern Tree Gully in 1949. It was this aspect of Kirtley's oeuvre that Alec admired. Although the stated edition size of *Heemskerck Shoals* was 85, Geoffrey Farmer estimates there were perhaps only around 20 copies that Kirtley considered were printed well enough to be put into circulation. A few more copies were sold many years later, after Kirtley's death, but the book remains both excessively rare and much admired.[3]

Early in 1984 Alec began a discussion with Farmer about possibly publishing an essay by him on Kirtley, to be called *A True Printer*, perhaps after completing the Christina Stead story.[4] A little later his interest had become firmer and he was hoping to include it in the work to be done after he became a full-time printer, although the size of the project worried him slightly. Because of their length he also turned down Farmer's initial counteroffer of the manuscript of his bibliography *The Literature of Australian Private Presses and Fine Printing*, later published by the Book Collectors' Society of Australia (1986), and the chance to do a new edition of his *Private Presses and Australia*, first published in an edition of 450 by the Hawthorn Press in 1972. At that time the Kirtley essay had been promised elsewhere.[5] Alec also reluctantly decided he could not accept the offer of a group of poems by Douglas Stewart at about this time, because his forward program was so full with the proposed Kirtley title as well as the Elizabeth Riddell and Christina Stead publications.[6]

Instead, in December he suggested to Farmer that his essay might perhaps accompany a half-size facsimile of the Kirtley edition of *Heemskerck Shoals*. The facsimile would be printed from blocks, except for one large map, which might be printed lithographically. He and Rosemary had been friends of R.D. FitzGerald and his wife for many years. He wrote asking for permission to proceed with either a half-size facsimile or a limited number of reproductions to illustrate Farmer's essay soon afterwards.[7] Despite the lack of an immediate response from FitzGerald, he also secured agreement from Geoffrey Ingleton, who had illustrated the original book, and, after a long delay and several letters, from Kirtley's widow, Janet Kirtley, to the project.

But in May 1986 it all fell apart. FitzGerald's wife rang to say they were unhappy with the idea of a half-size facsimile, and also with the notion of combining it with someone else's text. Initially Alec thought the issue was a misunderstanding of the nature of the project: 'that it is not a reprint for the poem's sake, but a book about a book'. And FitzGerald indeed seemed mostly uncomfortable with the notion of 'my poem being used as an illustration for the article' in a friendly letter that followed the phone call. But FitzGerald apparently expressed quite different sentiments to Geoffrey Ingleton: he was adamantly opposed to any use of his poem to promote Kirtley's work as a printer, Ingleton wrote to Alec. And this had its roots in bitter personal animosities that went back to the time of the original printing of the book.

Alec had no choice but to give up the idea of the facsimile, and seems to have made no further effort to change FitzGerald's mind. After all, apart from the copyright issues, his and Rosemary's friendship with the FitzGeralds was of long standing. Nevertheless, he told Ingleton:

> *I have been keenly interested to learn from you more of the inner history of Heemskerck Shoals. I suppose it is no surprise to hear that there were frictions at the time; but I am sorry to realise that in some sense they still seem to matter. Well, well. It is no disrespect to Fitz to say that it was the book that made the poem. The poem did not make the book.*

Ingleton's report of the 'inner history' of *Heemskerck Shoals* in these letters to Alec is at odds with Geoffrey Farmer's account, which was to be published some years later by the Book Collectors' Society of Australia.[8] Here he suggests a mostly easy collaboration between printer, poet and artist. Farmer had no real knowledge of its difficulties, Ingleton suggests. And although Alec kept the notion of publishing Farmer's essay alive for a while, he eventually came to the conclusion that such a publication without the facsimile probably would not sell well enough to justify the expense. 'My printing is now my main activity and interest; but there is no spare cash, and every project must finance its successor,' he told Ingleton.

He discussed the same issue in more detail with Farmer, who apart from being the author of the proposed text was also a long-standing correspondent and friend. It is a passage that needs full quotation, for it says much about the state of the press at the time.

> *I have a long-standing commitment to this project and would like it to go forward. It would be a pleasure to be associated with a tribute*

> *to Kirtley's heroic but rather crazy enterprise. The question is, how to put it across? Expensively? Modestly? 100 copies? 150 copies? I don't feel I have the right answers. Also I should mention that since I left the Library to devote myself to printing, there is a change in my circumstances. I don't have any spare cash with which to subsidize my printing ventures. They get more and more costly, but essentially each project must pay for its successor. Direct outgoings on the Serle book are close to $9,000; and direct outgoings on the Les Murray cycle of poems that comes next, with seven wood engravings, hand-made endpapers of blady-grass fibre done specially for the book, and goodness knows what else besides, will be close to $12,000. It is all great fun, but the risks increase. A failure could more or less shut me down. I had a touch of failure with the Geoff Page poems, of which about 50 of the 260 are still to be sold. I thought it was one of my better productions, thanks in large part to Ron Eadie's elegant binding. People are obviously not so interested in the younger author. My experience with the Page sounded a note of caution for me.*

As it happened, the first edition of Farmer's essay on Kirtley was not released after it was realised copyright had not been cleared on the use of illustrations, and it was replaced by a second edition without illustrations. Farmer's reflections after its launch at a meeting of the Book Collectors' Society of Australia in Sydney in August 1990 are a coda to this story. Much as he would have liked to have seen *A True Printer* 'elegantly hand set and printed', he was above all pleased to see it in print at all after seven years' work. And his regard for Alec, who spoke at the event, was unchanged: he was 'a gentle man of quiet printing achievement … a happy man', he wrote.[9]

22

'Exactly what the poem was expressing'

Judith Wright, *Rainforest* (1987)

Despite his new concerns about the need for each project to pay its own way, the next Brindabella publication was designed to net only a small amount for Alec, with the bulk of copies given to the Friends of the ANU Library. This was the first Brindabella broadside, Judith Wright's poem 'Rainforest', with a wood engraving by Rosalind Atkins, a young Melbourne artist with whom Alec soon afterwards began working on an ambitious edition of poems by Les Murray.

Rosalind Atkins wrote to Alec out of the blue in June 1986, saying that she had seen one of his books, admired its quality, and had learnt that he was looking for engravers.[1] A recent graduate in Fine Art from RMIT, where she had studied under Tate Adams, she had already been elected to membership of the Society of

Wood Engravers (England) in 1983 and was working on a book of her own engravings for Adams' Lyre Bird Press.[2] He responded quickly and with delight, asking for more information on her work, sending her the prospectus for *The Palace with Several Sides* ('literally the first to be issued, and possibly not quite dry'), which included the second of Mike Hudson's three wood engravings for that volume, and telling her 'it is a matter of great interest to me to have more of my books illustrated with engravings'.[3]

Atkins replied promptly to say that she was keen to work with him: 'I am aware of the low return for work like this, but the most important thing for me is the opportunity of doing another book'.[4] Although Alec immediately thought of pairing her work with the poetry of Les Murray, with whom he was at the time negotiating the possibility of a Brindabella edition, the first Atkins appearance as a Brindabella artist was the *Rainforest* broadside, which the two discussed when they met for the first time soon afterwards. He offered a fee of $200, with the block and the copyright to revert to Atkins after publication, and was anxious for a candid response:

> *Is $200 enough? You must say frankly what you feel, as it is important to our future relationship that the arrangements made should give you a practical as well as a 'spiritual' satisfaction.*

He also had tentative ideas about the image he had in mind:

> *I suppose we are thinking of something that will express rather than literally illustrate the idea of a rainforest. I think of something not closed on four sides, but perhaps open at the top. I think of the treefrog and the*

> *python as being heard rather than seen; but from your point of view you may feel the need of a visual element here.*[5]

Atkins' image skilfully fits this overall concept into the 4 x 5 inch dimension imposed by the woodblock. It was a highly successful beginning to a harmonious working relationship that would last for the rest of Alec's life.

Judith Wright was a long-time friend of the Boltons as well as living near Canberra, on the road to the South Coast. (She was a donor to the ANU, leaving it 'Edge', her property at Mongarlowe near Braidwood.) 'Rainforest' had previously been used as a poster in 'Poems on the Underground' in London. The poet John Rowland, whose *Times and Places* was the press' third book, chaired the Friends' committee and was Alec's main contact for this project. Of the edition of 275, 150 were given to the Friends and 100 copies sold by the press at $20 each. The edition was printed on Arches paper, with the poem set in 18 point Baskerville. Alec printed a prospectus on the same paper to promote the 100 copies available to supporters of the press. With overall costs of $815, this appears to have netted him approximately $1,185.[6] As for the Friends of the ANU Library, copies were given free as part of a membership package costing $25 a year. All but a few were distributed in this way, and the remainder sold to a local bookseller.[7]

'Judith is very happy with the result, and said very nice things about your work,' Alec told Atkins. 'She particularly praised the tonality of the engraving, and said that you had caught exactly what the poem was expressing … Things don't always turn out as you envisage, but this certainly has.'[8]

23

'I am trying to do books up to a standard rather than down to a price'

Geoff Page, *Smiling in English, Smoking in French* (1987)

Now that he was retired from the Library Alec was increasingly working on several projects at the same time. When the Canberra poet Geoff Page offered him a small collection of travel poems in late 1986 Alec replied that he had 'two and a half books in front of me', so could not contemplate beginning work on them until at least a year later, and suggested that Page explore other alternatives in the meantime.[1] Page was not concerned about the delay, which was as long as most publishers would take. Alternative small presses seemed increasingly scarce and Page thought they might have problems distributing their output. (He had mostly been published by mainstream presses, although his output had included a broadside printed on a hand press in Canberra in 1975 by the Open Door Press.[2])

Retirement from his busy job at the Library also meant that Alec was more aware of his isolation as a craftsman active in the book arts. Reflecting on this to Darrell FitzHardinge-Bailey of St Mark's Press in Sydney, he looked back to his visit to San Francisco:

> *When I was there briefly in 1982, I found it enormously stimulating to see a little bit of what was going on, and to realise what a wealth of interest there is in the book arts. I mention San Francisco because it happened to be where I was; but of course there are hand printers all over the country. It tempts me to try to go to America again, just for the heady charge of interest and encouragement you get from meeting people with similar interests. The scene in Australia is rather poverty-stricken, as we have often agreed. It has meant a great deal to me to meet you, and also Mike Hudson ... And then in Canberra I have met a couple of young women who are making a living as hand binders, while in Melbourne I am in touch with a very good young wood engraver named Rosalind Atkins. Also I have started corresponding with Margaret Lock (haven't met her yet). These contacts are very important to me.*[3]

It is noteworthy that he maintained a membership of the Book Club of California in these years, and sent it copies of his publications. 'I hope to revisit San Francisco one day,' he said when renewing his 1988 membership, 'as the inspirational value of contacts with your west coast printers is very important to me.'[4] His gift of a copy of *Something to Someone* had earlier been noted by the club in its newsletter as 'an unusually handsome example of private printing … with a very professional frontispiece engraved on wood by Michael McCurdy'.[5] At the same time, as he said to the letterpress printer Margaret Lock (then Brisbane-based, she returned to Canada in 1987), he was also interested in expanding his network of direct buyers:

> *The high discounts and often slow payments associated with bookshop sales do not thrill me. As I am leaving the National Library to become a more or less fulltime printer, I am more interested than I used to be in sales and promotion. To be in touch directly with the buyer/subscriber/collector is more satisfying than to be selling through a shop to an anonymous customer.*[6]

As well as continuing to produce his usual prospectuses, he also printed a small general promotional flyer in mid-1987 to announce that the press was 'now conducted full-time and has entered upon a more productive phase' and which invited recipients to join his mailing list.[7] Like *Smiling in French, Smoking in English*, it was printed in red and blue, suggesting it coincided directly with the book.

The negotiation with Page over the price of the new book underlines the importance of these customers in Alec's thinking. Page was a little taken aback by the $45 cost of *Occasions of Birds*, and said he was uncomfortable with the idea that his book might be priced similarly. Alec replied at length, in a letter that Rosemary Dobson later annotated as 'important, informative':

> *I plan that your book will be bound in paper, not hard covers. It certainly won't be $45, but it will be $25 to $30, and that has a lot to do with*

> *the high cost of hand binding. Also it will be 56 pages and the papers used will be expensive. If you are unhappy at this prospect, it is probably better if we don't proceed, although I would be sorry. I am trying to do books up to a standard rather than down to a price. That is what my subscribers expect. The content of the book is my first interest, but after that, the production has to come out right, and I am not willing to work within price ceilings and limitations. At the same time, I am not aiming at absurd prices. And I should just add that up until now I have not made any profits personally out of my printing.*

In the same letter he also explained that there would be no proofs: 'the final edited MS, approved by the author for setting, is the proof. I guarantee no mistakes!'

He designed a compact book, reflecting the short line length of Page's poems and setting one poem per small page, and commissioned a former colleague at the National Library, the designer Christian Preuschl von Haldenburg, to illustrate it with pen and ink drawings. He then had line blocks made from the drawings. The small page size allowed him to print four pages at a time on the Chandler & Price, the only time he ever did this. It was a 'light-hearted book, with a clever and entertaining binding that reflected its text', he said later.[8]

Ron Eadie bound the book in a limp, hand-sewn and non-adhesive binding with navy blue ribbon threaded through flecked beige cover paper. In common with Robin Tait's earlier binding of *The Palace with Several Sides*, its construction was based on the limp vellum method used for the majority of medieval books, although in this case influenced by a version of the method developed by the Swiss binder Hugo Peller rather than Christopher Clarkson, whom Tait had referenced. In a telephone conversation with the author on 6 October 2015, Eadie recalled that he offered Alec two mock-ups, the one used and the other a stiffer and more ambitious version of a laced binding, which would have cost a couple of dollars more per unit. The choice was based entirely on cost, for which Alec had budgeted $11 per unit.[9] One of the two unnumbered binder's copies Eadie was allowed to keep was later bound by him in full leather with coloured leather onlays and black embossing, during a ten-month stay in 1988 at the Centro Del Bel Libro school of fine binding in Ascona, Switzerland. It is now held by the National Library.

It was not Eadie's first encounter with Alec. He had helped his friend Helen Wadlington during two hard-working weeks when she was binding *Occasions of Birds* against its deadline and was looking after her bindery in Queanbeyan while she was overseas when Alec asked him to quote for the Page volume. He had been a binder since 1979, and had first studied in Switzerland in 1983, which led to a role in facilitating the exhibition *Contemporary Designer Bookbindings: Europe & Australia*, discussed earlier in relation to its important showing in Canberra in late 1984, and in which he was himself represented. Eadie recalled his working relationship with Alec as a good one: they shared a dry sense of humour, and Alec was always open to discussion of his preferences.

As anticipated, *Smiling in English* retailed for $35, although Alec expected most of his private sales would be to 90 or so subscribers at a ten per cent discount. Trade sales would net him only $23.33 per copy, and he anticipated the sale of 195 copies overall would bring in $5,564. This was a very small profit margin over costs of $5,031, the largest expenses being binding

($2,970), royalties ($791) and the artist's fee ($450). He relied heavily on a prospectus for advertising, putting aside only $250 for advertising.[10] The prospectus went to bookshops and to a mailing list, which had grown to about 270 people.[11] As before, general advertising consisted of a single ad in *The Weekend Australian*.

The book did not sell quickly, and some time later, as noted, there were still 50 copies unsold. Its only substantial review did not help. Peter Pierce did not quite know what to make of it: it 'distractingly commands attention first as an object, a piece of unusual book-making', and the poetry was 'something of a let-down … [which] suffers from a determination to be consequential'.[12] It is now quite scarce, and to my mind worth seeking out as an intriguing memoir of travel as well as being a lovely example of the art of the book in small form.

24

Interlude: Alec Bolton as Oral History Interviewer and Valuer

Alec's projects in retirement were not all printing-related. In 1987 he had indicated his willingness to work occasionally as an oral history interviewer for the National Library.[1] One of his first interviews was with veteran Library staffer Pauline Fanning, who had joined the Library when it was still the Parliamentary Library and who worked there and in the National Library, with a gap after marriage, for most of the time between 1936 and 1980. He began interviewing her on 16 February 1988, after nearly 30 hours of preparation, and over the next ten days recorded some seven hours with her.[2] It is an impressive debut as an interview: Alec is sympathetic and highly responsive, alert to the direction of the conversation, and deeply respectful of the life story of his subject and the difficulties in her early years. His style is gentle but thoughtful and, where necessary, probing. Fanning had been one of the treasures of the Library, an important part of its corporate memory as it grew into the statutory independence of its new role as the National Library of Australia, and Alec's performance as an interviewer led to several more highly significant interviews during the early years of the consolidation of its pioneering work in oral history.[3]

In May 1988 he recorded another long interview with the Rev. Fred McKay, John Flynn's successor as Superintendent of the Australian Inland Mission (1951–1973) and afterwards the moderator-general of the Presbyterian Church of Australia.[4] Another valuable interview, this one epitomises his later advice to interviewers to 'strive at all times to listen attentively', and not to 'rush in with another question to fill the silence'.[5] McKay preferred the fireside conversation style of interview, perhaps because he had some reluctance to speak, even though he fully acknowledged the importance of the task, and Alec's sensitive, gentle style led him into passages that at times seem to reveal rather more than the speaker at first intended.

In 1994, by now a veteran oral history interviewer for the Library, Alec was asked to prepare a short guide to interviewing techniques. Although very much about the specifics of the Library's program and its particular needs, especially in relation to interview documentation, the pamphlet is also a useful history of the early years of oral history at the Library and a thoughtful guide to researching and conducting interviews. 'Interviewing for oral history is an investigative process,' he proposed:

> *It does not have the aggression of current-affairs journalism as we know it from the electronic media, but this does not mean that it should be soft. Some interviewers are loath to ask tough questions that might disturb a comfortable atmosphere. But often the tough question, if it is calmly put, will uncover truths that otherwise might not surface. Almost any question can be asked and almost any point can be made by an interviewer whose demeanour is transparently fair-minded and unprejudiced. The person being interviewed may feel initially that the probe is too deep, but nevertheless respond openly. The risk is worth taking. The person must be encouraged to tell the whole story and not hold things back. A fault of many interviews is that they are not searching enough.*[6]

His few pages on technique merit close study by anybody embarking on an oral history interview.

Alec also took on occasional work as a valuer of manuscript collections offered to the Library, beginning with a valuation of papers offered by Les Murray that he reported on in September 1988. His wide knowledge of Australian and world poetry is strongly evident in his assessment of the collection: 'This sizeable, chaotic bundle of papers covers the years 1985 to mid-1988. Nearing 50, and still on the highest plateau of regard in Australia, the poet during this period has acquired a growing reputation overseas. That is the underlying theme of the collection'.[7] Such comments also show an ability to quickly grasp the enduring significance of a manuscript collection, born of years of working as an editor and surely also of his close contact with the Library's Manuscripts section (also at that time home of the Oral History program) during his tenure as the Library's publisher. He was a registered valuer of manuscripts and photographs under the Commonwealth's Taxation Incentives for the Arts Scheme, and in later years was to do valuations outside the literary sphere, such as that of the Eddie Koiki Mabo Papers (1995), as well as others including the papers of Katharine Susannah Prichard (1990) and Nene Gare (1994). He also valued a photographic collection of works acquired in the course of a major publishing project, for the Department of History at the Australian National University in 1990.[8]

25

'The thrill of the text buoyed me along'

Geoffrey Serle, *Percival Serle: A Memoir* (1988)

The next title was Alec's first use of a new press, and was also his first publication of a non-literary text since Manning Clark's obituary for David Campbell. 'I became a full-time printer in 1987,' he later told people on his mailing list, 'and celebrated by acquiring a Wharfedale press.'[1]

Geoffrey Serle approached him in 1986 to inquire whether he would be interested in publishing a short memoir he had written about his father Percival Serle, 'biographer, bibliographer, anthologist and art curator', as the subtitle of the book put it. It had been written for the benefit of family and friends, although Serle thought there might be larger interest in an edition of 300 to 400 copies, 'printed cheaply but decently', which he could publish and distribute himself, aiming only to recover most of the cost.

'Then I thought I should at least consider fine printing (especially given my father's interests).'[2]

Alec was interested in the manuscript, but sought a quote for machine setting of the type before he responded: at some 17,000 words it was too long for him to contemplate hand-setting. His reply to Serle suggested that such a book would have to sell for around $40, and also sought in-principle agreement for some editorial changes. He offered either a royalty of ten per cent on the sale copies, copies in lieu, or a combination of the two. 'The cost and the risk are mine,' Alec emphasised.[3] Despite his caution about the scale of the task, he was enthusiastic about the book. 'I had always been interested in Percival Serle and felt as if I knew him,' he said later. Angus & Robertson had published Serle's biographical dictionary shortly before Alec started there, and he much admired it:

> *It was an amazing single-handed achievement. So when I was approached by Geoffrey Serle to publish this memoir of his father, I was very happy. I also wanted to do another volume of prose. It was another of those books in which the thrill of the text buoyed me along: a masterpiece of concise biographical writing.*[4]

Although he had some editorial queries on first reading the text, he also sought detailed comments from F.B. Horner, a distinguished retired statistician and historian. Most of Horner's suggestions appear to have been accepted by the author, along with Alec's own.[5] The use of a typesetter, again C.D. FitzHardinge-Bailey of St Mark's Press, Sydney, was prompted by the length of the text, and Alec was still committed to printing letterpress. But for the frontispiece (a duotone image of Serle) and the photographic endpapers Alec made use of offset lithography, done by Goanna Print, a Canberra commercial printer. This was mentioned in both the prospectus and the colophon of the book; he was not a letterpress purist. The book itself was printed on the 'newly acquired, less than perfectly mastered Wharfedale press'.[6]

Alec's previous aspiration in seeking another press had been to look for a hand-fed art platen with parallel action such as a Vicobold or a Victoria. 'Quality of impression and not speed of printing is my consideration,' he told the firm that had supplied him with his Chandler & Price platen[7], but such a press proved hard to find. When Jim Walker of the Croft Press at Cobargo offered him a Wharfedale press he was keen to buy it, paying a little over $1,000 for the machine.[8] The new press caused a few problems, mainly because of inexperience, he commented to his friend Arthur Stokes, a book designer with whom he had worked on various National Library titles.

> *By the time I felt I was in control of what I was doing, I was putting the last forme on. I had some difficulty with unevenness of colour, but I have now fitted new cylinder bearers, which has overcome the problem. The next book ought to be all right. Always that hope that the next book will wipe away all sin!*[9]

The addition of this stop-cylinder press to Alec's printshop meant that he was now potentially better equipped for book production and longer runs. In the traditional sizing parlance, it could handle a demy size sheet of paper, 22.5 by 17.5 inches (444 x 571 millimetres), and it was also safer to operate than the

Chandler & Price platen press, which has the potential to crush its operator's hand while feeding paper. The Wharfedale style of printing press was developed in the mid-nineteenth century and was built by several firms, who all called their machines Wharfedales after the district of Yorkshire where they were first manufactured. A Wharfedale is a flat-bed press, which can be very large, in which either the forme remains stationary while imposition is achieved by it making contact with paper when a cylinder is rolled over it under pressure or (mostly in later versions) in which the forme travels backwards and forward beneath the cylinder. Because this contact is confined to a narrow strip directly under the cylinder as it moves across the type, less power is required to achieve considerable pressure.[10] Later improvements in the Wharfedale style of press particularly suited it to fine art printing, with heavy and solid impression combined with improved inking arrangements.[11] The Wharfedale is a 'stop-cylinder' press because the cylinder around which the paper is wrapped stops turning while it returns to a position to make the next impression on the next sheet of paper, which has in the meantime been fed into place. This concept is older than that of the Wharfedale and was invented in Germany early in the nineteenth century.[12]

Made at Reddish in England about 1900 by Furnival & Co. (and thus also referred to as a Furnival), this Wharfedale press had previously been used to print a newspaper at Koroit, in Victoria. Jim Walker later used it for the first books he printed after he retired from Melbourne University Press and moved to Cobargo on the South Coast of New South Wales, before he replaced it with a Vertical Miehle.[13] Alec had also seen a larger Wharfedale press in use at the Whittington Press, where it was used for the bulk of their longer titles such as the journal *Matrix* until they upgraded to a machine-fed Heidelberg cylinder press in 1985.[14]

The new press required a good deal of work, including repairs to the delivery system.[15] Fortunately, Alec could call on the help of Peter Finlay in its restoration. Finlay had been the head teacher of printing at the Reid campus of the Canberra TAFE, and was later on the staff of the Graphic Investigation Workshop at the School of Art, Canberra. He was a skilled professional printer and Alec often turned to him in moments of difficulty.[16] Although he had hoped that the Western could from then on be reserved primarily for printing illustrations, the Wharfedale turned out not to be as versatile as anticipated. A four-page imposition diagram for *Percival Serle* in his files is labelled 'Western' in Alec's hand, so perhaps at one stage he planned to use the Western press when faced by the restoration challenge of the new machine. Even though he persevered in using it for this and some later work, in the long run he was to describe the Western as his main press, and the Chandler & Price as his always reliable back up.[17]

Alec first used a pressmark designed by Arthur Stokes in this book, and in newsletters to his mailing list. (It was later also used on the inside wrappers of *A Licence to Print*.) Stokes offered him several hand-drawn versions of the initials OB, for Officina Brindabella. Alec's reply is interesting in what it says about his attitude to design and lettering issues:

> *On the whole I don't like the lower-case ob forms so well … I suppose I just prefer capital to lower-case forms for this kind of use. I think the italic B works better than the roman, and perhaps allows the enclosing shape to be slightly flattened rather than a pure circle … I must say that*

> *I do like the reversed forms … But when I think of the practicalities of using a press mark or colophon on, say, a title page, the reversed form would in many cases be too dominant an element unless printed in something other than black, and this would seem to be an undesirable limitation.*[18]

Stokes refused to send a bill for the design: 'I can never repay my debt to you & Rosemary,' he said.[19] While it is not clear what this refers to, Stokes should be noted as another figure in the Brindabella book arts network. (He was also a sculptor and did a bust of Rosemary in 1987.[20]) He designed National Library of Australia publications such as the elegant *Private Journal of James Burney* (1975) and *French Plays 1701–1840 in the National Library of Australia: A Bibliography* (1973). Stokes' passion for typography is recalled by designer Dominic Hofstede:

> *Arthur taught typography for many years at Chisholm Institute (now Monash University) and I was fortunate to have him in my first year. He spoke about type with the fervour of a zealot, and I cite him as a significant figure in my design education. I guess I absorbed some of Arthur's enthusiasm for the craft, and we see typography as the glue that binds our work.*[21]

Percival Serle marked a new development in Alec's own passion for type, being his first book set in 11 point Baskerville. 'I started off my printing in 10 pt Baskerville, then moved up to 12 pt,' he later told fellow printer Bob Summers, 'which however is a very big-looking face and needs a large page size. It was years and years before I realised that the ideal size in Baskerville is

11 pt.'[22] The book was machine-set in Monotype Baskerville by FitzHardinge-Bailey with 2 point leading, and Alec had enough 11 point Baskerville from previous projects to make corrections in-house. 'It has taken me a while to get into a satisfactory rhythm of operating this press, and to understand its idiosyncrasies,' he told his typesetter, 'but I think I am just about on top of it now and it is a dream to print from new type!'[23]

Alec was offered a good deal on a large consignment of Mohawk Superfine paper at this time and contemplated an edition as large as 425 copies, using 900 sheets of the 1700 on offer. He had nowhere to store such a large amount of paper, however, and ultimately decided to buy enough paper for 350 copies—which makes this book his largest edition, apart from the short obituary for David Campbell discussed elsewhere.[24] A little later he also bought a 23 inch Chandler & Price manual guillotine, having previously relied on paper suppliers to cut sheets to size or, earlier on, making use of a large guillotine in the bindery at the National Library.[25] With this and the later purchase of a paper-folding machine he completed the set-up of his printshop.

Helen Wadlington bound the book, as well as making its paste paper sides. Binding cost $14.30 a copy. Actual outgoings, without allowing anything for his own time, would be $8,500, he reported to Serle, which he calculated allowed the book to be sold for a recommended retail price of $45. This was based on Serle not receiving any royalty, as he had requested.[26] Alec estimated that he would clear $9,855 on sales. For the first time he recorded his own labour cost, calculated as 15 per cent of total production costs, which at $1,286 took the book to break even point. It represented a $3.67 return to himself per copy—hardly a princely wage for many hours of printing. This was still a labour of love. Unfortunately, there is no record of just how many hours printing took. Alec said later, however, that he printed in the mornings on most days of the week, finishing about midday. He began paging and making up *Percival Serle* about 21 April 1988, and printing about 26 April, having already spent some time correcting mistakes in the machine setting of the type. He finished printing on 26 July 1988. So three months' work, five days a week, give or take a few days for trips away, possibly added up to around 200 hours of printing alone. He therefore paid himself little more than $6 an hour for this book, making no allowance for time spent proofreading, editing, or on administration and distribution.

Percival Serle was advertised in both *The Age* and *The Weekend Australian*, with the tag line 'Fine short life of the Melbourne man of letters and cultural pioneer by his son, the noted historian and biographer'. These ads (which were only single insertions) were headed 'Brindabella Letterpress Editions', a rubric that would remain constant in advertising the rest of Alec's publications, even after he reclaimed the name Brindabella Press.[27] By now he was not keen on sending out review copies, he told Serle: 'usually by the time a book is noticed (if it is noticed at all) the edition is out of print'.[28] He was confident that the book would sell quickly through these ads and the prospectus sent to the Brindabella mailing list. He also told Serle that he sometimes deliberately kept the numbers low for sales through bookshops, even though the support of booksellers such as Kay Craddock in Melbourne was often very helpful, because such sales only covered his costs and made no profit. He drafted short plugs for the book for several journals suggested by Serle, and the inclusion of a full

Cataloguing-in-Publication entry on the imprint page suggests that he was hoping for good sales to libraries.

It sold well, he later recalled.[29] It was praised generously by Peter Ryan in the *Financial Review*[30], but does not appear to have been noticed elsewhere in the press. (Alec's usual meticulous list of recipients mentions only one press copy, but as Ryan and Serle had known each other since the 1940s, and Serle was one of Ryan's major authors as publisher at Melbourne University Press, it is likely that the copy he reviewed came from the 45 allocated to the author.[31])

However, ten copies in folded sheets (that is, unbound) bought by the Crafts Council of the ACT for individual binding and display in the exhibition *Fine Books, Fine Bindings* at the ANU's Drill Hall Gallery (March 1989) later won praise from Meredith Hinchliffe in *The Canberra Times*. She particularly liked Ron Eadie's binding of a 'gentle, restrained memoir' because it spoke eloquently of Serle, perfectly mirroring the biography it contained, and liked also another unassuming binding by Juhani Roininen from Finland that reflected 'the spareness of the writing'. It was Helen Wadlington who had suggested the choice of title to the Crafts Council, but Hinchliffe preferred her standard binding to that which she submitted for this exhibition. She criticised Hugo Peller's elaborate concept: 'the binding is superb, but it bears no relation to the contents'.[32] (Peller was a leading Swiss binder, associated with the Centro Del Bel Libro in Ascona.) Three of the six Australian binders to whom copies were sent were binders with whom Alec had already worked—Ron Eadie, Robin Tait and Helen Wadlington—and the project was a mark of respect for Brindabella in the Australian book arts community of the time.[33]

In similar terms, at about this time the National Library included several of the press' works in its major travelling exhibition for the Australian Bicentenary, *People, Print & Paper*, as an epitome of the private press tradition of sparse elegance and 'the loving interpretation of a text that the printer believes is important'.[34] (Full disclosure: the present writer was curator of that exhibition and selected its content, which was then approved by senior management, including the then director-general, Warren Horton. It was on this occasion that Alec suggested that Mary Quick, whose work at the Juniper Press he greatly admired, should be considered for inclusion in the exhibition.)

26

'The first wood engraver I have ever come across who has a sense of Australianness in her work'

Les A. Murray, *The Idyll Wheel* (1989)

With Alec now fully settled into a full-time avocation as a printer, the best years of the Brindabella Press began. His accomplishments of those years brought a renewed confidence in expressing strong views on the book arts, at least within his own circle. Perhaps this was also one of the results of leaving the Australian Public Service. There was no return to the pseudonymous writing of the 1970s, but by now he was a senior and highly respected figure in the Australian book world.

One of his first steps as a full-time printer was to publish the first checklist of his publications to date.[1] He prefaced the list with a short note on the history of the press. 'Letterpress was already well on the way out when I began to learn it in 1970–71, as an evening student at the London College of Printing,' he noted, before describing the presses he had acquired over the years and explaining the change of name to Officina Brindabella. His best work to date had been printed on the Western proof press, he said. 'With the addition of a folding machine and a fourth type cabinet in 1988, I seem to have run out of room.' It was in this period, too, that international interest in his work became more evident, notably with a selection of seven titles appearing in a Joshua Heller list in 1991. 'All productions are carefully designed and beautifully printed books,' noted Heller, one of the world's leading specialists in fine printing and private press books. Heller included four titles from 'this excellent Australian private press' again in 1995, in a list largely devoted to Leonard Baskin and his Gehenna Press—fine company indeed.[2]

One of the books that attracted Heller's interest was *The Idyll Wheel*, poems by Les Murray, a writer with a growing international reputation. Alec first approached Murray for a book in 1986. He preferred to be the first to publish a work in book form, he said, but alternatively it was perhaps possible that Angus & Robertson, Murray's usual publishers, might be interested in doing an offset edition based on his letterpress proofs, although he had not made any such suggestion to them. 'Behind this pedestrian account of the way in which my private press operates lies a sincere and eager interest on my part in any possibility of printing some work by yourself,' he told Murray.[3] Murray offered a sequence of twelve poems based on a year at Bunyah, a valley in the coastal north of New South Wales where his people had long farmed. He and his family had returned to live there in

1985, with great happiness, after 29 years away.[4] However he had contractual obligations with Angus & Robertson. Alec agreed to approach Richard Walsh, managing director at Angus & Robertson. He also sent Murray examples of Rosalind Atkins' work as the proposed illustrator, explaining why he was so enthusiastic about her work:

> *I was really overjoyed to hear from her. Besides being very talented and skilful in this difficult art of endgrain engraving, she is the first wood engraver I have ever come across who has a sense of Australianness in her work. Wood engraving has been a rare and little practised art in Australia. Even a brilliant practitioner like Lionel Lindsay had little sense of Australian place in his blocks. Thus to me she is an important find.*[5]

While Walsh was agreeable, he wanted the Angus & Robertson edition of Murray's next book, which would include the Bunyah poems, to come out either simultaneously with the Brindabella edition or a couple of months ahead of it.[6]

In the middle of these negotiations, Walsh's departure from Angus & Robertson was announced (he moved to Australian Consolidated Press as a director and publisher). Although Murray was confident this would not cause any problems, it was nearly a year before Angus & Robertson formally agreed, thankfully without demanding the separate contract between them and the press that had first been suggested by Walsh, nor requiring a right of first publication.[7] In the end, ten of the Bunyah poems were included in *The Daylight Moon*, which Angus & Robertson published in 1987; two additional poems, as well as a verse preface, were published for the first time in *The Idyll Wheel*, which ultimately appeared in 1989, and which stands as the most complete statement of Murray's happiness in coming home. The negotiations, however, were not the major cause of the time taken before publication, as Murray intended from the start to take a year to write the poems, one a month, and they were not completed until May 1987. This coincided with a visit by Atkins to Bunyah. She was, Murray reported, 'a hit with all of us. Friendly, unfussed and deeply professional'.[8]

Before going on to discuss progress with the book, it is necessary to explore briefly some logistical issues. The first of these, and the subject of a good deal of the early correspondence between Alec and Atkins, concerned her difficulty in finding suitable woodblocks for engraving. The last remaining maker of boxwood blocks in the UK was T.N. Lawrence & Son of Bleeding Heart Yard in Holborn, London, who was both expensive, given the state of the Australian dollar, and, as others have reported, at times wary of new customers.[9] American suppliers were an unknown quantity, and there were no Australian suppliers. Alec had a few blocks from Lawrence he was able to give her, but they also discussed the possibility of finding a substitute. Les Murray's father cut her a piece of brush box to experiment with when she visited Bunyah, and she tried ivory wood, a dense timber from Southern Africa, but found it softer than box.[10] So too was a maple block Alec had got from New York.[11] Wood engraving requires an extremely hard end-grain block for sharp detail, unlike woodcuts, which can be engraved along the grain in softer timber. Atkins had also tried engraving mulga, like box a slow-growing tree with dense wood, but in the end between them they found sufficient boxwood blocks for the seven engravings in *The Idyll Wheel*.[12]

This difficulty in finding basic necessities mirrored Alec's own issues with limited supplies of paper and type, and perhaps the shared adversity helped build the growing friendship between the two. Rosalind Atkins, like Mike Hudson and Barbara Hanrahan, became a regular partner in Brindabella projects from then on. The relationship survived Alec's horror when he discovered that her book *Recollections* had been printed offset and not letterpress, even though the edition was only 80. He would have urged her to withdraw it from Tate Adams' Lyre Bird Press if he had known, he told her, until he could have printed it himself.[13]

Another logistical issue causing concern for Alec at this time was the growing difficulty in getting hot metal typesetting done in Australia. Although he was again able to get Darrell FitzHardinge-Bailey of St Mark's Press to compose and cast *The Idyll Wheel* in Monotype Perpetua, and he hand-set Bulmer himself for display, FitzHardinge-Bailey had told him that he was selling most of his equipment and going out of business. An associate would continue, but in a limited way. By now there were almost no Monotype composition-casting resources left in Australia. This meant he would be restricted to only a handful of businesses still running Monotype Super Casters and a limited range of typefaces, or he would have to start using Linotype. In Sydney, Alec learned, he would probably be able to specify Baskerville, Bembo, Garamond, Perpetua and Plantin, but he had no idea of what sizes would be available. He resisted switching to Linotype, even though it was more varied; as he told Mike Hudson, 'Lino has always scared me because of the factors of distance and unchangeableness', and close inspection of even well-printed local Linotype suggested that the matrices used to cast the type were worn. One alternative was to set everything by hand, with type imported from Mackenzie & Harris in California, but this was expensive (especially so given the current exchange rate), and large type consignments were liable to be assessed for customs duty. Another possibility was to return to the notion of setting up as a typecaster himself: he was still a co-owner of the Monotype Super Caster which Jim Walker of Croft Press had bought in the early 1980s, and Walker also owned another caster.

> *I decided years ago that I had my hands more than full trying to print decently, and would give up all thought of learning to cast type as well. But keyboarding might be possible if there was someone to put the tapes through the caster? The trouble is, I am half a lifetime too late with all this stuff.*[14]

A few words of explanation may be necessary at this point for those not familiar with typesetting technology of the letterpress era. Hand-setting type to be used in a platen press as evoked in the first pages of this book involves setting individual letters (also referred to as sorts) and spacing material by hand, and demands exact calculation of the length of each line of metal—otherwise the forme will simply collapse as soon as it is moved, because it is held in the chase by lateral pressure. This justification is done by adding spacing material until every line is exactly the same length. Hand-setting was the norm for most of the history of letterpress printing, and was Alec's first practice.

By the 1890s the production of large texts such as newspapers had been increasingly taken over by Ottmar Mergenthaler's Linotype or similar typesetting machines, in which an operator worked a keyboard instead of setting previously cast type (cold metal) and line-length slugs of type were produced (hot metal). After printing, the type was melted down for re-use instead of being distributed into typecases. This was faster and cheaper than individual hand-composition. 'The Linotype justified its lines by mechanically expanding its interword spaces to fill the measure after the matrices that formed the text of the line had been assembled.'[15]

The Monotype system, invented by Tolbert Lanston, is different. 'Like the Linotype, Lanston's system produced a newly-cast printing surface in which the text was correctly justified; but this surface, unlike that from Mergenthaler's machine, was made up of individual sorts (that is, letters) and spaces.'[16] Justification is achieved by the keyboarding machine automatically varying the widths of sorts and spaces, and recording this on a perforated paper roll. This is then used in a separate machine to cast them. All this meant that a press operator, such as Alec, could make corrections in the text without having to go back to the typesetter, just as if it had been set by hand, provided he had the correct individual sorts. It also made kerning automatic, which Linotype could not do. This is the ability to adjust the width of letters that stretch to one side such as f, which often hangs over the next letter (as in the word 'often'), without moving the letter an awkward distance away from its neighbour.[17] But it was this sort of typographic elegance that was disappearing as casting machines were scrapped.

A Monotype Super Caster, such as the one Alec had a share in at the Croft Press, was 'designed specifically for casting type for case [that is, type cast for later setting by hand, stored meanwhile in a type case, the correct name for what is often referred to as a type tray], also leads, rules, borders and spacing material'.[18] One great advantage was that it was designed to cast display type (type intended for use in headings rather than body text) in larger sizes than were possible with the Monotype Composition Caster, up to 72 point, versus 24 point with the Composition Caster. (As David Jury and others have described, for much of its history the casting of type was dominated by the need for book text. The growing demand for larger typefaces from jobbing printers creating commercial and advertising material produced a vast industry in cutting large wood typefaces, as well as larger metal type. Wood type could be enormous but was often out of sympathy with the traditional serif faces that were favoured by people like Alec.[19]) Because it was used to cast type for repeated hand-setting, the Monotype Super Caster used a harder metal suitable for re-use, and thus was a versatile and useful adjunct to a hand-printing operation not set up for regular re-casting of type. The Monotype Composition Caster, such as Whittington Press possessed, was designed to set long texts for books and the like.

Both types of caster were substantial machines, weighing nearly 700 kilograms and requiring a working area of at least five square metres. Neither were particularly suitable for use in a small printery attached to domestic premises (and nor was, it has to be said, the Linotype Alec had previously speculated about acquiring in his retirement—most models weigh between one and two tonnes, and although their footprint is not huge, most are around two metres or more high. All such casters require molten metal to function, of course, and the Linotype was celebrated for occasionally blasting its operator with a jet of molten lead.)

As letterpress resources disappeared from commercial usage from the 1970s on, such machines were sometimes salvaged by private press printers and are still in use today. Some commercial type-casting operations do survive worldwide, and type can now be obtained from not-for-profit ventures such as The Printing Museum/*Whare Taonga Perehitanga* in Wellington, New Zealand.

However, both Linotype and Monotype machines are complex and require skills in operation and maintenance that once took years for apprentices to develop. They are not for the faint-hearted. A simpler alternative, common in Australia, was the Ludlow, 'a semi-mechanical composing machine'. With this, 'the matrices are assembled and justified by hand in the Ludlow stick, automatically cast in the form of a slug, and then distributed back into case by hand'.[20] One still needs to own sets of matrices in different sizes and faces, but the casting operation is simpler and, again, some letterpress printers still run Ludlows.

By the 1980s the transition from letterpress to offset printing was well and truly over in Australia. This meant that the extensive infrastructure that had once sustained letterpress printing as a major aspect of commercial life in Australia was mostly gone. A printer committed to letterpress had either to become self-sufficient or to find alternative techniques. It was this very transition to phototypesetting and offset litho printing that had created opportunities for small presses such as Brindabella to pick up high-quality equipment at affordable prices, but that era had now ended.

In one way Alec side-stepped the issue. His contacts with a small group of wood engravers eventually meant that he no longer depended on commercial line block makers, such as he had used in his first books, who were also disappearing. And there are private press printers who have argued that the best work is done by exploring the possibilities of a single, or at least of a limited range, of typefaces. As long as he could still specify his beloved Baskerville, and had Centaur and Arrighi in his cases, he would be able to keep on printing from the metal. Nevertheless, this issue was to continue to be a concern for him until he decided to explore the possibilities offered by photopolymer in the 1990s, and as late as 1992 he was still searching for Monotype casting resources elsewhere in Australia and lamenting the shortcomings of Linotype.

> *I … would give a lot to have a Monotype shop available. New type every time, and that total control over revision. We are in the wrong country—that is the trouble.*[21]

As it turned out, however, he was able to get typesetting done in Sydney for a while longer, albeit in Linotype. He also briefly explored the possibility of buying used magazines of Linotype Baskerville, hoping that they could be used on an Elektron II Linotype owned by a local Queanbeyan printer, who might also teach him how to key the machine for use at an hourly rate.[22] There is no evidence that this came to anything. Later, Alec bought two Intertype magazines to run on a C4 Intertype machine (similar to a Linotype)[23], and at the time of his death also owned Monotype Baskerville matrices in 10 and 12 points.[24] 'This was never a great Monotype country,' he told John Randle, 'and we never had large numbers of people with Monotype skills. I feel a bit uncomfortable in turning to Linotype, but it can't be helped.'[25]

His dilemma was that of many who loved fine printing, one shared by Penelope Fitzgerald's character Tvyordov, chief compositor at a small printing office in Moscow just before the Revolution:

> *Linotype, he felt was not worthy of a serious man's carefully measured time. It was only fit for slipshod work at great speed. To make corrections you had to reset the whole line, therefore you had orders not to do it. The metal used was a wretchedly soft alloy. Monotype, after some consideration, he tolerated. The machine was small and ingenious, and the letters danced out as they were cast from the hot metal, separate and alive. They weren't as hard as real founder's type, still they would take a good many impressions, and they could be used for corrections in the compositors' room. When, or even whether, Tvyordov had been asked for his views was not known, but Reidka's did monotype, and no linotype.*[26]

The *Idyll Wheel* was Alec's largest book to that point, at 268 x 190 millimetres. This was partly dictated by the length of lines in Murray's verse, he commented: 'I don't like breaking lines in setting poetry, which was a real challenge with this work'.[27] Although he briefly considered the possibility of printing it on Australian handmade paper from Alan Walker's Bemboka mill, after successfully printing the *Rainforest* engraving on one sheet as an experiment, the high cost of the paper worried him.[28] Atkins was also critical of the Bemboka paper, suggesting it would not print as clearly as the Arches used for *Rainforest*.[29] Alec may also have been mindful of Jim Walker's previous difficulties in printing with it, because he found it varied in thickness.[30] So in the end he used a creamy mould-made Zerkall paper at 145 gsm, which he bought directly from a paper supplier in London, and which he knew would be 'extremely sympathetic to the printing of wood engravings'.[31] He turned to Margaret Lock of Locks' Press in Brisbane for advice on importing paper, which he had not done before. She helped him with advice on how to clear it through customs and on sales tax exemption. [32] The paper merchants were slow to respond, and it was six months before the paper arrived, but he had made a small saving on its cost by importing it himself.

Although the drawings that Rosalind Atkins prepared were based on her visit to Bunyah and the photographs she took then, Alec's design sense helped shape them also. They had one face-to-face meeting to discuss them in Melbourne in July and exchanged numerous letters and trial drawings. Thus, while always deferring to her judgement, he asked if there could be more of a dimension of landscape in the illustration of the book. Later he just as gently asked, 'is it possible to suggest human presence, or animal presence perhaps? A distant person or an animal such as a cow in, say, August? Maybe not'. Fields with cattle eventuated for the March poem.

These were only suggestions: Alec was adamant that Atkins' response to her visit to Bunyah should be the key driver of her illustrations. 'The book can be replanned or rethought altogether in terms of what *you* want to do or think best after visiting Bunyah,' he wrote before her visit.[33] Artist and poet in conversation with a landscape, with a farm: here perhaps was a formula to avoid the creative tensions of the past? And in his prospectus for the book he emphasised the fact that Atkins had visited Bunyah to make the drawings.

But one drawing was rejected by him, Atkins' portrait of Murray's father, a rejection Atkins accepted with equanimity. Alec felt it did not work as a portrait, and also that the book as a whole might be 'more of an entity' without it. Murray's response to the first batch of sketches was also highly enthusiastic. His only reservation was that he did not want the farm to look too run-down, or as if it had no continuing life, and he also queried the use of an image of a dry gully for August, when it would normally be wet, and proposing February instead, which was accepted. Murray's bush knowledge was also drawn on by the engraver for the title-page vignette, 'Leaf Spring', which was repeated on the front cover. Atkins wrote:

> *Reading Les' poems again, I remembered a conversation I had with him about Leaf Spring (April). Leaf Spring refers to the new shoots that grow on gum trees in April.*[34]

Later, however, Murray vehemently rejected a proof of the gully engraving, complaining that it made the trees along his creek look completely dead.

> *I reckon she should either get the tops of those trees right, that is, lacy and millionfold with lights, or go back to the loop of barbed wire she originally had for Feb.*[35]

Alec was sympathetic, but explained that it was too late to ask for a new engraving. It had been based on a photograph, a copy of which he enclosed, which he thought overall showed as much foliage in the engraving as in the photograph. 'Unfortunately,' he reminded the poet, 'nothing can be put in where the wood has been engraved away.'[36] He sent more proofs in November, and to Murray's joy the creek trees now appeared to have more leaves and to look 'less like bushfire stumps'.[37]

Although Alec had earlier decided not to pursue the idea of using an Australian handmade paper in this book, the notion returned when it came to its binding. Canberra paper maker Katharine Nix 'achieves some very strong effects with local plant fibres', he told Murray[38], and she made paper for the endpapers with blady grass harvested near Braidwood.[39] (Later Nix sent Alec a photograph of the site where she had harvested the blady grass, showing that it was 'all shooting up strong and green again'.[40]) The binding was done by Robin Tait, who suggested a different colour palette after reading the poems.[41] Later she recalled that she had been responsible for finding the leather used on the spine, proposing a rust red oasis goatskin that Alec then matched in printing the title.[42] The paper used to cover the boards was his choice and not something she would have chosen. 'Looking at this purpley-grey paper it works extraordinarily well … Alec always surprised me with his choices and yet they always worked, something I really admired about him.' She was assisted in binding this and her later Brindabella editions by Bill Thorn, who had himself retired from the National Library at the end of 1987 and had taken up bookbinding.[43] Although at first the plan had been to bind the book with blue-green paper sides, as Alec specified in ordering the endpapers, he left the final choice to follow on from the colours of the endpapers when made, and the final selection was quite different.[44]

The Idyll Wheel was published in May 1989 at a recommended retail price of $75, with the usual 10 per cent discount to libraries and standing order subscribers. The discount to booksellers was 33⅓ per cent. The edition of 290, of which 260 copies were for sale, sold quickly. Although more than half had been ordered before publication[45], Alec took out a small ad in *The Weekend Australian*.[46] Murray suggested the Brisbane *Courier-Mail* and *The West Australian* for review copies. A half-hour program with Murray reading his poetry and talking about Bunyah was broadcast on the ABC show Radio Helicon in April, which perhaps also helped boost sales.[47] By August 1990 only seven copies remained for sale. The bulk had sold through booksellers (131 copies), 65 had gone to subscribers and libraries, and 57 were direct sales at full price to individual customers—that is, non-subscribers who had ordered either in response to the prospectus or an advertisement.[48]

Alec decided that with *The Idyll Wheel*, and from then on, the prospectuses he sent out to booksellers and his mailing list would be simple one-page affairs, although he did not always maintain this resolution in later years. Previously he had printed four-page samples of the book, but they were expensive to print and to post. 'You take a world of trouble with an announcement, and it seems to drop into a void,' he lamented to Mike Hudson. After 15 years he had built up a mailing list of about 300 names:

> *but many of these people are unreliable as buyers, and treat my prospectuses with disdain … It is always a mystery to me where the press book collectors in Australia are, and indeed if they exist at all as an identifiable species. The membership of the Book Collectors' Soc'y*

of Australia is a washout for my sort of book ... I resent posting quite elegant material to people who then ignore it—especially when, like you, I have included little personal notes in a high proportion of the total mailing. This must be in some way similar to suffering the pangs of unrequited love, don't you think?[49]

Although he made a smaller return from selling through booksellers than directly, it was the bookshops that contributed most to sales. His list of reliable booksellers, shared on this occasion with Hudson, showed that some stalwarts of the past had closed: he recommended Peter Tinslay, Louella Kerr, Nicholas Pounder and Hordern House in Sydney; Kay Craddock and Ken Hince in Melbourne; Michael Treloar in Adelaide; and Dan and Michael Sprod in Hobart—although some took only one or two copies.

The Idyll Wheel made a modest profit of $2,206. Actual costs of production were $11,669, the bulk being binding ($4,555 at $15.60 a copy) and royalties ($2,925). The blady grass endpapers, at $1,200, cost considerably more than the Zerkall paper (which was $659, plus $339 to clear through customs). Alec estimated his overheads at ten per cent to get a final production cost of $12,836, thus giving him a unit cost of $49.37. As of 8 November 1989, he had invoiced $15,042 in sales.[50] His initial attempt at costing the book in July 1988 had put costs at $13,882, not far out from the actual, but had been based on a 15 per cent overhead for the press, so costs had grown somewhat.[51] The book had 'cleaned me out', he told Mike Hudson, and he would need to sell more copies before he could afford to order more type.[52]

The book was reviewed favourably by Heather Cam in *The Sydney Morning Herald*—it was 'a superb instance of craftsmanship', and she liked Murray's ability 'to see things afresh and askew' as well.[53] Martin Duwell reviewed it in *The Australian*[54] and Geoff Page in *The Canberra Times*. Page's review recognised Alec as an artist of the book in his own right for the first time: the book is 'really three works of art in one', Page wrote.

> *For the majority of readers the most important of the three will be Murray's poems, but hardly less significant are the understated and painfully evocative wood engravings of the Bunyah landscape by Rosalind Atkins and the printing and book production by Alec Bolton.*[55]

Its cost might seem 'astonishing', but the book was easily worth 'the equivalent of a meal for two at a good restaurant'. Christopher Pearson also asked for a copy for *The Adelaide Review*.[56] And Barrett Reid, poet, friend and editor of the literary magazine *Overland*, told Alec he had excelled himself with *The Idyll Wheel*:

> *I've lost count of the number of people who have had the book proudly put into their (clean) hands—on Saturday it was John Perceval, the painter. Everyone agrees it's a lovely book. I liked the size of the page: it seems to suit these rather large sprawling poems and the fine wood engravings which in the firmness complement Murray's formal qualities.*[57]

The Idyll Wheel was later translated into German[58] and Murray used several of the poems in subsequent collections of his work. It was 'certainly the handsomest and best-made book I've ever appeared in', the poet wrote to the printer. 'So marvellous, to have a *real* book at last! Thanks again.'[59]

Bunyah's importance to Murray's verse was again emphasised recently, with the publication of his *On Bunyah.*[60] This includes two poems from *The Idyll Wheel* (both of which, it should be noted again, had first appeared in book form in *The Daylight Moon* in 1987).

27

'So strong and yet so tender'

Barbara Hanrahan, *Twelve Linocuts* (1990)

Alec's gift of a copy of *The Idyll Wheel* to Barrett Reid raised the question of whether the latter might have poems suitable for publication, and a little earlier he had been involved in an inconclusive correspondence with Sydney poet Robert Gray on the same subject.[1] He also approached Gwen Harwood in Hobart for a manuscript. She was interested but uncertain as to when she might have material available.[2] Although none of these tentative approaches went anywhere, by this time he was deeply immersed in a major new project; 'It is wonderful work,'[3] he told Reid. The new work was a suite of 12 large linocuts by Barbara Hanrahan, which was to be published as an edition of 100 boxed sets.

Twelve Linocuts had its genesis in a note by Alec to Hanrahan accompanying the prospectus for Elizabeth Riddell's poems, at the time when he was completing *Rainforest*. This prompted him to ask her if she would consider providing him with an image to use with 'an Australian poem as a broadside'—he contemplated doing two or three broadsides a year, he told her.[4] She was too busy with a new novel to do any engraving, she told him on that occasion.[5] Next he sent her the prospectus for *Percival Serle*, which this time drew the response that she was working on linocuts again—large ones, that were difficult for her to print with sufficient blackness. He replied quickly to ask if the linocuts might be suitable for a book after she had done them as prints: 'perhaps a quite small printing of something in a large format? There would be interest in it, if the integrity of the prints was not violated'. This did not interest her: she would not want to reproduce prints in book form that were being sold in galleries, she replied. Moreover, after a telephone conversation between her partner Jo Steele and Alec, it appeared the size he had in mind would be a good deal smaller than the work she was doing at the time. She did not have the time to devote to a separate series for a book, and found it difficult to work in small format on lino.

It looked as if this idea was going nowhere, despite Alec's obvious keenness to work with Hanrahan again, but even before he could have received her reply he had reconsidered his approach and returned to the discussion. On reflection, he could print large images, hand-inking them on his Western cylinder press, which could just take a 15 x 20 inch sheet. He proposed printing on one side only of each sheet and then joining them in concertina fashion for an unsewn binding:

> *It is the Japanese 'butterfly' style of binding. When the book is open, it lies perfectly flat. If you want to, you can stand it on edge and draw the*

> *concertina out for fun or decorative effect. But otherwise it handles like an ordinary book.*

A collection of twelve images all on right-hand pages, faced by titles and captions, plus other matter such as title and colophon, would thus add up to a 56-page book, and if the paper was 250 or 300 gsm it would be quite a substantial book, he added. Titles and captions could be a second colour, and she might want to think about hand-colour in the printed images.

This was the breakthrough for Hanrahan. She quickly responded to say she was excited about the concept, and she clearly was taken with the butterfly book idea in particular. She deferred judgement on the use of colour until the work was underway, but expected that black and white would be best. All she asked was not to be confined to a set date for completion. She was preparing work for two exhibitions, and still working on her novel. Left unsaid in this letter was anything about the state of her health. Early in 1988 she had again been diagnosed with cancer, for which she had been treated in 1984. *Twelve Linocuts* and later *Iris in Her Garden*, her final book with Brindabella, would be completed in the face of mortal illness. For now, though, her biographer notes, she and Jo Steele were convinced she would survive the cancer.[6] And despite a brief crisis in September, when she wrote a sad postcard to Alec withdrawing from the project after discovering that her tumour had grown[7], she kept working on *Twelve Linocuts*. (Annette Stewart's excellent biography of Hanrahan seems to me to somewhat conflate *Twelve Linocuts* with *Some Poems of Shaw Neilson* and suggests that she was working on *Iris in Her Garden* at Alec's suggestion at this time.[8] However, that came later, with the bulk of the *Iris* etchings being worked on in 1990, the year before Hanrahan's death.)

By November Hanrahan was able to send proofs of five linocuts. She was perhaps still a little uncertain of the likely response, assuring Alec that if he thought they were unsuitable for a book she would not mind. She was returning to images she had drawn early in life, when a student at the South Australian School of Art on Adelaide's North Terrace:

> *The images I am working with are all adaptions of some of my earliest prints of the 1960s—many of these were linocuts (though some were etchings). Most had just one or two prints pulled from them, and then they were lost or abandoned as I went on to something new. It was a very exciting period … evening classes in the new printmaking department & really my first taste of 'art'. So these new prints are a little homage to that first work. Though the new images are the old ones strengthened and added to, I have ideas for the other seven.*[9]

He thought the prints were simply wonderful: 'so strong and yet so tender, so rich in their diversity of detail and texture, and so characteristic of your work'.[10] One unresolved issue was the financial basis of the book: he suggested that there be no royalty but that the profits should be shared 60:40, with 60 per cent going to Hanrahan, whereas she thought he should take an equal share. The project would be a mildly expensive one, he thought. Costs were likely to be close to $8,000, but he thought 90 copies could be sold for $240 to create a net profit of around $10,000. (In the end Alec prevailed and Hanrahan received 60 per cent. And although costs rose, their earnings were to be four times Alec's original estimate.)[11]

Another unresolved issue was the question of whether the book would be just linocuts or would incorporate some sort of text, either commenting on each print or linking them. Alec completely deferred to Hanrahan on this issue, simply asking questions as the project evolved. He liked her explanation of the genesis of the first batch of five prints, and suggested a brief preface along the same lines, especially if the prints had titles only with no further explanation: 'the book could be simply entitled Twelve Linocuts'.

Early in 1989 he sent Hanrahan proofs of one linocut, 'Girl with Birds'. He mounted the lino on well-seasoned 7-ply blocks to bring it up to type-height, using double-sided tape, and was a little nervous, 'never having attempted an image of this size before!'[12] He was reasonably happy with the results. He pulled the first proofs on damp Aquarelle Arches satine paper, but he also tried the softer Velin Arches and in the end opted for the latter 'which I know from experience behaves well after dampening'.

> *The slightly textured surface of this sheet is more sympathetic to look at, and the softer feel is more sympathetic too … Of course, the dampening process is a chore, but I think it just has to be regarded as part of the printing cycle.*

He used a Van Son rubber-based black ink, with a little reducer, and Hanrahan approved both it and the Velin Arches paper. She finished the final linocut in May, part of a burst of productivity she described in her diary as 'a flowering of my printmaking'.[13] By now the two couples had become friends. Hanrahan and Steele came to Canberra in March, visiting the National Gallery exhibition *Prints and Australia: Pre-Settlement to*

Present, in which she was represented. 'Last night we had such a nice evening with Alec and Rosemary,' she recorded in her diary:

> *He is lovely and so is she. He liked the line blocks so much. His favourite of the ones I took out was 'Cat and the Sun' ... Rosemary has lost the sight in her right eye. She does not drive a car now. She must rest her eye, and at night she knits long scarves while Alec reads Proust aloud. We had such nice food. The pink wobbly mousse with basil we had before (and you squeeze on lemon juice) and then lovely onion and tomato pie and dish of green beans and almonds and carrots and small potatoes. And then we had stewed apples and cream. They were both so sensitive. We told them all about the Meditation. She is so beautiful and he was so perky and happy with his bow tie.*[14]

Hanrahan was meditating for at least four hours a day as therapy for her cancer. She was a follower of Ainslie Meares, a Melbourne psychiatrist whose pioneering work on the benefits of meditation as a cancer therapy attracted many followers. Although he had died in 1986, Hanrahan continued to see Mrs Vere Langley, who kept his practice going.[15]

Alec's first estimate of how long *Twelve Linocuts* would take to produce had been seven months, of which four months would be on the linocuts alone[16], but overall the project took somewhat longer to complete. He began printing the linocuts on 1 July 1989[17] and completed them in time for Hanrahan to sign them during a visit to Canberra in November. The heavy brayer (roller) he used for hand-inking tired him, so he aimed at about 30 prints a day, although on one occasion set a record of 51.[18] Peter Finlay helped him with make-ready for the first print, which was 'Girl with Birds'.[19]

In the meantime, the nature of *Twelve Linocuts* changed from its original conception as a book. In May, Alec commissioned Helen Wadlington to make two dummies: one as a book and another as a boxed suite of linocuts. Although he still preferred the butterfly book notion, it had been suggested to him that prospective buyers might prefer prints they could hang. (He had been quietly canvassing views on the best selling price, having realised that costs were going to be higher than anticipated.) But it would be Hanrahan's decision:

> *obviously we want to produce something that will sell, but I suppose the main question should be what is best for the work. As you are the creator of the work, I think the ultimate decision should be yours.*[20]

Hanrahan had been planning the sequence of prints, and for now still preferred the book.[21] A boxed set would require every print to be titled, signed and numbered, and might be more expensive to produce, Alec agreed. But after seeing both dummies and consulting with Canberra gallerist and art curator Helen Maxwell, who had recently hosted a show of Hanrahan's work at her gallery aGOG (Australian Girls' Own Gallery), he changed his mind. The scarlet and black canvas-covered box looked handsome and would allow a heavier weight of paper, 250 gsm instead of 160 gsm. 'Against the book is the fact that it does not open and close with quite the ease that I had hoped,' he wrote, perhaps mindful of this issue in some of his earliest productions. Although she liked the book, Maxwell thought the box was more practical and likely to sell. She suggested it could be priced higher, as each print on its own might be resold by some dealers for $200. And Hanrahan agreed, once she had seen both dummies. The book looked fragile, given the size and weight of its pages, and she preferred the heavier paper for the prints. She left the question of pricing completely up to Alec, as he would be the person responsible for sales.[22]

Given Alec's passion for book production, this decision might appear to be unexpected. He did not conceive of himself as a printmaker, after all. But he was prepared to let the project grow as its creator wished it to, and was above all by now deeply appreciative of Hanrahan's art and happy to trust her judgement. Much later, while promoting sales of *Twelve Linocuts*, he discussed the prints with Hanrahan in terms that tell of his engagement with them while also suggesting they remained a little mysterious to him:

> *It is interesting that so many friends and others to whom I have shown the inspection set have commented on the European-ness of some of the imagery, and an underlying folk element in the work generally. They ask me how this got into the consciousness of a girl growing up in Adelaide, and I am at a loss for an answer. Roger Butler told me that he thought that elements of folk art (this is over-simplifying him) are the same wherever they occur, so why should Adelaide be different from Eastern Europe or elsewhere. What do you say to this?*[23]

'About the "folk element"—though I never think of it as this in my own work. I agree with what Roger Butler says,' Hanrahan replied.

> *To me it's something that comes from inside the person, not from outside influences, so of course it can occur anywhere in the world. I don't really like to analyse it, because then I become self-conscious + the image hardens up. I seem to work in 2 styles anyway with 2 separate*

> *viewpoints. When I was at Art Sch[ool] in London I can remember worrying about the split, but now I just accept it. It seems quite natural—there are so many viewpoints in a single novel.*[24]

Another thing that changed once printing began was the size of the edition. He started out with 120 in his mind and printed 129 copies of 'Girl with Birds' to allow for a few extra artist proofs. But the possibility of a higher price also suggested a smaller edition, perhaps of 100, with 80 for sale. Hanrahan agreed. Her note arrived as he was printing 'Lovers with a Bird', so he stopped forthwith, at 121. 'I loved printing that cut,' he told her:

> *it is one of my favourites. There is a marvellous oneness about the composite framed by the girl's hair. I do like that, and the look of innocence and surprise on the lovers' faces, and the way that the tail feathers of the bird seem to caress her breast. It is a very beautiful and tender image—and a technical marvel too, I would say.*

And he chose it as one of the illustrations in his prospectus for *Twelve Linocuts*. Later impressions were a little over 100.[25]

The next print, 'Tiger Lady', gave him a little trouble, with a tiny break in the lino: 'about an eighth of an inch of a piece of wavy ground between the tiger's front and back legs just broke off. However it is a flaw that will pass unnoticed, I am sure of that.' A further variation was a brief cessation of dampening, after completing 'Girl with Birds', as he could not see any difference in the result once the paper had dried. With 'Butterfly Hunter' he reverted to dampening. 'When there are solids, it seems just a little easier to print after all. The paper is just a bit more receptive.'

'Acrobat' turned out rather lighter than Hanrahan's proof: 'the edition as printed is somewhat lighter and more airy, though everything is there that should be and there is no loss of detail. I think it looks better now, and believe you will agree,' he told Hanrahan, somewhat belatedly offering her a set of what he had printed to date. But she had complete trust in him: 'I am sure an airy Acrobat is much better than the dark one,' she replied. There was no need to send a set—she would look at them when she visited Canberra. This visit evidently did reveal a minor problem, possibly with the final print, 'Autumn', which had more large black areas than the others and about which Bolton had some trepidation before printing. This was a small amount of spotting that he had overlooked. 'It has come home to me that I don't see as acutely as I used to! I thought everything was OK.'[26]

With printing underway, the major unresolved matter was the pricing and distribution of the linocuts. Hanrahan gave him details of galleries that had handled her works, some of which Alec visited to take soundings, mostly in Sydney. He sought further advice from Sam Ure Smith, who suggested a price of $1,250 might be more realistic than $1,500, given the state of the economy, with a pre-publication offer of $1,000. By this stage total outgoings looked to be in the vicinity of $12,000, including rather more on advertising than usual, but they would not have to sell many sets to recover this. 'Of course, these calculations do not allow anything for your work, and mine, which between us would add up to an astronomical amount; but I believe—hope—that all that will be well repaid,' he told Hanrahan.[27]

In the end he settled on a recommended retail price of $950, less one third to commercial galleries and booksellers, and a pre-publication price (including to public institutions) of $800. Standing-order customers could pay this off in four quarterly instalments.[28] A pre-publication price under $1,000 had been advised by Hanrahan and Steele, who also suggested he might have to consider sending sets to commercial galleries on consignment rather than expecting up-front sales. They too worked hard to promote the work, visiting galleries that they had experience with, and passed on the expectation of such galleries that the suite would be advertised in local media as well as nationally.[29]

Hanrahan worried about the prospect of low sales and the extent of Alec's outlay in advance, although she was also relieved when it was agreed that there would be no exhibitions of the suite to promote it.[30] Still in ill health, at times low in spirits, she needed to guard her time carefully if she was to continue working. But she remained committed to the project, reporting in September that she had visited Rosemary Sorensen, editor of *Australian Book Review*, who wanted to feature 'Girl with Birds' on the cover of its November issue.[31] It was in fact to be a Hanrahan issue of this influential journal. Alec agreed to place a small ad there because it gave so much attention to her work, although he thought it was not aimed at Brindabella's target market. Five articles on Hanrahan, including an interview with her by Sorensen, dominated the *ABR* for November 1989, which was also extensively illustrated with her artworks.[32] He also placed a small notice in the *Australian Financial Review*, partly because 'it is read by the monied classes (if that is the right description), some members of which seem to have investing/collecting interests'.[33]

Alec reverted to four pages for his prospectus for *Twelve*

Linocuts. The cover again featured 'Girl with Birds', by now a favourite of his, and one that he speculated might be, consciously or unconsciously, a self-portrait. 'I can remember making the original drawing for Girl with a Bird on her Head—back in 1960,' Hanrahan replied:

> *I jumped out of bed one night, and used my cocker spaniel's drinking water to dip my brush into! Poor Tinker would have been there too, getting in the way of my inspiration in the sleep-out. It probably does look a bit like me—though not intentionally. I still have the drawing and the lithograph I made from it.*

He included a photograph of the artist, something he only did once again, with Helen Ogilvie's *Wood Engravings*. Faced by a request from one gallery for 600 copies of the prospectus for its own mailing list and wanting to get it out before he had finished printing the linocuts, he had 1,500 copies of the prospectus printed offset by a local printer, 500 with full details and 1,000 with details of the recommended retail price only for use by resellers, and began mailing it out in late November 1989. Pre-publication orders came rapidly –18 within a little over a week, most from galleries and booksellers—and he felt confident enough to decide that anybody asking for sets on consignment would be told their order would be filled last.

Alec had never worried about getting a decent number of orders for *Twelve Linocuts*. Indeed, he had departed from his normal practice in costing a book because of this. Usually he estimated his costs, added ten per cent or so as a notional overhead cost, and then worked out a unit cost price that was then the basis of a sale price.

> *With this project I am disregarding the overheads component, because the selling price is clearly so much greater than the actual costs. I am just considering that this is an art object and that it is different.*[34]

(Although neither approach made any real effort to cost the time involved in engraving and then printing the works. As he had said to Hanrahan, if that was properly costed the portfolio would be astronomically expensive.)

When Hanrahan visited Canberra in November to sign the linocuts there was talk of a new book. Alec later recalled that he had wanted to do another book with Hanrahan, that she had initially refused, and then had thought better of it a few days later.[35] Her diary suggests that she was thinking of a 'book of poetic bits from the diaries' when in Canberra. Her diary entry for 13 November 1989 records her impressions:

> *Always on proper behaviour with Alec and Rosemary. Their son Ian was home on holiday from the Sydney Opera Orchestra. He plays the viola, lives at Glebe, is a Scorpio. Very reserved. Proper people. When I sit there signing at the table with the rug on it I feel like giggling, saying something coarse. But we are ladies and gentlemen. They are classical. Alec liked the relief etching of 'Flora'. I think of a book of poetic bits from the diaries. Poppies ...*
>
> *And sometimes Alec is a Brontë clergyman with strange twisted expressions on his face. Rosemary—tall, gliding walk—remembering days at Angus & Robertson with Slessor and Eve Langley and all the rest. The fan Thea [Proctor] gave them as a wedding present in the passage. Alec in a pink shirt sitting opposite as I keep signing …*

I feel interested in the new Alec project. One of the sections could be on Frida Kahlo's dresses. Bits from my diary—still images, calm …

Both so nice. Talked to Rosemary about Sylvia Plath … To Alec's workroom and I see the type he will set the introduction to my prints in. Has to work out how to pack them now … R. is a very beautiful woman—that sounds queer written—as set as a jelly. Hair piled up grey, a little girl smile, shy. Tall … Alec looks like a goblin. Puckish face.[36]

Goblins appear to have been benevolent creatures in Hanrahan's personal spirituality. Caren Florance recalled in a conversation with the author in 2016 that Rosemary later took some exception to these remarks, when Hanrahan's diaries were published after her death, but more than anything else they demonstrate the Boltons' generous hospitality towards and acceptance of a younger person from a very different world, and their ability to meet with her over the work of writing and making art. Alec's likeness to a Brontë clergyman is not something that anybody else has commented on to me, but others do remember a personal trait that she might perhaps have interpreted in this way, of him sometimes turning away from a conversation while deep in thought. There was a certain watchfulness about him, Alan Gould recalls. To which one might add an intense concentration on what one was saying to him, and careful consideration of where that person's thought might be headed, along with restraint in jumping to a conclusion about what they were saying, and the respectful formality which often accompanies true civility. All this is characteristic of a good oral history interviewer, incidentally.

Alec's recollection of this visit highlights Hanrahan's stoical response to her ill health:

> *Barbara was ill over a period of many years, but she was a person who never mentioned being ill and you would really hardly have known that she was. When she came to sign those prints, she and her partner, Jo Steele, they drove up from Melbourne in their station wagon and she came and spent a day signing the prints and I think that she had really driven up lying down in the back of the wagon because it was not comfortable to her to sit up. She was completely self-effacing about those sort of difficulties, signed all these prints, was very happy about it and wrote to me a lot of letters— I've given them all to the National Library. So, that was a terrific collaboration.*[37]

The friendship between these two very different people strengthened as she began work on the autobiographical stories that became *Iris in her Garden*, even while her health worsened. By mid-December she had written six pieces and chosen the title, sometimes taping her recollections for transcription by Jo Steele.[38] But there was more to be done before the portfolio was finished with. Alec and Steele designed a strong carton for posting the portfolio and there was preliminary material to be printed. Meanwhile, Rosemary had been in hospital for an operation, and she and Alec returned from a recuperative week at Jervis Bay to find that her sister Ruth had just had a stroke and was in the Canberra Hospital. 'The illness of Rosemary's sister is grievous, and of course it absorbs us in a number of ways, so that I haven't got anything done lately,' he wrote to Hanrahan.[39] Ruth Dobson died on 14 December.[40] It was another month before Alec finished setting the title and imprint pages, by which time there were 28 advance orders—35 per cent of the sale copies—and the end of January before the rest of the printing was completed and the first 50 boxes made.[41]

The remaining correspondence regarding *Twelve Linocuts* between Hanrahan, Steele and Alec primarily concerns sales of the portfolio. The 80 copies reserved for sale had all been sold by August 1993 (and possibly a good deal earlier). Sales after that were from the sets reserved for artist and printer, or of a handful of unboxed sets. The slow response of the Art Gallery of South Australia drew comment from Hanrahan. It would be worthwhile, she suggested, to stress the historical and autobiographical nature of the portfolio as reflecting her experience of Adelaide in the 1960s in approaching the gallery, but added that they had bought little of her work in recent years. Instead, she had been sorting through her earliest prints with a view to selling them to the National Gallery of Australia after curator Roger Butler had shown interest in them.[42] She and Steele spent a good deal of time pursuing gallery orders, both public and commercial.

Despite his confidence, Alec was just as assiduous in promoting possible sales, in which he was assisted by friends such as the potter Les Blakebrough, who bought a set and offered to show the prospectus to fellow members of the committee responsible for developing the University of Tasmania's art collection.[43] Alec was particularly keen for it to go into public art galleries, offering to delay invoicing until the following financial year in at least one instance[44], and worrying that a possible large overseas order (which did not eventuate) might exhaust supply before the state galleries had all had a chance to purchase. In the end, sets were purchased directly from him only by the National Gallery of Australia and the Art Gallery of NSW, but six regional galleries bought portfolios, all but two of them in Victoria—Bendigo, Ballarat, Warrnambool, Mornington Peninsula, Wagga Wagga and Burnie Art Galleries. He found gallery people '*hard* to deal with, in that they cannot be reached with words on paper', he told Mike Hudson.

> *There is just nil response. The thing has to be held in front of them—I mean, the portfolio with the images inside—and then there is a response and their eyes light up. They must be purely visual and non-verbal people.*[45]

Twelve Linocuts was nonetheless financially highly successful. In August 1994, by which time only a handful of sets remained, costs stood at $13,761.71 and receipts at $52,978.69 (this is actual receipts, as not all invoices were fully paid for). The largest single cost was for Helen Wadlington to make the portfolio boxes, at $45 each.[46] The surplus of $39,216.98 was distributed between artist and printer in the 60:40 proportions Alec had proposed. Because he reported in detail on sales to Hanrahan, and later to Steele, there is a more complete record than usual of who ordered copies—normally he kept a list, but this correspondence adds details of who people were and whether they were buying for themselves or as resellers (and whether they had paid in full or not!). This summary shows that the largest number went to commercial galleries (28), nearly half of these to the Kensington Gallery in Adelaide. Booksellers took almost as many (20), with Brindabella's usual customers accounting for many of these. Public institutions (the art galleries already listed plus the National

Library of Australia, the University of Melbourne, the Australian Defence Force Academy and the State Library of South Australia) took 11 portfolios. Only 15 appear to have been bought by private customers direct from the press, although some other sales may not have been recorded in the documentation available.[47] And Alec donated one of his own reserved sets to the State Library of South Australia, to be used as a prize for exhibition visitors.[48]

Talking about *Twelve Linocuts* with Heather Rusden for the National Library of Australia, Alec highlighted something other than the financial success of the project. 'The collaboration with Barbara was very significant to me,' he said, because the most rewarding facet of his work was the relationships he developed with writers and artists:

> *it is the most satisfying, intensely interesting thing. I have made some good friendships and had many, many really nice experiences working with authors, and also with artists, and finding at the end of the day how pleased they were that the thing turned out as it did.*[49]

28

'Moonlight and water'

Kenneth Slessor, *The Sea Poems of Kenneth Slessor* (1990)

In October 1989, while still printing the Hanrahan linocuts, Alec approached Mike Hudson to see if he was interested in illustrating 'a rather special edition' of the sea poems of Kenneth Slessor (1901–1971), either as wood engravings or linocuts. 'You would be absolutely the right artist for the work and could handle it superbly. And the poems are marvellous—really distinguished stuff, and widely known and loved.'[1] Hudson was interested in principle, although he asked for more detail of format and technical aspects of the proposed work:

> *From memory, Slessor has a dark prosaic undercurrent in his work and my kind of figurative subjects would lend themselves to a chiaroscuro treatment. I can't see me being successful with the Olsen/Klee 'Taking a line for a walk' (or swim in this case) method. Anyway, that sort of*

abstract imagery would compete for space with the text as well as being an uphill task to reproduce effectively.[2]

Next Alec approached Angus & Robertson for permission to use nine Slessor poems, offering a 15 per cent royalty to be shared between artist and copyright owners.[3] Their initial response was positive, so planning began in earnest.[4]

Alec had long admired Slessor's writing and had been his editorial assistant on the literary journal *Southerly* in 1956. (*Southerly* was published by Angus & Robertson at that time, although Alec apparently did the work voluntarily rather than as part of his employment.) 'Slessor's work was not printed with the distinction it deserved in his own lifetime,' he said, 'and although he once said he did not like illustrated books I think he would have appreciated this one.'[5] He expanded on this in the last session of his oral history interview with Heather Rusden for the National Library, just days before his death. Slessor was not an easy person to get to know, he recalled: 'he was a very reticent, monosyllabic sort of person … But he was a very interesting editor to work for. His editing of copy was remarkable I thought, he seemed to make very few alterations to things and yet he brought them to a higher level'.[6]

Apart from the tribute to Slessor, there are parallels to Alec's own story in this book. Like Slessor, he loved Sydney Harbour, and the poems are, above all, about Sydney Harbour. All apart from 'Undine' (1924) were first published in Sydney in the 1930s and 1940s, the years of Alec's own upbringing in that city, which were also the years of Slessor's maturity as a poet. Several first appeared in Slessor's collection *One Hundred Poems 1919–1939* (1944), published when Alec himself went to sea.

Coincidentally, two were first published in book form by Sydney-based private presses: 'Undine' in *Thief of the Moon* (The Hand-Press of J.T. Kirtley, 1924) and 'Five Visions of Captain Cook' in *Trio* (Sunnybrook Press, 1931). On the other hand, 'Passenger by "Greycliffe"', about a terrible ferry disaster on Sydney Harbour, had not reappeared at all after its first publication in *Smith's Weekly* in 1927.[7]

One should perhaps not make too much of all this; he said later it was Dennis Haskell who made the selection of the poems to fit the book's proposed maritime theme. The book may only incidentally mirror Alec's own formative years, although one recalls the poetry he himself wrote as a young man, and early correspondence before Haskell comes into the picture mentions all the poems selected apart from 'Undine' and 'Passenger by "Greycliffe"'. Be that as it may, it is also one of the few Brindabella books Alec signed as its printer, and he later judged it to be his best book. As a rule he preferred not to sign his books, feeling that his name printed on the colophon page was sufficient.

> *I'm pleased enough to do that, but I wouldn't want my name too prominently. I feel that I'm an agent who's brought the various possibilities together to achieve the book.*[8]

In this case it was his own notion to group Slessor's sea poems, which had never been done before, and he substituted for the deceased author with his own initials. And some time after *Sea Poems* appeared, Alec reflected on his memories of Sydney Harbour in words that underscore his sense of personal connection to the book, in a letter to the journalist Ian Healy.

Healy had interviewed him for a lengthy biographical piece that appears never to have been published.

> *Years of living on the Harbour and travelling by ferry influenced me a lot. The life of the port was intensely interesting to me. I knew all the ships that were regular visitors. I was familiar with the P&O and Orient ships, the Blue Funnel steamers, and the Burns Philp island traders, etc. The Harbour had much more working life in the 1930s than it does today, not only in shipping but in the variety of work boats that plied the waterways. For instance, Scandinavian timber carriers would unload logs directly into the water of Snails Bay, and long rafts of lashed logs would be towed by little steam tugs to the timber yards above Gladesville, sometimes, if they were against the tide, scarcely seeming to make way. I used to read the shipping notices and was always aware of the tides. I was an apprentice to [Slessor's] Captain Dobbin, I suppose.*[9]

His love of Sydney Harbour is also apparent in a diary entry written in 1958, long before his life as a printer began, along with his acuity as an observer. He was stopped in traffic at the Gladesville Bridge over the Parramatta River, waiting for it to open for a ferry. It was still the old low-level swing bridge of his childhood; a year later construction began of its high single-arch replacement, opened in 1964. In the passage that follows, 'V.J.' refers to a Vaucluse Junior, a classic Australian wooden sailing dinghy of the 1930s.

> *I had the luxury of a long look down river towards Ferry Street—a thing I never as a rule get, except furtively out of the corner of my eye while driving along … It was a clear warm afternoon, the sky pale blue with*

> *a few puffs of cloud about: the sort of afternoon that belongs to summer, yet carries a hint of colder days to come. The water was blue too, but in the way that muddy water looks blue; after a lot of rain (now some days past) there was still a hint of chocolate in the water's colour seen close at hand. There was a V.J. sailing near the bridge. Two enormous tugs lay at permanent anchor off Huntley's Point, and dominating the horizon over Hunters Hill were the transmitting masts of ABN and ATN; but what struck me greatly was that this scene, except for the tugs and the masts, fell upon my eye exactly as it used to do 20 years ago; I mean it filled me with the same rather poignant love that I used to feel for just that stretch of water and that shape of waterfront, of hills and houses. Thus one recaptures the past, or seems to. But it is only a momentary business. The Kameruka is soon through the bridge, and the halted procession of cars is soon jumping into life again and moving forward; and so one returns to present responsibilities. Faintly eddying in the mind for a few moments is a feeling of incredulity that so much time should actually separate one from the recalled past that a moment ago seemed so immediate; and regret, too, that the past is past.*[10]

Haskell, a poet and academic at the University of Western Australia, had a longstanding interest in Slessor and was in Canberra on a Harold White Fellowship at the National Library. He was recruited for the project probably in early March 1990, by which time there was already agreement with Hudson on which poems would be illustrated. His introduction expertly and succinctly (he was allowed one leaf) pulls the poems together.[11] Alec was particularly grateful for his discovery of 'Passenger by "Greycliffe"': 'it casts a shadow that ends in Five Bells,' he said. Haskell then found a variant in the typescript in Slessor's papers at the National

Library, and there was some discussion of the setting of the last stanza. Alec called on his editorial and printing skills to conclude:

> *Further reflection confirms my belief that the last stanza is of four lines, and that the third line is 'Who blows his frozen breath? Who's there? Who's there?' because this preserves the five-stress rhythm of the preceding lines. The double indentation of the second 'Who's there?' in Smith's Weekly is surely only a consequence of the measure (width) of the poem allowed in the paper.*[12]

Alec hand-set the book in his favourite typeface, using a larger page size than ever before (or after: it is his tallest book). 'I had earlier used 12 point Baskerville in formats that were smaller and it looked a bit excessive, but it seemed just right in that book and I was very happy with the look of that book, and indeed how it turned out altogether.'[13] He was finding 'a lot of enigmatic lines in Slessor's work of which I was not fully conscious until I came to brood over them as I hand-set them,' he told Barbara Hanrahan.

> *Hand-setting is a severe test of quality and clarity. It must be that I am dumb, but there are quite a lot of lines in Slessor that remain opaque to me. But the richness of so much else is truly rewarding.*[14]

'Opaque' was a word he had used before, to describe some of Philip Hodgins' poems.

Mike Hudson's first response to the Slessor suggestion had raised the question of the '*mise-en-page* aspect' of the book—that is, where the illustrations would appear and how they would interact with the text: 'a strategy of how many and where they'll fall ought to be arrived at'. First he would look at the poems selected to see which he thought he could illustrate, and if there was a fixed sequence there might have to be some compromise on his part to avoid them bunching up.[15] Although there was no fixed sequence for the poems, Alec replied, he had some ideas of possible illustrations—although he also assured Hudson they were only tentative suggestions. His proposals, and the way Hudson responded to them, say much about the sensibilities of both men, and their ability to work together. Hudson accepted most of Alec's suggestions and then added his own touches, lifting them to new heights and creating a coherent assemblage that, taken as a whole, brilliantly emphasises the unity of the poetic selection. Above all, from the very beginning Hudson had seen the poem 'Five Bells' as being 'more about the nature of time passing than anything else', and this theme runs through the whole book, parallel to and underpinning its maritime concerns with an understanding of the importance of time to navigation in the era before the invention of GPS technology.

Alec's suggestion for the title-page was 'the ever-restless sea, perhaps by moonlight, and without any human presence'. Hudson's response was a view of the sea by moonlight, through a window—with a silhouette of the head and shoulders of an observer, who is also looking out through the window to the moon and the sea. For 'Captain Dobbin', Alec thought of the harbour seen through a window: Hudson's marvellous engraving has the captain, holding a book, reflected in the window, which looks out over the harbour, with a picket fence between his suburban villa and the scene. He was trying to suggest enclosure, containment, even claustrophobia, he told Alec. 'The Atlas' suggested to Alec 'a cartographic fancy such as one finds in cartouches on old maps'. Hudson engraved a cheerful mermaid, holding a mirror. 'Five Visions of Captain Cook' suggested to Alec two images, perhaps one the sea from the deck of the *Endeavour*, 'and the other as arising from the chronometer poem'. Hudson combined these ideas in a complex view across the sea to *Endeavour*'s outline, with a clock in the background and a sand-glass in the foreground—with another vessel inside, on the sand of the lower bowl. He saw this as a 'metaphor for old time scale rendered useless by the setting sun of the new-age chronometer'. The somewhat cryptic tailpiece to the poem is of a decanter and five glasses, one upside down and with a spill of liquor—or is it blood? 'Somewhere in the murky greyness of my memory I seem to remember an old naval (military?) tradition of upending a lost comrade's drinking vessel, signifying his absence from the toast,' Hudson wrote. 'Metempsychosis' is of the '1920s–1930s period. I think of this as having a more human and even humorous dimension than other poems in the series,' Alec wrote, and we are presented with John Benbow's tattooed shoulder reflected in a boarding-house mirror and (someone else's?) hand holding a glass, a turf guide on the dressing table, the Holy Virgin in a frame on the wall, and Sydney Harbour again through the window—a playful assembly of elements from the poem. They are 'mundane "landlubber" objects and the man is only seen as a fragmentary reflection, suggesting (I hope) the rather poor trade that results when sailors get shore-bound', Hudson wrote.

'And finally there is a masterpiece, "Five Bells"'—'a dark and mysterious poem' to Alec.

I would be happy for this subject to be treated as indirectly or abstractly as you wished. Otherwise the last stanza might suggest an image? To a lot of people this is a rather sacred poem. I feel like that about it too, without being able to say quite why.[16]

Hudson brings together the sea, moonlight, a vast clock, harbour buoys, a ferry, the Sydney Harbour Bridge and the drowning face and body of Slessor's friend Joe Lynch. One buoy doubles as an hour hand for the clock, marking 10.30 pm—five bells of the first watch, in the old manner of marking shipboard time by striking the ship's bell every half hour, originally with the passage of time measured by a sand glass. It is an extraordinary work, as strong and as compelling as the poem it illustrates. That the bridge had not been completed when Joe Lynch drowned in 1927 is of little significance; perhaps it should be read as a promise of the bridge to come, which might have prevented the death (Lynch was on his way to Mosman when he went overboard).[17]

The unity of the illustrations is underscored by Hudson's title-page vignette. It prefigures the illustration for 'Five Bells', foreshadowing it but with less complexity, as Alec suggested in February. He was delighted with the eventual drawing: 'the man with the domed head is even a bit like Slessor (I knew him)!', as he was with the entire suite:

Thank you very much indeed for the engravings. They are superb. You have done a wonderful job. Five Bells is a triumph, and Captain Dobbin has added power in this version. I like all the others too … I am most grateful for all your trouble.[18]

Alec printed 25 additional sets of three engravings for sale as separate prints on heavyweight Arches 88 paper, as well as extra copies for himself and the artist. They were 'Five Visions of Captain Cook', 'Captain Dobbin' and 'Five Bells', numbered and signed by Hudson and available either as a set for $270 or individually for $75 (for the first two) and $120 for 'Five Bells'. The book itself was printed on Mohawk Letterpress, which Alec found to be not as sympathetic to engravings as he would have liked,[19] but of which he still had a large stock bought in hope of doing the Kirtley facsimile.

Alec expressed some doubts about including 'Five Bells' in the edition, as it alone was not printed by him from the wood.[20] Jadwiga Jarvis recalls that this was because the large woodblock used for this work (195 x 127 millimetres) had slightly warped, and Alec could not print it successfully. Hudson then printed a proof, from which Alec had a line block made.[21] Hudson had no reservations, pointing out that he had done so much over-engraving of the line block to get it right that it was 'virtually a new engraving'.

> *Whether the images are seen as simply illustrations or whether they are seen as the exclusive result of an arcane craft, or a combination of both I leave to your predilection. Suffice to say I'm glad to have been able to go some way to support the Brindabella cause and hope we can all earn a buck out of it (incident[al]ly, of course).*[22]

Neither the colophon nor the book's prospectus mentions this small discrepancy, nor does the prospectus for the separate edition of engravings.[23]

Printing of *Sea Poems* began on 24 April 1990[24] and was half done by the end of May 1990, but time taken to settle Ruth Dobson's estate, of which he was an executor, somewhat delayed its completion. (At this time he was also briefly busy with valuations for the National Library of a collection of Blubber Head Press papers and those of R.F. Brissenden.[25]) He sent sheets of the proposed paper to Helen Wadlington for a dummy binding also in April, before he started printing: 'moonlight and water are the things to think of in association with these poems, above everything else,' he told her. 'They will come through as important elements of the engravings.' He thought a heavier board than she had used in *Percival Serle* would be appropriate: something close to her binding for *Occasions of Birds*. Subsequent discussions decided on paste paper sides with quarter leather, although she initially demurred at a proposal to use kangaroo leather, because she objected to the way they were killed, and suggested European goatskin. Alec accepted this[26], but Wadlington then appears to have found a source of kangaroo leather she was comfortable with. After some slightly awkward discussions about the cost of the binding, quarter leather with paste paper sides was settled on, with a dark blue paper to give 'a watery effect' and at Wadlington's proposed unit cost of $27.20.[27] The design of her paste paper sides, in a cerulean blue with yellow accents, swirls like waves around what could be wharf piles. It is highly effective, and the Mylar wrapping that had also been used on *The Idyll Wheel* accentuates it. Sheets went for binding on 8 October 1990.[28]

The cost of the binding prompted Alec to set a recommended retail price of $85 for *Sea Poems*, his highest for a book to date. At that figure, the copyright fee payable to Angus

& Robertson on the 220 copies for sale was $1,202.50 and he paid an equivalent amount to the illustrator.[29] This, plus binding at $6,360, was the major cost of the book. Overall, including overheads of 12.5 per cent, he projected costs of $12,108 and a potential profit of $1,385.90. He briefly considered a final selling price of $90 a copy, which he calculated would increase his profit by a little over $600, and pay him a fraction more for his overheads, but decided against it.[30] These calculations exclude sales of the print portfolios, which at $270 a set could bring in up to $6,750, if all were direct sales. He offered 80 per cent of the net proceeds to Hudson.[31] Sales of the prints were slow. It is difficult to assess how much they made in the end, but Alec's notes suggest that perhaps as late as 1992 only half the edition had been sold, mostly through booksellers.

The transactions with Hudson over the Slessor prints later prompted his most complete statement of the monetary aims of his press:

> *I … sometimes think when I am sending out a book that I need assistance with the invoicing and packing; but there is no way in which help like all that can be afforded. When I am costing a book, I factor in a notional figure for overheads—i.e., my own labour, heating and lighting, etc.—but I have never been game to reckon it up afterwards in terms of dollars per hour. Nor indeed have I ever reckoned up the hours I spend on any project. If I did, it would probably all result in something like the $3 per hour that you have arrived at. I am luckier perhaps than you, in that I have income from investments and an annuity purchased with what I retired [on] from the National Library; but that income has dwindled with the big reductions in interest rates,*

> *and I am in the position of needing a return from the press. When I started the press, it was all for love; but now I am interested in money as well as love. I try not to worry too much about these things, but to concentrate on achieving the best possible printed result.*[32]

In contrast to the prints, *Sea Poems* sold quickly. When he analysed its sales in May 1992, six months after publication, 85 per cent of the total edition of 240 had gone. Even better, 82 had sold at full price, while 63 copies had gone to booksellers at a one third discount. Subscribers, who now received a 12.5 per cent discount, took 58 copies. At that stage his total return was $14,853, with only 17 of the 220 copies for sale remaining in stock.[33] This compares favourably with his earlier projection, and must reflect these higher than usual direct sales at full price.

The influential critic Don Anderson's enthusiastic advance notice for the book in *The Sydney Morning Herald* possibly helped. 'Slessor is the poet-laureate of Sydney Harbour,' Anderson wrote, in a wide-ranging piece that cited Ezra Pound, Homer and Walter Benjamin in considering the work of Alec Bolton and Rosemary Dobson as Australian craftspeople. Anderson had himself had a brief experience of printing, working with Philip Roberts on one of the Island Press' Poet's Choice volumes at Bundeena: 'the satisfaction of having the press "bite" the right impression into the paper is with me still'.[34] He had previously bought *The Idyll Wheel* and was familiar with earlier Brindabella titles such those by John Shaw Neilson, Geoff Page, Elizabeth Riddell and Christina Stead (mentioned in his typescript of the column but excised by an editor[35]), thought that the Murray was beautiful and the Slessor volume too would be handsome.

The article included Hudson's title-page vignette and, more prosaically but just as important, contact details for the press. As Alec said to Mike Hudson during early correspondence over this book, 'there is nothing more dispiriting all round when a bookseller answers an inquirer with "publisher not known"'. Apropos of which, he had then urged Wayzgoose to follow his own practice of applying for an ISBN so that librarians and booksellers would know how to locate the press after seeing reviews of its books. He had used an ISBN ever since *Starting From Central Station* (1973), and now also sent new title cards to the *Australian Bookseller & Publisher*:

> *which gets a book a listing on their microfiche Australian Books in Print, and gets you and your address a listing too. As this is a sort of Bible in the book trade, it means that virtually any bookseller can find you. I had a couple of newspaper reviews for the Les Murray book following which I got orders from booksellers in outlandish places who would never have heard of me by any stretch of the imagination, but who obviously were approached by Murray fans and who were able to locate me.*[36]

Hudson disagreed, owing to a dislike for middlemen in principle, and pointing out that he and his partner Jadwiga Jarvis 'have enough problems with collectors without getting involved with recalcitrant booksellers (P. Tinslay being the exception)'.[37] But he maintained his high regard for the press. As Jarvis puts it:

> *Mike spent the winter of 1990 on the exacting task of engraving some powerful images for Alec Bolton's The Sea Poems of Kenneth Slessor*

> *(Officina Brindabella, Canberra 1990). Following their happy collaboration on Palace with Several Sides, Brindabella emerged as the only Australian press to whose publications he was happy to contribute. The Slessor book pleased both artist and printer.*[38]

Sea Poems appears to have had no further reviews in the Australian media. Although not one of the hardest or most expensive Brindabella titles to find, it is consistently scarce on the market. Alec gave a copy to John Randle, the English printer he most admired, whom he saw while he and Rosemary visited Lissant (working on her doctorate in Manchester) for a fortnight in April 1991.[39] It was a book to be proud of. The same journey to Europe provided an opportunity to meet John Crombie of Kickshaws, an innovative and peripatetic private press established by Crombie and Sheila Bourne in France in 1979. Rosemary had met them previously, and they evidently had a stimulating visit, although Crombie later wrote that he had not shown Alec any of his books as he had been so frustrated at the state of his current printing project![40]

29

'I think the experiment is a success'

Barbara Hanrahan, *Iris in Her Garden* (1991)

The final partnership between Alec Bolton and Barbara Hanrahan, *Iris in Her Garden*, developed out of conversations in late 1989 as *Twelve Linocuts* was being printed. To begin with they discussed a book based on extracts from her diaries, accompanied by relief etchings, and Hanrahan brought a plate of one of these for proofing when she visited Canberra to sign *Twelve Linocuts*.[1] However, after reading through her diaries Hanrahan decided they were not really suitable:

> *to be of interest you need all the personal bits, + it's too soon for that! And it would be a terrible task, anyway, plucking out bits here + there + weaving them into some sort of whole.*

But she did have a group of autobiographical stories based on her childhood and her family that she proposed as an alternative. Three of them had been published before, but two of these were in obscure publications, and she was rewriting them anyway. Another had previously been published only in an anthology for children, and the last was new. Eventually they might all be included in a larger collection to be published by the University of Queensland Press (her usual publisher).

> *They have a 'poetic' (can't think of another word), fantastic tone and I think would suit accompanying relief etchings. I'd been wanting to rework these pieces for years, so your interest pushed me into it (though none of them are finished yet).*[2]

Alec later recalled that the proposal to work on another book had initially come from him, and that she had turned it down at first, changing her mind shortly afterwards.[3] This may be so, but Hanrahan's diary and her correspondence suggest considerable interest in publishing another book with Alec from the very start.[4] It was also at her suggestion that the book was illustrated with relief etchings, because injuries from a recent street accident had left her without the strength to engrave.[5] In the relief etching process, instead of directly engraving a zinc, copper or aluminium plate with an engraving tool (which requires considerable strength), the plate is covered with an acid-resistant ground through which the artist draws with an etching needle. This exposes parts of the plate, which then goes into an acid bath to bite into the exposed areas. 'Usually it would be printed intaglio,' Hanrahan explained to Alec, 'but if the line is deep enough (if it's left in the acid long enough) it works as a relief print.' It was almost impossible to stop small blemishes from occurring where a wax-based ground had broken down, she added, so she planned to use a stronger ground based on stop-out varnish instead.[6] Using a hard roller to roll the ink onto the surface of the plate only, thus not wiping the ink into the etching lines, creates a relief print in which the incised lines print white on a solid background.[7] It would once again be a new technique for Alec to master, but Jo Steele was confident that the roller on his press would be appropriate for the job.[8]

Alec was immediately enthusiastic about the change of direction and Hanrahan's proposed title of *Iris in Her Garden* (the name of one of her new stories), finding time to write a quick note in the midst of the upset caused by the death of Ruth Dobson.[9] Hanrahan kept on working on the stories through January and February 1990, keeping him informed of their progress, both rewriting and also selecting those that best suited the mood of the collection as a whole.[10] She would not be able to start on the relief etchings for some months, owing to pressure of other work and a short closure of the Victorian Print Workshop (later the Australian Print Workshop), she told Alec.[11] There was no hint in her letters to him of her growing ill health at this time. Rather, they discussed the page size and *mise en page* of the works: Alec's initial thought was of a page size of $8\frac{1}{2}$ x $5\frac{1}{4}$ inches, with a type area 6 x $3\frac{1}{2}$ inches—very close to what eventuated, and which she was happy with.[12] All depended on his trial printing, and in March 1990, before he began printing Slessor and little over a month after the final piece of printing for *Twelve Linocuts* (the label for the portfolio), he finally was able to proof the plate she had left for trial in November.[13] 'I think the experiment is a success,' he reported: there were some minor blemishes, but some of these were in her own proof too.

> *I get a sort of message from this exercise, which is that fine faint images are easier to 'read' in darker than in lighter colours. I had been thinking that it might be good to have two alternating colours according to whether they fell on the first or second side of each sheet and was vaguely contemplating lilac and sage green'.*[14]

And so by April, Hanrahan and Steele were 'working on small Alec stories' plates', as she recorded in her diary:

> *Jo does it, too, because he is in charge of the little acid baths on the balcony. In various plastic boxes, and they all have lids and there are plastic washing-out bowls filled with water. Jo does the proof-printing, I do the inking up. Most of them look very good.*[15]

To begin with Hanrahan had contemplated doing eight or so full-page illustrations, one opposite the beginning of each of her eight stories[16], but Alec suggested a different direction, with many more illustrations in vignette form. He sent her a photocopy of a page from the Folio Society edition of Stevenson's *Travels with a Donkey*, illustrated by Edward Ardizzone, as a possible model.

> *This is of course from a line drawing. I don't know if the vignetted effect would work with an image in reverse, which is what we contemplate with the relief etchings. It might not be possible to cut a plate to give this casual-looking effect. Anyway, it was just an idea for an experiment.*[17]

And there are similarities between the two books, although the impact of Hanrahan's vignettes, as Alec anticipated, is much bolder. The page sizes are quite similar, although the text block is shorter in *Iris in Her Garden*, and the type sizes too are close (10 point Caledonia in *Iris*, 11 on 13 point Monotype Bell for *Travels with a Donkey*). Above all, the profusion of illustrations is similar. There are 22 in the 59 pages of *Iris in Her Garden*, plus one on the cover and another on the colophon page. Seventeen of them are vignettes and six full-page, some of the vignettes printed in deep green and burnt orange, darker colours having been suggested by Hanrahan in response to Alec's lilac and green, but most in Hanrahan's preferred black. There is an exuberance of illustration in the book, which exceeds that of any other Brindabella book except for *Some Poems of Shaw Neilson*.

Knowledge of Hanrahan's circumstances at the time makes even more poignant an awareness of the themes of mortality and letting go that run through both her stories and her art. By June 1990, when she sent the final draft of the stories and proofs of many of the relief etchings to Alec, she was gravely ill with cancer, although, as her biographer Annette Stewart records, few of her friends knew this.[18] She was in dreadful pain and had difficulty walking by September, although she kept on working on her art and her penultimate novel, *Good Night, Mr Moon*. Stewart suggests she was also still working on the illustrations for *Iris in Her Garden* in early 1991, but apart from a request by Alec for a new etching to use as a label on the front cover in March, suggesting 'the figure of Iris floating above her garden' soon afterwards,[19] the work was essentially completed earlier. (Hanrahan sent three versions of a possible cover etching in May, leaving the choice to Alec.

He selected one of Iris floating above her garden.)

Only now, for the first time in their copious correspondence (apart from the printing of *Iris in Her Garden*, there were regular reports on sales of *Twelve Linocuts* as well as personal news), is there a suggestion of how ill she was, in a letter that mentions she was finding it hard to do the drawings for her new novel because her hand shook so much it made doing the small images difficult. Even so, it was not until July that Alec learned of the difficulty Hanrahan was having with walking, although 'somehow I inferred that all was not well'. She had not wanted to worry him, she replied, writing optimistically of the possibilities of rehabilitation and life in a wheelchair after further treatment. Soon afterwards she underwent massive surgery, to remove half her spinal cord, followed by radiotherapy and chemotherapy. Doggedly, and with incredible courage, she kept on working.[20] 'Barbara was utterly dedicated: a tireless, almost ceaseless worker until the end,' wrote one of her friends. 'I think she would agree that it is the art that makes the artist, and that what is of paramount value is the work that survives.'[21]

Alec loved the Iris stories, and his reception of them says much about the friendship that had grown up between the two as well as his professional skill as an editor:

> *You re-create the world of your childhood with a wonderful effect of truth and simplicity. It goes straight to the heart without ever becoming sentimental or whimsical. Really admirably done. And I do appreciate the very spare language—so much in words of one or two syllables. Not many people can do that. There is a nice balance in the stories, and I like the way you avoid a straight sequential arrangement of the*

> *material. Sad about your father, but he lives again in The Czar. And I feel I know Reece and your grandmother intimately—your grandmother better than your mother perhaps. Your amazing recall of the detail of everyday life comes through very strongly. You and Hal Porter are the winners of that particular prize … I love the etchings—and so does Rosemary. They are so full of life and appropriate to the texts. I feel a weight of melancholy in the full-page for The Czar. You have offered a bewildering range of choice—I make it 27 altogether.*[22]

Although he thought he might have to choose only about 16 of the etchings for printing, as noted he ended up using most of them. He had some concerns about printing the vignetted images, worrying that he might lose ink from the edges (presumably from the mechanical action of the roller, which has to be set at exactly the right height to avoid slurring the leading edge of large solid impressions), but decided to leave selection until he was ready to make up the pages, once the text was typeset. Now that he had all her proofs he also agreed with her that the etchings should be printed in black, although ultimately some of the vignettes were printed in colour.

> *It would be like printing a wood-engraving in colour—perfectly possible, but a waste of the richness that black offers. This relief-etching technique gives an effect not unlike the wood-engravings of Eric Gill.*

He had just finished reading Fiona MacCarthy's biography of Gill, he added: 'admirable book but not to me a very likeable man'.[23] Hanrahan was happy to leave the choice and positioning of prints to him—and agreed that she 'had a peculiar feeling about Eric Gill, too. He had an awful attitude to women, didn't he?', adding that she loved the work of David Jones, the writer and artist who was for many years associated with Gill.[24]

Alec sent the text (including the prospectus) to Bankstown Typesetting in Sydney to be set in 10 point Linotype Caledonia, justified, and specified tight word spacing.[25] Caledonia is a highly successful Linotype face, designed by William Dwiggins in 1938.[26] It is a modern serif face, with straight serifs, unlike the oblique serifs of his beloved Baskerville, with a 'simple, hard-working, feet-on-the-ground quality', in the words of its designer.[27] Although he spoke in positive terms to Hanrahan about the transition to Linotype, stressing that it meant the type was freshly cast for the job[28], it was a major departure from his previous practice. (It's true that he had previously used Linotype for the David Campbell eulogy, but this was not a literary work, and he had wanted to get it printed quickly.)

Typically, having reluctantly embraced the move to Linotype, he specified an excellent book type designed specifically for its production process, and then had the type completely redone at his own cost after the first setting, when the long descenders he had asked for turned out to have been set fractionally short on g, p and q. He had the job reset with short descenders—a comparatively simple task with Linotype setting, as it simply required a change of magazines, but still costly.[29] Then Hanrahan, who loved the choice of Caledonia, found a literal and asked to change some punctuation, meaning he had to get eight lines reset yet again and posted up from Sydney. He apologised to her in case he had sounded 'sharp on the phone over the corrections. It is a bit unnerving dealing with Linotype corrections, especially when mistakes come to light that one has missed oneself'.[30]

He started printing the text in March 1991, and over the next few months printed up to 12 pages a week. He was keen to get the text all printed by early July, he told Hanrahan, as he was feeling a little anxious about the etchings. He planned to begin with the smaller ones, and to have the book completed by October. The first etching was printed on schedule in early July, he reported a little later, although he needed to improve the inking. And although he had only partial knowledge of the difficulties under which Hanrahan was working, he pressed on apace. 'I was surprised and delighted to get your letter from hospital,' he wrote:

> *That was heroism beyond the call of duty! I get some idea from Jo of your problems, which I feel you are conquering by your mental attitude. I am sorry for the pain and inconvenience of it all, but I am glad that your work goes on. I won't embarrass you by telling you how much I admire you; we will stand that over to another day! I am sure you will manage the wheelchair successfully in no time; it will facilitate a lot of things for you.*

A few days later he reported that he was having difficulties with smudges outside the plate area in some of the illustrations, and if he could not solve the problem by grinding down the edges he would get line blocks made. In the end he used line blocks to print three of the etchings, which he mentioned in the work's prospectus: these were 'The Czar with cherub wings' (page 21), the tailpiece for 'Solomon's Little Sister' (page 30) and the tailpiece for 'Iris in Her Garden' (page 59). The blocks were made from Hanrahan's proofs in the case of the first two, and for the last he used a proof of his own, cut round and spotted out.

He had decided against grinding down the edges (where the etching was too shallow to avoid inking) for fear of damaging the plates, he told her.

Iris in Her Garden would be bound in two formats—a decision initially to do with the cost of the book. Although Alec would have preferred to use hard covers, 'an elegant sewn form of binding in paper covers would be cheaper', and the times suggested making the book as cheap as possible. (The Australian economy was in deep recession in the early 1990s, following the stock market crash of 1987, and in common with most OECD economies.) He had sought Hanrahan's views in March 1991: either they could do 220 copies in paper and 30 more expensive ones in quarter leather, perhaps with an extra signed etching; or 210 in paper, 30 cased and 10 in sheets for binders. They decided on the former, and, after a later suggestion by Alec, chose not to include a frontispiece ('the title page will be modest, and I feel that a full facing page of etching would overwhelm it'). The full-page 'Iris' etching originally intended as a frontispiece was used instead as a loose etching to accompany the 30 leather-bound copies. It is not present in the copies in wrappers.[31] Hanrahan was insistent that the loose extra etching must be signed and titled by her, as it was likely to be framed separately; anything else would be unprofessional, she felt.[32] Alec asked Robin Tait to bind both editions. She proposed a Coptic-sewn binding for the paper edition, inserted into non-adhesive folded paper covers (again drawing on the work of Christopher Clarkson as she had for *The Palace with Several Sides*), and recalled having to work in a tremendous hurry because Hanrahan was so ill.[33] She also bound the 30 special copies, in quarter oasis goatskin with cloth sides.

Alec finished printing the last vignette etching on 14 September. By then he had also completed the printing of 30 separate etchings to be included loose with leather-bound copies of *Iris in Her Garden*, and these had been sent to Hanrahan for titling and signing. He had begun negotiations with the University of Queensland Press for a trade edition based on his setting, with all royalties to go to Hanrahan. The two had even discussed a possible sequel, perhaps based on another set of her stories, or a selection made by Hanrahan of works from another Australian writer and illustrated by her.

But by then she was dying; there was a new tumour in her brain. She finished signing the 250 colophon pages of *Iris in Her Garden* (sent to her in sheets, unbound) and the separate prints for the specials (the quarter leather bound edition) on 11 August, while Alec was still printing etchings.[34] He was amazed by the speed with which she did this, but she was racing against death.[35] He finished folding and collating the sections at the end of September and sent her the first advance copy on 8 November.

Jo Steele wrote with her thanks. She was thrilled with it, he wrote: 'we both thank you most sincerely and gratefully for making this exquisite Barbara Hanrahan memento'.[36] Her eyesight had mostly gone by then, but the last thing she ever wrote, he said shortly afterwards, was a barely legible note of thanks beginning with the words 'Dear Alec' which he had rewritten for her.[37] She died on 1 December 1991. Alec flew to Adelaide for the funeral.

The prospectus for *Iris in Her Garden* had been printed in early October, with a short delay during a visit by the Boltons to Vanuatu (where Lissant was working)[38] and posted out shortly afterwards. In it Alec wrote eloquently of the work and its 'new and different glimpses of a childhood in the suburbs, at once tender and piercing … They sparkle with life'. Hanrahan's grandmother Iris is 'the centre of a feminine world', he wrote.[39] 'I have described your home in Ross Street as a feminine world, which was literally true' he had written to Hanrahan when sending her a draft of the prospectus blurb. 'I wonder would Iris have been a feminist had she lived longer or been born later? I just think she might have been; but your mother perhaps not.'[40] Hanrahan loved the description of the book: 'I was so pleased with its sensitivity—with Iris at its centre,' she wrote.[41]

By the time the first copies were bound the paper edition was already half sold, and there had been about 100 orders for the 30 copies in quarter leather.[42] 'It is too soon to say, but with this book we could be close to selling out before publication and before anyone has actually sighted it,' Alec had told Hanrahan. He had had a 'mighty tussle' working out which of the 101 orders for the 30 specials should be met. In the end he cut booksellers down to one copy each, so that special customers such as the State Library of NSW, now a standing-order customer, could get a copy. There were enough sheets left over for ten or twelve paper and four special out-of-series copies to be bound, he also reported, so she would get her author's copies plus full royalties on all the sales.[43]

Nevertheless, he again bought a small display ad in *The Weekend Australian*, describing the book as 'Eight stories of an Adelaide childhood'[44]—'as it gives a wider cross-section of your admirers a chance to know about the book'[45], he said in his last letter to her before she died—and it continued to sell well. His record of the distribution of copies (as usual, every copy enumerated with its recipient named in nearly every case) shows that private collectors appear to make up the largest group of buyers (127), with booksellers adding another 85 purchases. Libraries took 25 and art galleries (mostly Helen Maxwell) 8 copies. The specials, with copies numbered one to 30, went mostly to private buyers, although a handful were allocated to booksellers who had long supported the press such as Kay Craddock, Michael Treloar and the ANU Co-operative Bookshop. Number 30 went as a complimentary copy to the National Gallery of Australia: a typically generous gesture, but one wonders if it was not also to forestall his past experience of them ordering long after an edition was sold out.[46]

The final financial figures for *Iris in Her Garden* do not appear to be extant, but a forecast drawn up in August 1991 projects total costs of $10,822 and receipts of $12,490. The retail prices of both editions were set at levels that would return the press a modest profit of 15.4 per cent: $55 for the paper edition and $120 for the specials. Binding, as usual, was the biggest single cost at nearly $3,000, with a royalty payout projected at $2,715. Typesetting, including half the cost of the hand-set Bodoni type that was used for display, came to $1,671. (This included the cost of resetting the entire work for a second time.) Advertising (one display ad plus mailing the prospectuses) came to $875.[47]

The University of Queensland Press, Hanrahan's usual publisher, published a paperback edition of the book, printed offset but based on sheets of the Brindabella edition, in 1992. Alec (who had suggested the edition in the first place) had the imprint page reset by Bankstown Typesetting for this edition, which differed from the original in reproducing its front cover etching on the rear and substituting on the cover a coloured detail from

Hanrahan's 1977 etching 'Iris in Her Garden', showing Iris as a young girl. Hanrahan had been very happy at the suggestion: the University of Queensland Press had previously suggested the possibility of a similar facsimile of *Some Poems of Shaw Neilson*, she told Alec, but nothing had come of it.[48] The page sizes are slightly smaller than the original, and it varied also in using only black and green for the illustrations, substituting green for Alec's ochre. All royalties went to Hanrahan's estate, Alec asking only for a small payment for his original typesetting. Although a small part of Hanrahan's considerable opus as both author and artist, the work is highly regarded.

Alec also proposed publication of Hanrahan's diaries, saying to her publisher soon after her death 'I know she kept diaries. One day you may get to publish them? I feel that there is a deep spring here that will flow for a long time'.[49] The diaries, sympathetically edited by Elaine Lindsay, were published by the University of Queensland Press in 1998.

30

'I have been present at many battles royal'

Rosemary Dobson, *Untold Lives* (1992)

Alec's next book was deeply personal. *Untold Lives* is a collection of 25 of Rosemary Dobson's poems, most of them previously unpublished and most about people she had known. Some were autobiographical, and 'may be as far as I will go in writing an autobiography', she said in her preface. But the people in the poems were disguised as well, she said. And Alec told the artist Neil Moore, whom he first approached as a potential illustrator, 'the characters in the poems are both real and partly imagined. I think of them as faces in the crowd, brought together as in a group photograph'. If Moore agreed to engrave a plate, Alec proposed having the etching printed by Basil Hall at Studio One in Canberra. Moore, an award-winning Australian newspaper and magazine illustrator who had taken up etching in the early 1980s, was initially keen, provided the timing was not too tight.[1] But he had recently moved to a village in Umbria, and his time was fully committed to work for Italian publishers. In an email to the author he recalled:

> *Alec sent me some examples of Rosemary's work and while recognising their quality I thought they were deeply tied to their Australian context and thus not too well suited to the very European direction that I was then exploring in my work. I think I told Alec that I didn't want to embark on something simply as a commission that I might have done but not with real inspiration.*[2]

So they turned to Mike Hudson again, proposing a frontispiece, but later adding four poems as possibles for illustration: 'Chekhov's Sister', 'The Green Years', 'Memsahib's Memories' and 'Breakaway'. (All these poems are included in *Collected.*[3]) 'Rosemary feels the illustrations for this work should not be too minutely observed but should have a broader sort of treatment, in more of a linocut style,' Alec said to Hudson. 'She is very pleased that you are interested.'[4] He got on with designing the book while Hudson began drawing. He was still selling sets of prints from *The Sea Poems of Kenneth Slessor*, and was delighted to be working with Hudson again.

The poems in *Untold Lives* are mostly quite short, nearly all fitting onto one page. It is printed in generously leaded 12 point Linotype Granjon, and was composed by Bankstown Typesetting with hand-set Castellar and Garamond for display (the 30 point Castellar purely for the title on the title-page). The text paper is Mohawk Superfine at 118 gsm and the stiff black endpapers are by the French firm Canson & Montgolfier, the first time Alec had used this distinctive paper. (It was possibly bought in a small quantity from the Canberra School of Art, which at that time Alec used for his more exotic paper supplies. The Mohawk came from the Raleigh Paper Company in Silverwater in western Sydney, one of his regular suppliers. The original plan had been to use Velin d'Arches at 160 gsm, but this was changed for unknown reasons.) The book is both small and tall, in his preferred format, with generous margins and only one poem per page.

An unexpected problem emerged after Hudson sent in his first rough drawings: Rosemary rejected them. 'I think the reality of the illustrations is somehow too close to home, particularly in the autobiographical images,' Alec wrote. Rosemary had even proposed calling the book off altogether, which he did not want to do. 'I feel uneasy and unhappy, and so does she … I will write again later in the week, when the debris from the bombshell has settled around me.'[5] It was an unexpected development, and one that clearly caused both of them considerable discomfort. Years later Rosemary put two regretful notes with the relevant folder in the Bolton papers before sending them to the National Library. 'Parts of this correspondence re *Untold Lives* are rather painful,' she said, and elsewhere: 'I have always regretted my responsibility for this difficult situation. Except for this occasion all ATB's relations with authors, artists, binders etc. for the Press were harmonious, as was his way'.[6]

Mike Hudson responded calmly. 'DON'T PANIC!' he wrote in bold capitals. 'I've been far too long "on the street" to be [fazed] by rejection slips':

> *The biggest problem is still to get the job done right. And that involves a whole plethora of ideas and attitudes that need reconciling when offering work to other creatives.*

Now! ... how can we succeed I ask? ... How about if I explain my position vis-à-vis interpretation. It might give you a clue as to where we go next ... that is, subject versus object.

Of the Chekhov piece: My understanding of the man is that by today's terms he'd be considered mildly neurotic (aren't we all). The poem suggests this by mentioning his (non)reaction to his witless sister's matrimonial perquisites. I immediately made the connection with Russian iconography. The central sainted figure dominating the landscape and any other 'lesser' characters. Obviously to be pictured in the manner of the traditional icon—which means just such a facial expression (even all the virgin Mary's look like that) and with the little sister in the position of an angel, here adjusting or supplying the halo to the anointed head of big brother. Whether Chekhov was a nay-sayer about other things or not, the fundamental theme of the poem is better served by the negative stance implied in the documented reaction to his sister's request. The poem is a wry celebration of female devotion. Implicit is the suggestion that such devotion could have been misplaced or else over solicitous; whichever, my purpose was to make that point by exaggerating the moment that suggests the irony of such a relationship. Hence the quasi-religious aspect (iconoclasm?) of adoration/deification/obedience/subservience etc ... the fact that the subject is Russian is a real deus ex machina for the choice of object.[7]

Notwithstanding his explanation of serving 'the fundamental theme of the poem', Rosemary remained adamant. She drafted a reply for Alec, although he did not use it verbatim. In this she spells out the reason for her discomfort:

> *She says that, never having had her poems illustrated before, she did not realise how much she would be affected by extension of her images, especially as the majority of these poems are specially personal.*

The only illustration she would be comfortable with was the relatively 'impersonal' drawing for 'Breakaway', if it was to be used as a frontispiece.[8] In two apologetic letters on the issue, Alec also emphasised how happy they were with the 'Breakaway' drawing. It was a wonderful image, and he greatly hoped Hudson would agree to engrave it as a frontispiece. 'I feel chastened and somewhat hollowed-out by this experience. Rosemary would say the same,' he wrote. A few days later he returned to a point Rosemary had suggested in her draft: 'she has not had poems illustrated before, and finds it strange to see these strong visual extensions of her images, especially as they relate to herself,' adding 'I don't want to do anything against her wishes, and you will understand that'.

Whatever his private feelings, Hudson accepted the suggestion that his drawing for 'Breakaway' should be a frontispiece, far removed from the poem it illustrated and with no other illustrations in the book, and proposed a conversation some time in the future (preferably over 'a glass or two of good Australian plonk') about the relationship between visual and literary roles in publishing. He had often been puzzled by the decisions of mainstream publishers in this regard, he said. Alec responded quickly and with feeling (and perhaps with some relief) to this more generalised question. It was all a matter of ownership, he suggested:

> *You raise an interesting point about editorial inflexibility when issues of visual treatment occur. I have had quite a lot of experience of this, often*

as the go-between. Authors and editors tend to be very proprietorial about text. They can't own the way readers may visualise characters and events, but they do want to own how it is all presented. I have been present at many battles royal over dustjackets, and especially over illustrations for children's books. Sometimes I thought the author was right, sometimes the artist. It is a strange thing, this assertion of ownership.

It was an awkward episode in an otherwise harmonious relationship between printer and artist, as Rosemary noted. It demonstrated the need for a printer such as Alec to be ready to renegotiate at all times, and the importance of his personality in smoothing out conflict. He was always ready to apologise when he thought there was a need, and his sincerity was so apparent that few could hold a grudge. Hudson had no difficulty in agreeing to the suggestion of a separate printing of the 'Breakaway' engraving, for sale on its own and with the same 80/20 split of the proceeds as with the Slessor engravings—in Hudson's favour. (The idea had been floated earlier, but was firmed up after Rosemary's veto of the remaining illustrations.) The edition was 25, on a heavy Magnani paper (the 220 gsm Incisioni, suggested by Hudson) and it was offered for sale at $120.

The text of *Untold Lives* was printed by mid-June 1992, although the cold weather had made it hard to get his workshop up to a reasonable temperature, Alec told Hudson. (A comment reflecting more than a desire for personal comfort: ink can be difficult to work with when it and presses are cold.) The frontispiece

looks really good. Not much makeready was required. It seems to need a fair amount of ink to get all those solids really black, and some of the fine

> *detail on the fingers and towards the top of the trees tends to fill in. I find it desirable to clean the block periodically.*[9]

He remarked to another correspondent that the engraving

> *was a very difficult one to print consistently; some of the fine detail was cut very shallowly, and tended to fill-in despite fairly frequent cleaning off. The prints are okay … The subject probably strikes some people as rather severe. Technically I think it is a tour de force.*[10]

Alec signed *Untold Lives* on the colophon page, along with Rosemary. This was not his usual practice, although he had signed *Times and Places*, *Greek Coins* and *Time Given* previously. (He would later also sign Helen Ogilvie's *Wood Engravings* and initial *For Prisoners*.) Although he was to tell Heather Rusden that 'the signature of the printer is meaningless to me' and that he was simply 'the agent who's brought the various possibilities together to achieve the book', one wonders if his signature on this occasion might perhaps reflect a particularly strong sense of accomplishment in salvaging the various possibilities.[11]

Robin Tait bound *Untold Lives*, with only minor delays caused by the birth of a daughter just as she started. It has a black cloth spine with sides in a patterned paper designed for the press by Adrian Young, after a wood-engraved patterned motif by Rosalind Atkins. This was similar to 'Leaf Spring', which she had previously engraved for *The Idyll Wheel*. (Young was no longer a graphic designer at the ANU, which he had left to go into partnership with Kathie Griffiths in the design firm Griffiths & Young.) The paper was silk-screened by hand by Allan Grant, the owner of Leader

Graphics in Queanbeyan (and a one-time letterpress printer himself). Tait supplied the paper, a deep primary red on one side, on which Grant screened the leaf pattern in brown and light magenta in two printings, through two indirect photographic stencils made from Young's artwork. All Grant's direct dealings were with Young, but he recalled in a telephone conversation in 2016 that he had to leave the stencils on the frame, to his surprise, while Young took test prints away for approval by Alec. He worked with Young regularly at this time, often on small one-off projects, and also remembers that on this occasion the task had been brought to him without a clear brief on how to achieve the desired result. Certainly Alec was at one stage uncertain as to how the printing would work. The colours then under consideration were a darker and a lighter olive-green, with a terracotta, a sketch of which is to be found in his papers along with the colours finally selected, and which Alec envisaged would all have to be printed on white paper.[12]

Robin Tait had some difficulty with the binding, recalling that 'the paper moved around quite a bit and we ended up putting the sides down and then cutting the corners rather than trying to do it all in one go'[13], but it is a striking and original design, which Alec also tipped in as the sole illustration of the four-page prospectus for *Untold Lives*. He mirrored the red background of the paper in the red used for the title-page rules and ornament, and the book as a whole is a powerful work in which the sombre, brooding frontispiece and the bold patterned paper sides complement each other and Rosemary's haunting poems well.

The completion of *Untold Lives* coincided with Alec's reclamation of the name Brindabella Press, but it was too late for this book, which was the last published under the Officina

Brindabella imprint. The first 50 copies had been bound and the first orders despatched by mid-September 1992. Orders were down a little to begin with, even after the usual small display ad in *The Australian*, which Alec attributed to the recession—a state of affairs that prompted one of his rare political statements:

> *I think it all reflects the present hard times, and I do wonder what is ever going to change those general hard times. Personally I don't really wish to vote for anyone at the next election.*[14]

The availability of 'Breakaway' as a separate print was mentioned in the prospectus and in a later announcement, and again orders were slow: by November six had been ordered, three by booksellers.[15] But by the end of November there were only 19 copies of the book left unsold, even though Alec commented to Kay Craddock that there had been 'only one repeat from the trade, which I think says something about the general condition of things rather than anything about this particular book. On the whole I was satisfied with it, but some copies are better than others, as is usually the way'.[16] His records show that in the end 63 copies went to standing order subscribers, producing a substantially better return to the press than those that went to booksellers and galleries and close to Alec's early projection of 60 copies to subscribers (which was based on averaging the results of *The Idyll Wheel* and *The Sea Poems of Kenneth Slessor*). Resellers took 65 copies (the projection had been 110), but only two of them, Kay Craddock and Michael Treloar, put in repeat orders. Sales were to both long-standing and relatively new outlets for the press, such as La Maison du Livre (in Balmain, Sydney), Fullers (Hobart) and Roy Farrell (Mornington Peninsula,

Victoria). These figures thus show that at the time Alec compiled his sales list, by which time 13 copies remained unsold, 96 had been sold at the full price of $75, more than double the 40 predicted (plus copies for Lissant, Robert and Ian).

Although Alec had projected a return on his outlay of as low as 4 per cent in his first costings, in the end the book did reasonably well by Brindabella Press standards. His first calculation of total cost put it at $11,887 (including half the cost of type and the patterned paper design as well as general overheads), and predicted revenue at $13,185 (including sales of prints). However, the greater number of direct sales than anticipated should have boosted the return somewhat, estimated to be at $14,584, a return of a little over $2,000 or 6.2 per cent on the book. The major costs were binding ($5,400), royalties (to both Rosemary and Mike Hudson, total $2,300), and $972 for paper ($488 for the Mohawk and $209 for the Canson endpapers, and a total of $575 for the patterned paper).[17]

Untold Lives was republished in 2000 by Brandl & Schlesinger, along with a group of later poems. In this form it won the Dinny O'Hearn Poetry Prize in The Age Book of the Year Award (2001), and was shortlisted for the C.J. Dennis Prize for Poetry in the Victorian Premier's Literary Awards (2001). The new edition was dedicated 'For Alec Bolton, Printer', and in its preface Rosemary spoke briefly of its earlier history. 'Alec Bolton encouraged his authors to seek commercial publication later, since he retained no rights to their texts,' she explained. 'All the poems honour the memory of Alec Bolton and his judgement and generosity of mind, which contributed so much to my poetry overall.'[18]

31

'I feel a deep satisfaction in reclaiming something of which, for the past seven years, I felt unluckily deprived'

Philip Hodgins, *The End of the Season* (1993)

The next Brindabella project was to be a return to publishing a young poet: the first since *The Spring-Mire*. Philip Hodgins' direct and unsentimental writing both challenged and appealed to Alec. 'I have had the keenest pleasure from living with the poems during these past few months,' he told Hodgins towards the end of the project. 'They have taken root in me.'[1] *The End of the Season* also became the occasion of a new epistolary friendship, cut short by Hodgins' death from leukaemia in 1995. (They joked between themselves that both worshipped the God or Goddess of letterboxes.) Hodgins also shared a background in publishing with Alec, having worked for many years for Macmillan. He was diagnosed with leukaemia at the age of 24 and some of his poems reflect the experience of his illness. He also suffered from chronic back pain, which made travel difficult. He and his wife, the writer Janet Shaw, had moved to the central Victorian countryside at the time of this book, and its pastoral poems (as the subtitle described them) were often based on that experience as well as his childhood on a dairy farm.

There had been a previous but unsuccessful discussion about the possibility of a book in 1987, when Lynn Hard, then head of the Australian Defence Force Academy Library, suggested Hodgins talk to Alec about possible publication.[2] (ADFA was later to acquire Hodgins' papers.) Hodgins approached Alec again in 1990, saying that in the three books he had published, along with new poems not yet published, there was a substantial body of pastoral poetry. The Brindabella edition of *The Idyll Wheel* suggested to him that the press might be interested in such a collection.[3] (Indeed, Les Murray was an early champion of Hodgins' poetry and its grounding in rural life.[4]) It took a considerable time for Alec to agree to the book—he was heavily committed to his forward publications program, he told Hodgins in April 1990, and Hodgins too was slow to respond—but by early in 1992 Alec said he had seen enough poems for a book. 'I do like them,' he wrote, 'they are original and strong, sometimes even a bit too strong for me.'[5]

Once they were committed to the book, Alec and Rosemary went into full editorial mode. Rosemary reported in detail on the manuscript, suggesting which poems should be retained and which discarded, and Alec sent a lengthy critique combining their two views. (The absence of such a report from most other records of the press' books suggests that this was somewhat unusual.) Alec was direct in his critique: 'I like this very much, but to me a couple of lines read unmusically,' he said of the poem Hodgins first proposed as the title piece, 'Milk Cream Butter'. Hodgins retained one line and made a small change in the other. Did he mean bearing or gears were grinding in low ratio, Alec asked of another. The line was changed. And he suggested that the shooters in 'The Verandah' would be prone, not supine: 'you have to lie prone to shoot'. Hodgins was happy to make such changes where it was a matter of meaning, but less willing to accommodate Alec's preferences in rhythm and his occasional inability to understand what was meant by notions such as machines promising rain in 'After a Dry Stretch'. The machines in question were meteorological equipment, he explained, and kept the line. Later Alec remarked to one of his customers:

> *Philip's sometimes bumpy rhythms worried me too, and I gave him quite a long list of queried lines, with suggested smoothings. But these effects were deliberate, and he did not wish to change anything of that kind. In the end I have got used to them. It is all part of his voice. He has recently cracked the New Yorker with a poem about a sheep parasite field day—an unlikely poetic subject for that magazine, you'll agree. I am looking forward to seeing it.*[6]

And to Gerald Fischer he remarked: 'Philip is a very impressive poet. He is plain and direct, and I like the unsentimental truth of his writing. Did you notice that the pronoun "I" never once appeared in that book?'[7]

The paper and design of *The End of the Season* presented Alec with some challenges. There were very long lines in some of the poems, he told Mike Hudson, and he wanted to use a larger format than was possible with the Mohawk Superfine paper he had used for the last two books. (The Mohawk mill also made a letterpress paper that would be in a better size, but he had found it less sympathetic to engravings when he printed the Slessor, he said.) He preferred to print four pages at a time, but this would be too big for the 25 x 38 inch sheet, and the larger Superfine size (35 x 45 inches) was no longer available from the mill. He was wary of importing paper such as Zerkall, which he had used for *The Idyll Wheel*, because of the cost of importing a small batch for one book. And then he made a typically Alec confession, both self-deprecatory and reflective:

> *At the back of my mind … is an unexpressed feeling that one should be using different papers and formats and binding styles in our kind of work. (Not that that atones for a lack of originality of conception, from which I rather feel that I suffer.)*[8]

So ultimately he stayed with Mohawk Superfine, reducing the size of the type so he could still print four pages per sheet in the modest format he chose, but he did innovate with both the type and the binding. The type he chose was Linotype Palatino, the first time he had used Hermann Zapf's most famous type, machine-set by Bankstown Typesetting in 10 point for the text and 12 point italic caps for poem titles. 'I seem to have a lot of projects, and as time is passing and I am ageing, I have more or less quit on hand-setting, except for small or special jobs,' he told one acquaintance.[9]

(Alec had asked that the title of the book be set in 36 point Palatino caps on a Ludlow caster, and had hoped to also get the poem titles set in 18 point Palatino italics, but the Ludlow was not working. After another attempt to order the title lines in the same size from another supplier, he settled on 24 point.) Elsewhere, he commented that even though hand-setting 'is often regarded as a *sine qua non* of private press work', the reality was that supplies of Monotype for future use were simply not available in Australia anymore.[10]

Robin Tait came up with a slightly experimental binding for the book, described in the prospectus as 'an unusual Ethiopian style, with a cloth spine and paper sides over boards'. She explained further when I interviewed her:

> *Occasionally [I] would put something in front of him, and in fact with the Philip Hodgins he fell in love with the material so much he just had to use it … The boards are actually a fold of card which is sewn at the same time as the actual text and then the spine was put over, and in order to capture the boards together … the siding paper went on and around and then the endpaper was put over the top of that, so actually in effect there's quite a lot of air in this binding because the boards are actually just a folded piece of card rather than being a stiff solid board—I actually think it's a really beautiful edition … I was so pleased he got it.*[11]

The 'Yellow Peter Thomas' handmade siding paper suggested by Tait was supplied by the Sea Pen Press & Paper Mill of Seattle, who made 75 sheets to Alec's order. Sea Pen was a small, specialist paper mill founded in 1977, which operated until the

1990s and specialised in paper for letterpress printing. At US$8 a sheet, and a total cost of A$1,356 (the Australian dollar was buying less than 70 cents US at the time, and as well as freight there were high customs duties), it was one of his most expensive paper purchases when looked at in terms of the unit cost of $6.25 per book for the siding paper alone. Although Alec still thought it was beautiful, he later told Gerald Fischer he would not use it again, 'as the cost was horrendous, and out of proportion to the other costs of binding'.[12] But he trenchantly defended the binding when Geoffrey Farmer appears to have commented on its plainness.

> *I admit to some tension within myself about the binding. It was meant to be very plain, and the result is perhaps too austere for some. But I stick by it.*[13]

The End of the Season was illustrated with wood engravings by Victoria Clutterbuck, a young artist who lived at Braidwood, a small country town on the road between Canberra and the South Coast. Alec approached her soon after agreeing to publish the book:

> *I think there is a lot of strength in the poems, and an element of dry humour, but I get an impression of a fairly hard life in a sometimes beautiful landscape.*[14]

He had not yet met the poet, he explained, but he knew there had been a long battle with leukaemia, now hopefully over. And, as he had done with Rosalind Atkins, he thought the commission should include a journey to the country where the poems were set, around Maryborough. Clutterbuck liked the poems very much and visited Maryborough for two days at Alec's expense at the end of May.

The subsequent correspondence between poet, artist and printer is useful for the light it throws on Alec's approach to negotiating the *mise en page* of the book. He liked all Clutterbuck's first drawings except for one that suggested too much starkness, he felt, in relation to the person dying in 'Leaving'. Clutterbuck also wanted to illustrate several poems that were close together in the current agreed sequence of poems, he remarked to Hodgins. 'I like if possible to spread the illustrations fairly evenly, and it may be that I will ask you to consider making one or two transpositions.' Hodgins was happy with the transpositions, he replied, and with nearly all the drawings, but he shared Alec's view of the dying figure in 'Leaving'. He explained that to him, the central image in the poem was the pastoral landscape being reflected on and returned to mentally—not the death of the thinker.[15] After some discussion and a meeting between the three of them in Canberra in July, agreement was reached to substitute an engraving for the poem 'Verandah' rather than 'Leaving', which was left unillustrated. The final order of poems was not decided until just before printing began, largely because of the way the illustrations worked and Alec's aim to have most of them on right-hand pages except for a couple of vignettes and the large engraving for 'The Farmer'. This was placed on a left-hand page so that the farmer in question 'should face the poem opposite, and not face out of the book'.[16]

The End of the Season was the first book since *Some Poems of Shaw Neilson* to carry the reclaimed imprint Brindabella Press.

The Officina Brindabella imprint that Alec had had to use for the previous seven years had always seemed a little pretentious, he told Hodgins, and some people had trouble pronouncing the Italian 'officina'.[17] The same news featured in a small circular he printed in September 1992 for distribution to his mailing list, illustrated with a wood engraving from the forthcoming book. 'I cannot say why it seems to mean so much, but I feel a deep satisfaction in reclaiming something of which, for the past seven years, I felt unluckily deprived,' Alec wrote.[18] The imprint, with the Brindabella pressmark Arthur Stokes had designed for him in 1988, is prominent on the prospectus he printed for the book, featuring two of Clutterbuck's wood engravings. The prospectus announced an edition of 230 copies, with ten copies reserved in sheets for hand binding, and the engraving for 'After a Dry Season' available as a separate signed and numbered print in an edition of 20 copies. The book was priced at $90 and the print at $80.

There were renewed concerns about Hodgins' health at the end of 1992, and perhaps for this reason, remembering his experience with Barbara Hanrahan, Alec printed the book as quickly as possible, working six or seven days a week. He also wanted to finish printing and folding before a visit to England (where both Lissant and Robert were now living) in late March.[19] He had difficulty printing some of the engravings, as they were on recycled blocks that had been rendered slightly uneven at the edges and corners by sanding, but met his deadline with time to spare.[20] There was little printing-related contact on this trip, he told Jadwiga Jarvis after his return, but he did fit in a return visit to Simon Lawrence at the Fleece Press, 'whose work I admire a lot'.[21]

Alec on his way to Coogee Boys' Preparatory School; during his service on HMAS *Echuca*, c.1945; with his mother Amy Bolton.

Australian Encyclopaedia staff in the Angus & Robertson offices, c.1953, with Alec standing in the middle; Rosemary Dobson and (likely) Henry Mund in the Angus & Robertson offices.

Alec with Yvonne Boyd, Arthur Boyd, Penelope Hope and Professor Alec Hope at Bundanon in 1978; Poets Judith Wright, Rosemary Dobson and Denise Levertov at Mongarlowe, 1981, photograph taken by Alec; Sally McCann, Alec and Dave Brown of the National Library of Australia publishing team, in the Library's Ferguson Room in 1982.

Alec working with the Chandler & Price in 1987; the Furnival Wharfedale press in the foreground of the Brindabella Press printery in 1997 before being dismantled; Alec holding a copy of Geoff Page's *Smiling in English, Smoking in French* (1987), open to an illustration by Christian Preuschl von Haldenburg.

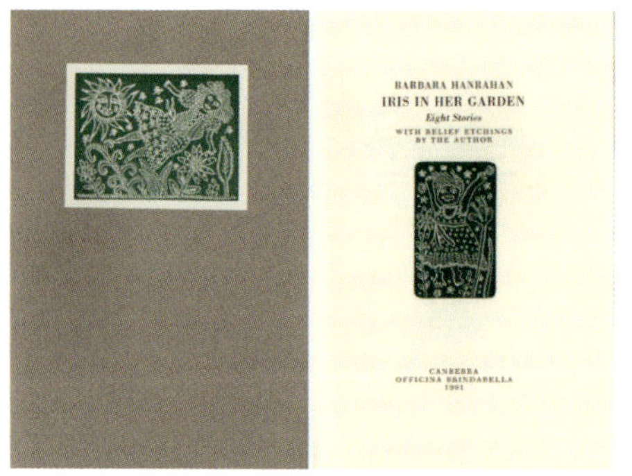

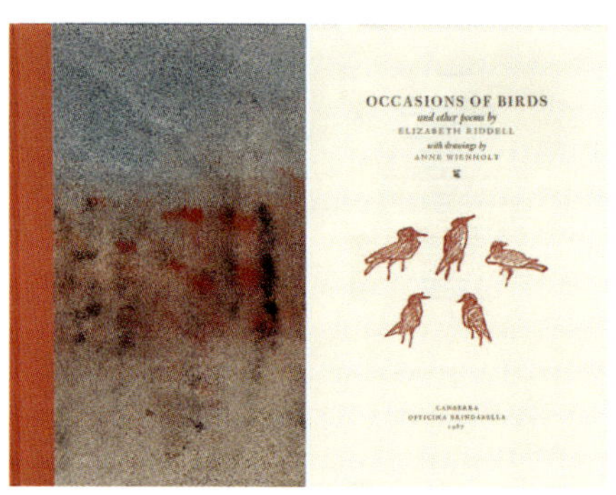

Cover and title-page of Barbara Hanrahan's *Iris In Her Garden* (1991); cover and title-page of James McAuley's *Time Given* (1976); cover and title-page of Elizabeth Riddell's *Occasions of Birds* (1987); frontispiece and title-page of John Shaw Neilson's *Some Poems of Shaw Neilson* (1985); spread and binding of Kenneth Slessor's *The Sea Poems of Kenneth Slessor* (1990).

Cover of Les Murray's *The Idyll Wheel* (1989).

Alec at work in 1987; with Rosemary outside their Deakin home in 1993.

Philip Hodgins had been amazed to discover that Alec did not necessarily set out to make a profit on all his books, but *The End of the Season* was priced to make a modest return of 11.7 per cent profit on outlays. The expensive siding paper, including freight and 20 per cent customs duty, cost $1,356, and typesetting almost as much, at $1,050. Hodgins' royalties would be $2,045 and Clutterbuck's $1,022, but the biggest cost, as always, was hand binding at $4,320. Overall, the book cost $13,211 to produce, which meant the unit cost was calculated to be $57.44. Alec assumed 85 per cent of the edition would sell: perhaps 51 to subscribers and libraries at 12.5 per cent discount, 80 to booksellers, allowing one third discount, and 61 direct sales at full price, producing a projected return of $14,761.[22]

The book sold well: in July Alec sent the author a royalty cheque for the entire edition.[23] His usual meticulous running summary of the distribution of copies, which he kept up to date as copies were sent out, accounts for all but 23 copies of the 220 for sale, but suggests that bookshops were not quite as keen on the book as he had anticipated, with 49 copies ordered by the trade. Victoria Clutterbuck's print sold almost completely, with five copies retained by the press, and six of the copies in sheets were taken by bookbinders, two of them by Robin Tait.

Although not one of the great rarities for collectors, it is now a scarce book. Its reception was muted. It was Hodgins' ongoing battle with leukaemia that dominated the only major article in the press to mention *The End of the Season*, a year after publication.[24] One needs to bear in mind, though, that Alec was no longer in the habit of sending out review copies, as previously discussed. He placed his usual ad in *The Weekend*

Australian, and sent out the prospectus: these were enough to almost sell the edition out.

It is evident from the surviving correspondence in the National Library that the friendship between the Boltons and Hodgins continued, with warm letters being exchanged at least up until November 1994.

32

'In this rather solitary occupation there is a lot of time to think about the people whose work one is printing'

Les A. Murray, *The Sleepout* (1994)

By the beginning of 1994 Alec had a year's work in hand, he remarked to the librarian, editor and poet Barrett Reid. (He was sending back a manuscript they had discussed many years earlier and that he liked but now thought was too short for the press as it had become.) There was a new book by John Rowland; an illustrated broadside of Les Murray's poem 'The Sleepout'; and a selection of wood engravings by Helen Ogilvie, all at different stages of production.[1] All were to present familiar challenges.

Alec approached Les Murray with the idea of printing a short poem in broadside format in July 1993. The poem need not be new, he said: something well known might be best. 'It would be important to have something amenable to illustration by a wood engraving—not too literally or descriptively, perhaps.' One motive in making the suggestion, he told Murray, was market-related:

> *I have been lucky in the selling of Brindabella publications, and my customers have mostly stuck to me despite prices that have got closer and closer to the dreaded $100 mark. However, I should like to vary the performance by offering something different and manifestly not dear, as I think this would be appreciated in the present hard times.*
>
> *I apologise for the prosaic nature of this letter, which seems to be all about money and other practical considerations. What I want to say is that I should love to be associated with another work of yours, and to produce something that, exceeding the sum of its parts, would reverberate in the heads of readers and viewers.*[2]

Murray was delighted at the suggestion they might work together again, the only problem being that few of his poems were short enough for the broadside format. But he nominated ten that might suit and asked Alec to look through them. Alec narrowed the choice to two, 'Lyre Bird' and 'The Sleepout', the first from the book *Translations from the Natural World* and the second from *The Daylight Moon*, published by Isabella Press (1992) and Angus & Robertson (1987) respectively. Once Murray had agreed to this shortlist, Alec and his artist, again Rosalind Atkins, opted for the latter, which the poet agreed would 'probably be my preference, too, by a short half-nose'.[3] 'The Sleepout' evokes 'childhood sleeps in a verandah room', as its first line puts it. 'That image of the forest as a great house with lamps seems to come from deep within me—it's in other poems too, e.g. Toward the Imminent Days. Dunno what it means. I suspect dreams mostly don't "mean" in daylight terms,' Murray wrote later.[4] However, he had specific ideas about what meaning there should be in the way it was illustrated, and this was to cause Alec considerable dismay. His brief to Atkins had been broad:

> *It is a challenging poem. There is the literal sleepout, and then there is the sense of presences in the bush beyond, in the perceptions of childhood. I guess the words rather than the illustration must be the main vehicle for the magic in this piece, but I hope we can convey some element of mystery and imagination in the broadside as a whole. Easy for me to say that!*[5]

He liked her first drawing and gave her the go-ahead—without checking with Murray. But Murray's vision was far more specific, as he pointed out in one of his characteristic postcards:

> *Rosalind's engraving shouldn't, if possible, be too 'inside'—remember that a sleepout is essentially on a verandah only partly closed in … Mine had 3 walls & was open at the north end, over my toes. The one at the other end of that same verandah had 2 walls & a wardrobe serving as a third! Stars & possums and full moons & night air, & bats, all visit you in a sleepout. Girls may not understand. They, & parents, often think a sleepout is too exposed for girls to sleep there. Sleepouts are great for demon lovers, & probably the more civil kind too.*[6]

He rejected Atkins' first engraving as

exquisite, but it's of a room. A verandah room, or as we used to say a "done-in" verandah. She comes from cold country, too far south to have had true sleepouts. Please, I know it'll cost time, but I can't accept a false picture. Ask her for another, with my apologies.[7]

Alec was mortified. The cutting of the block represented at least a fortnight's work, he told Murray, and he was responsible for having given her the go-ahead after seeing and commenting on her rough drawings. He felt he would need to compensate her for this work, but Murray's veto had been so decisive he knew it would be pointless to try to change his mind.[8] He was quite abject in his apology to Atkins, and rejoiced when she agreed to engrave another block. By way of some recompense, he printed twelve engravings from her original block and gave all but one to her: this is one of the great rarities of the Brindabella Press.[9] Happily Murray was happy with the second version, and loved the first pull from the woodblock.[10] This time Alec and he had exchanged detailed comments on her drawings. Future biographers of Murray might like to note the existence in the Bolton papers of a plan of the poet's childhood sleepout, including a drawing of the bamboo corner what-not on which he kept his kerosene lamp and books!

The broadside is in landscape orientation and printed in two colours on Arches 88 paper. The type is hand-set Monotype Baskerville for both text and display. Alec considered using a grey paper, as being 'more of Australian bush colour than any of the whites or soft-whites I have seen', but eventually chose a brilliant white for the sake of the printing surface and the weight of the paper, although he had concerns about Atkins' response to it.[11] He also considered printing on damp paper, and wrote to Simon

Lawrence of the Fleece Press, whom he had recently visited in his Yorkshire workshop and whose work he admired, to seek advice on dampening when there were three workings to handle.

> *I have dampened paper moderately successfully in the past, but only where there was a single working, and where a relatively small batch of sheets was prepared for each day.*

Simon Lawrence has no recollection of this letter reaching him and it is certain that Alec printed dry.[12] As with his earlier Judith Wright broadside, the colophon is perhaps a little more prominent than it might have been. This is partly because he was punctilious about acknowledging the previous publication of the poem, as required by Angus & Robertson, and this takes up a considerable amount of space. So too does his spelling out of the full address of the place of publication, a legal requirement. Nonetheless, the broadside is a lovely production, in which both the poem and the engraving work together to evoke childhood memory.

The to-ings and fro-ings regarding the illustration of the broadside caused delay, so it was not printed until February 1994. Alec printed the engraving first and then the text. At 360 x 479 millimetres, it was 'practically the limit of what will pass though the Western press', he said.[13] Both Les Murray and Rosalind Atkins visited in March to sign the broadside. It had been foreshadowed in 'News from Brindabella Press', a flyer that Alec sent out to his mailing list in November 1993, and he later also produced a prospectus. This included a colour photograph of the broadside and, for the first time, what Alec called his 'chop mark', a variant on the previous 'Officina Brindabella' pressmark with the reclaimed name 'Brindabella Press' in a circle around a capital B, all in blind embossing, which he used also on the broadside. He expected it would sell well to his subscribers, and at first queried the need for further advertising, but despite quickly securing 130 firm orders from subscribers he placed a small ad in *The Weekend Australian*.[14] He began distributing copies at the beginning of April.

The Sleepout was published in an edition of 200 numbered copies at $60, with six out-of-series copies each for author and artist and eight for the press. The standing order price was $52.50 and trade $40. The major costs, in total $3,900, were royalties of 20 per cent to Angus & Robertson and 10 per cent to Atkins, although he increased the latter to compensate for her extra wood engraving. The paper cost $475 and the prospectus some $500, including mailing. Overall, he estimated costs at $6,170 and revenue at $9,200: the broadside was, in a small way, a profitable venture and it quickly sold out.[15]

Despite its difficult moments, Alec was more than happy with *The Sleepout.* He particularly enjoyed the opportunity to work again with its illustrator. 'In this rather solitary occupation there is a lot of time to think about the people whose work one is printing,' he wrote to her. 'I like to feel some bond of closeness with them, and have always had that feeling about you.'[16]

33

'Memory and the mind'

John Rowland, *Granite Country* (1994)

With *Granite Country*, the twenty-first book of the press, Alec returned to the author of his third book. Like *Times and Places*—the earlier collection of poems by John Rowland that had been the first hard-bound Brindabella Press title—*Granite Country* was illustrated with line drawings by the author. Now retired from the Department of Foreign Affairs after a distinguished career that had included ambassadorships to the Soviet Union, Malaysia, Austria and France, Rowland lived in Canberra and spent much of his time on the South Coast, where he was also active as a campaigner on conservation issues such as opposition to woodchipping.[1]

Times and Places had been subtitled *Poems of Locality*, a description that could also be applied to the new collection. As Alec put it in his prospectus:

> *His landscape ranges widely, from the high country of the Monaro to the bays and beaches of the South Coast, and the New England tablelands where he grew up—celebrated in a fine sequence about his boyhood, 'Morunda'. The book also includes wry poems of European travel, and the witty long 'True Stories' about life in post-war Canberra, when he was a diplomatic cadet. But the essential landscapes here are those of memory and the mind: through life's hard country, Rowland maps a quest for understanding and intimacy in which disappointment is no stranger.*[2]

So in some ways the book represents a return to Brindabella's roots: poetry by a Canberra writer, an elder among a group of writers Alec and Rosemary had known for decades, and simply illustrated with blocks based on line drawings. Similar in format to *Times and Places*, it differed in that it was bound by Robin Tait in boards with screen-printed cloth covers, and also in that it was machine-set in Intertype Baskerville by Bankstown Typesetting rather than hand-set. Alec specified 11 on 12 point Baskerville for the bulk of the book and hand-set the title (in Castellar) and display text.[3] As previously mentioned, he liked 11 point Baskerville and owned a small quantity for hand-setting. This text was set using Intertype matrices that Alec owned but were kept in Bankstown for use as required. (In 1996, when he offered a long-term loan of these to Bob Summers of the Escutcheon Press and his son Nicholas, also a printer, he had Intertype Baskerville in 8, 9, 10, 11 and 12 point, although some were more complete than others. Baskerville was his most complete type family.[4])

Alec printed the line drawings in green, which he mixed himself from Van Son rubber base yellow, reflex blue and transparent white ink.[5] The title-page opening is one of his most dramatic, with a bouldered slope of hill country drawn by Rowland sprawling across both pages. The book is profusely illustrated: 'I would be happy to consider the drawings as many rather than few, so please lash out,' he told the author.[6] There are 13 drawings all told, plus the cover, printed with 'nylo' line blocks made by *The Canberra Times* from Rowland's line drawings and photographically reduced in size in some instances. (This use of nylon-based relief plates, a photopolymer-based system widely used in newspaper and magazine printing from the 1960s on, appears to have been his first venture into photopolymer printing.)

He began printing in May 1994 and completed sheets went to the binder at the end of September. *Granite Country* was published in late November. The cover cloth, with a drawing by Rowland of granite boulders and trees typical of the hills around Canberra, was screen-printed in black by Leader Graphics of Queanbeyan onto a light grey (almost a pale mauve) cloth, made by Fein Canvas in Germany. The text is on Archive Text Laid and the endpapers are smoke grey Grandee Text, both supplied by Edwards Dunlop. In an interview in 2015, Robin Tait recalls that Alec made the choice of book cloth and endpapers and that there was little need for further discussion about the project. The book is in a conventional case binding with a mylar dust jacket.

As usual with the later books, the biggest cost of production was hand binding (again by Robin Tait) at $6,133. Typesetting cost $1,105 and a 10 per cent royalty to the author came to $1,650. *Granite Country* retailed for $75: actual outgoings came to $10,950. An ad in *The Weekend Australian* cost $687, and a small prospectus, including mailing, $250. Alec calculated his receipts at

$11,881, which gave him a net profit of $931, a little less than the 10 per cent overhead of $1,095 he had hoped to recoup.[7]

The press records show that standing order subscribers supported the book strongly, taking 89 copies. Most of these went to individuals. Thirty-nine copies were ordered by booksellers. The book was still in print at the time of Alec's death, with 18 numbered copies unsold.[8] There appear to have been a further 22 copies out-of-series, which were also signed by the author. I have not been able to find any reviews.

34

'The Helen Ogilvie saga rolls slowly on'

Helen Ogilvie, *Wood Engravings* (1995)

Alec's next book was a lengthy task, with what he later estimated as upwards of 6,000 hand-inked impressions required for the illustrations alone. 'A mighty lot of work, but I enjoyed it,' he told Rosalind Atkins.[1] Although it was an artist of an older generation he was printing this time, not a poet, and while he did not explicitly describe the book in such terms, it can be seen as an extension of his earlier aims to publish work by older poets who were now untowardly overlooked. It is a lovely book, now much sought after, and still the only monograph devoted to Ogilvie's opus.

The genesis of Helen Ogilvie's *Wood Engravings* was an exhibition of her work in May 1991 at aGOG, Helen Maxwell's gallery in Kingston, Canberra, which was also a significant retrospective tribute to her long life as a working artist. Born in 1902, Ogilvie trained at the National Gallery Art School in Melbourne (1922–1925), and later ran the Peter Bray Gallery there while continuing with her own work. As a gallery director she aimed 'to show the most exciting contemporary work', exhibiting such artists as Margo Lewers, Helen Maudsley, John Brack, Sidney Nolan, Arthur Boyd, Charles Blackman and Ian Fairweather.[2]

She was largely self-taught as a printmaker and came up against the same difficulties in finding materials such as suitable woodblocks as younger Brindabella artists would encounter many years later. For some years, as Maxwell recounts, she used 'a vegetable paper with lumps and bumps' imported by Chinese traders in Little Bourke Street 'to record their abacus calculations', before being given a supply of fine Japanese tissue paper, a paper used by many linocut printers.[3] As a printmaker she worked extensively in linocut as well as wood engraving, and was one of a number of modernist Melbourne artists (often associated with Napier and Christian Waller) influenced by Claude Flight's 1927 book *Lino-Cuts*.[4] Wood engraving appealed to her, Helen Maxwell wrote after interviewing her, because 'it was done so directly with the hand. It seemed to her that the direct connection between the brain and the hand was even more apparent in wood engraving than in other mediums such as painting'.[5]

Although she produced few wood engravings after the 1950s, she continued to work as an artist into the 1980s and had solo exhibitions as well as participating in group shows. Despite this extraordinary longevity, she shared the experience of other Melbourne printmakers of the time, mostly women, who, as curator and gallery director Ron Radford puts it, were largely overlooked during their most productive years and again later during the revival of interest in Australian printmakers in the 1970s. 'Helen Ogilvie's intimate studies of poultry are such a delight, that it makes one regret that she did not produce more,' Radford commented in 1976.[6] Her work was best known in Melbourne and across Bass Strait at Launceston, where John McPhee, curator of art at the Queen Victoria Museum and Art Gallery, had become friendly with her in the 1970s.[7] It was McPhee who later introduced her to Helen Maxwell.[8]

The aGOG exhibition, which opened on her eighty-ninth birthday, was her first major solo show for many years. The exhibition included colour linocuts from the early 1930s and wood engravings done as editioned prints, as book illustrations, and as bookplates. Drawings (pen and ink with watercolour) and paintings came from later decades, mostly the 1960s. Many were studies of small buildings in the Australian countryside. Her 'gentle art' produced a 'loving record of humbler times and lifestyles', wrote the *Canberra Times* reviewer, and the exhibition was much admired by its visitors.[9]

Alec was always on the lookout for Australian wood engravers and in February 1992 asked Helen Ogilvie if she might be interested in a book based on 20 or so of her wood engravings. He introduced himself to her as a friend of Helen Maxwell and mentioned that she was interested in editing such a collection. He added a caveat: he had recently met Jonathan Stephenson of the Rocket Press (during his visit to England in 1991), who in the late 1980s had printed 250 sets of Tenniel's illustrations to *Alice in Wonderland* and *Through the Looking Glass* from the original blocks, which had been 'an anxious task'. He held some fears about the integrity of her blocks as they too would be quite old, but he 'would hope not to damage anything'.[10] It was a characteristic note of caution: he wrote again two days later to add that perhaps his first letter had been too businesslike, and that the main reason he wanted to do the book was that he liked the engravings.[11] He also asked Kay Craddock what she thought of the idea, as it would have a distinct Melbourne flavour about it, and after a visit to Helen Ogilvie in April asked Rosalind Atkins to have a look at the blocks still in Ogilvie's possession so she could report on their suitability for printing.[12] (She later helped prepare some blocks for printing by routing the edges.) Given his long-standing interest in the potential of Australian hardwoods for engraving, Alec was intrigued to find that Ogilvie had used yellow box, sassafras and possibly myrtle beech as well as the more usual English boxwood.

Alec designed the book in his preferred tall and narrow shape, of a size to suit the portrait format of the largest of the wood engravings (the frontispiece to *Stolne & Surreptitious Verses*, which was 13.8 x 9.5 centimetres). Captions and short commentaries recorded by Helen Maxwell are on generously uncluttered facing pages, which unusually for him do not include page numbers. A short introduction by Maxwell is still the most substantial account of Helen Ogilvie extant, and, unusually, Alec himself contributed a 'Printer's Note', explaining the difficulties involved in printing some of the blocks and describing the woods Ogilvie used. He also signed the edition himself, something he was generally loath to do, mainly because the artist had died before the work was complete, but also because it had taken such a long time to print.[13] The type is again Intertype Baskerville, composed from his matrices held by Inter-Typesetting Service, and the paper is Mohawk Superfine. The title-page is one of his best, with display type hand-set to mirror an engraving of a balcony. He 'only discovered that vital characters [that is, from his Baskerville type] were missing when I was irreversibly launched into the text of the Ogilvie book', he later told Bob Summers[14], although it is hard to discern what is missing.

To begin with, Alec was under the impression that most of Helen Ogilvie's woodblocks survived, in particular those used for two books illustrated by her and printed at Melbourne University Press in 1947 and 1952, *Flinders Lane* and *Stolne & Surreptitious Verses*, but this turned out not to be the case and for some time the project was in some doubt.[15] Eventually he decided it would be possible to proceed with a small number of line blocks copied from vintage proofs, providing the bulk of the engravings were printed from the original blocks. He and Helen Maxwell began looking for other surviving blocks. Meanwhile, Helen Ogilvie searched her house in South Yarra and made inquiries of people who had been involved in the printing of the two books, or who might know of the fate of these blocks in particular. Inquiries at the National Gallery of Victoria and the Baillieu Library were unsuccessful, but five blocks for Christmas cards for the Grimwade family were located in the University of Melbourne Gallery collection, three of which were used. Another was found being used as a paperweight by Peter Ryan, a former director of Melbourne University Press. (Although one of the missing blocks from *Stolne & Surreptitious Verses*, it was not used in the final book.) Later, Ogilvie's artistic executor, John McPhee, also assisted in the search and a few more blocks were found at South Yarra.[16]

Ultimately five of the 23 prints in the book (this figure includes three decorations) were made from new line blocks: two from each of the aforementioned books, and one from Helen Ogilvie's own bookplate. In most cases they are noticeably less successful than the excellent impressions Alec printed from the wood, with much of the white line detail lost and the blacks lacking the rich density of wood engravings. Here was the downside of his decision to have line blocks made from vintage proofs in the artist's collection, in part because the proofs were themselves somewhat problematic. This is evident from a comment, in a letter to Rosalind Atkins asking her to examine the five blocks at the University of Melbourne Gallery, that 'quite a lot of the old Ogilvie proofs that I have seen are not especially well printed; the solids aren't always solid. In some cases the blocks themselves may have been at fault'.[17] (Although Ogilvie owned a benchtop Albion press later in life, the earlier prints were made without a press.) 'Some of them are pretty well impossible to print properly,' he explained to his friend Bob Summers, 'as the surfaces must have been sanded by hand, which lowered the corners.'[18] And when sending the five proofs to be made into line blocks, he noted in particular that the 'image of the train gives me the most concern: it is a poor print, and there is no alternative. Please try to hold the white line and not let it all fill in … Best possible care of these originals, please,' he added.[19]

He might have been better off having the line blocks made from copies of the books concerned rather than vintage proofs, or even perhaps to have used a means other than relief printing to represent them. Using photoengraving processes to make a line block suitable for relief printing from a proof, and then printing with that block, takes a printer three steps away from the original wood engraving, as opposed to one step in printing directly from the block as he was able to do for the majority of works in the book. The end result is bound to be a compromise, even more so if the original proof is less than satisfactory. (It appears Alec did not consider using the original books as the basis for line blocks.) One needs to bear in mind, though, that part of the rationale for the book, as Helen Maxwell wrote in her introduction, was 'to give a good representation of Helen's oeuvre'. The inclusion of these line blocks achieved that end, albeit at some cost in printing terms. As Roger Butler comments, Ogilvie's wood engravings for *Flinders Lane* in particular, and also *Meanjin Papers* (in 1949 and 1950), had taken the genre as practised in Australia from the world of limited edition books and editioned prints into commercial printing.[20] It was important to represent this brief moment of her somewhat higher visibility. Two of the decorations in the book were from blocks used in the journal *Meanjin*, vol.8, no.1, 1949. The title-page decoration, a balcony, came from an exhibition announcement.

In April 1993 Helen Maxwell spent a morning with Helen Ogilvie, recording her recollections of the final selection of works, and from this began writing the brief commentaries on each work and her introduction to the book.[21] Alec planned a further visit in July to ask for a more detailed account of the cards done for the Grimwades, and to photograph her, but she died just three days before he was due to visit. 'In spite of her great age, it was unexpected,' Alec said.[22] But at an earlier stage he had joked to Rosalind Atkins that there were so many delays with the book production 'we could all be dead before the book is ready to go on the press'.[23]

And indeed production of the book also took a long time, just as the initial research and loan negotiations had done. The discovery of several blocks in Ogilvie's house after her death, including 'Chrysanthemums' (number four in the book) led to changes in its contents, causing further delay.[24] Alec wrote to Rosalind Atkins:

> *I am not complaining really as in the end the book will be better in every way. But these days I am more aware in myself of the phenomenon of age that it breeds impatience. We have all struck it, but it is odd to be striking it in oneself.*[25]

And although the choice of images was finalised in January 1994, Alec's doubts about the printability of some blocks meant completion of the text could not be finalised until after they had all been printed. It was not feasible to do trial proofs of doubtful blocks before printing commenced, he explained to Helen Maxwell, because doing the make-ready on the cylinder press was going to be so time-consuming.[26] The unevenness of some of the blocks meant that despite 'my best efforts and elaborate makeready, I have not been able to print some of this work to its best advantage', as he remarked in his Printer's Note. Printing the images was not complete until mid-April 1995, with the text due to be printed soon afterwards.[27] The first copies of the finished book were despatched to Helen Ogilvie's family in August 1995.[28]

Wood Engravings was bound in Melbourne by a third Helen, Helen Wadlington, the fourth Brindabella project she had worked on. Discussion of the binding began with consideration of the possibilities of using pictorial siding paper, but Alec wanted to feature Helen Ogilvie's own bookplate on the front cover so preferred a non-pictorial treatment. Wadlington proposed several decorated papers made by herself—the path they had followed successfully in two of their previous collaborations, *Occasions of Birds* and *The Sea Poems of Kenneth Slessor*. Alec worried about the additional cost for what was going to be his first book to sell for three figures, and briefly considered using an undecorated Bugra paper. However, in the end he chose one of her ideas for a decorated paper, in a warm brown with grainy stripes suggesting wooden boards, and agreed to her suggestion of green quarter leather titled on the spine in gold. The title label on the front board features the most successful of the line blocks used in the book, the bookplate of Helen Ogilvie, copied from an original in the possession of the National Gallery of Australia. The tipped-in frontispiece, a Melbourne *Argus* photo of Helen Ogilvie painting in her Little Collins Street studio in 1938, was printed in duotone by Goanna Print in Canberra. Photo and bookplate were also included in the modest prospectus.

This was the most expensive book produced to date by the press, retailing for $100, but nonetheless it sold well. Standing-order customers were offered the option of payment in two instalments on top of their usual discount. The total cost of production was $12,597. Binding accounted for half this, at $6,545. Other costs included fares to and from Melbourne, amounting to $1,099, and insurance of blocks on loan from Melbourne University Gallery at $230. Alec paid $2,000 in royalties, $716 for paper, $417 for line blocks and block preparation, and only $230 for advertising, which appears to have been for mailing the prospectus alone—there was no ad in

The Australian this time. Typesetting by Inter-Typesetting Service cost $520. As of 31 August 1995, when he reckoned up his total costs, Alec had invoiced $15,775.86 for copies sold, giving him a surplus of $3,178.86. This was rather more than he had originally estimated and must reflect greater than anticipated sales at full price.[29] The usual punctilious record of the distribution of copies shows that 57 copies were sold to libraries and booksellers and that by 1996 only eight numbered copies remained unsold, plus 13 of 15 out-of-series copies.[30] It bears repeating, however, that the enterprise was still only barely profitable from the printer's point of view. A profit of around $15 a copy was meagre compared with the hundreds of hours he had spent on this book. All that really mattered to Alec was that costs were fully recovered: 'I can't afford for the press to make a loss,' he told Heather Rusden soon afterwards, 'it's important to me that the books that I do sell, and sell out, because in a real sense the book that I'm doing now is the book that finances the next book'.[31]

Although I have not been able to find any reviews of the book, it was well received by his customers. Kay Craddock thought it was lovely and predicted it would be much sought after in years to come.[32] The comment that likely pleased him most came from Rosalind Atkins, who said that he had done such a good job of printing the blocks that there was no indication of how difficult they must have been to print.[33]

35

'I was fortunate to know her and to learn from her'

Nan McDonald, *For Prisoners* (1995)

One of the first aims of the Brindabella Press had been to print the work of poets who had been unwontedly overlooked. This was avowedly Alec's aim in printing the pamphlet *For Prisoners*, a single poem by Nan McDonald (1921–1974). It was also a return to the beginnings of his career in publishing, when McDonald was 'the senior member of the staff of Beatrice Davis at Angus & Robertson, Sydney, where I was fortunate to know her and to learn from her'.[1] McDonald had been the first winner of the Grace Leven Prize for Poetry, for her book *Pacific Sea* (1947), but published only two more books before her last collection, her *Selected Poems*, appeared in 1969. She had not been 'remembered or memorialized as her work deserves', Judith Wright commented in a note Alec solicited for the preface to his pamphlet. 'It is long overdue for a re-evaluation of poems which still retain their power to move and to recall the times we have lived through.'

McDonald had died in 1974, but it seems that it was not until 1995 that the poem in its present form came to Alec and Rosemary's attention, when her sister, Margaret McDonald, sent Rosemary copies of several unpublished poems found in Nan's papers at her home at Mount Keira, near Wollongong. Nan McDonald and Rosemary Dobson were lifelong friends and frequent correspondents—there are 13 folders of letters between them in Rosemary's papers at the National Library. There were earlier drafts of the poem found at Mount Keira, but this had been signed by her and could be considered to be final. Although Alec planned a small edition of 150 copies, none for sale and to be distributed to McDonald's family and friends and 'friends of the press', he intended also to send it to 'a few people who might be in a position to promote the republication of Nan's work'.[2]

For Prisoners is an unpaginated 8-page pamphlet in the usual tall format, with a one-page note by Alec and two pages of poetry hand-set in Centaur. Canberra graphic designer Kathie Griffiths designed an initial capital T, in the shape of a human figure with outstretched arms behind a barred window, which Alec printed from a line block.[3] The paper was Archive Text, sewn by Alec into ochre wrappers. He initialled the colophon. The poem itself is a prayer in remembrance of people imprisoned, and especially those who die in prison, contrasting their lack of freedom with the beauty and liberty of the poet's surroundings.

It is interesting to compare the distribution of this poem with that of *Three Poems on Water-Springs*, the press' first work printed after the Boltons settled in Canberra. There are only a handful of names in common, among them the librarians Geoffrey Farmer, Pauline Fanning and Jean Whyte, and Canberra crafts writer and close family friend Meredith Hinchliffe. Who, in what was unexpectedly to be the penultimate year of the press' history, were the 'friends of the press'? Overwhelmingly they were the faithful standing-order subscribers of recent years. Sixty-five had bought either all five or four of the most recent publications of the press: of these 41 had bought everything, sometimes in two copies. Among them were several libraries: ADFA, the Friends of the ANU Library, the Barr Smith, Swarthmore College in the US and the state libraries of South Australia, New South Wales and Queensland. (The National Library, of course, received the usual legal deposit copy.) Alec also sent copies to others who had contributed to the press over the years, people such as Rosalind Atkins, Mike Hudson and Jadwiga Jarvis, and Les Murray; and some (but not all) of the booksellers who had been his regular distributors, such as James Bennett, Roy Farrell and Kay Craddock.[4]

While *For Prisoners* did not inspire republication of her poetry by a commercial publisher, the poet Robert Gray, who greatly admired McDonald's work, told Alec he was attempting to interest Heinemann in bringing out a new selected edition.[5] This does not seem to have got anywhere. (The possibility of a Brindabella edition of Robert Gray's own poems and drawings, which had been under discussion for years, was also briefly revived around this time. Alec was interested but had too many commitments to print such a volume before a new Heinemann edition of Gray's poems came out in late 1995 or early 1996.[6]) A limited edition (90 copies) of 14 of McDonald's poems was published by Caren Florance under her imprint of Ampersand Duck in 2008, under the title of *Transmigration*. Apart from one poem in an anthology published by Penguin in 2009, this is the major appearance of Nan McDonald's poetry subsequent to the pamphlet. *For Prisoners* is now one of the scarcer Brindabella titles, with only a handful of copies on the market at any given time.

One element of Nan McDonald's persona reflected something of growing importance to Alec at this time. She was, as he pointed out in his prefatory note, a religious poet and a lifelong Christian. He himself had found his way back to what he called a 'qualified' Christianity when he published the poem, as he told Heather Rusden in the final moments of his oral history interview with her in 1996.

> *Under my mother's tutelage I was a church-goer from age zero and in my adolescent years became a Christian. At the age of about 19 or so, became an agnostic and remained an agnostic for most of my life, but in the last few years I have returned, in a questing sort of way, to an interest in religious ideas, and actually to the practice of religion. Rosemary and I are parishioners of the Anglican church of St Paul's here in Manuka and we go to church—we go to church less frequently than we go to the gallery perhaps, but we go to church, say, every two or three weeks.*
>
> *It's hard for me to say what that means to me. I suppose it's a kind of quest or questioning business. I'm probably such a qualified Christian that I would not be counted as a Christian. What I worship as God is a spirit of goodness and love and truth and I would like to think that my life was a pursuit of that God, or a wish to live in that way, in the lightness of goodness and love and truth. I think that for us, in the tradition that we've grown up in the West, that spirit is exemplified in the*

> *life of Christ and that is what it is good to try to emulate. For some reason it now seems to me that a way to try to do this is through the practice of organised religion and through the fellowship of worship … I think it was art that drew me back in a sense to religion because in a cathedral in Autun in France there are wonderful sculptures that were done in the twelfth century by a sculptor named Gislebertus and Rosemary's had for many years a … book of sculptures of Gislebertus, of the three kings being awakened by the angel to go to Bethlehem … I used to look at it and that perhaps drew me back, helped to draw me back.*[7]

He and Rosemary attended the 7am service at St Paul's. A simple, almost austere service based on the Book of Common Prayer, this gave him the opportunity to look 'for something we might have found', as Rosemary put it in her oral history interview three years after his death. St Paul's was also the church where both Alec's and Rosemary's funerals were to be held.

36

'Everything takes longer than is foreseen'

Gavin Souter, *A Torrent of Words* (1996)

A Torrent of Words was intended to be Alec's last book printed from hot metal but instead became his last book of all. It was also, in some ways, a return to the Sydney of his youth.

Gavin Souter had suggested a memoir of the writer Leon Gellert in mid-1994. Alec was immediately interested, seeing him 'as an ideal subject for a short book of the Percival Serle kind', while assuring Souter that he did not want to constrain him in terms of length. He was printing *Granite Country* at the time, and had Helen Ogilvie's *Wood Engravings* due next, so thought the book was likely to be a project for 1995. 'My experience (from which I seem never properly to learn) is that everything takes longer than is foreseen. Over-optimistic forecasts are as much a factor of life here as in real publishing,' he added.[1]

A Torrent of Words is in the usual tall, narrow Brindabella format, this time case-bound by a trade binder (The Bindery, Burwood, Victoria) in a charcoal Cialux rayon cloth. (The Bindery was a subsidiary of Brown Prior Anderson, whom Alec knew and trusted from past experience when at the National Library.[2]) The front board is blocked with a light blue foil panel, on which is superimposed a smaller line image of Gellert's head blocked in silver. The endpapers are Outback spinifex green, supplied by Raleigh Paper.[3] Goanna Print printed an 8-page section of offset duotone photographs on Parilux Dull Silk cream paper, which had been suggested by Raleigh Paper as the best match for the Mohawk Superfine of the text. (Alec investigated the possibility of printing the photographs on Mohawk Superfine as well, but decided against this because the extra cost did not guarantee a better result.)[4] 'I am looking for a richness of black, nothing reddish or sepia,' he told Goanna.[5] As usual, the book was supplied with a mylar dust wrapper. The line portrait of Gellert, taken from a greeting card used by him in 1953–1954 and lent by Joan Phipson, is repeated in blue on the title-page. Alec printed the headings in blue also.

The text was set in Linotype Granjon keyed by Inter-Typesetting Service (Intertype machines could run Linotype matrices[6]), using second-hand matrices Alec had imported from Canada in 1995[7], but he was not particularly happy with the result. He was now convinced there was no long-term future for hot-metal letterpress in Australia. 'I have fallen to brooding again about typesetting,' he told Bob Summers, halfway through printing *A Torrent of Words*:

But the results are not perfect, as the word spacing is not always exactly what I would wish, and then from time to time a worn mat (or something) produces a line where the alignment of the letters is not one hundred percent. This is to some extent perhaps the imperfection inherent in Lino when compared with Mono, where if there is a character that seems in any way blemished, you just hoist it out and insert another.

I would like to get control of my setting again. Of course, hand-setting, where I began, is an answer. But not an answer with which I can now be satisfied, as I am attempting longer and longer texts. The Souter book, for instance, is 20,000 words. I don't have enough type, and more importantly enough life left, to contemplate hand-setting prose of anything like that length.

Freight and customs costs ruled out having typesetting done in the US, and it was too late to set up his own Linotype machine. Instead, he now wondered if he should embrace computer typesetting, at his own desk:

and then send it away to have photopolymer plates made. Expensive? I expect so. And time-consuming, too, as my computer skills are pretty fundamental. I used to think that the photopolymer method was somehow unreal or false. The elegant Bookways magazine convinced me that I was wrong, because when they printed a Mono sample and a computer-set sample side by side, I couldn't tell which was which. I realised, while still feeling sceptical, that the result is more important than the question of how it was achieved … You may think that my best plan is to keep on as I am at present, using other people's Lino

> *skills. That could well be what will happen. All the same, I have this recurring dissatisfaction at not being in control.*[8]

The title of the book was set in Linotype Palatino, although with an unusual lower-case f with a straight descender, which makes it something of a mystery. Alec did own Linotype Palatino matrices in 10 and 12 point sizes but the title is 14 point. His source is not known to me. However, by now he was definitely moving away from hot-metal letterpress, and when the Inter-Typesetting Service closed soon after the Gellert job was complete he resolved to set out 'on this rather daunting exercise of computer setting and photopolymer platemaking'.[9] He told subscribers of his decision in September, in an announcement called 'News from Brindabella Press: September 1996', which was itself printed from photopolymer plates.

> *Not without anxiety as to my ability to master the software, I have taken this step to regain personal responsibility for the typesetting process, and also to escape from the growing difficulty of obtaining type fonts and hot-metal setting … I am using the same presses as before.*

At the same time, he forecast smaller editions. 'Frankly, I would like to try to produce Brindabella books to a higher standard'—which also meant higher prices.[10] The announcement was itself both 'opportunity for a test-run and demonstration', as he told Rosalind Atkins. 'I have been working hard at the new computer and gradually mastering—if only in an elementary way—the software. It is very sophisticated; quite takes my breath away.' He had also bought a second-hand photopolymer platemaker. 'If it all works, and I can master the software, I will have regained control of my setting and reverted to a different kind of hand setting.' [11]

He bought Adobe Garamond (Roman and Italic) fonts on disk for Mac, telling his supplier that although he was 'a bit confused by this welter of Garamonds', he had 'spent quite a few pleasant hours browsing in the Monotype Font Index, and will look forward to choosing one or two more in the future'. For the moment, he confessed:

> *I am fully stretched by the cost of changing to computer setting and polymer platemaking, to say nothing of the steepness of the learning curve involved in mastering the software … The closure of one hot metal resource after another has pushed me to this change, together with a wish to regain control of my setting … Such is life. I think of this change as an exciting development.*[12]

The transition was indeed expensive for him: the Adobe Garamond fonts cost him $450. A digital download of the same fonts today would be less than a quarter of that. (Although he had not used Garamond much previously, it was evidently a typeface he liked, because he had once bought six fonts of used Garamond. He told Mike Hudson in 1992 that 'One was missing lower case o, one was missing lower case h and two were Goudy'.[13] Such are the perils of buying second-hand type, and none were listed in the inventory compiled by his family after his death.)

Alec had personal knowledge of some of the people discussed in the Gellert memoir, which is reflected in some of his editorial comments. He was keen to get a sense of Gellert 'as a productive editor', and for the book to present every aspect of his personality. 'I am very happy with the manuscript,' he told Souter.

It is so succinct, and witty, and amazingly detailed. One gets a picture of the times that is as interesting as the picture of the man. He is not a very attractive character, but your portrait of him seems absolutely fair.

Thus Gellert's ungrateful assessment of Sydney Ure Smith as 'practically illiterate' should stay in, despite its churlishness, he thought. The only thing he insisted on were endnote references to quotes rather than just a brief guide to sources.[14]

Finding images for the book caused some difficulties. It proved to be impossible to locate the original of the portrait of Gellert by Norman Carter, a finalist in the Archibald Prize competition for 1923, so this was reproduced in black and white from the colour image in the March 1924 issue of *Art in Australia*. Unhappy with a photo taken by Souter of the view from Gellert's house at 22 Burran Avenue, Mosman (a view that features largely in Gellert's life), Alec commissioned the noted Sydney photographer Jill White to do a replacement, and had it printed as a two-page spread. (It was at about this time also that the Bolton family commissioned White to take an important series of photos of Alec at work at the press, and also of him with Rosemary.) His critique of the 'depressingly awful' drawings by Norman Lindsay in Gellert's *The Isle of San*, one of which he reproduced in the book, included a revealing comment to Souter:

It is hard not to feel that for a poet to be championed by Lindsay was an unfortunate fate. Closer to our own time, Rosemary was one who resisted his offers of illustration. It required some moral courage, considering that Doug Stewart would have been urging acceptance: practically a doubling of the pressure.

He also thought Lindsay was completely mistaken about Gellert's worth as a poet; that Lindsay's 'hymn of praise' in the introduction to *The Isle of San* was excruciatingly wide of the mark, and the book was very hard to read.[15] Despite the fame of Gellert's earlier war poetry, the point of this book was his larger role as a writer and editor, as the prospectus pointed out.

Gavin Souter's short life of Leon Gellert re-creates an interesting period in the history of Australian literary and artistic life. Admirers of Souter's many historical books will relish his mastery of detail, his ability to find the revealing quotation, the lightness of his touch. It is a lovely piece of writing.[16]

The prospectus itself, while modest, was attractive, reproducing the blue line drawing of Souter's head and, on the next page, Max Dupain's 1937 photograph of 'Gellert and a life mask of his younger self'. (The tipped-in photograph was also printed offset by Goanna Print. Although it is not attributed to anyone, it is possible that the blue line drawing was a self-portrait by Souter himself.)

Although the colophon mentions an edition of 270, correspondence with the binder suggests only 257 or 258 copies were bound after a large number of spoils.[17] This must have been a little frustrating, given Alec's hopeful expectations of a reliable job: the intended larger size of the edition was because Melbourne University Press had declined the offer of a Miegunyah Press edition based on the Brindabella letterpress, so Alec thought he could sell a few more copies than usual. (A similar offer was then made to the University of Queensland Press, but this too was declined.[18]) Nonetheless, he told Rosalind Atkins that he was generally happy with the binding job, apart from a few issues with blocking. There were fewer spoils with hand binding but the cost was much more: $20 to $25 for hand binding as opposed to $6 to $7 for machine binding.[19]

A Torrent of Words retailed for $69.95, with the usual discounts. When Alec estimated his costs in April 1996, the unit cost per copy was $40.32 (based on 260 copies). Typesetting cost $1,670 and royalties, at 12.5 per cent, amounted to $2,361 (for the sake of the royalty calculation, Alec treated all copies as selling for the full retail price[20]). Other major costs included printing the duotones ($1,198) and binding ($1,650). An ad in *The Weekend Australian* cost $744, and he later advertised also in *The Sydney Morning Herald*. The projected cost of the edition, including 10 per cent overhead (but not, as usual, labour) was $10,483.[21] Alec did not record income, but his detailed list of the distribution of copies suggests that fewer than 30 copies remained unsold at the time of his death. Booksellers and libraries took 70 copies.[22]

A Torrent of Words is now relatively easy to find second-hand and does not command high prices, although it remains the only substantial biography of Gellert. It was well received by critics. Peter Ryan praised it in *Quadrant*, likening its publication to finding a jewel among the crass rubbish of most contemporary events: 'the book prompts reflection on the debt which civilised Australians owe to private scholars (like Souter) and to small, quality publishing houses'.[23] It was also praised by Clement Semmler in *The Australian* as setting 'a standard of book production that could hardly be bettered'.[24] And Don Anderson gave the whole of his weekend column in *The Sydney Morning Herald* to the book, while recognising its somewhat ambivalent nature rather more: 'Gavin Souter manages the precarious art of the affectionate but not uncritical memoir with grace,' he wrote.

> *Ever-courteous Gavin Souter leaves the most intriguing sentence of his humane book hanging in the air. Imagine, if you will, a short story, or a novel, beginning with the 'unguarded' remark by Gellert that Gavin Souter reports, but does not pursue: 'I can never remember actually being proud of my wife'.*[25]

One is reminded of a remark Alec made to Souter during the editing process, discussing an episode that revealed Gellert's unpleasant side. Gellert may have been

> *one of those self-absorbed people who don't think through the implications of what they say and do. To me, his slighting references to Kathleen are more outrageous than this. Unfeeling is one word that describes Gellert to me.*[26]

37

Last Days of the Brindabella Press

The year 1996, which ushered in a time of change, also included recognition for Alec's work, beginning with his induction into the Hall of Fame of the Australian Book Publishers Association (now the Australian Publishers Association).[1] The award was for an 'outstanding and continued contribution to Australian book design and production'. 'Alec Bolton has devoted more than forty years to producing fine Australian books,' reads the citation. 'For the last twenty years he has designed and hand-printed books for his own small but renowned literary press, Brindabella. The books of the Brindabella Press … are each works of art. Alec Bolton's lifetime commitment to classical book design is legendary,' it concludes.[2]

Alec was somewhat taken aback. 'I am very pleased, but also somewhat embarrassed, as I am not a designer at all, only a rather mediocre printer,' he told one correspondent, just before going to Melbourne to receive the award.[3] 'I am as amazed as I am pleased,' he told Rosalind Atkins, and he was happy to tell her also of the award of an honorary doctorate to Rosemary by the University of Sydney a few days earlier. 'A big ceremony, gorgeous academic robes, the Great Hall organ pealing forth. Her occasional address was greeted with prolonged applause.'[4]

Then, on 8 November 1996, the Australian Academy of the Humanities elected him an Honorary Fellow, 'in recognition of his contribution to quality printing and book production over almost half a century, and for his willing work on the Academy Editions Project'.[5] The Academy Editions of Australian Literature was a ten-volume partnership between the Academy and the University of Queensland Press, launched with the publication of a definitive critical edition of *The Recollections of Geoffry Hamlyn,* by Henry Kingsley, in 1996. The series was the first to encompass such a gathering of key Australian colonial texts, and was coordinated by Professor Paul Eggert of the Australian Scholarly Editions Centre at University College, Australian Defence Force Academy.

In an interview on 24 October 2014, Eggert recollected that Professor John Mulvaney, Honorary Secretary of the Academy and a keen supporter of the project, had suggested that Alec's advice be sought for the page design of the first volume. At that time a dummy of the Hamlyn title had already been prepared to show potential sponsors, along with a blad to show booksellers (a blad is a promotional flier). The dummy was in a substantially larger format. Alec suggested the page size be reduced. He suggested the setting be tighter but the leading and margins (especially top and bottom) more generous, and overall the volume became rather more readable. Eggert made the point that such volumes are highly complex, with extensive scholarly apparatus and a need for absolute clarity, as well as economy in setting so no page is wasted in an 800-page text. Local graphic designer Caren Florance, who had recently completed an MA under Eggert's supervision, then realised Alec's design ideas in PageMaker. The constant to-ing and fro-ing between the three of them produced many iterations, until they were all happy with the result.

Alec saw the book in proof, and also made suggestions for *The Journal of Annie Baxter Dawbin*, next in the series. Florance and Eggert designed the rest of the series in the spirit of what they had learned from Alec. It was Eggert who proposed Ehrhardt as a typeface, partly because he was already familiar with it in the context of the Cambridge University Press Lawrence editions:

> *However [Alec] surprised me by improving in so many ways on the design of those Cambridge editions: better type block dimensions and thus fewer number of words per line, and leading (the latter, smaller than I expected) … The Cambridge design was less daring (e.g. nothing on the reading page but text) and far less handsome (e.g. smaller type for front and end matter) … It was an education to really know for sure that the page has an aesthetic of its own, and that anticipating the reader's needs is a vital part of the design.*[6]

The quid pro quo for Alec was that Caren Florance helped him with learning how to use a computer in preparation for his transition to photopolymer typesetting, while she in turn absorbed everything he shared with her about letterpress. She was already immersed in printing, but this was an invaluable learning experience. (Florance had done a short course in printing with Peter Finlay at the Graphic Investigation Workshop of the Canberra Art School during her study for a Masters in Literature, and later enrolled full-time in the Art School, adding a BA with Honours in Visual Arts and later still a doctorate to her formidable list of qualifications.[7]) And thus, just before his death, Alec passed the torch to someone who would later become one of Australia's leading exponents of letterpress printing.

Just a few days after his election to the Academy of the Humanities, on 18 November 1996, Alec Bolton died suddenly of a heart attack. He was 70. Frank Thompson, who had known him for 38 years, recalled his 'extraordinary generosity of spirit' in his *Canberra Times* obituary:

> *Authors universally admired him and were genuinely fond of him. Many of Australia's most distinguished authors have worked with Alec and some were notoriously difficult. However, he never once made a disparaging comment about authors but preferred to dwell on how interesting they were.*[8]

The funeral took place at St Paul's Anglican Church, Manuka, where he and Rosemary had worshipped. Robert Bolton and John Mulvaney delivered eulogies and Ian read a prayer of thanksgiving written by Lissant. The service began with Psalm 23 and finished with Whittier's hymn, 'Dear Lord and Father of Mankind'. The funeral program was illustrated with two Rosalind Atkins engravings and the Brindabella Press pressmark.

The shock of his unexpected death is remembered by those who knew him, including this writer. His family was left with the melancholy task of disposing of the printery. Rosemary and her children planned the disposal of Alec's equipment carefully and found appropriate homes for everything. Some items were given to friends: the Baskerville type to the printers Phil Day and Ingeborg Hansen, then living at Goulburn (later to be acquired by Caren Florance); the Centaur type to Bob Summers. Alec's guillotine was given to Robin Tait. The Australian Scholarly Editions Centre at the ADFA bought the three big presses and most of the ancillary equipment to use in its teaching of analytical bibliography, a not uncommon practice at academic institutions concerned with the study of the history of printed texts, while the family kept only the little Adana (now at the National Library of Australia). The ADFA later disposed of at least one of these presses, the Furnival Wharfedale, which was in 2018 in the possession of Canberra printer Millan Pintos-Lopez, proprietor of the Raspincho Press. I have not been able to ascertain the whereabouts of the other two presses.

There was no thought of the press continuing. As his family put it in a final card distributed to 'Alec Bolton's family, friends and colleagues, and for the friends and supporters of the Brindabella Press', 'the Brindabella Press concludes with Alec', although he had been working on several books when he died. It was the last use of the BP pressmark, and again featured an engraving by Rosalind Atkins.[9]

Given this, Rosemary was unhappy when one of these books, a collection of poems by Lynn Hard, appeared in 1998 with the suggestion that the author saw it 'as the last publication of the Brindabella Press'. *Australia Suite* was published by Tom Thompson of ETT Imprint in a signed edition of 100 copies, illustrated by Garry Shead, with an original signed etching by Shead loosely inserted. Shead had certainly been Alec's choice as artist, and the book was bound by Robin Tait, who pencilled the words 'For Alec, Robin Tait' on the title-page verso.[10] Printing details are not given, but *Australia Suite* appears to have been printed offset. Design is credited to Mike Connolly, of Watson's Bay. Rosemary noted in 1998 that the Brindabella Press edition had reached 'an advanced stage of preparation', and the surviving proofs suggest it would have looked quite different from the published edition, with poem titles in italic and dedications in small caps.[11] Alec had in mind a format 'slightly wider than it is high—with many or most of the poems set in two columns', which again is not replicated.[12]

After the Brindabella Press link was mentioned in a *Canberra Times* review of *Australia Suite*, Rosemary wrote to the paper to reiterate that the Brindabella Press had ended on Alec's death. 'I appreciate that Lynn Hard's comments are intended as a tribute,' she said. 'However, I would like to make it clear that although Alec Bolton planned to publish the poems he had no part in the design or production of this edition.'[13] She also left a note for 'Readers of the Archive held in the National Library' to reiterate the point. 'Alec Bolton was the founder and sole operator of the Press. As the compiler of the Archive I am most anxious to state that the claim made by Lynn Hard … cannot be substantiated and should not have been made.'[14] Rosemary nonetheless lent the Brindabella Press mail list to Tom Thompson so he could promote the book, but only a handful of subscribers bought copies.

The two other projects that had been underway at the time of Alec's death were at a less advanced stage. One was a collection of four short stories by David Malouf, whom both Alec and Rosemary had known for many years and to whom they sent copies of Brindabella books as gifts from time to time. He had particularly appreciated *The Palace with Two Sides*, he wrote in 1986.[15] Alec approached him in 1993, asking for either a short story or for a poem to print as a broadside. Although it took some time for the project to gel, it was announced in his last newsletter to subscribers in September 1996, and he had begun to discuss possible illustrations with the wood engraver Patsy Payne after sending her a copy of the manuscript.[16] (Both he and Payne found the stories just a little 'Delphic', he wrote to Fay Zwicky, asking for her thoughts on what might be going on below the surface: 'they have similar, mythic qualities of style. I do like them, and am excited at the prospect of printing them'.[17])

The four stories were eventually published in 1999 by Paper Bark Press as *Untold Tales*, with the dedication 'For Alec Bolton, 1926–96'.[18] (The first story, 'Buxtehude's Daughter', was itself originally entitled 'An Untold Tale'. It was Alec who suggested its eventual title, after receiving the manuscript from Malouf.) He had difficulty deciding which story was his favourite, he told Malouf. 'An Untold Tale' was for him 'the most resonant and accessible', while 'Epimetheus' held 'the deepest wells of meaning'. He had planned to set the book in Adobe Garamond in PageMaker prior to making photopolymer plates, and, given the shortness of the book, thought it should be in a small format. 'I would not like to have a huge type-size floating about on a large page,' he had written.[19] *Untold Tales* was set in Aldine 721 BT typeface, 11.5 point on 19. Given the similarities between Garamond and Aldine, and despite its lack of illustrations and offset printing, the Paper Bark Press edition was resonant with its unrealised Brindabella Press antecedent although not claimed as such.

The other unfinished project was *Terang Revisited*, a book by Rosalind Atkins about her childhood in western Victoria. It would have been a return to the scene of her earlier book of wood engravings, *Recollections*, but this time printed letterpress. 'Proofs I have seen of early engravings she has made for this new series are outstanding,' Alec told his subscribers. 'I am looking forward more than I can say to working on this book. It is still some way off.'[20] *Terang Revisited* was never completed and has not been published.

Epilogue

How, then, to sum up this life? In the memorial card sent to friends and the press' supporters after Alec's death, Rosemary and her children began by reiterating that he had been 'a creative force in Australian publishing over a long period: as editor for major publishers, as Director of Publications at the National Library of Australia and, most creatively, as founder and sole operator of the Brindabella Press. His skills and experience were joined in the search for the perfect book'. 'Alec contributed to Australia's cultural life in many areas,' they went on to say:

> *His advice was sought and always given thoughtfully, but diffidently. He was humane and selfless, but also strong of mind and realistic … Elements of his quality as a person can be seen in his most memorable achievement—the making of books in which all elements worked together towards the highest standards, and in harmony. Asked to sum up his principles of design, he nominated simplicity, a minimum of ornament, restraint, a search for joy and esprit. It could be said in truth that these were the principles he applied to his whole life.*[1]

A few years earlier, in 1993, the Friends of the National Library had celebrated Alec's achievement over a lifetime in publishing, producing a small memoir (my first opportunity to write about him at some length) and hosting a congenial event at the Library. Many nice things were said on that occasion, but one letter in particular stands out to me, written by Allan Fleming, who had recruited Alec to the Library in 1971 and who could not be there on the night.

> *I feel very proud that I was able to render to the NLA the enduring service of inviting you to join us, to welcome you in, and later to be able to register it as one of our lucky NLA history making days. Even in my short time you did so much that we could never have done without you. I had known about your skills, but as you took over our publishing I realised that the word 'skills' was just the name of an ingredient—it was a word on the way to acknowledging and admiring your great gift of creativity. And all that came to us in someone whose head never swelled under praise, and whose quiet smile and modesty were maintained through the inevitable tension of office. It was wonderful to have you as a colleague.*[2]

To these words one can add something about legacy. Alec kept alive a commitment to the book as one of the supreme products of human culture at a time when we can now see that the centrality of the book as a mode of expression was about to be challenged. He did not belong to an artistic or intellectual avant-garde. He had little sympathy for the experimental and the adventurous, even when made by friends. Instead, and from the very beginning with such early books as *Time Given*, he set out to show that good writing deserved to be treated with respect and dignity rather than being hastily printed as if it had no lasting value. His faith was in the book as the most significant, coherent, persistent and transparent bearer of meaning in his culture.

His passion for a well-printed book was no Arts-and-Crafts yearning for a medieval past, however. Good printing and design could be achieved by modern means of relief printing: unlike many private press printers of his day, he did not look for a large iron hand press but worked with the letterpress technology that had reached its heights in his own lifetime, and he simply sought to become more proficient in its use. His advocacy of wood engraving also links him to its revival in the early years of the twentieth century, not to any notion of a golden age of medieval printing.

He thus built a bridge between the book-oriented culture of the early twentieth century and those of us who, in these challenging times, continue in the perhaps quixotic belief that the book can be one of the great triumphs of the human spirit and that we should not surrender automatically to the ceaseless demands of modernity and technological change. His was a life of dedication to his craft as a maker of books, and of singular achievement in that goal. Just as Rosemary decided she should do, in her poem 'Museums', he sought to 'Put past to present purpose. Make'.[3] There is much that the letterpress revival of recent years can learn from his example, and much of value to all who seek to live an ethical, sustainable and productive life.

The last word should be with Rosemary, whose poem 'Reading Aloud' comes from a sequence she called 'Poems of a Marriage'[4]:

Low, clear and free of self your voice went on
At night you read, and for how many years
From Sterne to Kipling, Flaubert, Boswell, Proust —
Proust a whole year, and finishing you said

'One of the great experiences of my life.'
And mine, and mine.

Intent to listen, quieting my hands
With plain and purl, I followed your low voice,
Knitting unmindfully long scarves for friends
Sent off as signs of that shared calm content
Still looked for in the un-shared books I choose
Reading alone.

Well, we gave up once, stalled on Chuzzlewit.
How wrong it felt. You sensed a binding need
To take books to the end. Faced with reverses said,
'We must press on.'
From books to life, your thought:
'Forgive, learn from the past. Press on.'
And I press on.

Acknowledgements

I pay respect to the Elders of the Ngunnawal people, past and present, and acknowledge their long stewardship of the beautiful country where I write.

This work began when Alan Loney asked me to give a talk on Alec Bolton. I am grateful to him for his call to action. Dr Lissant Bolton AM, Robert Bolton and Ian Bolton gave me full access to Alec's papers and generously welcomed the project into their already busy lives. Their contribution has been substantial but they have never sought to alter how things were described. I am deeply grateful to them. I also owe a considerable debt to Dr Caren Florance. Her enthusiasm for the project and her wide-ranging knowledge of the letterpress and book arts scene in Australia have been invaluable. She is one of many who have answered questions about events of long ago, a gift of memory and insight that I treasure. Others of Alec's friends, along with printers, book binders and book arts colleagues who have helped include Rosalind Atkins, Bill Chambers, Ron Eadie, Paul Eggert, Alan Gould, Meredith Hinchliffe, Bill Huff-Johnston, Mike Hudson, Jadwiga Jarvis, Simon Lawrence, Helen Maxwell, Geoff Page, Robin Tait, Jim Walker and Adrian Young.

Alec's and my own former colleagues at the National Library have for many years encouraged my enthusiasm for the Brindabella Press. Judith Baskin, Gordon Bower, Kevin Bradley,

Diana Carroll, Warwick Cathro, George Clark, Mark Cranfield, Diana Dack, Margaret Dent, George Donda, Jan Fullerton, Andrew Gosling, Pauline Haldane, Philip Jackson, Janet Kahler, Jan Lyall, Indulis Kepars, Anthony Ketley, Graeme Powell, Marie Sexton, Beth Stone, Richard Stone, Ross Swindley, John Thompson, Bill Thorn, Bill Tully, Ted Vellacott, Eric Wainwright and Kerry Webb have all contributed to my understanding either of Alec or the Library, or both, often perhaps without realising it! The National Library's oral history interviews with Alec conducted by Heather Rusden have been invaluable and I have drawn on them extensively. I also thank Jill White for her generous gift to the National Library of the photos she took of Alec and Rosemary in 1993, one of which illustrates the cover of this book.

More times than I can count I have found inspiration in the pages of the Whittington Press journal *Matrix*, just as Alec did. *Matrix* is no more but I thank John and Rosalind Randle for their immense gift to the world of letterpress printing over nearly four decades. In a more general sense, writing this book has taken me deeply into the complex technical and social histories of the 'Printing and Kindred Industries' and I have relied heavily on the published work of historians and practicing printers. I am grateful for their knowledge, which is acknowledged throughout the text: mistakes and misunderstandings are my own.

The National Library of Australia has been a lodestar for me ever since I first visited as a reader in the 1970s, and numerous staff members have been unfailingly courteous and helpful. Jürgen Wegner of the Brandywine Archive has also been of great assistance. Lauren Smith at NLA Publishing has been an enthusiastic advocate for the project, and I thank Amelia Hartney and Tricia Dearborn for their skilful editing, and Jemma Posch for image research and coordination. I greatly admire Filip Bartkowiak's elegant design of the book, which I am sure Alec too would have praised.

My greatest debt is to Helen. She has lived with this book for most of the last decade and has been unstinting in her support of its significance. A passionate grammarian, she has been a superb copy editor as well! Our daughter Christabel shares our love of books and writing, and leads me to hope that the book will remain central to our culture into the future.

The Brindabella Press: A Brief Bibliography

I have chosen to organise this bibliography in a single chronological list. This is partly for simplicity; the total output of Alec Bolton's press was not enormous, after all. Primarily, though, it is to underscore one of the main themes of the work as a whole, which is to describe the development of the press. Alec learned from each production, no matter how simple, and positioning them in a narrative sequence, as in the biography, aims to underscore this aspect of his work as a private press printer. Thus the list begins with his first publication as a letterpress printer: ephemeral, tiny in number and pre-dating the move to Canberra and the subsequent naming of his press, yet characteristically a work by Rosemary Dobson and circulated among their circle of friends. Titles are listed in order of imprint date, which in four early instances varies from the actual dates of publication as noted.

Michael Richards

A full bibliography can be found at: nla.gov.au/stories/national-library-publishing/book-title/a-maker-of-books.

1971

KNOSSOS by Rosemary Dobson
Hand-set in Univers and printed in London on the Adana
24 hand-numbered copies, 265 x 188mm, printed in black on light grey-green Abbey Mills Greenfield Text laid paper
Collation: single leaf, unfolded

1972

VENITE, ANGELI SANCTI
Hand-set in Monotype Baskerville and printed in Canberra on the Adana
Unknown number of copies, 149 x 105mm, with the title poem set in alternate Roman and Italic lines, printed in black (Roman) and red (Italic), on pale grey Glastonbury Antique laid paper watermarked 'Glastonbury'
Collation: single leaf, folded once into 4pp.
Note: on p.3, printed in red, 'CHRISTMAS GREETINGS FROM THE BOLTONS'

1973

THREE POEMS ON WATER-SPRINGS by Rosemary Dobson
Hand-set in Monotype Baskerville
150 unnumbered copies, 203 x 288mm (unfolded, 203 x 96 folded), printed in black with the title and a single illustration by the author printed in red, on an unknown warm grey laid paper with no watermark noted
Collation: single leaf, folded twice into 6 pp.
Note: on p.4 a line drawing, printed from line block of two women filling a pot at a waterspout

STARTING FROM CENTRAL STATION by David Campbell, illus. by William Huff-Johnston
Hand-set in Monotype Baskerville
220 numbered copies, 203 x 128mm, printed in black, with illustrations in ochre, on Beckett Text laid paper watermarked 'Beckett'.
Collation: ten leaves, sewn in a single gathering into grey cover paper, wrappered and overlapped into brown laid paper sides with title printed on a label on the front wrapper in black inside an irregular ochre rule 65 x 46mm, overprinted on a light ochre linocut of the interior of Central Station
Note: on title-page, linocut print of Central Station, Sydney, in a ruled box 54 x 50mm, in ochre

FIVE DAYS OLD by Francis Webb
Hand-set in Monotype Baskerville
About 150 unnumbered copies, 137 x 197mm, printed in black, with title and rules in red, on cream Glastonbury Antique laid paper watermarked 'Glastonbury'
Collation: single leaf folded once into 4pp.
Note: on title-page, 'Christmas is in the air …'; Webb signed 21 or 22 copies shortly before his death

1974

ELEGIES by R.F. Brissenden, illus. by Robin Wallace-Crabbe
Hand-set in Monotype Baskerville
303 numbered copies, 222 x 125mm, printed in black with red section titles and, on t.p., 'Elegies' and 'Brindabella Press mcmlxxiv', on white Monadnock Paper Mills Caress Text machine-made paper and bound in stiff black cover paper
Collation: five leaves sewn in a single gathering into two leaves of black card (the outer leaf heavier than the inside one) with a cream label on the front in red
Note: on title-page, a brush drawing of a head and a hand printed from line block; publication appears to have taken place in 1975 although *Elegies* was mostly printed on weekends during 1974. The final number of copies published was 303

BRINDABELLA by Douglas Stewart, illus. by Margaret Coen
Hand-set in Monotype Baskerville with title in Imprint Shadow
100 copies, 126 x 168mm, printed in black and blue (title and initial letter of poem), on cream Glastonbury Antique laid paper watermarked 'Glastonbury'
Collation: single leaf folded once into 4pp.
Note: on p.2, a pen and ink drawing of trees by Margaret Coen printed in black from a line block

1975

TIMES AND PLACES by J.R. Rowland, 'with decorations by the author'
Hand-set in Monotype Baskerville with title in Perpetua Light
230 copies, 158 x 248mm, printed in black with illustrations in brown, on white Monadnock Paper Mills Caress Text machine-made paper and case-bound in navy blue cloth boards (253 x166mm) with maroon endpapers and an acetate wrapper
Collation: eight leaves folded and sewn into three gatherings [a-b^4, c^2] with a white label on front board, all in a double rule printed in brown
Note: on title-page, a line drawing of a steeplecock printed in brown from a line block; on p.7, a drawing of hills and trees printed in brown from a line block; despite colophon date, published in 1976

1976

TIME GIVEN by James McAuley
Hand-set in Monotype Baskerville with title and two section titles hand-written in italic and printed from line blocks
238 copies, 145 x 237mm, printed in black with title and section titles in cadmium red, on white Basingwerk Parchment paper machine-made by Grosvenor, Chater & Co. Ltd, England, and case-bound by E.C. Chapman & Co. in navy blue cloth boards (246 x 150mm) with grey endpapers and an acetate wrapper
Collation: 11 leaves folded and sewn into three gatherings [a-b^4, c^3] with a white label on front board in double rule, cadmium red
Note: on p.44, 'The hand-written titles were the gift of the calligrapher, Rod Shaw'; 'This is the fourth book of the Brindabella Press. It was begun with the generous collaboration of the author and is finished to his memory, Christmas Day 1976'

1977

GREEK COINS by Rosemary Dobson, 'with line drawings by the author'
Hand-set in Monotype Baskerville with title in Imprint Shadow
240 copies, 122 x 179mm, printed in black with title and illustrations in red ochre, on white Basingwerk Parchment machine-made paper and case-bound by E.C. Chapman, Sydney, in brown Winterbottom buckram boards 127 x 184mm, with pale yellow ochre Glastonbury Antique endpapers and in a dustwrapper of the same colour. The drawing of *Hera Enthroned* on p.13 is gold-blocked on the front board and in red ochre on the dustwrapper
Collation: eight leaves folded and sewn into two gatherings [a-b^4] with a dustwrapper including a drawing of *Hera Enthroned*
Note: on p.7, a line drawing of a dolphin in harbour; on p.13, a line drawing printed from line block of *Hera Enthroned* holding a pomegranate in her right hand and a staff in her left

1979

THE DRIFTING CONTINENT by A.D. Hope, illus. by Arthur Boyd
Hand-set in Monotype Baskerville
285 copies, 246 x 151mm, printed in black on white Curtis Rag machine-made acid-free paper and case-bound by hand by Peter Marsh, the Dove Bindery, Melbourne, in brown quarter leather with green buckram sides 253 x 160mm, with black Grandee Text endpapers, and in an acetate wrapper. The title-page drawing is gold-blocked on the front board. Gilt-lettering on the spine
Collation: 12 leaves folded and sewn into three gatherings [a-c^4]
Note: on title-page, a line drawing printed from line block of a person asleep under hay; further drawings printed from line-and-tone blocks, plus, on pp.43 and 45, two drawings printed from halftone blocks; on p.48, 'Engravings by A.A. Lawson, Sydney'

DAVID CAMPBELL [Words spoken at his funeral] by Manning Clark
Machine-set in Linotype Baskerville with title hand-set in Imprint Shadow
About 400 copies, 203 x 119mm, printed in black on white Glastonbury Antique machine-made paper and pamphlet-sewn at the press into Lusterkote cover paper of the same dimensions. The cover is printed in two colours, with the title and a ruled box in red ochre and the remainder in black
Collation: two leaves folded and sewn into a single gathering
Note: on title-page, photograph of David Campbell by Graeme Kinross Smith printed from a halftone block and in a ruled box

1981

THE EXILED IMMORTAL by Harold Stewart
Hand-set in Monotype Baskerville
240 copies, 235 x 138mm, printed in black on white Basingwerk Parchment machine-made paper, pamphlet-sewn at the press into brown card and glued into light brown turned-in cover paper of the same size printed in red ochre and light cobalt blue. Harold Stewart's *inkan* (i.e. his signature seal) is printed in red on the colophon page
Collation: eight leaves folded and sewn into a single gathering with front cover printed in blue and ochre
Note: a printed label, present in most copies, reading 'MANUSCRIPT MISTYPING Page 21 line 15: *For* jewels *read* fruits'; there is some variation in size and an early copy seen is 231 x 144mm. (This is number 12, one of the first batch sent to Harold Stewart in Kyoto.) Published the year after the imprint date

THE CONTINUANCE OF POETRY by Rosemary Dobson
Hand-set in Monotype Baskerville
275 copies, 190 x 208mm, printed in black with illustrations in cobalt green, on cream Abbey Mills Greenfield Text laid paper watermarked with a triple-pointed crown and 'Abbey Mills Greenfield', and case-bound by Stanley Owen & Sons, Sydney, in dark blue buckram boards 196 x 213mm, with sage Glastonbury Antique endpapers and in an acetate dust-wrapper. A drawing of grass in seed is gold-blocked on the front board. Gilt-lettering on the spine
Collation: eight leaves folded once and sewn into four gatherings [a-d^4]
Note: on title-page, a line drawing of a plant printed from line block; further line drawings of grasses printed in green from line blocks and halftone photographs printed in green tipped-in; on p.28, 'The decorations are by the author; the photographs, taken at David Campbell's property The Run and at Lilli Pilli on the South Coast, are by the printer'

1982

THE SPRING-MIRE by Philip Mead, illus. by Ian Sharpe
Hand-set in Monotype Baskerville
236 copies, 241 x 157mm, printed in black with illustrations in a deep violet blue on white Curtis Rag acid-free machine-made paper and case-bound by hand by the Dove Bindery, Melbourne, in brown quarter leather with brown and white crash canvas sides 248 x 168mm, brown laid Curtis Tweedweave endpapers and an acetate dustwrapper.
The title-page drawing of a rose is blocked on the front board in dark brown.
Gilt-lettering on the spine
Collation: eight leaves folded and sewn into two gatherings [a-b^4]
Note: on title-page, a line drawing of a rose, printed from line block; on p.32, 'Gee Graphics, of Sydney, made the engravings of the drawings'. Despite colophon date, published in 1983

1983

SOMETHING TO SOMEONE by Dorothy Auchterlonie
Hand-set in Monotype Centaur and Monotype Arrighi
Probably 238 copies, 232 x 165mm, printed in black with title in light red, on white mould-made Arches paper watermarked ARCHES FRANCE ∞ and case-bound by the Dove Bindery, Melbourne, in Oxford Library buckram boards 241 x 168mm, in two sections, quarter bound in black with front and back in terracotta with a gold rule at the join of the two cloths. Endpapers are Brigadoon Ancient Red machine-made paper.
Gilt-lettering on the spine. Glassine dustwrapper
Collation: 9 leaves folded and sewn into three gatherings [a-c^3]
Note: on p.2, a frontispiece, a wood engraving by Michael McCurdy printed in black

1985

SOME POEMS OF SHAW NEILSON by John Shaw Neilson, illus. by Barbara Hanrahan

Hand-set in Monotype Centaur and Arrighi

230 copies, 215 x 137mm, printed in black with title and printer's ornament on title-page printed in green, on white Basingwerk Parchment machine-made paper and case-bound by hand by Brian Hawke in brown quarter leather with blue buckram sides 220 x 142mm, with a gold rule at the join of the leather and cloth, and with pale green endpapers of cream Abbey Mills Greenfield Text laid paper watermarked with a triple-pointed crown and 'Abbey Mills Greenfield'. Gilt-lettering on the spine. Glassine dustwrapper

Collation: 11 leaves folded and sewn into three gatherings [$a^4b^3c^4$]

Note: on p.2, a frontispiece, *Green Singer*, wood engraving by Barbara Hanrahan, printed from the wood; further wood engravings printed from the wood

1986

THE PALACE WITH SEVERAL SIDES by Christina Stead, illus. by Mike Hudson

Machine-set in Monotype Bembo with title hand-set in Imprint Shadow

220 copies, 191 x 115mm, printed in black with title and printer's ornament on title-page in red purple, on white machine-made Basingwerk Parchment paper and hand bound by Robin Tait, the Tait Bindery, in a limp non-adhesive wrapper binding folded into cool violet Kilmory text paper wrappers 192 x 116mm and with two grey Kilmory text endpapers. The cover has a two-colour label in red purple

Collation: nine leaves folded and sewn into three gatherings [a-c^3]

1987

RAINFOREST by Judith Wright

Hand-set in Monotype Baskerville

275 copies, 412 x 255mm, printed in black with title and rules in green, on white mould-made Arches paper

Collation: single leaf broadside

Note: on title-page, a wood engraving by Rosalind Atkins of a rainforest scene printed from the wood, plate-mark 126 x 101mm

OCCASIONS OF BIRDS by Elizabeth Riddell, illus. by Anne Wienholt
Hand-set in Monotype Centaur with Monotype Arrighi for italic (p.4 and colophon) and Monotype Bulmer for display
275 copies, 250 x 160mm, printed in black with illustrations in rust red, on white laid Rising Paper Company letterpress paper made at the Rising Mill and hand-bound by Helen Wadlington in brown quarter cloth with paste paper sides over boards 265 x 165mm, with endpapers of the same paper as the text. On the spine is a printed label in rust red
Collation: 12 leaves folded and sewn into four gatherings [a-d^3]
Note: on title-page, a soft pencil drawing of five birds printed from line block; further pencil illustrations printed from line blocks

BRINDABELLA LETTERPRESS EDITIONS (flyer)
Hand-set in Monotype Centaur with Monotype Arrighi for italic
Unknown number of copies, 108 x 150mm, printed in red on an unknown cream wove paper
Collation: single leaf printed on one side
Note: on p.1, 'The Officina Brindabella is the private press of Alec Bolton, devoted to publishing hand-printed editions of significant Australian texts, mostly poetry, to a high standard of production …'

SMILING IN ENGLISH, SMOKING IN FRENCH by Geoff Page, illus. by Christian Preuschl von Haldenburg
Hand-set in Monotype Plantin with poem numbers in Imprint Shadow
260 copies, 184 x 101mm, printed in black with author's name and imprint on title-page in blue, on Mohawk Letterpress machine-made paper and hand bound by Ron Eadie in a limp non-adhesive binding with navy blue ribbon threaded through flecked beige cover paper and with grey endpapers. The front cover has title details printed in blue, white and red. The spine is blank
Collation: 14 leaves folded and sewn into five gatherings [a-d^3e^2]
Note: on title-page, a line drawing by Christian Preuschl von Haldenburg, of a man at a café table with the Eiffel Tower, a castle and a soldier in the background, detail of a larger drawing used inside the book and printed from line block

1988

PERCIVAL SERLE [A Memoir] by Geoffrey Serle

Machine-set in Monotype Baskerville composed by C.D. Fitzhardinge-Bailey

350 copies, 236 x 147mm, printed in black on white Mohawk Superfine machine-made paper and hand-bound by Helen Wadlington in grey quarter cloth with paste paper sides made by the binder over boards 241 x 150mm with brown endpapers and a photograph printed by offset lithography by Goanna Print, Canberra. On the spine is a label printed in black

Collation: 15 sheets folded and sewn into four gatherings [a-b^{4}c^{3}d^4]

Note: on p.2, a frontispiece, a duotone portrait printed by offset lithography; on p.61, 'The press mark printed above for the first time was drawn by Arthur Stokes'

1989

THE IDYLL WHEEL by Les A. Murray, illus. by Rosalind Atkins

Machine-set in Monotype Perpetua composed and cast by C.D. Fitzhardinge-Bailey with hand-set Bulmer for display

290 copies, 261 x 183mm, printed in black with title and imprint details on title-page in rust red, on white Zerkall mould-made paper and hand-bound by Robin Tait in rust red quarter goat skin with grey paper over boards 268 x 189mm and endpapers of blady grass paper hand-made by Katharine Nix. The cover has a two-colour label in rust red and black. Acetate dustwrapper

Collation: nine leaves folded and sewn into three gatherings [a-c^3]

Note: on title-page, a wood engraving of eucalyptus leaves, printed from the wood; further wood engravings printed from the wood; the prospectus envisaged a total of 14 poems, instead of the 12 published

PUBLICATIONS FROM 1973 TO 1989 OF THE OFFICINA BRINDABELLA

Machine-set in Linotype Baskerville

Unknown number of copies, 226 x 113mm, printed in black with illustrations in red and green, on white machine-made paper and pamphlet sewn into grey laid paper covers. The title is taken from a label on the front cover 47 x 74mm

Collation: two leaves folded once and sewn into a single gathering [a^8]

Note: two copies seen have a slip inserted, dated October 1989, apologising for a delay in issuing the list and noting that two books described as being still available in it have since gone out of print

1990

TWELVE LINOCUTS by Barbara Hanrahan

100 sets, each consisting of 12 linocuts, two letterpress prelims and one letterpress colophon page, all on deckle-edged sheets 510 x 380mm, on cream wove Arches paper watermarked 'Arches ∞', individually titled, numbered, dated and signed in pencil by the artist. The linocuts are printed in black from one block on one side of each sheet. Enclosed in a scarlet and black portfolio box made by Helen Wadlington 620(h) x 472(w) x 200(d)mm. The box is covered with French canvas and cloth and is fastened by toggles. The front of the box has a label 108 x 152mm, bordered with a rectangular Oxford rule
Collation: 15 loose sheets in portfolio box
Note: the number of individual prints made began at around 120 (*Girl with Birds* and *Lovers with a Bird*) but otherwise was a little over 100 copies

THE SEA POEMS OF KENNETH SLESSOR by Kenneth Slessor, illus. by Mike Hudson

Hand-set in Monotype Baskerville
240 copies, 280 x 188mm, printed in black with title and rule on title-page in blue, on white Mohawk Letterpress paper machine-made paper and hand-bound by Helen Wadlington in black quarter kangaroo leather with paste paper sides made by the binder over boards 286 x 144mm with grey endpapers. Gilt-lettering on the spine. Mylar dustwrapper
Collation: 12 leaves folded and sewn into four gatherings [a-d^3]
Note: on title-page, a wood engraving by Mike Hudson, of a moon-lit harbour seen through a window, printed from the wood; further wood-engravings printed from the wood and one from a reworked metal block

SLESSOR WOOD ENGRAVINGS BY MIKE HUDSON

An edition of 25 sets of three engravings printed on heavy Arches 88 paper titled, numbered, dated and signed in pencil by the artist was issued separately. They were *Five Visions of Captain Cook*, *Captain Dobbin* and *Five Bells*. There were also an unknown number of Artist's Proofs. The prints were offered to purchasers of the book, with priority to buyers of complete sets. The offer was mentioned in the prospectus for the book, with a separate announcement giving details dated November 1990

1991

IRIS IN HER GARDEN by Barbara Hanrahan, 'with relief etchings by the author'

Machine-set in Linotype Caledonia, composed by Bankstown Typesetting, with hand-set Bodoni for display

250 copies in two bindings by Robin Tait at the Tait Bindery, Queanbeyan, 212 x 139mm, printed in black with four etchings in green (title-page and three tailpieces) and four tailpieces in red on white machine-made Mohawk Superfine paper

220 copies in a Coptic sewn binding folded into grey paper wrappers 219 x 140mm and with green endpapers. The cover has a green etching as a label and there is a label on the spine, printed in green

30 copies casebound in very dark green quarter oasis goatskin with brown cloth sides 222 x 141mm and grey endpapers, with a separate etching signed and numbered in pencil, 152 x 89mm image on stiff Arches paper 234 x 165mm. The case-bound edition has gilt-lettering on the spine

Collation: 16 leaves folded and sewn into eight gatherings [a-h^2]

Note: on title-page, an etching of a young girl in a garden printed from zinc plate; on p.8, an etching of Iris with three children; further etchings

1992

UNTOLD LIVES by Rosemary Dobson

Machine-set in Linotype Granjon, composed by Bankstown Typesetting, with title set in hand-set Monotype Castellar and Garamond for display

240 copies, 236 x 140mm, printed in black on white machine-made Mohawk Superfine paper, case bound by Robin Tait, the Tait Bindery, in black quarter cloth with Brindabella siding paper designed by Adrian Young from a wood-engraved motif by Rosalind Atkins and silkscreened in three colours by Leader Graphics, Queabeyan, over boards 239 x 145mm and with black endpapers made by Canson & Montgolfier. Gilt-lettering on the spine. Mylar dustwrapper

Collation: ten leaves folded and sewn into five gatherings [a-e^2]

Note: on title-page, a wood engraving by Mike Hudson, *Breakaway*, printed from the wood

'BREAKAWAY' WOOD ENGRAVING BY MIKE HUDSON

An edition of 25 copies of the frontispiece wood engraving printed on heavy Magnani Incisioni paper, numbered, titled, dated and signed by the artist in pencil, was issued separately. The image is 178 x 101mm on a sheet 290 x 209mm.

BRINDABELLA PRESS: THE NAME REGAINED

Machine-set in Linotype Caledonia
Unknown number of copies, 108 x 150mm, printed in black on white machine-made paper and pamphlet sewn into white wrappers 104 x 152mm folded over grey card. The front cover text is printed in red
Collation: two leaves folded once and sewn into a single gathering [a^4]
Note: on p.2, a wood engraving by Victoria Clutterbuck printed from line block; issued to subscribers in September 1992. The publications still available were the Hanrahan *Twelve Linocuts* portfolio and the separate wood engravings by Mike Hudson from *The Sea Poems of Kenneth Slessor*

1993

THE END OF THE SEASON by Philip Hodgins, illus. by Victoria Clutterbuck

Machine-set in Linotype Palatino, composed by Bankstown Typesetting
230 copies, 252 x 144mm, printed in black with title and pressmark in red ochre, on soft white Mohawk Superfine machine-made paper and Coptic-bound by Robin Tait in dark brown quarter cloth with hand-made Yellow Peter Thomas siding paper from Sea Pen Press and Paper Mill over boards 252 x 146mm. The endpapers are also Mohawk Superfine. Gilt-lettering on the spine
Collation: 12 leaves folded and sewn into four gatherings [a-d^3]
Note: on title-page, a wood engraving of a wedge-tailed eagle printed from the wood

'AFTER A DRY SEASON' WOOD-ENGRAVING BY VICTORIA CLUTTERBUCK

An edition of 20 copies of the wood engraving on page 17 of the book, printed on heavy Arches paper, numbered, titled, dated and signed by the artist in pencil, was issued separately. The image is 76 x 103mm on a sheet size 304 x 194mm (measurements taken from a printer's proof). The forthcoming availability of the wood engraving was mentioned in the prospectus for the book.

NEWS FROM BRINDABELLA PRESS
Machine-set in Helvetica.
Unknown number of copies, 164 x 116mm, printed in black on white machine-made paper
Collation: one leaf folded once [a^4]
Note: on title-page, a line drawing of Morunda homestead by J. R. Rowland, printed in black from nylo block; issued to subscribers in November 1993. The sole Brindabella Press publication still in print was Philip Hodgins, *The End of the Season*

1994

THE SLEEPOUT by Les Murray
Hand-set in Monotype Baskerville
200 copies plus fourteen out-of-series, 360 x 479mm, printed in black with title, initial letter and rules in blue, on white mould-made Arches paper
Collation: single leaf broadside
Note: a wood engraving by Rosalind Atkins, of a sleepout, printed from the wood, plate-mark 135 x 161mm; on colophon, a circular 'Brindabella Press' pressmark, blind embossed

GRANITE COUNTRY by J.R. Rowland, 'with drawings by the author'
Machine-set in Intertype Baskerville by Bankstown Typesetting, with title hand-set in Castellar and display hand-set in Monotype Baskerville
220 copies (plus 22 out-of-series), 248 x 162mm, printed in black with illustrations printed from nylo line blacks in green, on white Archive Text machine-made laid paper watermarked 'Archive' and case-bound by Robin Tait in light grey cloth made by Fein Canvas over boards, 261 x 167mm, with smoke grey endpapers of Grandee Text. A line drawing of granite boulders is screen-printed onto the cloth (continuing over front and rear) and the spine is gilt-lettered. Mylar dustjacket
Collation: 16 leaves folded and sewn into eight gatherings [a-h^2]
Note: on title-page, a continuation of frontispiece line drawing of a hillside with hills in the distance, printed in green and spread across title and facing pages

1995

HELEN OGILVIE WOOD ENGRAVINGS by Helen Ogilvie (ed.) and introduced by Helen Maxwell

Machine-set in Intertype Baskerville, composed by Inter-Typesetting Service, with title hand-set in Monotype Castellar

200 copies with a further 15 out-of-series, 250 x 151mm, printed in black on white Mohawk Superfine machine-made paper and case-bound by hand by Helen Wadlington in quarter leather with decorated paper sides over boards 256 x 162mm, with Mohawk Superfine endpapers. Duotone frontispiece printed by Goanna Print, Canberra and line blocks by Modern Reproduction, West Melbourne. The cover has a two-colour label 83 x 59mm, printed in light cadmium red, with Helen Ogilvie's bookplate printed in black from a line block. Gilt-lettering on the spine. Mylar dustwrapper

Collation: 14 leaves folded and sewn into seven gatherings [a-g^2]

Note: on title-page, a wood engraving of a balcony, printed from the wood, fills the left-hand side; on p.ii, a tipped-in duotone photo of Helen Ogilvie in her Little Collins Street studio, 1938

FOR PRISONERS by Nan McDonald

Hand-set in Centaur

150 numbered copies, 239 x 149mm, printed in black, with main title and initial letter T printed in blue from a line block, on Archive Text machine-made laid paper watermarked 'Archive'. Numbered and initialled by the printer

Collation: 2 leaves, sewn in a single gathering into orange laid machine-made paper wrappers 242 x 152mm, with title printed on front, in a plain blue ruled box 30 x 60mm

Note: on p.5, the initial letter T is a drawing by Kathie Griffiths of a person behind bars with arms outstretched

1996

A TORRENT OF WORDS: Leon Gellert: A Writer's Life by Gavin Souter
Machine-set in Linotype Granjon, keyed by Inter-Typesetting Service, with title in Linotype Palatino (with a straight descender on the lower-case f) and display hand-set in an unknown bold italic font
270 copies (stated, but no more than 258 bound), 235 x 145mm, printed in black with title and display text in blue, on white machine-made Mohawk Superfine paper and case-bound by The Bindery, Burwood, Victoria, in charcoal Cialux rayon cloth over boards 243 x 155mm, with spinifex green Outback endpapers from Raleigh Paper. The title-page drawing of Gellert's head is silver-blocked over a blue background on the front board and the spine is silver-lettered. Mylar dustwrapper
Collation: 18 leaves folded and sewn into nine gatherings [a-i^2]. Gathering [d] consists of offset duotone photographs printed by Goanna Print, Canberra, on Parilux Dull Silk paper
Note: on title-page, a line drawing of Gellert's head, printed from line block in blue; further photographs

NEWS FROM BRINDABELLA PRESS: SEPTEMBER 1996
Computer-set in Adobe Garamond and printed from photopolymer plates
Unknown number of copies, 220 x 110mm, printed in black with cover in red, on an unknown white paper and pamphlet-sewn into grey laid paper wrappers 225 x 112mm
Collation: 4pp., a single leaf folded once into four pages
Note: on p.1, 'With this announcement the press inaugurates a change in its production methods: from traditional letterpress using hot-metal type to computer typesetting and printing from photopolymer plates'

Endnotes

Introduction

1 Maryanne Wolf, *Proust and the Squid: The Story and Science of the Reading Brain.* London: Icon Books, 2008, pp.69–78.

Chapter 1

1 Stanley Devlin, *Multiple Stains: The Story Of the Devlin and Associated Families in Australia.* Canberra: S.L. Devlin, 1999, pp.411–412, 436–473. As a child he was also ignorant of a distant connection to the Windeyer family, through Mary Bolton (1837–1912), a daughter of Robert and Jane Bolton, who married the politician and judge William Charles Windeyer in 1857. In later years he was to discover a distant cousinship, through the Windeyer/Le Gay Brereton connection, with his friend the poet R.D. FitzGerald (1902–1987), a nephew of J. Le Gay Brereton.

2 Tony Moore, *Death or Liberty: Rebels and Radicals Transported to Australia 1788–1868.* Sydney: Pier 9, 2010, pp.95, 121.

3 Alec Bolton to Gerald Fischer, 11 March 1984, Box 11 Folder 40, NLA MS 7426 Addition 25 February 1998. NB: the numbering of folders in the Bolton Papers at the National Library is ambiguous, owing to the sequence being started again from the third addition to the collection (i.e. folders 1–37 cover the original deposit and two further additions, while another series from folder 1–46 stem from a further three additions). For this reason, box number and date of accession are given in endnotes. A further series of papers, deposited in 2015, lacked folder numbers at the time of writing.

4 *The Daily Advertiser* (Wagga Wagga), 18 April 1933, p.2; *The Sydney Morning Herald*, 17 April 1933, p.9. However, the latter source says he 'joined the staff of the Sydney office of the Peninsular and Oriental Steam Navigation Co in 1909'.

5 Alec Bolton, interview with Heather Rusden, 11 October 1996. All direct quotes by Alec in the remainder of this chapter are from this interview, unless otherwise acknowledged.

6 His estate was valued for probate at £44,992 (*The Daily Examiner* (Grafton), 3 February 1922): a substantial sum, but hardly wealth beyond the dreams of avarice, especially when divided among ten children.

7 Obituary of Frederick George Crouch, *Casino and Kyogle Courier and North Coast Advertiser*, 4 January 1922.

8 *Casino and Kyogle Courier and North Coast Advertiser*, 8 September 1923, p.2.

9 Harry Crouch, 'Family notes', 1965, Bolton Family Papers, p.7.

10 Also known as *The Departure*, it in fact depicts RMS *Otranto* leaving Woolloomooloo. See nla.gov.au/nla.obj-140187379/view This version differs from other Cazneaux images with the title *Departure*.

11 Ruth Park, *The Companion Guide to Sydney.* Sydney: Collins, 1973, p.358.

12 Gavin Souter, *Times & Tides: A Middle Harbour Memoir.* Sydney: Simon & Schuster, 2004, p.215.

13 P.R. Stephensen and Brian Kennedy, *The History and Description of Sydney Harbour.* Sydney: Reed, 1980, p.266.

14 Park, *The Companion Guide to Sydney*, 378. Kylie Tennant, who moved to Hunters Hill in 1953 and lived there for many years, set her novel *Tantavallon* (South Melbourne: Macmillan, 1983) in 'Balm Point', a fictional location similar to Hunters Hill in many respects.

15 Alec Bolton, 'Fruit Boat, Hawkesbury River', published in *The Bulletin*, 12 December 1951, clipping in Box 1, NLA MS Acc14.052 Alec Bolton.

16 She died on 18 June: obituary in *The Daily Examiner* (Grafton), 24 June 1933, p.6.

17 It was advertised for sale in the *Sydney Morning Herald*, 29 July 1933, p.22.

18 New South Wales. *Widows' Pensions Act* 1925; *Family Endowment Act* 1927.

19 Crouch, 'Family Notes', p.3. According to Harry Crouch, Amy's investments did well under his care, including a one third share in Liverynga, a large house in Elizabeth Bay, which they bought as an investment for £4000 in 1940.

20 *The Sydney Morning Herald*, 22 April 1969, and *New Idea*, 13 December 1969, p.17. Beulah believed that Kareela was one of the sandstone houses built in Hunters Hill in the 1850s by stonemasons from Lombardy employed by the Joubert brothers.

21 R.D. FitzGerald, *To Meet the Sun.* Sydney: Angus & Robertson, 1929, p.i.

22 Mairi MacInnes, *Clearances.* New York: Pantheon, 1992, p.75.

23 Alec Bolton, diary entry for 20 January 1960, *Diary 1958–60*, Bolton Family Papers.

24 *The Sun* (Sydney), 6 October 1933, p.12, where he is listed as Bolton II.

25 *A Record of the Victoria League in New South Wales, 1917 to 1961*. Roneoed document in Box 1, NLA MS Acc14.052 Alec Bolton.

26 John Mackenzie, *Propaganda and Empire.* Manchester: Manchester University Press, 1986, pp.152–153.

27 Michael Gleeson-White, interviewed by Robert Bolton, 14 March 2021.

28 Quoted in Averyl Whitnall (ed.), *Max Dupain Modernist.* Sydney: State Library of NSW, 2007, p.4.

29 John Story, 'Open Letter'. *Grammar Foundations: Newsletter of the Sydney Grammar School Foundation*, no.31 (November 2004).

30 *The Sydneian*, cited in *Directory of Old Sydneians.* Sydney: Alumni Directories for Sydney Grammar School Foundation, 2000, p.6.

31 Service records at National Archives of Australia: A6769, Bolton AT. He would have been liable for service in the Citizen Military Forces as soon as he turned 18, but volunteering for the navy meant he could be sent to serve overseas and not just in Australia, or those areas in the Southwest Pacific that conscription had been extended to cover in 1943.

Chapter 2

1 A.G. Stephens, *Along the Castlereagh.* Sydney: The author, 1924. For more on Castlereagh Street as the heart of Sydney bookselling, see Michael Richards, 'All Our Strength, All Our Kindness and Our Love: Bertha McNamara, Bookseller, Socialist, Feminist and Parliamentary Aspirant', in Joy Damousi, Kim Rubenstein and Mary Tomsic (eds), *Diversity in Leadership: Australian Women, Past and Present*, Canberra: ANU Press, 2014, pp.109–128.

2 Alec Bolton, 'Publishing in an Age of Innocence: Angus & Robertson in the 1950s', *Publishing Studies*, no.1 (Spring 1995), pp.12–14.

3 Anthony Barker, *One of the First and One of the Finest: Beatrice Davis, Book Editor.* Carlton: The Society of Editors (Vic.), 1991, p.21.

4 Bolton, 'Publishing in an Age of Innocence', p.13.

5 Bolton, draft of an untitled talk on Australian publishing (probably for a meeting of the ABPA), p.3, c. 1980, Box 2, NLA MS Acc14.052 Alec Bolton.

6 Barker, *One of the First and One of the Finest*, pp.10–11.

7 First published in 1914. Sales topped a million by 1960, according to Craig Munro and Robyn Sheahan-Bright, *Paper Empires: A History of the Book in Australia, 1946–2005.* St Lucia: University of Queensland Press, 2006, p.13.

8 Elizabeth Wood-Ellem, 'How I Became an Editor', in *At the Typeface: Selections from the Newsletter of the Victorian Society of Editors.* Carlton South: Society of Editors (Victoria)

Inc., 2005, p.154. (Wood-Ellem took over Rosemary Dobson's job after she left Angus & Robertson.)

9 Alec Bolton, interview with Heather Rusden, 11 October 1996, National Library of Australia, available online at nla.gov.au/nla.oh-vn2834398

10 Neil James, '"The Fountainhead": George Ferguson and Angus & Robertson', *Publishing Studies*, no.7 (Autumn 1999), p.9.

11 Arthur Upfield, *An Author Bites the Dust.* Sydney: Angus & Robertson, 1948, p.3.

12 Not 1948, as is incorrectly stated in many sources: *The Sydney Morning Herald*, 11 January 1947, p.12. It was published in the newspaper in three installments, between 15 February and 1 March 1947. Angus & Robertson published her book *Ship of Ice* in 1948, which has confused some. The poem was also broadcast by Sydney's ABC radio station 2BL in 1949 (*The Sunday Herald*, 30 January 1949, p.12).

13 One is at the National Library of Australia, the other in private hands. She comments in her oral history interview that this was very much a Sydney circle: there was little interchange with writers in Melbourne, Brisbane, or elsewhere outside New South Wales.

14 W.H. Wilde, *Courage a Grace: A Biography of Dame Mary Gilmore.* Melbourne: Melbourne University Press, 1988, p.392.

15 James, '"The Fountainhead"', p.10. The exact figure is 46 per cent. Not one of these books made a profit.

16 Alec Bolton to Philip Hodgins, 14 November 1992, Box 5, Folder 32, NLA MS 7426, Addition 12 September 1995.

17 Rosemary Dobson, *Child with a Cockatoo.* Sydney: Angus & Robertson, 1955, p.50.

18 The first of his poems to be published in *The Bulletin* was 'The Lutine Bell', on 9 August 1950. Later came 'The Oarsman', 20 September 1950; 'Old Wares', 23 May 1951; 'Fruit Boat, Hawkesbury River', 12 December 1951; 'Lion Island', 19 September 1951; and finally 'The Old Destroyer', 9 January 1952. Clippings and an original typescript of 'Old Wares' (first titled 'The Sextant') are in Box 1, NLA MS Acc14.052 Alec Bolton. The people who worked and lived along the Hawkesbury River in the 1950s feature in a wonderful series of photographs by Axel Poignant: see his and Roslyn Poignant's *Mangrove Creek 1951: A Day with the Hawkesbury River Postman.* Sydney South: Hawkesbury River Enterprises, 1993.

19 Arthur Dobson wrote a textbook on railway engineering, according to Rosemary. He was christened Austin Arthur Grieves Dobson. This information, and all other biographical information about Rosemary Dobson not separately footnoted in this section, comes from an oral history interview with her by Heather Rusden conducted

for the National Library beginning on 1 September 1999: NLA TRC 3943.

20 Marjorie was a serious reader. She began her diary for 1914, the year she met Arthur Dobson, with a list of 'Some books I want. Anthology of Australian Poetry/Shelley's Poetical Works (with biography)/Keats Poems/Boswell's Life of Johnson/The Newcomes (Thackeray)/Thoreau's "Walden or Life in the Woods"/Fabre's Life of a Spider': Bolton Family Papers.

21 Joy Hooton, *Rosemary Dobson: A Celebration*. Canberra: Friends of the National Library of Australia, 2000, p.4.

22 Rosemary Dobson, *A World of Difference: Australian Poetry and Painting in the 1940s*. Sydney: Wentworth Press, 1973, p.3.

23 Hooton, *Rosemary Dobson: A Celebration*, pp.5–6. Hooton suggests that she went to Angus & Robertson 'in the early 1940s'. Rosemary Dobson said she worked at 'RAN HQ in Elizabeth Bay', which I have not been able to locate apart from the CO's official residence.

24 Leicester: Dryad Press, 1931. Her suggestion that he ought to have his own press is mentioned in her interview with Heather Rusden. *Printing Explained* was the first substantial introduction to letterpress printing aimed at English-speaking schools and amateurs (as opposed to apprentice printers) since early in the nineteenth century, and still has value despite the publication of other popular texts in recent years. It is almost certainly the reference book Rosemary and Joan Phipson would have used at Frensham. For Carter, see Martyn Thomas, *Harry Carter, Typographer*. Hinton Charterhouse, Bath: The Old School Press, 2005, p.12. For the Frensham Press, see Rosemary Dobson and Joan Phipson, 'The Frensham Press', *Biblionews and Australian Notes and Queries* vol.17, no.4 (December 1992).

25 Dobson, *A World of Difference*, p.4.

26 Often republished, 'The Alphabet' was also set to music in 2006. Geoffrey Allen, *Four Songs to Poems of Rosemary Dobson*. Perth: Keys Press, 2006, pp.11–15.

27 A.H. Chisholm, *The Australian Encyclopaedia*. Sydney: Angus & Robertson, 1958, vol.1, p.v.

28 *Southerly* was the quarterly journal of the English Association, in which Alec and Rosemary were active. It was closely associated with Angus & Robertson in Alec's time: he worked to Kenneth Slessor (editor 1956–1962).

29 *The Bulletin*, 9 April 1958, p.11.

30 Alec Bolton, diary entry for 5 January 1958, *Diary 1958–60*, Bolton Family Papers.

31 Alec Bolton, diary entry for 20 February 1958, *Diary 1958–60*, Bolton Family Papers.

Rosemary Dunlop was a friend of Alec's from his time at Sydney University.

32 Jacqueline Kent, *A Certain Style: Beatrice Davis, A Literary Life*. Ringwood: Viking, 2001, p.225. Kent interviewed Alec in September 1996, shortly before he died.

33 Kent, *A Certain Style*, 229.

34 Alec Bolton, interview with Heather Rusden, 15 October 1996.

35 The best short account is by Craig Munro, in Munro and Sheahan-Bright, *Paper Empires*, pp.13–19.

36 Masanobu Tsuji, *Singapore: the Japanese Version*. Sydney: Ure Smith, 1960. Highly successful, there was a UK edition in 1962 (Constable) and an OUP edition in 1988.

37 NLA oral history interview with Rosemary Dobson, track 2.

38 Keith McKenry, *More than a Life: John Meredith and the Fight for Australian Tradition*. Dural: Rosenberg Publishing, 2014, p.218. The book was published in 1967.

39 Bolton, draft of an untitled talk on Australian publishing (probably for a meeting of the ABPA), p.8, c. 1980, Box 2, NLA MS Acc14.052 Alec Bolton.

40 Change of address notice, 6 July 1966, Box 5, NLA MS Acc14.052 Alec Bolton.

41 Figures compiled by John Ferguson, cited in James, '"The Fountainhead"', p.12.

42 Alec Bolton, interview with Heather Rusden, 14 October 1996.

43 Alec Bolton, interview with Heather Rusden, 11 October 1996.

44 Kent, *A Certain Style*, p.215. It is interesting to put Mund's work alongside the transformation of British art publishing caused by the arrival of émigrés, mostly from Germany and Austria, fleeing Nazi persecution in the 1930s and 1940s. See Anna Nyburg, *Emigrés: The Transformation of Art Publishing in Britain.* London: Phaidon, 2014. Mund had previously been editor of *The Dictionary of Terms Used in the Printing and Allied Trades*, published in London by Linotype in 1936 and revised in 1948. Although Jacqueline Kent describes him as a German immigrant, Alec said he was Polish.

45 Alec Bolton, interview with Heather Rusden, 11 October 1996.

46 Kent, *A Certain Style*, p.215.

47 Bolton, 'Publishing in an Age of Innocence', pp.16, 19.

48 Quoted in James, '"The Fountainhead"', p.7.

49 Alec Bolton, interview with Heather Rusden, 15 October 1996.

50 Alec Bolton, interview with Heather Rusden, 14 October 1996.

51 Standard accounts from the UK of the period largely ignored offset other than for

reproduction of illustrations: see e.g. Sean Jennett, *The Making of Books.* London: Faber & Faber, 1964.

52 Alec Bolton, interview with Heather Rusden, 14 October 1996.

53 Alec Bolton to Mike Hudson, 2 April 1992, Alec Bolton to Mike Hudson, 31 July 1990, Box 7, Folder 15, NLA MS 7426, Addition 25 February 1998. See also Richard Kennedy, *A Boy at the Hogarth Press.* Whittington: Whittington Press, 1972.

54 Elizabeth Wilton, *Red Ribbons and Mr Anders.* London: Angus & Robertson, 1970. Kennedy later illustrated two more children's books for the firm.

55 Alec Bolton, interview with Heather Rusden, 14 October 1996.

56 Conversation with Lissant and Robert Bolton, 14 August 2014.

57 Alec Bolton to Mike Hudson, 2 April 1992, Alec Bolton to Mike Hudson, 31 July 1990, Box 7, Folder 15, NLA MS 7426, Addition 25 February 1998. In 1987 Bolton suggested inclusion of Mary Quick in the National Library's Bicentennial exhibition (see Michael Richards, *People, Print & Paper: A Catalogue of a Travelling Exhibition Celebrating the Books of Australia, 1788–1988.* Canberra: National Library of Australia, 1988, pp.49, 82.) For Quick, see Geoffrey Farmer, 'Three Women Printers', *Biblionews and Australian Notes and Queries*, vol.8, no.3 (September 1983), pp.86–87.

58 The Adana miniature jobbing platen was produced in various sizes by an English press maker, Donald Aspinall, from 1933 on, after he had success with a slightly larger flatbed press—originally designed as a working model, but immediately popular with amateur printers, and even produced in a format light enough to be parachuted into Occupied Europe for use by Resistance groups during the Second World War. He named his firm Adana after the Turkish town of that name, where he had served during the First World War. See James Moran, *Printing Presses: History and Development from the Fifteenth Century to Modern Times.* London: Faber & Faber, 1973, pp.244–245.

59 A variant of *Knossos* exists, known from a copy in a collection of books formed by Sir Brian Hone, which is now at the Library. This is printed on a single leaf with much the same layout as the London edition but set in Garamond, and with the title and author's name printed in red. It is signed by Dobson but is neither dated nor numbered. With it are three other poems, all signed by their authors and printed in similar formats: 'Soliloquy of an Astronaut' by David Campbell; 'Iris' by Gwen Harwood; and 'Parabola' by A.D. Hope. All four poems were originally in a Canberra Grammar School envelope, and this is the clue to their origin. They were printed for the school by a local printer, not by Alec, for a series of poetry readings in about 1972. Guests were given signed copies of a poem by the appropriate poet. This information is from a conversation with Robert Bolton (21 April 2022), who remembers having to take 250 copies back to the school (where he was a student at the time) for reprinting

after Rosemary found a typo. I am grateful to Philip Jackson for drawing my attention to this variant. Hone was the founder of the Marlborough College Press, where John Randle first learned to print, and later became a distinguished headmaster in Australia. See Chris Harrison, 'Sir Brian Hone: The Scholar, His Press and His Books in the National Library', *National Library of Australia News*, February 1991, pp.11–13.

60 Alec Bolton to Walter Stone, 11 August 1979, Box 3, Folder 18, NLA MS 7426.

61 Conversation with Jan Fullerton, 3 October 2017.

Chapter 3

1 Conversation with Lissant and Robert Bolton, 14 August 2014.

2 Invoice, Dolphin & Hannan Pty Ltd, 8 September [1972], Box 1, NLA MS Acc14.052 Alec Bolton.

3 Alec Bolton, interview with Heather Rusden, 14 October 1996.

4 Peter Golding, *An Unqualified Success: The Extraordinary Life of Allan Percy Fleming*. Dural: Rosenberg Publishing, 2013, p.255.

5 In a conversation on 6 December 2016.

6 Harrison Bryan, 'The National Library of Australia: An Historical Perspective', *Australian Academic & Research Libraries*, vol.22, no.4 (1991), p.178, n.35.

7 Golding, *An Unqualified Success*, pp.219–63. Fleming was the last National Librarian: since amendments to the *National Library Act* in 1973 his successors have been designated as Director-General.

8 Alec Bolton, interview with Heather Rusden, 14 October 1996.

9 Dobson, *A World of Difference*, p.11.

10 Jim Hart, 'New Wave Seventies', in *Paper Empires*, p.53.

11 Hart, p.55.

12 Case study by Richard Walsh in Hart, 'New Wave Seventies', p.57.

13 Paul Turnbull, 'The Network and the Nation: The Development of National Bibliographical Resources', in *Remarkable Occurrences: The National Library of Australia's First 100 Years 1901–2001*. Canberra: National Library of Australia, 2001, p.258.

14 Turnbull, 'The Network and the Nation', pp.259–61.

15 The Library's aspirations for national leadership went back well before Fleming, of course. For a detailed account, see Bryan, 'The National Library of Australia'.

16 Frank Thompson, 'Case-Study: Government Publishing', in *Paper Empires*, p.341.

17 Sydney Ure Smith, *Book Design in Australia*. Canberra: National Library of Australia, 1972.

18 Alec Bolton, interview with Heather Rusden, 14 October 1996. Subsequent references to the Rusden interview are all to this source, conducted over several days in 1996.

19 'Sir Alister McMullin', *Australian Dictionary of Biography*, vol.18, 2012, Canberra: Australian National University, adb.anu.edu.au/biography/mcmullin-sir-alister-14900

20 Alec Bolton, interview with Heather Rusden, 24 October 1996.

21 Beatrice Warde, *The Crystal Goblet: Sixteen Essays on Typography*. London: Sylvan Press, 1955, p.13. Alec and Rosemary owned a copy of Aubrey West's *Written By Hand* (London: Allen & Unwin, 1951, now in the author's collection), which had been inscribed by Warde using her typographic nom de plume of Paul Beaujon during a visit to Sydney in 1957. She spent two months in Australia, representing the Monotype Corporation of London and spoke widely to printers, designers, librarians and publishers, including a visit to the Government Printing Office in Canberra. It is not clear whether she inscribed the book for them in Sydney in 1957, or if it was a later acquisition, but it is likely that the former was the case. For details of Warde's visit, see *The Canberra Times*, 23 October 1957. For a sympathetic portrait of Warde and an account of the fractious world of North American and British typography in the early twentieth century, see the biography of her husband, whom she left for Stanley Morison: Simon Loxley, *Printer's Devil: The Life and Work of Frederic Warde*. Boston: David R. Godine, 2013.

22 Christopher Burke, *Active Literature: Jan Tschichold and New Typography*. London: Hyphen Press, 2007, p.276.

23 Published in 1967, this was an English translation based on Tschichold's *Typographische Gestaltung* (1935), which was in some ways the beginning of his subsequent transition from being the leading proponent of the New Typography (a term coined at the Bauhaus) to a 'New Traditionalism'. It was published soon after his flight from Nazi Germany to Switzerland. See Burke, *Active Literature*, pp.286–88. See also Alston Purvis, 'Tschichold and the New Typography', in Cees W. de Jong (ed.), *Jan Tschichold: Master Typographer. His Life, Work & Legacy*, London: Thames & Hudson, 2008, pp.60–63.

24 Founded in 1967, and known as *The Journal of Typographic Research* until 1971. The Library subscribed briefly to this important American scholarly journal, but ceased to do so before Alec's arrival in Canberra. No other Canberra library appears to have subscribed after 1970.

25 *The Canberra Times*, 24 June 1981; 30 June 1982. For Pat Croft's role in establishing the ANU Press see Shirley Purchase, 'Croft, Patricia (Pat) (?–1995)', Obituaries Australia, National Centre of Biography, Australian National University, oa.anu.

edu.au/obituary/croft-patricia-pat-264/text265. The ANU Press was established in 1967 after beginning as an offshoot of Melbourne University Press. It was taken over by Pergamon in 1984, a decision that many bitterly opposed. ANU Press was re-established, primarily as an e-publisher, in 2004.

26 Lifeline was established first by the Rev. Dr Sir Alan Walker of the Methodist Church in Sydney in 1963, and has spread throughout Australia and internationally. It now takes around a million calls for help a year at 60 locations around Australia. Canberra Lifeline began operations in 1971: *The Canberra Times*, 19 March 1983.

27 The *Canberra Times* reported income of $600 from rare books and manuscripts (sold at auction on the first evening) and a total of $2,100 overall by the end of the first day: *The Canberra Times*, 8 June 1973

28 Alec Bolton, 'Notes for the Auction Concerning the Poets and Their Manuscripts', typed MS in the possession of Anthony Ketley.

29 Rosemary Dobson, *Over the Frontier*. Sydney: Angus & Robertson, 1978, p.17.

Chapter 4

1 John Pope-Hennessy, *Sandro Botticelli: The Nativity in the National Gallery London*. London: Percy Lund Humphries, n.d., p.11. This is the only reference I have been able to find to the carol.

2 Alec Bolton to Nancy Bonnin, Fryer Library, 2 December 1975, Box 4, Folder 24, NLA MS 7426. The carol can be found among the tipped-in letterpress and paper samples in some copies of John Mason's Twelve by Eight Press edition of the book (Leicester, 1963). The ordinary edition sold for 30 shillings; for 50 shillings 'extra specimens' were inserted. I am indebted to Jim Owens, of Thorn Books, Tucson, Arizona, for confirmation that the text was present in a copy from his personal collection (email 26 July 2018), which he has now made available to me. There is no indication of who printed the Mason version, although it perhaps has the look of the Rampant Lions Press.

3 Alec Bolton, interview with Heather Rusden, 24 October 1996. That Brindabella was his first choice is made clear by correspondence with his solicitor in 1972, in which he asked for advice on whether it could be construed as passing off in relation to an existing firm named Brindabella Pty Ltd. He was prepared to consider Brindabella Mountain Press as an alternative. Alec Bolton to Messrs R.J.A. Dunn & Associates, 11 December 1972, Box 1, NLA MS Acc14.052 Alec Bolton.

4 Bolton, draft of an untitled talk on Australian publishing (probably for a meeting of the Australian Book Publishers Association), pp.8–9, c. 1980, Box 2, NLA MS Acc14.052 Alec Bolton.

Chapter 5

1 Note by Alec Bolton c. 1995[?], Box 1, Folder 7, Alec Bolton Papers, NLA MS 7426, National Library of Australia.

2 Alec Bolton to G.L. Anderson, 4 June 1974, Box 4, Folder 25, NLA MS 7426. He was also able to buy small stocks of paper from this firm of printers.

3 For Baskerville and its revival by Bruce Rogers, followed by its cutting for Monotype (1923), Stempel (1926), Mergenthaler Linotype and Intertype (1931) typefoundries, see Alexander Lawson, *Anatomy of a Typeface*. Boston: David R. Godine, 1990, pp.184–195. A recent survey by David Bolton of typefaces in 9,446 books described in *Private Press Books* between 1959 and 2010 shows that Baskerville was the second most used, at 6.73 per cent. The most common was Bembo, at 11.23 per cent. Bolton, '[Survey of Typefaces]'.

4 Walter Stone to Alec Bolton, 3 June 1973, Box 4, Folder 25, MS 7426. Subsequent citations of manuscript material in this chapter are from this folder, unless otherwise indicated.

5 Frank Webb to Alec Bolton, 15 August 1973.

6 Alec Bolton to Ian McLaren, 12 March 1975. There is a discrepancy in the number said to have been signed by Webb: in 1975 Alec told Nancy Bonnin that it was 21 or 22 (Alec Bolton to N. Bonnin, 2 December 1975, NLA MS 7426, Box 4, Folder 24), but when interviewed for *A Licence to Print* he recollected the number as 'about twelve'. The intention had been for him to sign 25, but he died eleven days after signing a first batch. Alec's carbon copy of the letter to Bonnin is unclear: the number printed may be 130.

7 Alec Bolton, 'Christmas Card, 1973', Box 2, NLA MS Acc14.052, Folder 'Distributions of Copies'.

8 Alec Bolton to Douglas Stewart, 28 September 1974. In the end Stewart and Coen took 40 copies.

Chapter 6

1 Rosemary Dobson and David Campbell, *Moscow Trefoil*. Canberra: Australian National University Press, 1975; Rosemary Dobson and David Campbell, *Seven Russian Poets: Imitations*. St Lucia: University of Queensland Press, 1979.

2 Michael Richards, *A Licence to Print*. Canberra: Friends of the National Library of Australia, 1993, p.21.

3 Alec Bolton to Bob Gormack, 16 June 1975, Box 4 Folder 25, MS 7426. Subsequent citations of manuscripts in this chapter are from this folder, unless otherwise indicated.

4 Alec Bolton to John Gartner, 14 April 1974.

5 Personal communication from Bill Huff-Johnston, September 2005.

6 Bolton, 'The Brindabella Press'. *Biblionews and Australian Notes and Queries* 7, no.254 (June 1982), p.28.

7 Alec Bolton to Gerald Fischer, 24 March 1974.

8 Jean Stone, *The Passionate Bibliophile*. Sydney: Angus & Robertson, 1988.

9 Alec Bolton to Walter Stone, 26 December 1973 and Walter Stone to Alec Bolton, 3 January 1974, Box 2, Folder 12, NLA MS 7426.

10 Alec Bolton to Geoffrey Farmer, 20 April 1974, Box 2, Folder 12, NLA MS 7426.

11 Geoffrey Farmer to Alec Bolton, 6 May 1974.

12 Alec Bolton to Bob Gormack, 16 June 1975.

13 Alan Gould, 'Ten Years of Poetry in Canberra', *Poetry Australia*, no.87 (April 1983), pp.67–68. The major public collection of Open Door imprints is at the National Library of Australia. For an account of this press, see Michael Denholm, *Small Press Publishing in Australia: The Early 1970s*. North Sydney: Second Back Row Press, 1979, pp.38–39.

Chapter 7

1 Richards, *A Licence to Print*, p.22.

2 This paper was imported from New Hampshire by VRG paper merchants: Alec Bolton to Bob Gormack of Nag's Head Press, 16 June 1975, Box 4, Folder 24, MS 7426. Subsequent citations of manuscript material in this chapter are from this folder, unless otherwise indicated. That it was a special order for Alec and not a regular inventory item is suggested in a later letter, Alec Bolton to Michael McCurdy, 10[?] July 1976.

3 Alec Bolton to Bob Brissenden, 19 May 1974, Box 4, Folder 25, NLA MS 7426.

4 Alec Bolton to Robin Wallace-Crabbe, 10 August and 3 June 1974, Box 1, Folder 5, NLA MS 7426.

5 Numbered distribution list for *Elegies*, Box 1, Folder 5, NLA MS 7426.

6 Alec Bolton to Manager, Margareta Webber's Bookshop, 5 February 1975.

7 Munro and Sheahan-Bright, *Paper Empires*, pp.214–217.

8 Dorothy Green to Alec Bolton, 7 May 1975, Box 1, Folder 5, NLA MS 7426.

9 Alec Bolton to David Chambers, 8 March 1975, Box 1, Folder 5; and John Ryder to Alec Bolton, 3 October 1975.

10 Among them, Justice K. Jacobs of the Punch Bowl Press (Alec Bolton to Justice Jacobs, 9 February 1975, Box 4, Folder 25) and Bob Gormack of the Nag's Head Press, Christchurch NZ (16 June and 5 October 1975, Box 4, Folders 25 and 24), NLA MS 7426.

11 Alec Bolton to David Chambers, 3 February 1975. There are similar letters to Chambers dated within days of each other, but it is not clear which one he sent.

Chapter 8

1 Alec Bolton to John Rowland, 31 March 1974, Box 1, Folder 6, NLA MS 7426.

2 Alec Bolton to John Rowland, 20 April 1974, Box 2, Folder 15, NLA MS 7426.

3 Alec Bolton to John Rowland, 1 November 1974, Box 2, Folder 15, NLA MS 7426.

4 Alec Bolton, data sheet for *Private Press Books*, [1976], Box 2, Folder 15, NLA MS 7426; and Alec Bolton to Bob Gormack, Box 4, Folder 25, NLA MS 7426.

5 E.J. Chapman to Alec Bolton, 28 January 1976, Box 2, Folder 15, NLA MS 7426.

6 Alec Bolton to George Anderson, Brown Prior Anderson, 9 May 1976, Box 4, Folder 24, NLA MS 7426. This firm supplied the type.

7 Richards, Michael, *A Licence to Print*, p.23.

8 Alec Bolton to James McAuley, 17 April 1976, Box 1, Folder 1, NLA MS 7426.

9 Beatrice Davis to Rosemary Dobson, 16 November 1976, Box 10, Folder 37, NLA MS 7426.

10 Alec Bolton to Aubrey Cousins, 30 April 1976, private collection of M. Richards.

11 Alec Bolton to Gerald Fischer, 2 May 1976, Box 4, Folder 24, NLA MS 7426.

12 Alec Bolton to Gerald Fischer, 23 February 1975. The device was to be a snowflake, but this did not eventuate.

13 The advertisement is referred to by Gwen Harwood in a letter written 1 December 1975, but I have not been able to find an appearance of it in the press of the day. It was to be signed by her, A.D. Hope and Dobson, among others. Gregory Kratzmann, *A Steady Storm of Correspondence: Selected Letters of Gwen Harwood, 1943–1995*. St Lucia: University of Queensland Press, 2001, pp.308.

14 Alec Bolton to R.S. Gormack, 16 June 1975, 5 October 1975, and R.S. (Bob) Gormack to Alec Bolton, 6 November 1975, Box 4, Folder 24, NLA MS 7426.

15 Alec Bolton to Michael McCurdy, July 1976, Box 4, Folder 24, NLA MS 7426.

16 Alec Bolton to Michael McCurdy, 10 July 1976; McCurdy to Bolton, 12 October

1976. Michael McCurdy (1942–2016) built a considerable reputation as a printer, publisher and illustrator, whose wood engravings and scratchboard drawings were published in more than 200 books.

17 Alec Bolton to Philip Hodgins, 13 March 1993, Box 5, Folder 32, NLA MS 7426, Addition 12 September 1995.

18 A.T. Bolton, 'The Resignation of Mr Utzon', *Art and Australia*, March 1966, p.286.

Chapter 9

1 Alec Bolton to James McAuley, 4 April 1976, Box 1, Folder 1, NLA MS 7426. Subsequent citations of manuscript material in this chapter are from this folder, unless otherwise indicated.

2 W.H. Wilde, *The Oxford Companion to Australian Literature*. Melbourne: Oxford University Press, 1985, p.515. The pamphlet was the first to appear in Series 1 of *Poets of the Month*, which by 1978 amounted to 24 slim volumes.

3 For the establishment of *Quadrant* see Cassandra Pybus, *The Devil and James McAuley*. St Lucia: University of Queensland Press, 1999, pp.142–55.

4 Pybus, *The Devil and James McAuley*, p.152.

5 NLA oral history interview, 7 November 1996.

6 Email from Ian Bolton to M. Richards, 15 November 2019.

7 Bolton, 'The Brindabella Press', p.29.

8 See also Alfred Fairbank, *A Handwriting Manual*. Leicester: Dryad, n.d., pp.8–11.

9 Unattributed quote, cited in Harry Stein, *From The Barn on the Hill to Edwards & Shaw: 1939–1983*. Sydney: State Library of NSW Press, 1996, p.27.

10 Bolton, 'The Brindabella Press', p.29.

11 For Shaw's friendship with McAuley, see Stein, *From The Barn on the Hill to Edwards & Shaw*, p.30. For Shaw's training at the National Art School in Sydney in the mid 1930s, see Rod Shaw, *The Windsor Group 1935–1945*.

12 Alec Bolton to Bill Chapman, 30 October 1977, Box 3, Folder 20, NLA MS 7426.

13 Alec Bolton to James Bennett, 26 March 1977, Box 1, Folder 1; and Alec Bolton to Bill Chapman, 30 October 1977, Box 3, Folder 20, NLA MS 7426. Chapman is sure that steps would have been taken to rectify faults had copies not been commercially acceptable.

14 It is not clear exactly how many copies were lost: 'more than 40' is the closest estimate given by Alec.

15 *Time Given* costing.

16 Walter Stone to Alec Bolton, 13 January 1978.

17 Alec Bolton to Geoffrey Farmer, 7 December 1976, Box 4, Folder 24, NLA MS 7426.

18 Ian Healy, 'Alec Bolton: Extremes of Adventure', unpublished article, 1992, p.29; Alec Bolton to Ian Healy, 19 April 1992; both Box 1, NLA MS Acc14.052, p.28. Although Rosemary Dobson annotated this article as 'NOT successful', and there are numerous corrections in correspondence between Healy and Alec, it is not clear why it was not published. Healy had written a piece about the National Library for *Good Weekend* (4–6 April 1986), when he met Alec. For the comment on *Greek Coins* being better than *Time Given*, see Bolton, 'The Brindabella Press', p.29.

19 Alec Bolton to James McAuley, 7 June 1976; Alec Bolton to Aubrey Cousins, 30 April 1976, private collection of the author.

20 Alec Bolton to Jim Adams, B.J. Ball Ltd, 19 September 1976, Box 4, Folder 24, NLA MS 7426.

21 Beatrice Davis to Alec Bolton, 23 August 1977, Box 4, Folder 26, NLA MS 7426. For Davis' departure from A&R, see Kent, *A Certain Style*, pp.277–279.

22 Dorothy Green to Alec Bolton, Easter Sunday 1977.

23 Alec Bolton to Fay [Zwicky?], 22 May 1977.

Chapter 10

1 Alec Bolton to Bob Muir, W.A. Currie & Co, 7 October 1977; and Alec Bolton to Walter Stone, 19 December 1977, Box 4, Folder 26, NLA MS 7426.

2 Alec Bolton to K. Sparks, Dominion Press, 7 October 1977, Box 4, Folder 26, NLA MS 7426.

3 Alec Bolton to Bob Muir, W.A. Currie & Co., 7 October 1977, Box 4, Folder 26, NLA MS 7426.

4 A similar trajectory in the maintenance of typographic standards through letterpress printing while all else fell apart under the assault of technological change is described in John Walters, *Alan Kitching: A Life in Letterpress*. London: Laurence King Publishing, 2016.

5 'Peter Pica' was Andrew Fabinyi, a Hungarian refugee from the Nazis who came to Australia in 1939 and who built the Melbourne bookshop FW Cheshire into an innovative and significant publishing firm. See John McLaren in Munro and Sheahan-Bright, *Paper Empires*, pp.19–21.

6 Alec Bolton to John McLaren, editor *Australian Book Review*, 26 February 1979, Box 3, Folder 16, NLA MS 7426.

7 *Cazneaux*, reviewed in *Australian Book Review*, April 1979, p.35.

8 Martin Em, 'BookShapes', *Australian Book Review*, December 1978, pp.32–33.

9 *Australian Book Review*, October 1979, p.37.

10 Personal communication from Philip Jackson, 2020.

11 *Australian Book Review*, April 1979, p.36.

12 Alec Bolton, draft of an untitled talk on Australian publishing (possibly for a meeting of the ABPA), pp.9–11, c. 1980, Box 2, NLA MS Acc14.052 Alec Bolton.

13 Alec Bolton to Gerald Fischer, 2 January 1994, Addition 25 February 1998, Box 11, Folder 40, NLA MS 7426.

14 Alec Bolton, notes for a talk on Australian book production, possibly to the Colophon Society, Canberra, early 1980s. Box 2, NLA MS Acc14.052 Alec Bolton.

Chapter 11

1 Dobson, *Over the Frontier*.

2 Marie-Louise Ayres , 'Dobson, Rosemary de Brissac (1920–2012)'. *Obituaries Australia*. oa.anu.edu.au/obituary/dobson-rosemary-de-brissac-15206.

3 Peter Kirkpatrick, 'Guide to the Classics: The Poetry of Rosemary Dobson'. *The Conversation*, 13 September 2018. theconversation.com/guide-to-the-classics-the-poetry-of-rosemary-dobson-100581

4 Rosemary Dobson, *Focus on Ray Crooke*. St Lucia: University of Queensland Press, 1971, p.1.

5 Quoted in Ayres, 'Dobson, Rosemary de Brissac (1920–2012)'.

6 Alec Bolton to Miles Little, 13 November 1977, Box 4, Folder 28, NLA MS 7426.

7 A comment made by Caren Florance in conversation on 16 December 2016. Florance printed and published Rosemary Dobson's *Poems to Hold or Let Go* under her imprint of Ampersand Duck in 2008. She was a close friend of Rosemary's for many years, and helped sort Alec's papers for donation to the National Library.

8 Dobson, *Over the Frontier*, pp.42–44.

9 Dorothy Green to Alec and Rosemary Bolton, 3 January 1978, Box 3, Folder 20, NLA MS 7426.

10 Rosemary Dobson, *Greek Coins*. Canberra: Brindabella Press, 1977, p.8.

11 Ray Crooke to Alec Bolton, 8 February [1978], Box 4, Folder 28, NLA MS 7426. See also Dobson, *Focus on Ray Crooke*. The earlier Dobson/Cooke collaboration appeared

in *Australian Letters*, a South Australian literary quarterly that featured 19 such partnerships between artist and poet over the 11 years of its existence (1957–1968). See Wilde, *The Oxford Companion to Australian Literature*, p.59.

12 'Greek Coins', Box 3, Folder 20, NLA MS 7426.

13 Alec Bolton to Walter Stone, 19 December 1977, Box 4, Folder 26, NLA MS 7426.

14 *The Sydney Morning Herald*, 21 January 1978.

15 Australian Book Publishers Association, *Book Design Awards 1978–9*, pp.17–18.

16 Alec Bolton to Bill Chapman, 30 October 1977, Box 3, Folder 20, NLA MS 7426.

17 Alec Bolton to Tom Shapcott, 4 November 1976, Box 4, Folder 24, NLA MS 7426. Emphasis in original. See also telegram, James McAuley to Alec Bolton, 16 September 1976, Box 1, Folder 1, NLA MS 7426.

18 Miles Little to Alec Bolton, 11 April [1977], Box 4, Folder 28, NLA MS 7426.

19 Miles Little, *Round Trip*. Carlton, Vic.: Melbourne University Press, 1977.

20 Alec Bolton to Miles Little, 20 March 1977, Box 4, Folder 26, NLA MS 7426.

21 For Little's friendship with Drysdale, see Klepac, *Russell Drysdale*. Sydney: Bay Books, 1983, p.183. Leonie Kramer provided a generous foreword to *Round Trip*, and the collection includes a poignant tribute to James McAuley in his final illness.

22 Alec Bolton to Miles Little, 13 November 1977, Box 4, Folder 28, NLA MS 7426. Although Little offered a new selection of poems in 1981, nothing came of it. Miles Little to Alec Bolton, 9 December 1981, Box 4, Folder 27, NLA MS 7426.

Chapter 12

1 Alec Bolton to Jim Adams, Edwards Dunlop and B.J. Ball, 7 January 1979, Box 4, Folder 26, NLA MS 7426.

2 Richards, *A Licence to Print*, p.24.

3 Geoffrey Glaister, *Glaister's Glossary of the Book*. London: George Allen & Unwin, 1979, p.106.

4 Alec Bolton to A.D. Hope, 24 May 1978, Box 3, Folder 18, NLA MS 7426.

5 A.D. Hope to Alec Bolton, n.d. (June 1977), Box 4, Folder 24, NLA MS 7426.

6 Alec Bolton to Kaye Mortley, 27 June 1977, Box 4, Folder 24, NLA MS 7426. Mortley's important career in *auteur* radio-making is discussed in Virginia Madsen, *SCAN: Journal of Media Arts Culture* vol.6, no.3 (3 December 2009).

7 Alec Bolton to A.D. Hope, 27 June 1977, Box 4, Folder 24, NLA MS 7426.

8 Alec Bolton to A.D. Hope, 27 June 1977, Box 4, Folder 24, NLA MS 7426.

9 R.D. FitzGerald, *Product: Later Verses*. Sydney: Angus & Robertson, 1977.

10 Alec Bolton to Beatrice Davis, 6 August 1977, Box 1, Folder 1, NLA MS 7426. He expressed similar sentiments in a letter to Bob Gormack of the Nag's Head Press, 16 June 1975, Box 4, Folder 25.

11 A.D. Hope, interview with Ann McCulloch, [1988?], *Double Dialogues*, Issue 5, Summer 2003, available online at www.doubledialogues.com/article/in-dialogue-with-a-d-hope-dialogue-one-childhood-adolescence/

12 Alec Hope to Alec Bolton, 3 June 1978 and 15 June 1978, Box 3, Folder 18, NLA MS 7426.

13 Alec Bolton to Arthur Boyd, 28 December 1978, Box 3, Folder 18, NLA MS 7426.

14 Clifford Burke, *Printing Poetry: A Workbook in Typographic Reification*. San Francisco: Scarab Press, 1980, p.76. Alec does not appear to have been familiar with this book.

15 Burke, pp.76–77.

16 Alec Bolton to Jim Adams, 7 January 1979, Box 4, Folder 26, NLA MS 7426

17 Michael McCurdy to Alec Bolton, n.d. [1977?], Box 10, Folder 36, NLA MS 7426, Addition 25 February 1998.

18 It is sometimes difficult to establish whether a paper used was acid-free at the time.

19 It is worth noting that Alec later came to the view that he had also asked for a leather that was too stiff. Alec Bolton to Peter Marsh, 17 February 1982, Box 3, Folder 22, NLA MS 7426.

20 'The Drifting Continent' Costing and Distribution List, Box 3, Folder 18, NLA MS 7426.

21 *The Sydney Morning Herald*, 18 August 1979.

22 Prospects for *The Drifting Continent*, p.4.

23 Alec Bolton to Arthur Stokes, 5 August 1980, Box 3, Folder 18, NLA MS 7426.

Chapter 13

1 Alec Bolton to Harold Stewart, 22 May 1977, Box 3, Folder 16, NLA MS 7426. Unless cited differently, subsequent references to correspondence in this chapter are to this folder.

2 Alec Bolton to Harold Stewart, 7 January 1978, Box 3, Folder 20, NLA MS 7426.

3 Harold Stewart to Alec Bolton, 13 January 1978, Box 3, Folder 20, NLA MS 7426.

4 Harold Stewart to [Ron Harrison], [1981], accompanying an amended presentation copy from the first batch (number 12 of 240), personal collection of the author.

5 Published by Tuttle in 1969, and frequently reprinted.

6 Alec Bolton to Harold Stewart, 8 April 1979, Box 3, Folder 16, NLA MS 7426.

7 Alec Bolton to Tom Shapcott, 21 November 1976, Box 4, Folder 24, NLA MS 7426.

8 Alec Bolton to Harold Stewart, 27 April 1980, Box 3, Folder 16, NLA MS 7426.

9 Bolton, 'The Brindabella Press', p.30.

10 This consisted of 'four Chinese characters, which in Japanese pronunciation give the sounds: Su-Chiu-Wa-Tõ, which is the nearest Japanese equivalent to the name Stewart; but these characters can also be read as meaning: Great Emptiness, the Japanese Way—which forms a Buddhist proverb'. Harold Stewart to Alec Bolton, 15 November 1980, Box 3, Folder 16, NLA MS 7426.

11 Alec Bolton to Geoffrey Farmer, 28 April 1981, Box 3, Folder 16, NLA MS 7426. Michael Ackland, who suggests *The Exiled Immortal* was intended to show that Stewart 'could write short as well as epic-length verse', also draws attention to its failure to attract praise. See Michael Ackland, *Damaged Men: The Precarious Lives of James McAuley and Harold Stewart*. Sydney: Allen & Unwin, 2001, p.260.

12 Marianne Yamaguchi to Alec Bolton, 5 July 1982, Box 3, Folder 16, NLA MS 7426.

13 Datasheet for *Private Press Books*, 1981, Box 3, Folder 16, NLA MS 7426.

14 Alec Bolton to Rosalind Atkins, 23 July 1987, Box 7, Folder 12, NLA MS 7426, Addition 25 February 1998.

15 Ackland, *Damaged Men*, p.185.

16 For a sympathetic view of Stewart, informed by a long-term friendship and his own practice of Zen Buddhism, see Milton Moon, *The Zen Master. The Potter & The Poet*. Stepney, South Australia: Axiom Publishing, 2006, pp.171–229. For a detailed discussion of Stewart's embrace of Pure Land Buddhism, see Paul Croucher, *A History of Buddhism in Australia: 1848–1988*. Kensington, NSW: New South Wales University Press, 1989, pp.73–75.

17 Hope cited in Ackland, *Damaged Men*, pp.247–248.

Chapter 14

1 Note by Alec Bolton on Manning Clark, *Words Spoken at the Funeral of David Campbell*, Box 3, Folder 21, NLA MS 7426. Clark's eulogy was republished in Manning Clark,

Occasional Writings and Speeches. [Melbourne?]: Fontana/Collins, 1980, pp.265–269.

2 Bolton, 'The Brindabella Press', p.28.

3 Douglas Stewart to Alec Bolton and Rosemary Dobson, 23 January 1982, Box 2, Folder 14, NLA MS 7426. They had sent him and Margaret Coen copy number 6, now in the collection of the author.

4 David [?] to Alec Bolton and Rosemary Dobson, 5 January 1982, Box 2, Folder 14, NLA MS 7426. For White's friendship with Campbell, see David Marr, *Patrick White: A Life*. Sydney: Random House, 1991.

5 Richards, *A Licence to Print*, p.16.

6 Conversation with Lissant and Robert Bolton, Canberra, 14 August 2014.

7 H.M. Green and Dorothy Green, *A History of Australian Literature: Pure and Applied.* Sydney: Angus & Robertson, 1984, vol.2, p.998.

8 Alec Bolton to Bernard Smith, 25 April 1977, Box 4, Folder 24, NLA MS 7426.

9 Dobson, *A World of Difference*, p.23.

10 Bolton, 'The Brindabella Press', p.31.

11 Alec Bolton, note on *The Continuance of Poetry*, Box 2, Folder 13, NLA MS 7426.

12 Alec Bolton to Jim Walker, 21 April 1981, Box 4, Folder 27, NLA MS 7426.

13 Alec Bolton to Norman Ward, A.A. Lawson Pty Ltd, ordering the halftone blocks, 13 April 1981, Box 4, Folder 27, NLA MS 7426. The blocks for Rosemary's four line drawings were made by Gee Graphics.

14 J.S. Mertle and Gordon Monsen, *Photomechanics and Printing: Practical Information on Platemaking and Presswork by Recognized Procedures.* Chicago: Mertle Publishing Company, 1957, p.97.

15 Although there is a discrepancy: in the colophon Alec says 210 were for sale, but in his later entry for Private Press Books the number for sale is given as 225.

16 Alec Bolton, 'Continuance of Poetry—Costing', 15 November 1981, Box 2, Folder 14, NLA MS 7426.

17 Alec Bolton to Detlef Thieme, 3 January 1982, Box 2, Folder 14, NLA MS 7426.

18 Alec Bolton to Scott Walker of Greywolf Press, 1 February 1982, Box 4, Folder 29, NLA MS 7426.

19 *The Canberra Times*, 30 June 1982, p.3.

20 Alec Bolton to Jim Walker, 23 February 1982, Box 4, Folder 30, NLA MS 7426.

Chapter 15

1 Philip Mead to Alec Bolton, 2 April 1981, Box 3, Folder 22, NLA MS 7426. Unless cited differently, subsequent references to correspondence in this chapter are to this folder.

2 Philip Mead, *Songs From Another Country*. Canberra: Open Door Press, 1975. The edition was of 375 copies.

3 Philip Mead to Alec Bolton, 27 July 1982, Box 3, Folder 'Something to Someone', NLA MS Acc14.052 Alec Bolton.

4 Alec Bolton to Philip Mead, 23 January 1983, Box 3, Folder 22, NLA MS 7426. The colophon states printing concluded in December 1982.

5 Alec Bolton to Philip Mead, 7 November 1982, Box 3, Folder 22, NLA MS 7426. The typo is 'sussuration' on p.22.

6 Richards, *A Licence to Print*, p.26.

7 Alec Bolton to 'Fitz' [R.D. FitzGerald], 6 August 1983, Box 3 Folder 22, NLA MS 7426.

8 ibid.

9 Alec Bolton, 'The Spring-Mire Cost Estimate', 24 December 1982, Box 3, Folder 22, NLA MS 7426.

10 *The Age*, 18 June 1983; clipping in Box 3, Folder 22, NLA MS 7426.

11 In August 1981 Levertov gave the Boltons a copy of her Copper Canyon title, *Wanderer's Daysong* (1981), now in the author's possession. Beautifully printed by Tree Swenson in an edition of 240 copies, using Centaur type, this elegant book would have been much approved of by Alec.

12 Alec Bolton to Jim Walker, 23 February 1982, Box 4, Folder 30, NLA MS 7426.

13 Lewis Allen, *Printing with the Handpress*. New York: Van Nostrand Reinhold, 1969.

14 Alec Bolton to Lewis and Dorothy Allen, 23 February 1982, Box 4, Folder 29, NLA MS 7426.

15 Alec Bolton to Michael McCurdy, 19 June 1982, Box 4, Folder 30, NLA MS 7426.

16 Alec Bolton to Geoffrey Farmer, 2 January 1983, Box 4, Folder 29, NLA MS 7426

17 See Raben Harlan, 'The Example of Fine Print', *Fine Print*, no.4 (April 2000). Bolton first mentioned this journal in a letter to Jim Walker in February 1982, suggesting that his knowledge of it is through the Library's subscription and not one of his own. Alec Bolton to Jim Walker, 23 February 1982, Box 4, Folder 30, NLA MS 7426.

18 Alec Bolton to Michael McCurdy, [10?] July 1976, Box 4, Folder 24, NLA MS 7426.

19 Adrian Wilson, *The Work & Play of Adrian Wilson: A Bibliography with Commentary*. San Francisco: The Press in Tuscany Alley, 1983. Bolton also owned a copy of a 1982 printing of Wilson's influential book *The Design of Books*. Layton, UT: Peregrine Smith, 2nd edn, 1974 (copy with his ownership signature in the author's collection.) Alas, there are no annotations!

20 Alec Bolton to Michael McCurdy, [10?] July 1976, Box 4, Folder 24, NLA MS 7426. Although Allen's book was first published in a limited edition, it is most likely that Alec was familiar with the later reprint: Allen, *Printing with the Handpress*.

21 Listed in a substantial collection of books on printing and typography presented by the Bolton family to the Australian National University Library after his death, list supplied by ANU to the author.

22 John Tranter to Alec Bolton, 15 April 1982; Rosemary Dobson, 'Report', n.d.; Alec Bolton to John Tranter, 15 May 1982; all in Box 4, Folder 30, NLA MS 7426.

23 Bolton, 'The Brindabella Press', p.31.

Chapter 16

1 Beatrice Davis to Alec Bolton, 23 August 1977, Box 4, Folder 26, NLA MS 7426.

2 Dorothy Green to Alec Bolton, 22 November 1977, apparently quoting AB's own words, 'low key, inconspicuous': Box 2, Folder 10, NLA MS 7426. Unless cited differently, subsequent references to correspondence in this chapter are to this folder.

3 Barbara Hanrahan to Alec Bolton, 10 July 1982, Box 2, Folder 11, NLA MS 7426.

4 Dorothy Green to Alec Bolton, 24 July 1982, Box 2, Folder 11, NLA MS 7426.

5 Alec Bolton to Dorothy Green, 18 July 1982, Box 2, Folder 11, NLA MS 7426.

6 Alec Bolton to Barbara Hanrahan, 18 July 1982, Box 2, Folder 11, NLA MS 7426.

7 Barbara Hanrahan to Alec Bolton, 31 July 1982, Box 2, Folder 11, NLA MS 7426.

8 Garrett, *A History of Wood Engraving*, pp.178–203.

9 Dorothy Harrop, *A History of the Gregynog Press*. Pinner: Private Libraries Association, 1980, pp.79–111.

10 Andrews, *The Life and Work of Robert Gibbings*, pp.57–58, 236.

11 Albert Garrett, *A History of Wood Engraving*. London: Bloomsbury Books, 1986, pp.263, 272. For a recent brilliant study of modernist linocuts in Britain between the wars, see Jenny Uglow, *Sybil & Cyril*. London: Faber & Faber, 2021). The definitive study is Stephen Coppel, *Linocuts of the Machine Age*. Aldershot: Scolar Press, 1995.

12 Alec Bolton to Barbara Hanrahan, 23 October 1982, Box 2, Folder 11, NLA MS 7426.

13 Barbara Hanrahan to Alec Bolton, 29 October 1982, Box 2, Folder 11, NLA MS 7426. Eric Gill had a somewhat similar view: 'engravings are as much a part of *book making* as of *illustration*. They don't merely illustrate the text, they also decorate the book. Therefore the engraver & printer *must* be one "firm"'. (Cited in Martin Andrews, *The Life and Work of Robert Gibbings*. Bicester: Primrose Hill Press, 2003, p.61.)

14 Hanrahan was less diplomatic in her personal diary: 'If I did something for her book surely it would seem as if I approve of her poems—that me, the writer, relates to them to allow me, the printmaker, to engrave for them. And A.B. says prints should be subordinate to text (he knows—or he is sure—I agree, he says). She is second-rate, not me. They are soft middle-brow poems and I can't do 'em'. Entry for 26 October 1982. Barbara Hanrahan, *The Diaries of Barbara Hanrahan*. St Lucia: University of Queensland Press, 1998, p.190.

15 The description of books flooding in is from William Thorn's eulogy for his father at his funeral, St David's Church, Red Hill, 25 August 2015 (personal observation). Bill Thorn's obituary is at Michael Richards, 'William Darbyshire Thorn'. *Obituaries Australia*. oa.anu.edu.au/obituary/thorn-william-darbyshire-bill-19120.

16 Jim Walker to Alec Bolton, 12 November 1981, Box 4, Folder 30, NLA MS 7426.

17 As Richard-Gabriel Rummonds has argued, this narrowness has been widespread. See his critique of the second edition of the standard English language history of the private press movement, Cave's *The Private Press*, in Richard-Gabriel Rummonds, 'The Eternal Dilettante', *American Book Collector*, May–June (1984). Cave's mention of Brindabella itself is perfunctory, to say the least: Roderick Cave, *The Private Press*, New York: Bowker, 1983, p.297. Even though published in 1983, with the best of the Brindabella work to come, his description was somewhat condescending.

18 For Wayzgoose involvement in TYPOMANIA, see Jadwiga Jarvis, *The Wayzgoose Affair*. Katoomba: The Wayzgoose Press, 2007, p.67. Also see Mike Hudson, 'The Wayzgoose Broadsides', *Matrix*, no.19 (1999).

19 Email from Jadwiga Jarvis to M. Richards, 17 April 2016.

20 Alec Bolton to Dorothy Green, 18 July 1982, Box 2, Folder 11, NLA MS 7426.

21 Alec Bolton to Dorothy Green, 22 February 1983, Box 2, Folder 10, NLA MS 7426

22 Alec Bolton to Dorothy Green, 6 March 1983, Box 2, Folder 11, NLA MS 7426.

23 Alec Bolton to Michael McCurdy, 4 April 1983, Box 2, Folder 11, NLA MS 7426.

24 Alec Bolton to Michael McCurdy, 23 June 1983, Box 2, Folder 11, NLA MS 7426.

25 Michael McCurdy to Alec Bolton, 12 July 1983, Box 1, NLA MS Acc14.052.

26 Michael McCurdy to Alec Bolton, 11 September 1984, Box 1, NLA MS Acc14.052. The pull McCurdy included in the parcel with the block, inscribed 'For Alec Bolton—who made all this possible!', demonstrates that Alec's editioning was fully equal to the quality of the artist's own. (Pull now in the author's collection, the generous gift of the Bolton family.)

27 Alec Bolton to Peter Marsh, Dove Bindery, 17 November and 12 December 1983, Box 2, Folder 11, NLA MS 7426.

28 Peter Marsh to Alec Bolton, 28 January 1984, Box 2, Folder 11, NLA MS 7426.

29 Alec Bolton to Peter Marsh, 5 February 1984, Box 2, Folder 11, NLA MS 7426.

30 Alec Bolton to Peter Marsh, 28 February 1984, Box 2, Folder 11, NLA MS 7426.

31 Alec Bolton to Peter Marsh, 2 February 1984, Box 2, Folder 11 NLA MS 7426.

32 Peter Marsh to Alec Bolton, 10 February 1984, Box 2, Folder 11, NLA MS 7426.

33 Peter Marsh to Alec Bolton, n.d. [early February 1984], Box 2, Folder 11, NLA MS 7426.

34 Peter Marsh to Alec Bolton, n.d. [late February 1984], Box 2, Folder 11, NLA MS 7426.

35 Alec Bolton to Peter Marsh, 28 February 1984, Box 2, Folder 11, NLA MS 7426.

36 Note by Bolton attached to Folder 10 in Box 2, NLA MS 7426.

37 Alec Bolton to Dorothy Green, 29 June 1984, Box 2, Folder 11, NLA MS 7426.

38 Alec Bolton to Dorothy Green, 29 June 1984, Box 2, Folder 11, NLA MS 7426.

39 Note in Box 3, MS Acc14.052 Alec Bolton.

40 *The Sydney Morning Herald*, 22 September 1984, p.44.

41 *The Weekend Australian Magazine*, 24–25 November 1984, p.16.

42 Alec Bolton to Neil [Bookshop of Margareta Webber], 8 May 1985, Box 2, Folder 11, NLA MS 7426.

43 *Sydney Morning Herald*, 22 April 1969. The house was also featured in *New Idea*, 13 December 1969, with speculation it was one of those built in the mid-nineteenth century by Jules Joubert, employing masons from Lombardy.

44 Alec Bolton to Gerald Fischer, 29 November 1982, Box 11, Folder 40, NLA MS 7426, Addition 25 February 1998.

45 Alec Bolton to Gerald Fischer, 27 February 1983, Box 11, Folder 40, NLA MS 7426, Addition 25 February 1998.

46 Jim Walker to Alec Bolton, 3 September [1982], Box 4, Folder 29, NLA MS 7426. The Super Caster had come from Brown Prior Anderson, 'where George Anderson … cast type for me until the eleventh hour of Monotype'. See Bolton, 'The Brindabella Press', p.31.

47 Jim Walker to Alec Bolton, 22 June 1982, Box 4, Folder 30, NLA MS 7426.

48 Alec Bolton to Jim Walker, 21 April 1981, Box 4, Folder 27, NLA MS 7426.

49 Judy Slinn, *History of the Monotype Corporation*. London: Printing Historical Society, 2014, p.242.

50 Mick Belson, *On the Press: Through the Eyes of the Craftsmen of Oxford University Press.* Witney: Robert Boyd Publications, 2003, pp.55–60.

51 Alec Bolton to Jim Walker, 29 August 1982, Box 4, Folder 30, NLA MS 7426.

52 Email from Jim Walker to M. Richards, 23 March 2016.

53 Turnbull, 'The Network and the Nation: The Development of National Bibliographical Resources', p.265.

54 Bryan himself was more generous regarding his predecessor, crediting his term with the foundation work of what became the Australian Bibliographic Network. See Bryan, 'The National Library of Australia', p.173. Others have pointed out that Chandler built much on Fleming's foundations with regard to science and technology, and credit him with gaining significant private sponsorship for the library for the first time. See Ted Vellacott's obituary for Chandler, *Australian Library Journal*, vol.42, no.1, February 1993.

55 Alec Bolton to Gerald Fischer, 11 March 1984, Box 11, Folder 40, NLA MS 7426, Addition 25 February 1998.

56 Robyn Holmes, 'Musical Dialogues', in *Remarkable Occurrences: The National Library of Australia's First 100 Years 1901–2001*. Canberra: National Library of Australia, 2001, p.222.

Chapter 17

1 Box 1, Folder 2, NLA MS 7426.

2 Wesley Pasko, *American Dictionary of Printing and Bookmaking* Detroit, Gale Research Co., 1967 (republished edn), p.359.

3 Alec Bolton to Barbara Hanrahan, 3 November 1982, Box 1, Folder 3, NLA MS 7426. Unless cited, subsequent references to correspondence in this chapter are to this folder.

4 Barbara Hanrahan to Alec Bolton, 5 November 1982. Emphasis in original.

5 Annette Stewart, *Barbara Hanrahan: A Biography*. Kent Town: Wakefield Press, 2010, p.191. However, a correction to Stewart's account of the Neilson book: Stewart posits that Bolton suggested the choice of Neilson in the first place (p.235), which was not the case, and that Green had suggested Hanrahan as an illustrator of her poems (p.294), which is incorrect. It was Bolton, and Green was reluctant from the start.

6 Barbara Hanrahan to Alec Bolton, 17 November 1982.

7 Barbara Hanrahan to Alec Bolton, 12 April 1983.

8 Although the copyright statement is dated 1984, the colophon says 1984–85, and the book was printed in February–March 1985, and published in August.

9 Alec Bolton to Gerald Fischer, 6 March 1985, Box 11, Folder 40, NLA MS 7426, Addition 25 February 1998.

10 Imposition plan and separate letter, Alec Bolton to Barbara Hanrahan, 7 February 1985.

11 Alec Bolton to Gerald Fischer, 6 March 1985, Box 11, Folder 40, NLA MS 7426, Addition 25 February 1998.

12 Alec Bolton to Gerard Fischer, 23 September 1984, Box 11, Folder 40, NLA MS 7426, Addition 25 February 1998.

13 Peter Marsh to Alec Bolton, 4 November 1984.

14 Alec Bolton to Barbara Hanrahan, 17 August 1985.

15 Ross Clendinning, *Contemporary Designer Bookbindings: Europe & Australia*. Sydney: Crafts Council of Australia, 1984.

16 Caren Florance, 'Flashdancing through Canberra's Material Book Cultures', *Axon: Creative Explorations*, vol.5, no.1 (March 2015), pp.4–10. On Petr Herel and the Graphic Investigation Workshop, see also Anna Gray, *Petr Herel: An Exhibition of Artist Books at the National Library of Australia 22 March – 30 June 1989*. Canberra: National Library of Australia, 1989. This moment in Canberra's history has been further discussed by Sasha Grishin. See *The La Trobe Journal*, no.95 (March 2015).

17 Alec Bolton to Jack McKimm, 8 December 1982.

18 Barbara Hanrahan to Alec Bolton, 6 December 1982.

19 Louis Lothian to Alec Bolton, 9 March 1983.

20 'Neilson—Provisional Costing', 4 February 1985; undated supplement; and 'Neilson—Costing', 11 August 1985, all at Box 1, Folder 3, NLA MS 7426. The final estimate of $5,546 in income was based on projected sales of 120 copies less 40 per cent, 40 less 33.3 per cent, and 40 sold to subscribers at the full price of $40.

21 Alec Bolton to Gerald Fischer, 6 March 1985, Box 11, Folder 40, NLA MS 7426, Addition 25 February 1998.

22 Mike Hudson to Alec Bolton, 12 August [1985], Box 1, Folder 4, NLA MS 7426.

23 However, sales were not always so brisk at bookshops: I bought my own copy at the University Cooperative Bookshop, Canberra, in May 1987, at the original price.

24 Alec Bolton to Barbara Hanrahan, 17 August 1985.

25 Alec Bolton to Barbara Hanrahan, 24 February 1985.

26 *Some Poems of Shaw Neilson* Prospectus, 1985.

27 *The Sydney Morning Herald*, 12 October 1985, p.46.

28 *The Weekend Australian Magazine*, 21–22 December 1985, p.13.

29 Cliff Hanna, *The Folly of Spring: A Study of John Shaw Neilson's Poetry*. St Lucia: University of Queensland Press, 1990.

Chapter 18

1 Alec Bolton to Gerald Fischer, 23 September 1984, Box 11, Folder 40, NLA MS 7426.

2 Alec Bolton to R.G. Geering, 9 January 1984, Box 2, Folder 9, NLA MS 7426. Unless cited differently, subsequent references to correspondence in this chapter are to this folder.

3 R.G. Geering, 'Editor's Note', in Christina Stead, *The Palace with Several Sides*. Canberra: Officina Brindabella, 1986. The story was later published in *Southerly*, vol.47, no.2 (1987) and again by Angus & Robertson (in a free pamphlet format, to introduce its new Imprint Classics series) in 1990. Place of publication of Officina Brindabella/Brindabella Press publications is given as shown therein, varying between Deakin and Canberra.

4 Jürgen Wegner, 'Another Rare Item of St. Mark's Press Ephemera', *The Shadowland Newsletter*, no.109:16 (May 2020).

5 This is implied in Alec Bolton to C.D. FitzHardinge-Bailey, 21 July 1985.

6 Alec Bolton to Jim Walker, 25 February 1984, Box 4, Folder 29, NLA MS 7426. This letter also suggests Bolton planned to cast enough 10 point Plantin to print the Stead, but nothing came of this idea.

7 Alec Bolton to Michael McCurdy, 21 July 1985 and McCurdy to Bolton, 2 August 1985.

8 Alec Bolton to Mike Hudson, 22 August 1985.

9 Alec Bolton to Secretary, Society of Wood Engravers, 23 January 1984, Box 4,

Folder 29, NLA MS 7426

10 Larry Macdonald to Alec Bolton, 24 March 1984; Alec Bolton to Larry Macdonald, 15 July 1984; both Box 4, Folder 29, NLA MS 7426.

11 Alec Bolton to Mike Hudson, 4 February 1985, Box 10, Folder 35, NLA MS 7426. For the history of Craftsman House, see Wyndham, 'The Fine Art of Survival'.

12 Schuller, 'A New Generation of Private Presses in Australia', p.86.

13 Mike Hudson's early career is described in Jarvis, *The Wayzgoose Affair*, pp.1–9. The quote is on p.3.

14 Mike Hudson and Jadwiga Jarvis, *Private Impressions*. [Leura]: Wayzgoose Press, 1989, p.1. From a copy inscribed by its authors 'to Alec + Rosemary/our version of a Christmas card', now in the possession of the author.

15 Mike Hudson to Alec Bolton, June 1986 (exact date not given). Emphasis in original.

16 James Taylor, 'Editions and Presswork in Australia: Private Presses and Contemporary Printing', *Craft Australia*, no. 2 (1986), p.87.

17 Proofs of Hudson's wood engravings for *Poitiers* can be found in Alec's papers at the National Library and one is reproduced in Jarvis, *The Wayzgoose Affair*, p.13. She describes the difficult relationship with Taylor on pp.11–18, and also the problems with *Poitiers*. The proofs are at Box 2, Folder 9, NLA MS 7426.

18 Mike Hudson, *The Battle of Poitiers: A Suite of 7 Wood Engravings*. Katoomba: Wayzgoose Press, 2018.

19 For discussion of the conference as a seminal moment in Canberra's history as a city of the book, see Florance, 'Flashdancing through Canberra's Material Book Cultures', pp.5–9.

20 Apart from matters specifically footnoted as being from the Bolton papers, all material relating to Robin Tait is from an interview with her by Michael Richards, Murrumbateman, 1 March 2015. The Clarkson volume was Christopher Clarkson, *Limp Vellum Binding and Its Potential as a Conservation Structure for the Rebinding of Early Printed Books.* Llandudnow: Red Gull Press, 1982.

21 Robin Tait to Alec Bolton, 15 January 1986.

22 Alec Bolton to Robin Tait, 27 January 1986.

23 Alec Bolton to Robin Tait, 27 January 1986.

24 Alec Bolton to C. Macphillamy, October 1984; Alec Bolton to Paul Richter, Brindabella Press and Publications Pty Ltd, 2 October 1984, Box 4, Folder 29, NLA MS 7426.

25 The bulk of the correspondence between Bolton and C.E. Macphillamy relating to registration of the business names, and relevant certificates is in Box 10, Folders 36 and 37, NLA MS 7426. Bolton's own account of the name change is in his circular of September 1992: Alec Bolton, *Brindabella Press: The Name Regained and Other News*. Canberra: Brindabella Press, 1992. The quote is from Bolton: Alec Bolton, interviewed by Heather Rusden, 25 October 1996.

26 Alec Bolton to Ron Geering, 23 January 1987.

27 'The Palace with Several Sides/Preliminary Costing', 18 May 1986, Box 11, Folder 36, NLA MS 7426.

28 Alec Bolton to Ron Geering, 26 January 1987.

29 The notion of 'long service leave' may need explanation outside Australia. It is an entitlement to three months' paid leave after ten years with an employer, at first the purview of senior colonial officials, then of officials (public servants) generally, and extended in the 1970s to the rest of the workforce in permanent positions.

30 Alec Bolton to Gerald Fischer, 27 February 1983, Box 11, Folder 40, NLA MS 7426.

31 Alec Bolton to Gerald Fischer, 25 July 1983, Box 11, Folder 40, NLA MS 7426.

32 Grishin, 'Books in the Canberra Region: The Golden Years', p.34.

33 Richards, *A Licence to Print*, p.28.

34 Alec Bolton to Gerald Fischer, 21 April 1987, Box 11, Folder 40, NLA MS 7426. Emphasis in original.

35 'Farewell to Alec Bolton. Mr Bolton's Speech'. National Library of Australia, *Staff Bulletin*, 28 May 1987.

36 Alec Bolton to Anne Wienholt, 22 September 1985, Box 6, Folder 5, NLA MS 7426, Addition 25 February 1998.

37 *The Canberra Times*, 17 November 1984.

38 Alec Bolton to Elizabeth Riddell, 2 December 1986, Box 6, Folder 5, NLA MS 7426, Addition 25 February 1998.

39 Rosemary Dobson, *Summer Press*. St Lucia: University of Queensland Press, 1987. Caren Florance recalls that late in life she dismissed the book as trivial and regretted its publication. Similarly, she regretted the publication of her first volume by the Frensham Press in 1937, and did not include it in her counting of published works.

40 It was reviewed by Peter Fuller in *The Canberra Times*, 25 November 1987, p.30.

Chapter 19

1 ATB, Desk Diary, 16 April 1966. Box 4, NLA MS Acc14.052 Alec Bolton.

2 'Schedule of Photographic Equipment', [1997?], Box 2, NLA MS Acc14.052 Alec Bolton.

3 NLA oral history interview, 7 November 1996.

4 NLA oral history interview with Rosemary Dobson, 1 September 1999, track 2.

Chapter 20

1 Elizabeth Riddell, Film Australia: Australian Biography Series, tape 5. Interview by Robin Hughes, 11 December 1992. www.australianbiography.gov.au/subjects/riddell/.

2 Rosemary Dobson, note dated November 1997, Box 6, Folder 5, NLA MS 7426, Addition 25 February 1998.

3 Alec Bolton to Anne Wienholt, 25 August 1985, Box 6, Folder 5, NLA MS 7426, Addition 25 February 1998. Unless cited differently, subsequent references to correspondence in this chapter are to this folder.

4 Joan Kerr, 'Anne Wienholt', in *Design & Art Australia Online*, 1995. www.daao.org.au/bio/anne-wienholt/biography/. Wienholt then studied at East Sydney Technical College and won the NSW Travelling Art Scholarship in 1944, which first took her to the US. See Sydney Ure Smith, *Present Day Art in Australia*. Sydney: U. Smith, 1945. pp.42–43.

5 Alec Bolton to Anne Wienholt, 25 August 1985.

6 For Randle's description of the process, see John Randle, 'The Four Fathers of Richard Kennedy', *Matrix*, no.9 (1989), p.5.

7 Richards, *A Licence to Print*, p.28.

8 Randle, 'The Four Fathers of Richard Kennedy', p.5.

9 Alec Bolton to John Randle, 7 March 1991, John Randle private collection.

10 Alec Bolton to Elizabeth Riddell, 9 November 1986.

11 Elizabeth Riddell, *From the Midnight Courtyard*. North Ryde, NSW: Angus & Robertson, 1989.

12 Alec Bolton to Elizabeth Riddell, 9 November 1986.

13 The Bulmer too came from Mackenzie-Harris: Alec Bolton to Helen Lee, Mackenzie-Harris, 28 April 1986, Box 10, Folder 37, NLA MS 7426, Addition 25 February 1998.

14 Alec Bolton to Helen Wadlington, 29 January 1987.

15 Alec Bolton to Elizabeth Riddell, 4 August 1987.

16 Elizabeth Riddell to Alec Bolton, 26 May 1987.

17 'Riddell—est of costs', n.d. and 'Riddell Sales Summary', n.d..

18 Wallace-Crabbe, 'Cottage Industry, With Muse', p.342.

19 25–26 July 1987: cited in Wallace-Crabbe, 'Cottage Industry, With Muse'.

20 Wilde, *The Oxford Companion to Australian Literature*, p.304.

Chapter 21

1 Craig Munro, *Wild Man of Letters: The Story of P.R. Stephensen*. Carlton: Melbourne University Press, 1984, p.224.

2 Munro, p.251.

3 See Geoffrey Farmer, *Private Presses and Australia*. Melbourne: Hawthorn Press, 1972, p.51. See also Richards, *People, Print & Paper*, p.50.

4 Geoffrey Farmer to Alec Bolton, 22 February 1984, Box 4, Folder 29, NLA MS 7426; Alec Bolton to Geoffrey Farmer, 13 June 1984, Box 6, Folder 2, NLA MS 7426, Addition 25 February 1998. Unless cited differently, subsequent references to correspondence in this chapter are to this folder.

5 Geoffrey Farmer to Alec Bolton, 22 February 1984; Alec Bolton to Geoffrey Farmer, 26 February 1984; both Box 4, Folder 29, NLA MS 7426. For Farmer's account of these discussions, see Farmer, *A Private Pursuit*. Pearl Beach: Escutcheon Press, 1995, pp.33–34.

6 Douglas Stewart to Alec Bolton, 26 October 1984; Alec Bolton to Douglas Stewart, 13 November 1984; both Box 4, Folder 29, NLA MS 7426.

7 Alec Bolton to R.D. FitzGerald, 3 January 1985, Box 6, Folder 2, NLA MS 7426, Addition 25 February 1998.

8 Geoffrey Farmer, *A True Printer: John Kirtley and Heemskerck Shoals*. Cremorne: Book Collectors' Society of Australia, 1990.

9 Geoffrey Farmer, 'An Interlude of Fine Printing and Other Activities', *Biblionews and Australian Notes and Queries*, vol.15, no.3 (September 1990), pp.70–71.

Chapter 22

1 Rosalind Atkins to Alec Bolton, 5 June [1986], Box 7, Folder 12, NLA MS 7426, Addition 25 February 1998.

2 Published as *Recollections*. Melbourne: Lyre Bird Press, 1986. Information on Rosalind Atkins' early career is from her CV available as a PDF download at australiangalleries.com.au/artists/rosalind-atkins/. Atkins thanked Bolton for his assistance in producing this volume in its acknowledgements.

3 Alec Bolton to Rosalind Atkins, 11 June 1986, Box 7, Folder 12, NLA MS 7426, Addition 25 February 1998.

4 Rosalind Atkins to Alec Bolton, 30 June 1986 (original has July, corrected by Bolton to June), Box 7, Folder 12, NLA MS 7426, Addition 25 February 1998.

5 Alec Bolton to Rosalind Atkins, 4 November 1986, Box 7, Folder 12, NLA MS 7426, Addition 25 February 1998.

6 'Rainforest—Costs', 2 May 1987, Box 6, Folder 6, NLA MS 7426, Addition 25 February 1998. These calculations are based on actual fees of $200 paid to Atkins and Wright rather than a total of $350 in royalties suggested by this summary. Because Atkins and Wright forwent royalties on the Friends' allocation, Bolton described these copies as being a gift from author, engraver and printer.

7 *The Canberra Times*, 21 October 1987, and email from Colin Steele to M. Richards, 23 September 2015.

8 Alec Bolton to Rosalind Atkins, 6 May 1987, Box 6, Folder 6, NLA MS 7426, Addition 25 February 1998.

Chapter 23

1 Alec Bolton to Geoff Page, 14 December 1986, Box 6, Folder 7, NLA MS 7426, Addition 25 February 1998. Unless cited differently, subsequent references to correspondence in this chapter are to this folder.

2 This was the poem *Daguerrotype Tennis*, the sixth broadside of Open Door Press, printed in an edition of 150.

3 Alec Bolton to Darrell FitzHardinge-Bailey, 23 January 1987, Box 10, Folder 37, NLA MS 7426, Addition 25 February 1998.

4 Alec Bolton to Ms Sheffield, Book Club of California, 16 January 1988, Box 10, Folder 36, NLA MS 7426, Addition 25 February 1998. See also Alec Bolton to the club, 9 January 1985, Box 10, Folder 37, NLA MS 7426, Addition 25 February 1998.

5 Book Club of California, *Quarterly News-Letter*, vol.50, no.4, Autumn 1985, p.108.

6 Alec Bolton to Margaret Lock, n.d. [1987?], Box 10, Folder 36, NLA MS 7426, Addition 25 February 1998. Margaret Lock describes the history of her press in 'Locks' Press 1979–2006', *The Private Library*, vol.10, no.1 (Spring 2007).

7 'Brindabella Letterpress Editions', one-sided flyer, 1987.

8 Richards, *A Licence to Print*, p.29.

9 The unused alternative mock-up and Eadie's working notes are now in the collection of the State Library of Queensland.

10 'SMILING—Final costing', 9 November 1987, Box 6, Folder 7, NLA MS 7426, Addition 25 February 1998.

11 The size of the mailing list is mentioned in Alec Bolton to Geoffrey Sawer, 21 October 1987, Box 6, Folder 8, NLA MS 7426, Addition 25 February 1998.

12 'Armed against the sour world', *The Canberra Times*, 19 March 1988.

Chapter 24

1 Mark Cranfield, National Library of Australia, to Alec Bolton, 5 June 1987, NLA File reference 465/1/449, in 'Important letters re Oral History', Box 3, MS Acc14.052 Alec Bolton.

2 Bolton, Desk Diary for 1988, Box 4, MS Acc14.052 Alec Bolton.

3 The interview with Pauline Fanning is available online at nla.gov.au/nla.obj-216003830/listen

4 The interview with Fred McKay is available at nla.gov.au/nla.obj-216031865/listen

5 Alec Bolton, *Interviewing for Oral History at the National Library of Australia*. Canberra: National Library of Australia, 1994, p.20.

6 Bolton, *Interviewing for Oral History at the National Library of Australia*, pp.19–20.

7 Alec Bolton to Graeme Powell, NLA, 22 September 1988, NLA File ref 203/13/156, copy in File 'Valuing', Box 3, MS Acc14.052 Alec Bolton.

8 Alec Bolton to Professor Ken Inglis, ANU, 27 June 1990, File 'Valuing', Box 3, MS Acc14.052 Alec Bolton.

Chapter 25

1 Alec Bolton, *Publications from 1973 to 1989 of the Officina Brindabella, with a Note on the Beginnings of the Press*. Deakin: Officina Brindabella, 1989, p.1.

2 Geoffrey Serle to Alec Bolton, 21 September 1986, Box 6, Folder 8, NLA MS 7426, Addition 25 February 1998. Unless cited differently, subsequent references to correspondence in this chapter are to this folder.

3 Alec Bolton to Geoffrey Serle, 15 January 1987.

4 Richards, *A Licence to Print*, p.29.

5 'Serle—Comments by F.B. Horner', n.d.

6 Prospectus for *Percival Serle*. Canberra: Officina Brindabella, 1988.

7 Alec Bolton to B. Hannan, Dolphin & Hannan Pty Ltd., 10 June 1985, Box 10, Folder 37, NLA MS 7426, Addition 25 February 1998.

8 Alec Bolton to Jim Walker, 6 October 1987, Box 10, Folder 36, NLA MS 7426, Addition 25 February 1998. This letter is annotated with the odd sum of $1099.22, perhaps representing residue after a deposit, or purchase of sundries with the press.

9 Alec Bolton to Arthur Stokes, 16 August 1988.

10 Harry Whetton, *Practical Printing and Binding: A Complete Guide to the Latest Developments in All Branches of the Printer's Craft*. London: Odhams Press, 1946, pp,101–104.

11 John Southward, *Modern Printing: A Handbook of the Principles and Practice of Typography and the Auxiliary Arts*. London: Raithby, Lawrence & Co., 1922, p.51.

12 Glaister, *Glaister's Glossary of the Book*, p.463.

13 Email from Jim Walker to M. Richards, 23 March 2018.

14 John Randle to Alec Bolton, 1 February 1985, Box 10, Folder 37, NLA MS 7426, Addition 25 February 1998.

15 Alec Bolton to Arthur Stokes, 27 January 1988, Box 10, Folder 36, NLA MS 7426, Addition 25 February 1998.

16 Alec Bolton to Arthur Stokes, 27 January 1988, Box 10, Folder 36, NLA MS 7426, Addition 25 February 1998. Ingeborg Hansen and Phil Day later named their private press The Finlay Press (1997–2009), in acknowledgement of his role in teaching letterpress in Canberra. See also Alec Bolton, interviewed by Heather Rusden, 25 October 1996, available online at nla.gov.au/nla.obj-217335183/listen/5-3401~5-3479

17 Alec Bolton, interview with Heather Rusden, 25 October 1996.

18 Alec Bolton to Arthur Stokes, n.d., Box 10, Folder 36, NLA MS 7426, Addition 25 February 1998.

19 Arthur Stokes to Alec Bolton, 8 February 1988, Box 10, Folder 36, NLA MS 7426, Addition 25 February 1998.

20 Alec's photos of the bust, and of Rosemary sitting for it, are in the NLA.

21 Paul Fuog, 'Studio Profile: Hofstede Design'. *Desktop: The Culture of Design*, 25 February 2012.

22 Alec Bolton to Bob Summers, 5 March 1995, Box 11, Folder 41, NLA MS 7426, Addition 25 February 1998.

23 Alec Bolton to Darrell FitzHardinge-Bailey, 28 May 1988.

24 Alec Bolton to Rod Williamson, Raleigh Paper Company, 21 December 1987; 'Serle—Estimate of paper requirement'; both in Box 6, Folder 8, NLA MS 7426, Addition 25 February 1998.

25 Alec Bolton to Barry Toombs, 4 December 1989, Box 10, Folder 37, NLA MS 7426, Addition 25 February 1998. He was introduced to Toombs by Mike Hudson: Alec Bolton to Mike Hudson, 10 October 1989, Box 7, Folder 15, NLA MS 7426, Addition 25 February 1998.

26 Alec Bolton to Geoffrey Serle, 28 June 1988.

27 Box 11, Folder 42, NLA MS 7426, Addition 25 February 1998.

28 Alec Bolton to Geoffrey Serle, 28 June 1988.

29 Richards, *A Licence to Print*, p.29.

30 *Financial Review* (now *Australian Financial Review*), 21 October 1988.

31 Peter Ryan, *Final Proof: Memoirs of a Publisher.* Sydney: Quadrant Books, 2010, pp.124–125.

32 *The Canberra Times*, 25 March 1989.

33 Stephanie Kille, Crafts Council of the ACT, to Alec Bolton, 22 July 1988.

34 Richards, *People, Print & Paper*, pp.49–51.

Chapter 26

1 Bolton, *Publications from 1973 to 1989 of the Officina Brindabella, with a Note on the Beginnings of the Press*.

2 Joshua Heller Rare Books, Inc., *List 13* (1991), p.28; *Tenth Anniversary Catalogue* (1995), p.20.

3 Alec Bolton to Les Murray, 12 June 1986, Box 7, Folder 12, NLA MS 7426, Addition 25 February 1998. Unless cited differently, subsequent references to correspondence in this chapter are to this folder.

4 The difficult circumstances of Murray's life at the time are described in Peter Alexander, *Les Murray: A Life in Progress.* South Melbourne: Oxford University Press, 2000, pp.215–226.

5 Alec Bolton to Les Murray, 6 July 1986. Emphasis in original.

6 Richard Walsh to Alec Bolton, 14 July 1986.

7 Jennifer Rowe, Angus & Robertson, 18 March 1987.

8 Les Murray to Alec Bolton, 4 May 1987.

9 Merlin Waterson, 'From Bleeding Heart Yard to Whittington', *Matrix*, no.31 (Winter 2012), p.54.

10 Rosalind Atkins to Alec Bolton, 18 December [1986].

11 Rosalind Atkins to Alec Bolton, 11 February [1987].

12 Rosalind Atkins to Alec Bolton, 22 July [1987].

13 Alec Bolton to Rosalind Atkins, 23 July 1987. *Recollections* was published in 1987.

14 Alec Bolton to Mike Hudson, 9 April 1989, Box 10, Folder 35, NLA MS 7426, Addition 25 February 1998.

15 Richard Southall, 'Technical History of Monotype Composing Machines', in *History of the Monotype Corporation*. London: Printing Historical Society, 2014, p.311.

16 Southall, 'Technical History of Monotype Composing Machines', p.311.

17 Sebastian Carter, 'Typeface Design for the Monotype Corporation', in *History of the Monotype Corporation*, London: Printing Historical Society, 2014, pp.203–204. See also Alice, *London Review of Books*, vol.42, no.13 (2 July 2020).

18 Whetton, *Practical Printing and Binding*, p.42.

19 David Jury, *Graphic Design before Graphic Designers: The Printer as Designer and Craftsman 1700–1914*. London: Thames & Hudson, 2012, pp.57–103.

20 Whetton, *Practical Printing and Binding*, p.42.

21 Alec Bolton to Mike Hudson, 8 March 1992, Box 8, Folder 18, NLA MS 7426, Addition 25 February 1998. In this instance he had discovered a printer in Port Lincoln, South Australia, who had both Monotype equipment and training—but evidently nothing came of this.

22 Alec Bolton to Dennis [?], 26 May 1989, Box 10, Folder 36, NLA MS 7426, Addition 25 February 1998.

23 Alec Bolton to Bruce Price, 19 July 1990, Box 10, Folder 36, NLA MS 7426, Addition 25 February 1998.

24 'Brindabella Press Disposal Strategy', [1997], Box 2, Folder 'Sales of Brindabella Equipment', NLA MS Acc14.052 Alec Bolton.

25 Alec Bolton to John Randle, 7 March 1991, John Randle collection.

26 Penelope FitzGerald, 'The Beginning of Spring', in *Offshore, Human Voices, The Beginning of Spring*. Everyman's Library 269. New York: Alfred A. Knopf, 2003, p.308.

27 Richards, *A Licence to Print*, p.30.

28 Alec Bolton to Rosalind Atkins, 8 May 1987.

29 Rosalind Atkins to Alec Bolton, 12 May 1987.

30 Jim Walker to Alec Bolton, 12 November 1981, Box 4, Folder 30, NLA MS 7426. For the Bemboka Paper Mill (1978–[?]), see Robert Morris, 'Hand Made Paper at Bemboka'. *Wayzgoose*, no.1 (1985).

31 Alec Bolton to Margaret Lock (Locks' Press), 11 June 1987; and Alec Bolton to John Purcell Paper, 24 June 1987.

32 Margaret Lock to Alec Bolton, 25 April 1987.

33 Alec Bolton to Rosalind Atkins, no date [April 1987].

34 Rosalind Atkins to Alec Bolton, 22 July [1987].

35 Les Murray to Alec Bolton, 2 September 1988, Box 7, Folder 13, NLA MS 7426, Addition 25 February 1998.

36 Alec Bolton to Les Murray, 11 September 1988, Box 7, Folder 13, NLA MS 7426, Addition 25 February 1998.

37 Les Murray to Alec Bolton, 7 December 1988, Box 7, Folder 13, NLA MS 7426, Addition 25 February 1998.

38 Alec Bolton to Les Murray, 25 June 1988, Box 7, Folder 13, NLA MS 7426, Addition 25 February 1998.

39 Ian Healy, 'Alec Bolton: Extremes of Adventure', unpublished article, 1992, Box 1, p.28, NLA MS Acc14.052.

40 Katharine Nix to Alec Bolton, 30 January 1989, Box 7, Folder 14, NLA MS 7426, Addition 25 February 1998.

41 Robin Tait to Alec Bolton, 9 August 1988, Box 7, Folder 13, NLA MS 7426, Addition 25 February 1998.

42 For the leather spine, Alec Bolton to Les Murray, 25 November 1988, Box 7, Folder 13, NLA MS 7426, Addition 25 February 1998.

43 Interview with Robin Tait, 1 March 2015.

44 Alec Bolton to Katharine Nix, 18 August 1988, Box 7, Folder 13, NLA MS 7426, Addition 25 February 1998.

45 Les Murray to Alec Bolton, 19 April 1989, Box 7, Folder 14, NLA MS 7426, Addition 25 February 1998.

46 13–14 May 1989.

47 Les Murray to Alec Bolton, 19 July 1989 and 23 August 1989; Alec Bolton to Les Murray, 2 August 1989; Box 7, Folder 14, NLA MS 7426, Addition 25 February 1998. The ABC broadcast on 9 April 1989 is confirmed in correspondence with the ABC Library Sales section, 20 November 2015.

48 Alec Bolton, 'Murray the Idyll Wheel, Analysis of Sales May '89 – Aug '90', Box 7, Folder 14, NLA MS 7426, Addition 25 February 1998.

49 Alec Bolton to Mike Hudson, 9 April 1989, Box 10, Folder 35, NLA MS 7426, Addition 25 February 1998. Emphasis in original.

50 'The Idyll Wheel: Final Costs', 5 June 1989, Box 8, Folder 21, NLA MS 7426, Addition 25 February 1998.

51 'Les Murray: A leap in the dark at costing it', 7 July 1988, Box 8, Folder 21, NLA MS 7426, Addition 25 February 1998.

52 Alec Bolton to Mike Hudson, 9 April 1989, Box 10, Folder 35, NLA MS 7426, Addition 25 February 1998.

53 *The Sydney Morning Herald*, 29 July 1989.

54 *The Australian Magazine*, 19–20 August 1989.

55 *The Canberra Times*, 7 October 1989.

56 Alec Bolton to Les Murray 3 April 1989, Box 7, Folder 14, NLA MS 7426, Addition 25 February 1998.

57 Barrett Reid to Alec Bolton, 2 August 1989, Box 10, Folder 35, NLA MS 7426, Addition 25 February 1998.

58 'Das Idyllenrad: Zyklus eines Jahres in Bunyah, New South Wales, April 1986–April 1987', translated by Margitt Lehbert, in Les Murray, *Ein Ganz Gewöhnlicher Regenbogen: Gedichte*. Munich: Carl Hanser, 1996.

59 Les Murray to Alec Bolton, 23 August 1989, Box 7, Folder 14, NLA MS 7426, Addition 25 February 1998. Emphasis in original.

60 Collingwood, Vic.: Black Inc., 2015.

Chapter 27

1 Alec Bolton to Barrett Reid, 25 June 1989, Box 10, Folder 35, NLA MS 7426, Addition 25 February 1998. This prospect emerged again in 1990, but without result

after Reid was diagnosed with cancer. See also Alec Bolton to Robert Gray, 7 January 1988, Robert Gray to Alec Bolton, 7 July 1988, and subsequent correspondence, all Box 10, Folder 35, NLA MS 7426, Addition 25 February 1998.

2 Alec Bolton to Gwen Harwood, 8 November 1989; Gwen Harwood to Alec Bolton, 23 November 1989, Box 10, Folder 35, NLA MS 7426, Addition 25 February 1998.

3 Alec Bolton to Barrett Reid, n.d. [August 1989], Box 10, Folder 35, NLA MS 7426, Addition 25 February 1998.

4 Alec Bolton to Barbara Hanrahan, 6 May 1987, Box 1, Folder 3, NLA MS 7426.

5 Barbara Hanrahan to Alec Bolton, 11 May 1987, Box 1, Folder 3 NLA MS 7426.

6 Stewart, *Barbara Hanrahan*, pp.236–249.

7 Barbara Hanrahan to Alec Bolton, 19 September 1988, Box 6, Folder 3, NLA MS 7426, Addition 25 February 1998. See also Hanrahan, *The Diaries of Barbara Hanrahan*, p.295.

8 Stewart, *Barbara Hanrahan*, pp.245, 266.

9 Barbara Hanrahan to Alec Bolton, 16 November 1988, Box 5, Folder 35, NLA MS 7426, Addition 12 September 1995. Unless cited differently, subsequent references to correspondence in this chapter are to this folder.

10 Alec Bolton to Barbara Hanrahan, 21 November 1988.

11 Cost estimate in Alec Bolton to Barbara Hanrahan, 15 September 1988.

12 Alec Bolton to Barbara Hanrahan, 11 December 1988.

13 Hanrahan, *The Diaries of Barbara Hanrahan*, p.305, entry for 15 May 1989.

14 Hanrahan, *The Diaries of Barbara Hanrahan*, p.304, entry for 19 March 1989.

15 Stewart, *Barbara Hanrahan*, p.237.

16 Alec Bolton to Barbara Hanrahan, 28 April 1989.

17 Alec Bolton to Barbara Hanrahan, 2 July 1989.

18 Alec Bolton to Barbara Hanrahan, 22 July 1989.

19 Richards, *A Licence to Print*, p.30.

20 Alec Bolton to Barbara Hanrahan, 14 May 1989. Emphasis in original.

21 Barbara Hanrahan to Alec Bolton, 18 May 1989.

22 Barbara Hanrahan to Alec Bolton, 20 June 1989, Box 6, Folder 3, NLA MS 7426, Addition 25 February 1998.

23 Alec Bolton to Barbara Hanrahan, 6 May 1990, Box 5, Folder 36, NLA MS 7426, Addition 12 September 1995.

24 Barbara Hanrahan to Alec Bolton, 15 May 1990, Box 6, Folder 3, NLA MS 7426, Addition 25 February 1998. Ellipsis in original.

25 'Tiger Lady' 106; 'Mother & Child' 108; 'Butterfly Hunter' 109; 'Acrobat' 111.

26 Alec Bolton to Barbara Hanrahan, 16 August 1989, Box 5, Folder 36, NLA MS 7426, Addition 12 September 1995.

27 ibid.

28 Prospectus for *Twelve Linocuts*. Canberra: Officina Brindabella, 1990. This was canvassed in a letter, Alec Bolton to Barbara Hanrahan, 24 August 1989.

29 Barbara Hanrahan to Alec Bolton, 18 August 1989.

30 Hanrahan, *The Diaries of Barbara Hanrahan*, p.315, entry for 23 August 1989.

31 Barbara Hanrahan to Alec Bolton, 13 September 1989.

32 Alec Bolton to Barbara Hanrahan, 30 September 1989. The issue focused on her new novel, *Flawless Jade*, and also advertised a 1986 book on her art: Alison Carroll, *Barbara Hanrahan, Printmaker*. Netley, South Australia: Wakefield Press, 1986. Still available was a limited specially bound edition of this (150 copies each with an original signed and numbered etching), which retailed for $125, as well as a trade edition at $25.

33 Alec Bolton to Barbara Hanrahan, 14 October 1989.

34 Alec Bolton to Barbara Hanrahan and Jo Steele, 1 December 1989.

35 Richards, *A Licence to Print*, p.31.

36 Hanrahan, *The Diaries of Barbara Hanrahan*, pp.319, 320, entries for 13, 16, 17 November 1989.

37 Alec Bolton, interviewed by Heather Rusden, 25 October 1996. This portion of the interview can be heard online at nla.gov.au/nla.obj-217335183/listen/5-3481~5-3542

38 Hanrahan, *The Diaries of Barbara Hanrahan*, p.321, entries for 12, 17 December 1989.

39 Alec Bolton to Barbara Hanrahan, 8 December 1989.

40 For Ruth Dobson's career as an indomitable pioneer women diplomat, see Sylvia Marchant, 'Ruth Violet Dobson', in *Australian Dictionary of Biography*, vol.17, Melbourne: Melbourne University Press, 2007.

41 Alec Bolton to Barbara Hanrahan, 9 January and 21 January 1990.

42 Barbara Hanrahan to Alec Bolton, 24 January 1990. The National Gallery holds a substantial collection of her work, including these early prints, purchased in 1991.

43 Alec Bolton to Barbara Hanrahan, 4 February 1990.

44 Alec Bolton to Janda Gooding (Art Gallery of Western Australia), 3 April 1990.

45 Alec Bolton to Mike Hudson, 30 May 1990, Box 7, Folder 15, NLA MS 7426, Addition 25 February 1998. Emphasis in original.

46 Helen Wadlington invoice, 5 March 1990.

47 'Hanrahan TWELVE LINOCUTS, Distribution of Copies', n.d., Box 2, NLA MS Acc14.052 Alec Bolton.

48 Alec Bolton to Jo Steele, 21 February 1994, Box 6, Folder 4, NLA MS 7426, Addition 25 February 1998.

49 Alec Bolton, interviewed by Heather Rusden. 25 October 1996. This portion of the interview can be heard online at nla.gov.au/nla.obj-217335183/listen/5-3605~5-3635

Chapter 28

1 Alec Bolton to Mike Hudson, 10 October 1989, Box 7, Folder 15, NLA MS 7426, Addition 25 February 1998. Unless cited differently, subsequent references to correspondence in this chapter are to this folder.

2 Mike Hudson to Alec Bolton, 17 October 1989.

3 Alec Bolton to Jane Scurr, 25 October 1989.

4 Jane Scurr to Alec Bolton, 19 December 1989.

5 Richards, *A Licence to Print*, p.31.

6 Alec Bolton, interview with Heather Rusden, 7 November 1996.

7 Douglas Stewart praised this last poem in his reflections on Slessor but thought it was 'on the whole … best left where it lies'. Douglas Stewart, *A Man of Sydney.* West Melbourne: Nelson, 1977, p.98. On 3 November 1927 the Sydney Harbour ferry *Greycliffe*, crowded with schoolchildren, collided with the liner *Tahiti* and 40 people died. The tragedy was also the basis of Eleanor Dark's novel *Waterway*. London: Collins, 1938.

8 Alec Bolton, interview with Heather Rusden, 25 October 1996.

9 Alec Bolton to Ian Healy, 12 April 1992, Box 1, Folder 'ATB Background Material', NLA MS Acc14.052, Papers of Alec Bolton.

10 Alec Bolton, diary entry for 16 February 1958, *Diary 1958–60*, Bolton Family Papers.

11 Alec Bolton to Dennis Haskell, 21 March 1990.

12 Alec Bolton to Dennis Haskell, 17 April 1990.

13 Alec Bolton, interview with Heather Rusden, 7 November 1996.

14 Alec Bolton to Barbara Hanrahan, 6 May 1990, Box 5, Folder 36, NLA MS 7426, Addition 12 September 1995. Emphasis in original.

15 Mike Hudson to Alec Bolton, 24 November 1989.

16 Alec Bolton to Mike Hudson, 1 January 1990, and Mike Hudson to Alec Bolton, 29 January 1990.

17 For events surrounding Joe Lynch's death, see Stewart, *A Man of Sydney*, pp.120–126.

18 Alec Bolton to Mike Hudson, 31 July 1990.

19 Alec Bolton to Mike Hudson, 13 July 1992, Box 8, Folder 18, NLA MS 7426, Addition 25 February 1998.

20 Alec Bolton to Mike Hudson, 31 July 1990, Box 7, Folder 15, NLA MS 7426, Addition 25 February 1998.

21 Email from Jadwiga Jervis to M. Richards, 17 April 2016.

22 Mike Hudson to Alec Bolton, 2 August 1990.

23 Alec Bolton, *Slessor Wood-Engravings by Mike Hudson*. Deakin: Officina Brindabella, 1990.

24 Bolton, Desk Diary for 1990, Box 4, NLA MS Acc14.052.

25 Bolton, Desk Diary for 1990, Box 4, NLA MS Acc14.052.

26 Alec Bolton to Helen Wadlington, 27 April 1990.

27 Alec Bolton to Mike Hudson, 28 June 1990. For a detailed breakdown of binding costs, see Alec Bolton to Helen Wadlington, 28 June 1990, and Helen Wadlington to Alec Bolton, 19 July 1990.

28 Bolton, Desk Diary for 1990, Box 4, NLA MS Acc14.052.

29 Alec Bolton to Jane Scurr, 21 August 1990; Annette Renshaw (Angus & Robertson) to Alec Bolton, 20 September 1990.

30 'Slessor—Final Costs', 20 October 1990, Box 7, Folder 15, NLA MS 7426, Addition 25 February 1998.

31 Alec Bolton to Mike Hudson, 31 July 1990.

32 Alec Bolton to Mike Hudson, 2 April 1992.

33 'Slessor Sea Poems: Analysis of sales, Nov. '90 – May '91', 25 May 1992, Box 7, Folder 15, NLA MS 7426, Addition 25 February 1998.

34 'Behind the Lines', *The Sydney Morning Herald*, 17 November 1990. Philip Roberts was a very occasional correspondent with Alec. His account of the Island Press between 1970 and 1975, when he gave up hand-printing, can be found in his 'Ten Years on an Island', *Poetry Australia*, no.74/75 (1980).

35 Don Anderson to Alec Bolton, 19 November 1990.

36 Alec Bolton to Mike Hudson, 26 October 1989.

37 Mike Hudson to Alec Bolton, 24 November 1989.

38 Jarvis, *The Wayzgoose Affair*, p.48.

39 Alec Bolton to John Randle, 7 March 1991, John Randle Collection.

40 John Crombie to Alec Bolton, 4 June 1991, Box 10, Folder 36, NLA MS 7426, Addition 25 February 1998.

Chapter 29

1 Alec Bolton to Barbara Hanrahan, 18 November 1989, Box 5, Folder 36, NLA MS 7426, Addition 12 September 1995. Unless cited differently, subsequent references to correspondence in this chapter are to this folder.

2 Barbara Hanrahan to Alec Bolton, 11 December 1989, Box 5, Folder 35, NLA MS 7426, Addition 12 September 1995.

3 Richards, *A Licence to Print*, p.31.

4 Barbara Hanrahan to Alec Bolton, 23 November 1989.

5 Richards, *A Licence to Print*, p.31. See also Alec Bolton, interview with Heather Rusden, 25 October 1996.

6 Barbara Hanrahan to Alec Bolton, 14 March 1990, Box 6, Folder 3, NLA MS 7426, Addition 25 February 1998.

7 John Ross and Clare Romano, *The Complete Intaglio Print*. New York: Macmillan, The Free Press, 1974, p.5.

8 Barbara Hanrahan to Alec Bolton, 7 June 1990.

9 Barbara Hanrahan to Alec Bolton, 12 December 1989; Alec Bolton to Barbara Hanrahan, 16 December 1989; both Box 5, Folder 35, NLA MS 7426, Addition 12 September 1995.

10 Barbara Hanrahan to Alec Bolton, 24 January 1990, Box 5, Folder 35, NLA MS 7426, Addition 12 September 1995. Her diary records finishing six stories on 12 February, but she later added two more: Hanrahan, *The Diaries of Barbara Hanrahan*, p.323.

11 Barbara Hanrahan to Alec Bolton, 9 February 1990, Box 5, Folder 35, NLA MS 7426, Addition 12 September 1995.

12 Alec Bolton to Barbara Hanrahan, 19 February 1990 and Barbara Hanrahan to Alec Bolton, 2 March 1990; both Box 5, Folder 35, NLA MS 7426, Addition 12 September 1995.

13 Bolton, diary entry for 11 March 1990, Box 4, NLA MS Acc14.052.

14 Alec Bolton to Barbara Hanrahan, 12 March 1990, Box 5, Folder 35, NLA MS 7426, Addition 12 September 1995.

15 Hanrahan, diary entry for 1 April 1990 in Hanrahan, *The Diaries of Barbara Hanrahan*, p.326.

16 Barbara Hanrahan to Alec Bolton, 14 March 1990, Box 6, Folder 3, NLA MS 7426, Addition 25 February 1998.

17 Alec Bolton to Barbara Hanrahan, 26 March 1990, Box 5, Folder 35, NLA MS 7426, Addition 12 September 1995.

18 Barbara Hanrahan to Alec Bolton, 7 June 1990, Box 5, Folder 35, NLA MS 7426, Addition 12 September 1995; Stewart, *Barbara Hanrahan*, p.261.

19 Alec Bolton to Barbara Hanrahan, 25 March 1991.

20 Stewart, *Barbara Hanrahan*, pp.264–265.

21 Andrew Taylor, 'Remembering Barbara Hanrahan', *The Adelaide Review*, June 1992, pp.24–25.

22 Alec Bolton to Barbara Hanrahan, 11 June 1990.

23 ibid. See Fiona MacCarthy's *Eric Gill: A Lover's Quest for Art and God*. London: Faber & Faber, 1989. MacCarthy exposed previously covered-up crimes in Gill's private life, including his incestuous abuse of two of his daughters.

24 Barbara Hanrahan to Alec Bolton, 15 June 1990, Box 6, Folder 3, NLA MS 7426, Addition 25 February 1998.

25 Marked-up copy of 'Sleeping Beauties' typescript, Box 5, Folder 34, NLA MS 7426, Addition 12 September 1995.

26 Neil Macmillan, *An A–Z of Type Designers*. London: Laurence King, 2006, pp.76–77.

27 Cited in Sebastian Carter, *Twentieth Century Type Designers*. London: Trefoil, 1987, p.69.

28 Alec Bolton to Barbara Hanrahan, 6 February 1991 and 12 March 1991.

29 Alec Bolton to Bruce [?], Bankstown Typesetting, 12 March 1991; Alec Bolton to Barbara Hanrahan, 16 March 1991.

30 Alec Bolton to Barbara Hanrahan, 25 March 1991.

31 Alec Bolton to Barbara Hanrahan, 21 June 1991.

32 Barbara Hanrahan to Alec Bolton, 9 July 1991. Bolton always intended this to be the case, but had failed to spell it out in his draft text for the prospectus.

33 Interview with Robin Tait, 1 March 2015.

34 Hanrahan, *The Diaries of Barbara Hanrahan*, p.358.

35 Alec Bolton to Barbara Hanrahan, 17 August 1991.

36 Jo Steele to Alec Bolton, 14 November 1991.

37 Jo Steele to Alec Bolton, 7 December 1991.

38 Alec Bolton to Barbara Hanrahan, 8 October 1991.

39 Prospectus for *Iris in Her Garden*. Canberra: Brindabella Press, 1991.

40 Alec Bolton to Barbara Hanrahan, 23 June 1991.

41 Barbara Hanrahan to Alec Bolton, 9 July 1991.

42 Alec Bolton to Laurie Muller, University of Queensland Press, 8 November 1991, Box 5, Folder 36, NLA MS 7426, Addition 12 September 1995.

43 Alec Bolton to Barbara Hanrahan, 2 November 1991.

44 *The Weekend Australian*, 16–17 November 1991.

45 Alec Bolton to Barbara Hanrahan, 8 November 1991.

46 'Iris Copies', Box 2, NLA MS Acc14.052 Alec Bolton. He had commented on the slowness of the gallery, and the Art Gallery of NSW, in a letter to Hanrahan, 2 November 1991, Box 5, Folder 36, NLA MS 7426, Addition 12 September 1995.

47 'Iris Costings', 25 August 1991.

48 Barbara Hanrahan to Alec Bolton, 3 August 1990, Box 6, Folder 3, NLA MS 7426, Addition 25 February 1998.

49 Alec Bolton to Rosanne Fitzgibbons, University of Queensland Press, 14 February 1992, Box 5, Folder 36, NLA MS 7426, Addition 12 September 1995.

Chapter 30

1 Alec Bolton to Neil Moore, 8 March 1991; Neil Moore to Alec Bolton, 22 March 1991; both Box 8, Folder 18, NLA MS 7426, Addition 25 February 1998.

2 Neil Moore to the author, 27 March 2016. Rosemary Dobson annotated the file copy of the July letter to say 'A tentative approach. I think NM finally too committed elsewhere'. Alec Bolton to Neil Moore, 22 July 1991, Box 8, Folder 18, NLA MS 7426, Addition 25 February 1998.

3 Rosemary Dobson, *Collected*. St Lucia: University of Queensland Press, 2012.

4 Alec Bolton to Mike Hudson, n.d., and 18 November 1991; both Box 8, Folder 18, NLA MS 7426, Addition 25 February 1998.

5 Alec Bolton to Mike Hudson, 14 January 1992, Box 8, Folder 18, NLA MS 7426, Addition 25 February 1998. Unless cited differently, subsequent references to correspondence in this chapter are to this folder.

6 Rosemary Dobson, cover note on folder 18; and note on draft letter to Mike Hudson.

7 Mike Hudson to Alec Bolton, 23 January 1992. Ellipses in original.

8 Draft in Rosemary Dobson's hand of an unsent letter to Mike Hudson, n.d. [January 1992].

9 ibid.

10 Alec Bolton to Kay Craddock, 25 November 1992.

11 Alec Bolton, interview with Heather Rusden, 25 October 1996.

12 The plan was originally to print the paper by process engraving, but there was some concern it might be too finely detailed for this. Alec Bolton to Rosalind Atkins, n.d., Box 7, Folder 14, NLA MS 7426, Addition 25 February 1998. See also Alec Bolton to Adrian Young, 15 June 1992, Box 8, Folder 18, NLA MS 7426, Addition 25 February 1998. Colour samples are in Box 2, NLA MS Acc14.052 Alec Bolton.

13 Interview with Robin Tait, 1 March 2015.

14 Alec Bolton to Mike Hudson, 31 August 1992 and 14 September 1992.

15 Alec Bolton to Mike Hudson, 14 October 1992 and 9 November 1992.

16 Alec Bolton to Kay Craddock, 25 November 1992, Box 8, Folder 18, NLA MS 7426, Addition 25 February 1998.

17 'Untold Lives, First shot at costing', 25 May 1992; 'Untold Lives, Revised costing', 1 June 1992; both Box 8, Folder 18, NLA MS 7426, Addition 25 February 1998, and 'Untold Lives—Copies', Box 2, NLA MS Acc14.052 Alec Bolton.

18 Rosemary Dobson, *Untold Lives & Later Poems*. Rose Bay, NSW: Brandl & Schlesinger, 2000, p.7.

Chapter 31

1 Alec Bolton to Philip Hodgins, 13 March 1993, Box 5, Folder 32, NLA MS 7426, Addition 12 September 1995. Unless cited differently, subsequent references to correspondence in this chapter are to this folder.

2 Philip Hodgins to Alec Bolton, 14 February 1992.

3 Philip Hodgins to Alec Bolton, 14 March 1990.

4 Alexander, *Les Murray: A Life in Progress*, pp.223–224.

5 Alec Bolton to Philip Hodgins, 15 April 1990 and 17 January 1992.

6 Alec Bolton to Andrew [possibly Taylor], 26 July 1993.

7 Alec Bolton to Gerald Fischer, 2 January 1994, Box 11, Folder 40, NLA MS 7426, Addition 25 February 1998.

8 Alec Bolton to Mike Hudson, 13 July 1992, Box 8, Folder 18, NLA MS 7426, Addition 25 February 1998.

9 Alec Bolton to James [?], 8 December 1992.

10 Bolton, *Brindabella Press: The Name Regained and Other News*, p.4.

11 Interview with Robin Tait, 1 March 2015.

12 Alec Bolton to Gerald Fischer, 2 January 1994, Box 11, Folder 40, NLA MS 7426, Addition 25 February 1998.

13 Alec Bolton to Geoffrey Farmer, 26 July 1993.

14 Alec Bolton to Victoria Clutterbuck, 10 March 1992.

15 Philip Hodgins to Alec Bolton, 20 June 1992.

16 Alec Bolton to Philip Hodgins, 22 November 1992.

17 Alec Bolton to Philip Hodgins, 28 August 1992.

18 Bolton, *Brindabella Press: The Name Regained and Other News*. The format for this is similar to Simon Lawrence's prospectus *Twelve Years Young: The Fleece Press in 1992*, printed in April. According to Lawrence, Alec sent him a copy of his own prospectus, 'saying he hoped I wouldn't mind that he'd copied the design and typography directly from one of my own!' Email from Simon Lawrence to M. Richards, 3 April 2017.

19 Alec Bolton to Philip Hodgins, 12 January 1993 and 21 February 1993.

20 Alec Bolton to Philip Hodgins, 13 February 1993.

21 Alec Bolton to Jadwiga Jarvis, 27 April 1993, Box 3, NLA MS Acc14.052 Alec Bolton.

22 'The End of the Season/Second costing 23.2.93'.

23 Alec Bolton to Philip Hodgins, 4 July 1993, Box 5, Folder 32, NLA MS 7426, Addition 12 September 1995.

24 Katrina Iffland in *The Canberra Times*, 17 July 1994, p.17.

Chapter 32

1 Barrie [Barrett] Reid to Alec Bolton, 28 December 1993 and Alec Bolton to Barrett Reid, 25 January 1994; both Box 10, Folder 35, NLA MS 7426, Addition 25 February 1998. He offered to consider a longer manuscript mentioned by Reid, should Angus & Robertson decline it, but *Making Country* was published by them in 1995.

2 Alec Bolton to Les Murray, 1 July 1993, Box 8, Folder 21, NLA MS 7426, Addition 25 February 1998. Unless cited differently, subsequent references to correspondence in this chapter are to this folder.

3 Les Murray to Alec Bolton, 16 July 1993 and 15 August 1993.

4 Les Murray to Alec Bolton, 30 August 1993.

5 Alec Bolton to Rosalind Atkins, 9 August 1993.

6 Les Murray to Alec Bolton, 16 October 1993.

7 Les Murray to Alec Bolton, 21 October 1993.

8 Alec Bolton to Les Murray, 26 October 1993.

9 Alec Bolton to Rosalind Atkins, 31 October 1993. This was confirmed by Atkins in an email to the author, 30 August 2017. Printed in 1993, some copies were sold through Helen Maxwell's gallery aGOG in Canberra.

10 Les Murray to Alec Bolton, n.d..

11 Alec Bolton to Rosalind Atkins, 25 August 1993 and 11 October 1993.

12 Alec Bolton to Simon Lawrence, 10 August 1993; email from Simon Lawrence to M. Richards, 3 April 2017. Alec's admiration for Simon Lawrence is mentioned in a letter to Jadwiga Jarvis, 27 April 1993, Box 3, NLA MS Acc14.052 Alec Bolton.

13 'News from Brindabella Press', folded one-page flyer. Deakin: Brindabella Press, November 1993.

14 Alec Bolton to Rosalind Atkins, 26 March 1994.

15 'The Sleepout/second thoughts on costs', 11 October 1993, with later annotation, Box 8, Folder 21, NLA MS 7426, Addition 25 February 1998

16 Alec Bolton to Rosalind Atkins, 26 March 1994.

Chapter 33

1 *The Canberra Times*, 29 May 1985, records his election as president of the Conservation Council of the South-East Region and Canberra.

2 Prospectus for *Granite Country*. Canberra: Brindabella Press, 1996.

3 Alec Bolton to Bruce McKenzie (Bankstown Typesetting), 8 November 1993, Box 8, Folder 22, NLA MS 7426, Addition 25 February 1998.

4 Alec Bolton to Bob Summers, 6 June 1996 and 13 June 1996, Box 11, Folder 41, NLA MS 7426, Addition 25 February 1998.

5 Alec Bolton to A.E. Hudson P.L., ordering ink, 6 June 1994, Box 8, Folder 22, NLA MS 7426, Addition 25 February 1998.

6 Alec Bolton to J.R. Rowland, 12 September 1993, Box 8, Folder 22, NLA MS 7426, Addition 25 February 1998.

7 'Granite Country: First shot at costing, 20-4-94', as amended, Box 8, Folder 22, NLA MS 7426, Addition 25 February 1998.

8 'Granite Country Copies', [1994–1996], Box 2, NLA MS Acc14.052 Alec Bolton.

Chapter 34

1 Alec Bolton to Rosalind Atkins, 28 April 1995, Box 10, Folder 34, NLA MS 7426, Addition 25 February 1998.

2 Helen Maxwell, 'Helen Elizabeth Ogilvie', *Design & Art Australia Online*. www.daao.org.au/bio/helen-elizabeth-ogilvie/biography/

3 Helen Ogilvie, *Wood Engravings*. Canberra: Brindabella Press, 1993, p.viii. The use of tissue paper for linocuts, backed onto heavier paper after printing, is described in Grishin, *Australian Art: A History*, p.230.

4 Sasha Grishin, *Australian Art*. Melbourne: Miegunyah Press, 2013, p.230.

5 Ogilvie, *Wood Engravings*, p.vii.

6 Ron Radford, *Outlines of Australian Printmaking*. Ballarat: Ballarat Fine Art Gallery, 1976, p.34.

7 John McPhee, Introduction to Helen Ogilvie Catalogue. Canberra: aGOG (Australian Girls' Own Gallery), 4–23 May 1991. Copy in Box 9, Folder 24,

NLA MS 7426, Addition 25 February 1998.

8 Helen Maxwell, Obituary for Helen Ogilvie, *Art Monthly Australia*, vol.63, September 1993, p.36.

9 Sonia Barron, *The Canberra Times*, 15 May 1991, p.26.

10 Alec Bolton to Helen Ogilvie, 14 February 1991, Box 9, Folder 24, NLA MS 7426, Addition 25 February 1998.

11 Alec Bolton to Helen Ogilvie, 16 February 1991, Box 9, Folder 24, NLA MS 7426, Addition 25 February 1998.

12 Alec Bolton to Kay Craddock, 28 February 1992; Helen Ogilvie to Alec Bolton, 29 May 1992; Alec Bolton to Helen Ogilvie, 14 February 1992 and 24 April 1992, Box 9, Folder 24, NLA MS 7426, Addition 25 February 1998.

13 Alec Bolton, interviewed by Heather Rusden, 25 October 1996.

14 Alec Bolton to Bob Summers, fax of 13 June 1996, Box 11, Folder 41, NLA MS 7426, Addition 25 February 1998.

15 The two titles were Russell Grimwade, *Flinders Lane: Recollections of Alfred Felton*. Melbourne: Melbourne University Press, 1947 and J.D.G. Medley, *Stolne & Surreptitious Verses*, privately printed by Melbourne University Press in an edition of 200 signed and numbered copies in 1953. 'Stolne' is correct.

16 John McPhee to Alec Bolton, 17 August 1993, Box 9, Folder 25, NLA MS 7426, Addition 25 February 1998.

17 Alec Bolton to Rosalind Atkins, 1 December 1992, Box 9, Folder 24, NLA MS 7426, Addition 25 February 1998. In a letter to Ogilvie's niece Gillian Grice he confirms that the line blocks were to be made from 'prints and proofs that your aunt also lent'. Alec Bolton to Gillian Grice, 22 August 1993, Box 9, Folder 25, NLA MS 7426, Addition 25 February 1998.

18 Alec Bolton to Bob Summers, 5 March 1995, Box 11, Folder 41, NLA MS 7426, Addition 25 February 1998. The two met in 1989 and became good friends. Summers, based in Sydney, was one of the few nearby printers Alec could discuss printing issues with.

19 Alec Bolton to Michael Ryan, 'Modern Reproduction', 23 January 1995, Box 9, Folder 26, NLA MS 7426, Addition 25 February 1998. The negatives used to make the line blocks are in the same folder.

20 Roger Butler, *Printed: Images by Australian Artists 1885–1955*. Canberra: National Gallery of Australia, 2007, p.157. Another who briefly broke through the same barrier was Tate Adams, who in the 1960s illustrated a high school civics text for Longmans,

Yesterday and Tomorrow (1965), with wood engravings.

21 Helen Maxwell to Alec Bolton, 9 April 1993, Box 9, Folder 24, NLA MS 7426, Addition 25 February 1998.

22 Alec Bolton to Kay Craddock, 3 August 1993, Box 9, Folder 24, NLA MS 7426, Addition 25 February 1998.

23 Alec Bolton to Rosalind Atkins, 1 December 1992, Box 9, Folder 24, NLA MS 7426, Addition 25 February 1998.

24 Rhoda Lord, 'List of Engraved Wood Blocks sent to Alec Bolton', 15 November 1993; Alec Bolton to Rhoda Lord, 17 November 1993; Alec Bolton to Clem Christesen, 3 December 1993; all in Box 9, Folder 25, NLA MS 7426, Addition 25 February 1998.

25 Alec Bolton to Rosalind Atkins, 19 November 1993, Box 8, Folder 21, NLA MS 7426, Addition 25 February 1998.

26 Alec Bolton to Helen Maxwell, 22 January 1994, Box 9, Folder 25, NLA MS 7426, Addition 25 February 1998.

27 Alec Bolton to Rhoda Lord, 17 April 1995, Box 9, Folder 25, NLA MS 7426, Addition 25 February 1998.

28 Alec Bolton to Rhoda Lord, 1 August 1995, Box 9, Folder 25, NLA MS 7426, Addition 25 February 1998.

29 'Ogilvie: First Shot at Costing', 7 March 1995, annotated with 'Final Costs', Box 9, Folder 25, NLA MS 7426, Addition 25 February 1998.

30 'Ogilvie—Distribution of Copies', Box 2, NLA MS Acc14.052 Alec Bolton.

31 Alec Bolton, interviewed by Heather Rusden, 7 November 1996.

32 Kay Craddock to Alec Bolton, 31 August 1995, Box 9, Folder 26, NLA MS 7426, Addition 25 February 1998.

33 Rosalind Atkins to Alec Bolton, 3 September [1995], Box 9, Folder 26, NLA MS 7426, Addition 25 February 1998.

Chapter 35

1 Nan McDonald, *For Prisoners*. Canberra: Brindabella Press, 1995. Prefatory note by Alec Bolton.

2 Alec Bolton to Judith Wright, 6 September 1995, Box 9, Folder 27, NLA MS 7426, Addition 25 February 1998.

3 Supplied by Modern Reproduction in Melbourne. The block is now in the possession

of the author, courtesy of the Bolton family.

4 'For Prisoners—Copies', Box 2, NLA MS Acc14.052 Alec Bolton.

5 Robert Gray to Alec Bolton, 4 January 1996, Box 2, NLA MS Acc14.052 Alec Bolton.

6 Alec Bolton to Robert Gray, 1 June 1995, Box 10, Folder 36, NLA MS 7426, Addition 25 February 1998. Gray's *New and Selected Poems* was published by Heinemann in 1995.

7 Alec Bolton, interview with Heather Rusden, 7 November 1996.

Chapter 36

1 Alec Bolton to Gavin Souter, 2 July 1994, Box 9, Folder 28, NLA MS 7426, Addition 25 February 1998

2 Alec Bolton to Rosalind Atkins, 31 January 1996, Box 10, Folder 34, NLA MS 7426, Addition 25 February 1998.

3 Alec Bolton to Rod Williamson, Raleigh Paper, 4 February 1996, Box 9, Folder 28, NLA MS 7426, Addition 25 February 1998.

4 Alec Bolton to Phil Abbott, Goanna Print, 7 November 1995, Box 9, Folder 28, NLA MS 7426, Addition 25 February 1998.

5 Alec Bolton to Phil Abbott, Goanna Print, 22 February 1996, Box 11, Folder 39, NLA MS 7426, Addition 25 February 1998.

6 Frank Romano, *History of the Linotype Company*. Rochester, New York: RIT Press, 2014, p.130.

7 Invoice from Don. K. Black Linecasting, 7 July 1995, Box 10, Folder 37, NLA MS 7426, Addition 25 February 1998.

8 Alec Bolton to Bob Summers, 30 December 1995, Box 11, Folder 41, NLA MS 7426, Addition 25 February 1998.

9 Alec Bolton to Bob Summers, 6 June 1996, Box 11, Folder 41, NLA MS 7426, Addition 25 February 1998.

10 'News from Brindabella Press', September 1996, p.1.

11 Alec Bolton to Rosalind Atkins, [?] and 9 June 1996, Box 10, Folder 34, NLA MS 7426, Addition 25 February 1998.

12 Alec Bolton to Harry Pearce, The Font Factory Pty Ltd, 12 June 1996, Box 1, NLA MS Acc14.052 Alec Bolton.

13 Alec Bolton to Mike Hudson, 17 February 1992, Box 8, Folder 18 NLA MS 7426,

Addition 25 February 1998.

14 Alec Bolton to Gavin Souter, 15 June 1995, Box 9, Folder 28, NLA MS 7426, Addition 25 February 1998.

15 Alec Bolton to Gavin Souter, 14 July 1994, Box 9, Folder 28, NLA MS 7426, Addition 25 February 1998.

16 Prospectus for *A Torrent of Words*. Canberra: Brindabella Press, 1996, p.3.

17 Alec Bolton to Rod Jenkins, 27 May 1996, Box 9, Folder 28, NLA MS 7426, Addition 25 February 1998.

18 John Currey, Miegunyah Press, to Alec Bolton, 18 October 1995; Alec Bolton to Laurie Muller, University of Queensland Press, 19 October 1995; both Box 9, Folder 28, NLA MS 7426, Addition 25 February 1998.

19 Alec Bolton to Rosalind Atkins, 9 June 1996, Box 10, Folder 34, NLA MS 7426, Addition 25 February 1998.

20 Alec Bolton to Gavin Souter, 9 May 1996, Box 9, Folder 28, NLA MS 7426, Addition 25 February 1998.

21 ATB, 'Souter A Torrent of Words/First Shot at Costing', Box 9, Folder 28, NLA MS 7426, Addition 25 February 1998.

22 ATB, 'Souter Copies', Box 2, NLA MS Acc14.052 Alec Bolton

23 Peter Ryan, 'A Torrent of Words', *Quadrant*, September 1996, pp.87–88.

24 Clement Semmler, 'Laureate to Legend of Anzacs', *The Australian*, 2 July 1996.

25 Don Anderson, 'Untold Stories of an Un-French wife: Behind the Lines', *The Sydney Morning Herald*, 20 July 1996.

26 Alec Bolton to Gavin Souter, 15 June 1995, Box 9, Folder 28, NLA MS 7426, Addition 25 February 1998.

Chapter 37

1 The annual Book Design Awards are now administered by the Australian Book Design Association, founded in 2014 after the Australian Publishers Association ended its sponsorship of the awards.

2 The citation and award certificate are in Box 5, NLA MS Acc14.052 Alec Bolton.

3 Alec Bolton to Peter Barker, Brown Prior Anderson, 11 March 1996, Box 9, Folder 28, NLA MS 7426, Addition 25 February 1998.

4 Alec Bolton to Rosalind Atkins, 5 March 1996, Box 10, Folder 34, NLA MS 7426,

Addition 25 February 1998.

5 John Mulvaney, 'Vale Alec Bolton 1926–1996', *Australian Scholarly Editions Newsletter*, no.2, April 1997, pp.9–10.

6 Email from Paul Eggert to M. Richards, 26 October 2014. For the history and aims of the Academy Editions Project, see Paul Eggert, 'Editing a Nation's Literature: The Academy Editions of Australian Literature Project', *Bibliographical Society of Australia and New Zealand Bulletin*, vol.20, no.2 (Second Quarter 1996).

7 Andrew Schuller, 'A New Generation of Private Presses in Australia', *Matrix*, no.31 (2012), pp.87–93. Florance holds a doctorate from the University of Canberra, where she studied in the Centre for Creative and Cultural Research, completing a thesis entitled 'Axonologue: 5 Years of Experiential Materiality'. See also Caren Florance, 'The Changing Face of Contemporary Letterpress in Australia', *The La Trobe Journal*, no.95 (March 2015).

8 *The Canberra Times*, 24 November 1996.

9 'Alexander Thorley Bolton', memorial notice, 1996. Copy in the author's collection.

10 Interview with Robin Tait, 1 March 2015. A trade edition in wrappers was also published, based on extra sets of sheets estimated by her to have been enough for 200 copies. This edition is now even scarcer than the hand-bound edition.

11 Note by Rosemary Dobson on proofs in Box 2, NLA MS Acc14.052 Alec Bolton.

12 Alec Bolton to Lynn Hard, 29 January 1996, Box 10, Folder 32, NLA MS 7426, Addition 25 February 1998.

13 *The Canberra Times*, 20 May 1999.

14 Note by Rosemary Dobson, 1 July 1999, Box 11, Folder 46, NLA MS 7426, Addition 16 July 1999.

15 David Malouf to 'Alex and Rosemary', 11 December 1986, Box 10 , Folder 33, NLA MS 7426, Addition 25 February 1998.

16 'News from Brindabella Press', p.4; Alec Bolton to Patsy Payne, 3 September 1996, Box 10, Folder 33, NLA MS 7426, Addition 25 February 1998.

17 Alec Bolton to Fay [Zwicky], 17 September 1996, Box 3, NLA MS Acc14.052 Alec Bolton.

18 In a conversation on 2 March 2015, David Malouf confirmed that this was the collection originally offered to the Brindabella Press. Paper Bark Press was established by Robert Adamson, Juno Gemes and Michael Wilding in 1986. Wilding withdrew in 1990. Three of the stories had been previously published in *Heat*.

19 Alec Bolton to David Malouf, 9 September 1996, Box 10, Folder 33, NLA MS 7426, Addition 25 February 1998.

20 'News from Brindabella Press', p.4.

Epilogue

1 'Alexander Thorley Bolton', memorial notice, 1996.

2 Allan Fleming to Alec Bolton, 15 November 1993, Box 3, NLA MS Acc14.052 Alec Bolton.

3 Rosemary Dobson, *The Three Fates & Other Poems*, 59.

4 Dobson, *Untold Lives & Later Poems*, p.72.

Credits and Courtesy Lines

Frontmatter images

(cover) Jill White, *Alec Bolton* [40], b&w negative, courtesy Robert Bolton; (title-page) Mike Hudson, *Breakaway*, wood engraving, 10 x 16.8cm, in *Untold Lives* by Rosemary Dobson, 1992, courtesy Wayzgoose Press

Image well

Bolton family photographs, courtesy Robert Bolton; *Australian Encyclopaedia Staff, Angus and Robertson, 1953*, sepia-toned photograph, 15.5 x 21.1cm, nla.gov.au/nla.obj-136705155; (likely) Alec Bolton, *Rosemary Dobson and (likely) Henry Mund*, courtesy Robert Bolton; *Portraits of Alec Bolton, Yvonne Boyd, Arthur Boyd, Penelope Hope and Professor Alec Hope at Bundanon, 1978*, gelatin silver photograph, 16.5 x 21.6cm, nla.gov.au/nla.obj-143781663; *Sally McCann, Alec Bolton and Dave Brown,* 1982, internal photograph, National Library of Australia; Alec Bolton, *Portrait of Judith Wright, Rosemary Bolton and Denise Levertov, Mongarlowe, NSW, 1981*, gelatin silver photograph, 20.3 x 25.3cm, nla.gov.au/nla.obj-144050951; Loui Seselja, Brindabella Press printery, b&w photograph, MS7426, Box 5, file 37, nla.gov.au/nla.obj-298485116; Henk Brusse, *Alec Holding a Brindabella Press Book*, 3 February 1987, b&w negative, 5.5 x 5.5cm, internal photograph, National Library of Australia; *Iris in Her Garden*, *Time Given* [right], *Occasions of Birds*, *Some Poems of Shaw Neilson*, Michael Richards private collection; *Time Given* [left], *The Sea Poems of Kenneth Slessor*, *The Idyll Wheel*, National Library of Australia; Henk Brusse, *Alec Bolton at Work at His Brindabella Press in Canberra, 3 February 1987*, b&w negative, 5.5 x 5.5cm, nla.gov.au/nla.obj-151329035; Jill White, *Alec Bolton and Rosemary Dobson* [93], b&w negative, courtesy Robert Bolton

Text permissions

Permission to reproduce the words of Ruth Park courtesy of the copyright owner The Niland Family Trust, c/- Tim Curnow, Literary Agent, Sydney

Permission to reproduce James McAuley letter by arrangement with the Estate of James McAuley, c/- Curtis Brown (Aust) Pty Ltd

References

Ackland, Michael, *Damaged Men: The Precarious Lives of James McAuley and Harold Stewart*. Sydney: Allen & Unwin, 2001.

Alexander, Peter F., *Les Murray: A Life in Progress*. South Melbourne: Oxford University Press, 2000.

Allen, Geoffrey, *Four Songs to Poems of Rosemary Dobson*. Perth: Keys Press, 2006.

Allen, Lewis, *Printing with the Handpress*. New York: Van Nostrand Reinhold, 1969.

Andrews, Martin J., *The Life and Work of Robert Gibbings*. Bicester: Primrose Hill Press, 2003.

Australian Book Publishers Association, *Book Design Awards 1978–9*, 1979. abdacdn-wpengine.netdna-ssl.com/wp-content/uploads/ABDA-Catalogue-1978-1979.pdf

Ayres, Marie-Louise, 'Dobson, Rosemary de Brissac (1920–2012)'. *Obituaries Australia*. oa.anu.edu.au/obituary/dobson-rosemary-de-brissac-15206

Barker, Anthony, *One of the First and One of the Finest: Beatrice Davis, Book Editor*. Carlton: The Society of Editors (Vic.), 1991.

Belson, Mick, *On the Press: Through the Eyes of the Craftsmen of Oxford University Press*. Witney: Robert Boyd Publications, 2003.

Bolton, Alec, 'The Brindabella Press'. *Biblionews and Australian Notes and Queries* vol.7, no.254 (June 1982).

———, *Publications from 1973 to 1989 of the Officina Brindabella, with a Note on the Beginnings of the Press*. Deakin: Officina Brindabella, 1989.

———, *Brindabella Press: The Name Regained and Other News*. Canberra: Brindabella Press, 1992.

———, *Interviewing for Oral History at the National Library of Australia*. Canberra: National Library of Australia, 1994.

———, 'Publishing in an Age of Innocence: Angus & Robertson in the 1950s'. *Publishing Studies*, no.1 (Spring 1995).

———, Alec Bolton interviewed by Heather Rusden. Sound recording, 1996. nla.gov.au/nla.oh-vn2834398

Bolton, David, [Survey of Typefaces]. *It's a Small World 67*, 2021, pp.57–58.

Bryan, Harrison, 'The National Library of Australia: An Historical Perspective'. *Australian Academic & Research Libraries* 22, no.4 (1991).

Burke, Christopher, *Active Literature: Jan Tschichold and New Typography*. London: Hyphen Press, 2007.

Burke, Clifford, *Printing Poetry: A Workbook in Typographic Reification*. San Francisco: Scarab Press, 1980.

Butler, Roger, *Printed: Images by Australian Artists 1885–1955*. Canberra: National Gallery of Australia, 2007.

Carroll, Alison, *Barbara Hanrahan Printmaker*. Netley: Wakefield Press, 1986.

Carter, Sebastian, *Twentieth Century Type Designers*. London: Trefoil, 1987.

———, 'Typeface Design for the Monotype Corporation', in *History of the Monotype Corporation*, pp.177–302. London: Printing Historical Society, 2014.

Cave, Roderick, *The Private Press*, 2nd edn. New York: Bowker, 1983.

Chisholm, Alec H. (ed.), *The Australian Encyclopaedia*. 2nd edn. 10 vols. Sydney: Angus & Robertson, 1958.

Clark, Manning, *Occasional Writings and Speeches*. [Melbourne?]: Fontana/Collins, 1980.

Clarkson, Christopher, *Limp Vellum Binding and Its Potential as a Conservation Structure for the Rebinding of Early Printed Books.* Llandudnow: Red Gull Press, 1982.

Clendinning, Ross (ed.), *Contemporary Designer Bookbindings: Europe & Australia*. Sydney: Crafts Council of Australia, 1984.

Croucher, Paul, *A History of Buddhism in Australia: 1848–1988*. Kensington: New South Wales University Press, 1989.

Denholm, Michael, *Small Press Publishing in Australia: The Early 1970s*. North Sydney: Second Back Row Press, 1979.

Devlin, Stanley L., *Multiple Stains: The Story of the Devlin and Associated Families in Australia*. Canberra: S.L. Devlin, 1999. www.netspeed.com.au/kdevlin/stanley/MultipleStainsComplete.pdf

Directory of Old Sydneians, Sydney: Alumni Directories for Sydney Grammar School Foundation, 2000.

Dobson, Rosemary, *Child with a Cockatoo*. Sydney: Angus & Robertson, 1955.

———, *Focus on Ray Crooke*. St Lucia: University of Queensland Press, 1971.

———, *A World of Difference: Australian Poetry and Painting in the 1940s*. Herbert Blaiklock Memorial Lecture 3. Sydney: Wentworth Press, 1973.

———, *Greek Coins*. Canberra: Brindabella Press, 1977.

———, *Over the Frontier*. Sydney: Angus & Robertson, 1978.

———, *The Three Fates & Other Poems*. Marrickville: Hale & Iremonger, 1984.

———, *Summer Press*. St Lucia: University of Queensland Press, 1987.

———, *Untold Lives & Later Poems*. Rose Bay, NSW: Brandl & Schlesinger, 2000.

———, *Collected*. St Lucia: University of Queensland Press, 2012.

Dobson, Rosemary and Campbell, David, *Moscow Trefoil*. Canberra: Australian National University Press, 1975.

Dobson, Rosemary, and David Campbell, *Seven Russian Poets: Imitations*. Brisbane: University of Queensland Press, 1979.

Eggert, Paul, 'Editing a Nation's Literature: The Academy Editions of Australian Literature Project'. *Bibliographical Society of Australia and New Zealand Bulletin* 20, no.2 (Second Quarter 1996), pp.146–53.

Fairbank, Alfred, *A Handwriting Manual*. Leicester: Dryad Press, n.d.

Farmer, Geoffrey, *Private Presses and Australia*. Melbourne: Hawthorn Press, 1972.

———, 'Three Women Printers'. *Biblionews and Australian Notes and* Queries, vol.8, no.3 (September 1983), pp.86–89.

———, *A True Printer: John Kirtley and Heemskerck Shoals*. 2nd edn. Cremorne: Book Collectors' Society of Australia, 1990.

———, 'An Interlude of Fine Printing and Other Activities'. *Biblionews and Australian Notes and Queries*, vol.15, no.3 (September 1990), pp.68–72.

———, *A Private Pursuit*. Pearl Beach: Escutcheon Press, 1995.

Fitzgerald, Penelope, 'The Beginning of Spring', in *Offshore, Human Voices, The Beginning of Spring*. Everyman's Library 269. New York: Alfred A. Knopf, 2003.

FitzGerald, Robert D., *To Meet the Sun*. Sydney: Angus & Robertson, 1929.

———, *Product: Later Verses*. Sydney: Angus & Robertson, 1977.

Florance, Caren, 'Flashdancing through Canberra's Material Book Cultures'. *Axon: Creative Explorations*, vol.5, no.1 (March 2015). www.axonjournal.com.au/issue-8-1/flashdancing-through-canberra%E2%80%99s-material-book-cultures

———, 'The Changing Face of Contemporary Letterpress in Australia'. *The La Trobe Journal*, no.95 (March 2015), pp.64–76.

Fuog, Paul, 'Studio Profile: Hofstede Design'. *Desktop: The Culture of Design*, 25 February 2012.

Garrett, Albert, *A History of Wood Engraving*. London: Bloomsbury Books, 1986.

Glaister, Geoffrey Ashall, *Glaister's Glossary of the Book*. 2nd edn. London: George Allen & Unwin, 1979.

Golding, Peter, *An Unqualified Success: The Extraordinary Life of Allan Percy Fleming*. Dural: Rosenberg Publishing, 2013.

Gould, Alan, 'Ten Years of Poetry in Canberra'. *Poetry Australia*, no.87 (April 1983), pp.65–72.

Gray, Anna, *Petr Herel: An Exhibition of Artist Books at the National Library of Australia 22 March – 30 June 1989*. Canberra: National Library of Australia, 1989.

Green, H.M., and Dorothy Green, *A History of Australian Literature: Pure and Applied.* Sydney: Angus & Robertson, 1984.

Grishin, Sasha, *Australian Art: A History*. Melbourne: Miegunyah Press, 2013.

———, 'Books in the Canberra Region: The Golden Years'. *The La Trobe Journal*, no.95 (March 2015). www.slv.vic.gov.au/sites/default/files/La-Trobe-Journal-95-Sasha-Grishin.pdf

Hanna, Cliff, *The Folly of Spring: A Study of John Shaw Neilson's Poetry*. St Lucia: University of Queensland Press, 1990.

Hanrahan, Barbara, *The Diaries of Barbara Hanrahan*. Edited by Elaine Lindsay. St Lucia: University of Queensland Press, 1998.

Harrison, Chris, 'Sir Brian Hone: The Scholar, His Press and His Books in the National Library'. *National Library of Australia News*, February 1991, pp.11–13.

Harrop, Dorothy A, *A History of the Gregynog Press*. Pinner: Private Libraries Association, 1980.

Hart, Jim, 'New Wave Seventies', in *Paper Empires: A History of the Book in Australia, 1946–2005*. St Lucia: University of Queensland Press, 2006.

Holmes, Robyn, 'Musical Dialogues', in *Remarkable Occurrences: The National Library of Australia's First 100 Years 1901–2001*. Canberra: National Library of Australia, 2001.

Hooton, Joy W., *Rosemary Dobson: A Celebration*. Canberra: Friends of the National Library of Australia, 2000.

Hudson, Mike, and Jadwiga Jarvis, *Private Impressions*. [Katoomba]: Wayzgoose Press, 1989.

James, Neil, '"The Fountainhead": George Ferguson and Angus & Robertson'. *Publishing Studies*, no.7 (Autumn 1999), pp.6–16.

Jarvis, Jadwiga, *The Wayzgoose Affair*. Katoomba: The Wayzgoose Press, 2007.

Jennett, Sean, *The Making of Books*. 3rd edn. London: Faber & Faber, 1964.

Jury, David, *Graphic Design before Graphic Designers: The Printer as Designer and Craftsman 1700–1914*. London: Thames & Hudson, 2012.

Kennedy, Richard, *A Boy at the Hogarth Press*. Whittington: Whittington Press, 1972.

Kent, Jacqueline, *A Certain Style: Beatrice Davis, A Literary Life*. Ringwood: Viking, 2001.

Kerr, Joan, 'Anne Wienholt'. In *Design & Art Australia Online*, 1995. www.daao.org.au/bio/anne-wienholt/biography/

Kirkpatrick, Peter, 'Guide to the Classics: The Poetry of Rosemary Dobson'. *The Conversation*, 13 September 2018. theconversation.com/guide-to-the-classics-the-poetry-of-rosemary-dobson-100581

Klepac, Lou, *Russell Drysdale*. Sydney: Bay Books, 1983.

Kratzmann, Gregory (ed.), *A Steady Storm of Correspondence: Selected Letters of Gwen Harwood, 1943–1995*. St Lucia: University of Queensland Press, 2001.

Lawson, Alexander, *Anatomy of a Typeface*. Boston: David R. Godine, 1990.

Little, Miles, *Round Trip*. Carlton, Vic.: Melbourne University Press, 1977.

Loxley, Simon, *Printer's Devil: The Life and Work of Frederic Warde*. Boston: David R. Godine, 2013.

McDonald, Nan, *For Prisoners*. Canberra: Brindabella Press, 1995.

MacInnes, Mairi, *Clearances*. New York: Pantheon, 1992.

McKenry, Keith, *More than a Life: John Meredith and the Fight for Australian Tradition*. Dural: Rosenberg Publishing, 2014.

Mackenzie, John M., *Propaganda and Empire*. Studies in Imperialism. Manchester: Manchester University Press, 1986.

Macmillan, Neil, *An A–Z of Type Designers*. London: Laurence King, 2006.

Marchant, Sylvia, 'Ruth Violet Dobson', in *Australian Dictionary of Biography*, vol.17. Melbourne: Melbourne University Press, 2007. adb.anu.edu.au/biography/dobson-ruth-violet-12424

Marr, David, *Patrick White: A Life*. Sydney: Random House, 1991.

Maxwell, Helen, 'Helen Elizabeth Ogilvie', in *Design & Art Australia Online*. www.daao.org.au/bio/helen-elizabeth-ogilvie/biography/

Mead, Philip, *Songs from Another Country*. Canberra: Open Door Press, 1975.

Mertle, J.S., and Gordon L. Monsen, *Photomechanics and Printing: Practical Information on Platemaking and Presswork by Recognized Procedures*. Chicago: Mertle Publishing Company, 1957.

Moon, Milton, *The Zen Master. The Potter & The Poet.* Stepney, South Australia: Axiom Publishing, 2006.

Moore, Tony, *Death or Liberty: Rebels and Radicals Transported to Australia 1788–1868*. Sydney: Pier 9, 2010.

Moran, James, *Printing Presses: History and Development from the Fifteenth Century to Modern Times*. London: Faber & Faber, 1973.

Morris, Robert, 'Hand Made Paper at Bemboka'. *Wayzgoose*, no.1 (1985), pp.71–76.

Munro, Craig, *Wild Man of Letters: The Story of P.R. Stephensen*. Carlton: Melbourne University Press, 1984.

Munro, Craig, and Robyn Sheahan-Bright (eds), *Paper Empires: A History of the Book in Australia, 1946–2005*. St Lucia: University of Queensland Press, 2006.

Nyburg, Anna, *Emigrés: The Transformation of Art Publishing in Britain*. London: Phaidon, 2014.

Ogilvie, Helen, *Wood Engravings*. Edited by Helen Maxwell. Canberra: Brindabella Press, 1993.

Park, Ruth, *The Companion Guide to Sydney*. Sydney: Collins, 1973.

Pasko, Wesley Washington, *American Dictionary of Printing and Bookmaking*. Facsimile edn. First published 1894. Detroit: Gale Research Company Co., 1967.

Pope-Hennessy, John, *Sandro Botticelli: The Nativity in the National Gallery London*. The Gallery Books 15. London: Percy Lund Humphries, n.d. archive.org/stream/sandrobotticelli00popeuoft/sandrobotticelli00popeuoft_djvu.txt

Purvis, Alston W., 'Tschichold and the New Typography', in Cees W. de Jong (ed.), *Jan Tschichold: Master Typographer. His Life, Work & Legacy*. London: Thames & Hudson, 2008.

Pybus, Cassandra, *The Devil and James McAuley*. St Lucia: University of Queensland Press, 1999.

Radford, Ron, *Outlines of Australian Printmaking*. Ballarat: Ballarat Fine Art Gallery, 1976.

Randle, John, 'The Four Fathers of Richard Kennedy'. *Matrix*, no.9 (1989), pp.1–7.

Richards, Michael, *People, Print & Paper: A Catalogue of a Travelling Exhibition Celebrating the Books of Australia, 1788–1988*. Canberra: National Library of Australia, 1988.

———, *A Licence to Print*. Canberra: Friends of the National Library of Australia, 1993.

———, 'William Darbyshire Thorn'. *Obituaries Australia*, [2014]. oa.anu.edu.au/obituary/thorn-william-darbyshire-bill-19120

Riddell, Elizabeth, *From the Midnight Courtyard*. North Ryde, NSW: Angus & Robertson Publishers, 1989.

———, Film Australia: Australian Biography Series. Interview by Robin Hughes, 11 December 1992. nfsa.gov.au/collection/curated/australian-biography-elizabeth-riddell

Romano, Frank, *History of the Linotype Company*. Rochester, New York: RIT Press, 2014.

Ross, John, and Clare Romano, *The Complete Intaglio Print*. New York: Macmillan, The Free Press, 1974.

Rummonds, Richard-Gabriel, 'The Eternal Dilettante'. *American Book Collector*, May–June (1984), pp.23–31.

Ryan, Peter, *Final Proof: Memoirs of a Publisher*. Sydney: Quadrant Books, 2010.

Schuller, Andrew, 'A New Generation of Private Presses in Australia'. *Matrix*, no.31 (2012), pp.85–93.

Shaw, Rod, *The Windsor Group 1935–1945*. North Narrabeen: Edwards & Shaw, 1989.

Slinn, Judy, 'Business History of the Monotype Corporation', in *History of the Monotype Corporation*. London: Printing Historical Society, 2014.

Smith, Sam Ure, *Book Design in Australia*. Canberra: National Library of Australia, 1972.

Smith, Sydney Ure (ed.), *Present Day Art in Australia*. Sydney: Ure Smith, 1945.

Souter, Gavin, *Times & Tides: A Middle Harbour Memoir*. Pymble: Simon & Schuster, 2004.

Southall, Richard, 'Technical History of Monotype Composing Machines', in *History of the Monotype Corporation*. London: Printing Historical Society, 2014.

Southward, John, *Modern Printing: A Handbook of the Principles and Practice of Typography and the Auxiliary Arts*. 4th edn. London: Raithby, Lawrence & Company, 1922.

Stead, Christina, *The Palace with Several Sides*. Canberra: Officina Brindabella, 1986.

Stein, Harry, *From The Barn on the Hill to Edwards & Shaw: 1939–1983*. Sydney: State Library of NSW Press, 1996.

Stephens, A.G, *Along the Castlereagh*. Sydney: A.G. Stephens, 1924.

Stephensen, P.R., and Brian Kennedy, *The History and Description of Sydney Harbour*. Sydney: Reed, 1980.

Stewart, Annette, *Barbara Hanrahan: A Biography*. Kent Town: Wakefield Press, 2010.

Stewart, Douglas, *A Man of Sydney*. West Melbourne: Nelson, 1977.

Stone, Jean E., *The Passionate Bibliophile: The Story of Walter Stone, Australian Bookman Extraordinaire*. North Ryde, NSW: Angus & Robertson, 1988.

Taylor, James, 'Editions and Presswork in Australia: Private Presses and Contemporary Printing'. *Craft Australia*, no.2 (1986), pp.81–89.

Thomas, Martyn, *Harry Carter Typographer*. Hinton Charterhouse, Bath: The Old School Press, 2005.

Thompson, Frank, 'Case-Study: Government Publishing', in *Paper Empires: A History of the Book in Australia 1946–2005*. St Lucia: University of Queensland Press, 2006.

Turnbull, Paul, 'The Network and the Nation: The Development of National Bibliographical Resources', in *Remarkable Occurrences: The National Library of Australia's First 100 Years 1901–2001*. Canberra: National Library of Australia, 2001.

Upfield, Arthur, *An Author Bites the Dust*. Sydney: Angus & Robertson, 1948.

Wallace-Crabbe, Chris, 'Cottage Industry, With Muse'. *Meanjin*, vol.46, no.3 (Spring 1987), pp.338–342.

Walters, John L., *Alan Kitching: A Life in Letterpress*. London: Laurence King Publishing, 2016.

Warde, Beatrice, *The Crystal Goblet: Sixteen Essays on Typography*. London: Sylvan Press, 1955.

Waterson, Merlin, 'From Bleeding Heart Yard to Whittington'. *Matrix*, no.31 (Winter 2012), pp.54–59.

Whetton, Harry, ed., *Practical Printing and Binding: A Complete Guide to the Latest Developments in All Branches of the Printer's Craft.* London: Odhams Press, 1946.

Whitnall, Averyl (ed.), *Max Dupain: Modernist*. Sydney: State Library of NSW, 2007. www2.sl.nsw.gov.au/archive/events/exhibitions/2007/dupain/docs/maxdupain_modernist_guide.pdf

Wilde, W.H., *The Oxford Companion to Australian Literature*. Melbourne: Oxford University Press, 1985.

———, *Courage a Grace: A Biography of Dame Mary Gilmore*. Melbourne: Melbourne University Press, 1988.

Wilson, Adrian, *The Work & Play of Adrian Wilson: A Bibliography with Commentary*. Edited by Joyce Lancaster. San Francisco: The Press in Tuscany Alley, 1983.

Wilton, Elizabeth, *Red Ribbons and Mr Anders*. London: Angus & Robertson, 1970.

Wolf, Maryanne, *Proust and the Squid: The Story and Science of the Reading Brain*. London: Icon Books, 2008.

Wood-Ellem, Elizabeth, 'How I Became an Editor', in *At the Typeface: Selections from the Newsletter of the Victorian Society of Editors*. Carlton South: Society of Editors (Victoria) Inc., 2005.

Wyndham, Susan, 'The Fine Art of Survival'. *Sydney Morning Herald*, 1 May 2002. www.smh.com.au/articles/2002/04/30/1019441367996.html

Index

Note: Titles of works in this index are Brindabella Press imprints unless another publisher is named.

A

B

C

D

E

F

G

I

J

K

L

M

N

O

P

Q

R

S

T

U

V

W

Y

Z

Published by NLA Publishing
Canberra ACT 2600

ISBN: 9781922507365

The National Library of Australia acknowledges Australia's First Nations Peoples—the First Australians—as the Traditional Owners and Custodians of this land and gives respect to the Elders—past and present—and through them to all Australian Aboriginal and Torres Strait Islander people.

Publisher: Lauren Smith
Managing Editor: Amelia Hartney
Editor: Tricia Dearborn
Designer: Filip Bartkowiak
Image Coordinator: Jemma Posch
Indexer: Sherrey Quinn
Printed in Australia by Ligare Book Printers, on Norbook 65gsm Cream, typeset in Baskerville

Find out more about NLA Publishing at nla.gov.au/national-library-publishing.

A catalogue record for this book is available from the National Library of Australia

The paper this book is printed on is in accordance with the standards of the Forest Stewardship Council®. The FSC® promotes environmentally responsible, socially beneficial and economically viable management of the world's forests.